ROY FULLER

Also by Neil Powell

POETRY

At the Edge

A Season of Calm Weather

True Colours

The Stones on Thorpeness Beach

FICTION

Unreal City

CRITICISM

Carpenters of Light

ROY FULLER
Writer and Society

NEIL POWELL

First published in 1995 by
Carcanet Press Limited
402-406 Corn Exchange Buildings
Manchester M4 3BY

A CIP catalogue record for this book
is available from the British Library
ISBN 1 85754 133 2

The publisher acknowledges financial assistance
from the Arts Council of England

Designed by Janet Allan
Set in 11/12pt Bembo by XL Publishing Services, Nairn
Printed and bound in England by SRP Ltd, Exeter

For my mother
and in memory of my father

'Like ordinary people, poets long to be loved.
But all that is necessary is that
they should be understood.'

ROY FULLER

Contents

❧❧ ❧❧ • ❧❧ ❧❧

Illustrations

Acknowledgements

Clearly, my first and greatest debt is to the late Roy Fuller himself: for numerous, wholly characteristic kindnesses over several years; for giving his blessing to this project (which he did not live to see or approve); and, of course, for providing the life and the works which jointly form my subject here. From his son and executor John Fuller I have received unstinting assistance without interference: my gratitude to him is deepened by the knowledge that this perfect combination is not always granted to the literary biographer. All quotations from the published and unpublished writings of Roy Fuller appear by kind permission of John Fuller and The Estate of Roy Fuller.

Though this does not aspire to be a scholarly book, it has taken a good deal of time to research and to write; and time, inescapably, is money. It could not have been undertaken without generous financial assistance from the Authors' Foundation and the Woolwich Building Society; my thanks are especially due to Mark Le Fanu, General Secretary of the Society of Authors, and to David Blake, Head of Corporate Affairs at the Woolwich.

I hope the many individuals who have given me so much help will accept, in a spirit of literary democracy, the alphabetical acknowledgement which follows shortly. They will also, I know, forgive me for mentioning separately my gratitude to Roy Fuller's oldest literary friend, the late Julian Symons, for his kindness and patience in dealing with my queries and for allowing me access to a correspondence file stretching over more than fifty years. I've suggested to doubting friends on more than one occasion that the extracts from Fuller's letters to Symons – which are engaging, perceptive, and often subversively funny – would be worth the price of this book, even if everything I've written is valueless; and I wasn't wholly joking.

To the following people who have answered questions, loaned material, set down recollections, located books or magazines, and helped in numerous other ways – some of which are more specifically detailed in the notes at the end of the book – I gladly record my most grateful thanks: Richard Austin, Jonathan Barker, Bernard Bergonzi, David Blake, A. Burt Briggs, Alan Brownjohn, Harry Chambers, Katharine Cooke, John Cornish, Brian Cox, John Dyer, Bobby Furber, K.W.Gransden, Stella Halkyard, Michael Hamburger, Richard Hamburger, John Heath-Stubbs, Minnie Hilton, Barry Hirst, Harold Kemble, Sir Frank Kermode, Mark Le Fanu, Eddie Linden, Herbert Lomas, Charles Monteith, Eric Norris, Adam Oliver, Charles Osborne, Hugh Parish, Mark Preston, Arnold Rattenbury, Neil Rhind, Alan Ross, Peter Scupham, Kenneth Shenton, John Stafford, Margaret Steward, Ann Thwaite, Anthony Thwaite, A.T.Tolley, Malcolm Walker, Martin Wright.

I am grateful for the editorial involvement of Michael Schmidt, Janet Allan and Robyn Marsack at Carcanet, and for the no less essential non-editorial help of Pam Heaton, Joyce Nield and Gillian Tomlinson. Thanks are also due to Lisa Eveleigh and Nora Child-Villiers of my agents, A.P. Watt Ltd.

One further acknowledgement should chronologically precede even that to Roy Fuller himself, and that is to the late Alexander Meikle, who was Chairman of the Woolwich Building Society and a near-neighbour of my parents when I was a student in the late 1960s. It was Sandy who rightly thought I might like to meet the Woolwich's Legal Director, whom he believed to be rather a good poet.

My parents, unreasonably tolerant of their fate in having a penniless freelance writer for a son, provided me with unwavering support and far too many lunches while I was working on this project. The book was to have been dedicated to them; it is a matter of the deepest sorrow that my father, who was almost exactly Roy Fuller's age and who was not unlike him in other ways, did not live to see its completion.

Aldeburgh, 1994   N.P.

Preface

❧❧ ❧❧ • ❦❦ ❦❦

It makes sense to begin at the end. When Roy Fuller died, on 27 September 1991, there was an unusual, and perfectly genuine, consensus of opinion: he was one of the finest poets of his time, a novelist of real if not major importance, and a man whose multi-stranded career – literary, cultural, professional – had been both distinguished and exemplary. His obituarists tried, and necessarily failed, to catch the essence of the man: as Arnold Rattenbury put it, 'an essential niceness that was never less than tough'.[1] His friends – a numerous and uncommonly diverse collection, ranging from writers of all ages to former building society colleagues – found themselves recalling all those elegantly laconic notes and postcards. 'No need to reply to this' was a recurring formula: many of us began to wish that we'd replied more often.

And yet this writer, of undisputed achievement and importance, had somehow never quite taken his central place in contemporary English literature. In the last ten years of his life, his books had appeared from five different publishers – a discontinuity due not to the whimsy of an elderly man but to simple, outright rejection. He seldom figured on academic syllabuses and was patchily antholo-gised. In short, he didn't quite fit: his first book had appeared in December 1939, just too late for him to be a 'thirties poet'; but then he certainly wasn't a 'forties poet', with all the rhetorical looseness and bardic posturing which that phrase too easily suggests. The 1950s – though that decade saw, with *Brutus's Orchard*, Fuller's arrival at indisputable poetic maturity and, in a poem such as 'The Ides of March', greatness – was a time charac-terised by writers several years younger, the poets who appeared in *New Lines* and who were gathered under the umbrella of 'The Movement': poets who admired Fuller, but somehow seemed not to mention him quite as often as they should have done. In the remaining three decades of his life, he became both more prolific and more confidently sure-footed; his later books are his best, and there isn't a trace of falling-off, even in his astonishing last sonnet-collection, *Available for Dreams*, which appeared in 1989: fifty years of publishing poetry – and then there were the novels, the memoirs, the Oxford lectures, the books for children. Suddenly it strikes you that this diffident, self-effacing man who looked exactly like (and was) a retired building society solicitor was simultaneously too *big* a writer to fit into the pigeon-holes of easy recognition.

Another way of putting this is to insist that Fuller was in fact a highly original, deeply unconventional literary figure. In a time when poets were popularly supposed to be eccentric, his crowning eccentricity was to appear to be so disconcertingly ordinary. He acknowledged and delighted in this species of reversed-out weirdness, recalling how, when he joined the BBC's Board of Governors at the same time as a businessman called Tony Morgan, the then Director-General, Ian Trethowan, had instantly decided which was which: 'the long-haired trendily dressed chap was the poet, Roy Fuller; the businessman was the short-haired, cropped-moustached, conventionally garbed other.'[2] Of course, Roy Fuller wasn't the only important poet to possess an impeccably, even dully respectable *alter ego*. There was Wallace Stevens, who joined the Hartford Accident and Indemnity Company in 1916 and stayed with it until his death in 1955; he, as Frank Kermode has pointed out, 'does seem to have kept his Hartford life clear of literary people',[3] just as Fuller did his life with the Woolwich; but that was another country, and an older generation – the generation in which T.S. Eliot could work, though more briefly, for Lloyd's Bank. Closer to home and only a decade away in age, there was Philip Larkin, who with typically ironic dryness cited both Fuller and Stevens as poets whose jobs were ordinarily mundane, like his: 'you can go away and be something very different like an accountant – I believe Roy Fuller is something like that, Wallace Stevens was an insurance man; I'm a librarian, I never see a book from one year's end to another.'[4]

The difference – and it is an absolutely vital one – is that Fuller was much more than 'just' a poet. He was an all-round writer of a kind all too rare in our time (our lamentably pigeon-holing mentality nags us into sorting writers too readily by genre as well as by chronology). Larkin dried up after two novels; Fuller published ten, as well as the memoirs and lectures and children's books, and the best of them are very considerable achievements indeed. Beyond even that, he was an important figure in wider cultural life: as Oxford Professor of Poetry, BBC Governor,

Chairman of the Arts Council Literature Panel, member of the Library Advisory Council. It was a life whose demands could only be met with the help of insomnia or an elastic day. Fuller's improbable and not altogether welcome ally was insomnia.

In his memoirs, Fuller recalled that as a fifteen-year-old schoolboy in 1927 'I proclaimed my allegiance to Labour, a position still highly unrespectable for the provincial middle classes.'[5] After the war, he joined the Labour Party, of which he remained a member until antagonised by an unspecified party political broadcast in the 1970s. By 1981 – when, he noted, as an instance of ludicrous union demarcation, a carpenter had to be fetched to move a chair a few feet in a television studio – he had become 'in many respects... an old bull of the right.'[6] But that, of course, is to simplify matters: 'I see now when I try to shock by uttering reactionary views as I once achieved a similar effect by leftism, that being part of a minority has always been for me a natural role.'[7] It comes as little surprise, however, to discover that many of the values supported by 'leftist' Fuller in the 1930s were not dissimilar from those advanced by the 'old bull' in the 1980s. His role was not so much that of pendulum as of counter-balance, seeking to correct, by teasing or challenging, successive follies and extremes while remaining true to underlying principles of social justice and cultural excellence. And because of this, because his work exists in a kind of constantly benevolent but critical tension with the society around it, he was an especially subtle chronicler and commentator – much more subtle than the polemicist locked into an apparently 'consistent', though in fact merely undeveloping, political viewpoint.

So I have subtitled this book 'Writer and Society' only partly in punning homage to Fuller's own title *Image of a Society* – which was, of course, about a building society not entirely unlike the Woolwich. My primary concern is with the work (of the *writer*, rather than only of the poet, giving some long-overdue attention to his undervalued novels) and the dialogue it conducts, often exasperatedly but almost always affectionately, with the society which informs and provokes it.

In April 1990 I wrote to Roy Fuller, seeking his blessing for what I then called a 'literary biography'; I'd met him on only two or three occasions, but had reviewed some of his books and very much wanted to write about him at greater length. He replied:

'You are one of a very few people I would be calm about undertaking the project you envisage. I ought to warn you, though, that
I may have stolen some of your thunder by writing my post-war
memoirs, which Sinclair-Stevenson are publishing I hope next
year...'[8] I was in fact almost as grateful for his thunder-stealing as I
was for his generous vote of confidence, since it enabled me to
think in terms of a different sort of book: one which would refer
back to the life from the work, rather than the other way round.
Two months later he added:

> A *literary* biography would be to my own taste: indeed, my life
> has otherwise been mildly uneventful. My own autobiograph-
> ical writings have sucked it fairly dry, though I suppose amuse-
> ment could result from investigating the views of those I've
> worked with in various fields.[9]

The four volumes[10] of his own memoirs are almost dismayingly
exhaustive in their command of recollected detail, shuffled and
muffled though it often is: they home in infallibly on the bizarre
and comic particularities of acquaintances and places, railways and
bus-routes, strange meetings and unlikely meals and the quirks of
what he memorably calls one's 'internal economy'. They marvellously describe the inner events of an outwardly uneventful war;
later, they offer valuable insights into the workings of three major
institutions – the Woolwich Building Society, the BBC, and the
Arts Council. They are reticent about the complexities of adult
emotional life, a subject which some future biographer may care to
excavate more fully but which should not, I think, be exhaustively
covered on this occasion. What remains to be done now is exactly
what I would have wished: an attempt to show why Roy Fuller is
among the most central English twentieth-century writers, and
among the finest.

Part One: North and South

1: Northern Boy

Calamitous, a bird's abandonment:
But what about my own young orphancy?
The unreachable corner where I hid or died?[1]

Claudius, in Act I of *Hamlet*, attempts for famously idiosyn-
cratic reasons to reassure his nephew that 'death of fathers' is
nature's 'common theme'. He fails, of course. Roy Fuller was eight
years old in 1920 when his father died, which makes the occur-
rence far from common, and what would have been called his
'circumstances' were as a result not so much altered as annihilated:
the house was sold, and he spent the rest of his childhood moving
with his mother and younger brother through a series of eccentric
lodgings, except when attending a no less eccentric local boarding-
school. His maternal grandfather was a Justice of the Peace,
Councillor and Alderman who would shortly become Mayor of
Oldham; but he was not especially wealthy, and he proved unable
to offer much practical assistance to his widowed daughter and her
children in their time of hardship. He had been initially unhappy
about her choice of husband, and although in time he seemed to
overcome his doubts, cheerfully noting (like Mr Wrigley, his
fictional counterpart in *The Perfect Fool*)[2] that his successful son-in-
law spoilt his taste for cheap cigars,[3] he may still have felt privately
that she had only herself to blame for the consequences.

For Alderman Fred Broadbent was in most respects a typical
provincial Conservative, affectionately remembered by his
grandson yet deeply suspicious of all oddities except his own; and
by his standards Leopold Charles Fuller was definitely an oddity.
He looked wrong: olive-skinned, with dark wavy hair and light
eyes, his 'foreign' appearance 'caused consternation' when he was
first introduced to his prospective parents-in-law.[4] Such outlandish
physical characteristics were entirely consistent with his shadily
exotic background: he and his elder sister had been brought up as
'remittance children' in Caithness, mysteriously though quite pros-
perously illegitimate, and he was even rumoured to be the son of
that Loie Fuller whose 'Chinese dancers' so memorably 'enwound

a shining web' in Yeats's 'Nineteen Hundred and Nineteen'.[5] But
the truth was rather different. He was born in the socially
ambiguous London borough of Fulham on 23 May 1884, the son
of Minnie Augusta Fuller – the father's name does not appear on
the birth certificate[6] – while she in turn had been born on 30
March 1863 in Soham, a village between Ely and Newmarket on
the Fenland side of Cambridgeshire, where her father Richard
Fuller was a police constable. The illegitimacy indisputably proven
but the foreignness essentially repudiated, it seems a sufficiently apt
pedigree for so English a writer as Leopold Fuller's son.

Precisely how two children from Fulham were transplanted to so
startlingly remote a place as Caithness is unclear. Their Scottish
upbringing was financed by a shadowy individual named Meyer,
presumed to be their father, which must have contributed to the
tendency for Leopold to be thought Jewish when he was not being
equally tenuously identified as Spanish: Roy Fuller would recall
how his 'goy grandfather' was 'Inclined, when my exogamous sire
appeared, / To think him Jewish, with putative, black beard.'[7] On
Leopold's marriage certificate, his own names are also anachronis-
tically assigned to his father – 'Leopold Charles Fuller – deceased,
Furrier' – which looks less like a deliberately contrived fiction than
an inept clerical attempt to fill in an embarrassing blank.[8] When the
remittances to maintain them eventually ceased, at or before the
time of Minnie Augusta's death in 1904, the children travelled
south to Manchester, where their guardian's nephew, Alfred Fraser,
had a business interest in a rubber-proofing mill. Of all the rapidly
expanding industrial towns of Lancashire, Manchester had grown
the fastest during the the nineteenth century (between 1801 and
1851 alone, the population of Manchester-Salford had increased
from 84,000 to 367,000),[9] so it was a place in which two necessarily independent young people might reasonably expect to earn
their livings, if not their fortunes.

They set about the task with conspicuous diligence. In the academic year 1904–5, Leopold was awarded a prize (somewhat incongruously, a copy of Thackeray's *Vanity Fair*) 'for success in Practical
Inorganic Chemistry', an extramural course run by the Manchester
School of Technology, which suggests he had a clear-headed
commitment to obtaining academic knowledge with some practical relevance to his probable career.[10] He married Nellie
Broadbent on 21 September 1910; by the time his first son Roy

Broadbent Fuller was born on 11 February 1912, he had become Assistant Works Manager at the rubber-proofing mill at Hollinwood near Manchester of which he, like Alf Fraser, would later be a Director. Fuller recalled that 'the firm name originally included that of an elderly Jew who I think had died or retired';[11] this was perhaps a link with the mysterious Meyer, and it was certainly a contributory factor in Fred Broadbent's suspicious hostility towards his son-in-law. Leopold's sister Minnie, a year older and named after her mother, became Matron of the Manchester Royal Infirmary; she subsequently married and emigrated to Australia. Both brother and sister thus overcame their initial disadvantages of birth, absence of family and lack of geographical roots to create independent, successful careers based on ability. An interestingly similar pattern was to recur in the siblings of the next generation.

The progress of Leopold's career, a strikingly successful instance of what a more vulgarly self-assured generation would call 'upward mobility', was very naturally reflected in his domestic surroundings. Failsworth, midway between Manchester and Oldham, had already earned a footnote in literary history as the place where William Stevenson, Unitarian minister at the Dob Lane Chapel, met Elizabeth Holland, whom he married: they were the parents of the region's most celebrated nineteenth-century novelist, Mrs [Elizabeth] Gaskell. It had also 'always been noted for its love of music and poetry,' according to a local historian, Sim Schofield, in 1905: 'There are few places in Lancashire that have produced so many local poets as Failsworth', he added, naming 'our revered and renowned author, Ben Brierley' as well as 'Elijah Rydings, John Rydings, Nathan Rydings, Ned Wright, Sam Collins, and a number of very minor poets'.[12] The house in Timpson Street, Failsworth, where Roy was born, and which he would later track down in a search for solidly proletarian roots, half-expecting to find it demolished during slum clearance, he found on the contrary to be 'red brick, semidetached, with a little front garden – small but perfectly respectable';[13] it is indeed a neat, houseproud-looking residential street, with well-tended privet, roses and conifers in its gardens, and bright burglar-alarms conspicuously abundant among the upper windows of its substantial Victorian terraces. Yet within four years, the family had moved into a more prosperous neighbourhood in Frederick Street, Oldham, which was and remains (as a present-day resident and local historian puts it) 'the most impressive street in town'. At this time,

> there were three hundred and twenty cotton mills in Oldham…
> In some places there was a kind of humming in the air when the
> factories started up… But there were other things that seemed
> to make Frederick Street a pleasant place to live, a large
> Grammar School (close to where Roy must have lived), trees,
> gardens, no trams or buses, so relative quiet… You could be
> proud to live on Frederick Street.[14]

And in 1919 the Fullers moved once again, to a large mock-Tudor
house in Waterhead, with a view of the Pennines, a day nursery for
Roy and his brother (its floor 'laid with a patent green material…
ideal for bare knees, as a foundation for Lotts' bricks and Hornby
train lines'),[15] two maids and a chauffeur. This was 'the house
whose superiority, though best displayed by its fanciful elevation,
was indubitably demonstrated by the remoteness of its rear access'
so cherished by young Alan Percival in the opening pages of *The
Perfect Fool*;[16] for him, as for Roy, 'The moors' green shoulder filled
half the sky that he saw from his bedroom window.'[17] From here,
Leopold took his young son to rugby league and association football matches at Watersheddings and Boundary Park, and on a
memorable occasion 'to see the pictures' – which to Roy's disappointment turned to be not at the Imperial cinema but at the
Oldham Municipal Art Gallery, then celebrated for its acquisition
of John Collier's 'The Death of Cleopatra' (1890): 'Perhaps,' Fuller
would later speculate, 'its sensuous splendours were something my
father particularly wanted to see'.[18]

Leopold's material progress was, however, outweighed by personal misfortunes of a sort much commoner then than now but no less
devastating. His second and fourth sons, born in 1914 and 1920
respectively, both died in infancy from the then-undiagnosed though
in fact simply operable congenital hypertrophic pyloric stenosis (his
surviving son, Roy Fuller's younger brother John, was born in 1916).
By 1920, Leopold himself was found to have cancer of the bowel,
and he died after unsuccessful surgery and considerable suffering on
18 December. He was thirty-six years old and left a widow of thirty-
two. 'My father's death,' wrote Fuller, 'shattered my mother's existence: it also caused his children to lead lives that were for many years
divided and too narrow in scope.'[19] In so emotionally reticent a

memoir, those stern and simple words carry a special resonance.

Would Leopold have been more kindly regarded by Alderman Broadbent if the speculation about his foreign-exotic ancestry had been replaced by the prosaic certainty of his descent from a Cambridgeshire policeman? Probably not, given the Alderman's inexhaustible though engaging quirkiness. More serious and distressing than any mere quirk, however, was the fact that he suffered from Dupuytrin's Contracture, a progressive disorder in which the fibrous lining of the palm thickens so that the patient is unable to straighten some or all of his fingers. His professional life comprised a succession of worthy-sounding occupations which turn out, on closer inspection, to be less than taxing: schoolmaster at Waterhead Church School and Royton Church School; Clerk and subsequently Master of Oldham Workhouse; Superintendent Registrar of Births, Marriages and Deaths for Oldham. Elected to the Town Council in 1908, he became a magistrate in 1921 and served as Mayor of Oldham in 1924–5. He was fond of bridge, and inclined to punctuate this game as well as other even less suitable occasions with quotations from *The Merchant of Venice*, apparently the only literary work with which he was intimately acquainted: his grandson recalled how his usually demotic street-greeting ("Ow do, Albert?') would sometimes be incongruously replaced by 'How now Tubal! what news from Genoa?'[20] Otherwise his accomplishments included a repertoire of comic songs and sayings (such as 'I'll have some of that scanamanah, commonly known as lobjaw' when offered a choice of pudding[21]), the regular concoction on Sunday afternoons of a dish principally comprising cheese, onions and potatoes, and the annual insistence on New Year's Eve that at that precise moment there was a man standing in Oldham market-place with as many noses as there were days in the year.[22] He also held the eccentric though strangely plausible belief that an individual's political convictions could be infallibly deduced from his manner of cutting cheese: with the rind denoting a conservative, without a radical. Each morning, he would don a hat knitted for the purpose, announce that he was going 'golfing', and proceed to fetch in the coal. His most conspicuous civic monument, an apt enough one perhaps, was the completion of underground public lavatories near the Theatre Royal in Oldham, which on account of their protruding twin glass domes were popularly known as 'Alderman Broadbent's Two-Valve Receiver'.[23]

Roy Fuller's mother, Nellie Broadbent, was thus able to claim cheerfully that she had been born in the Workhouse, as was indeed the case, on 28 October 1888, the third child of Fred Broadbent and his wife Emily (née Jenkins). Fuller, with what may strike us as odd over-emphasis, was inclined to stress her cultural background of 'small-town Tory politics, low Church of England, parlour music and a general style of enforced modesty'[24] and her 'detestation of the unconventional',[25] phrases which tell us more about his sympathy with the ordinary surfaces of middle-class life than about hers. Her marriage to Leopold and her unsettled, nomadic existence after his death were far from conventional by small-town Tory standards. Her mother, Emily Broadbent, who had turned down the chance of becoming a professional actress before her marriage, had an exceptional singing voice – she joined the choir of St James', Oldham, as a girl of eight and went on to sing in 'practically every church in town'[26] – and in later life took up drawing and painting: these talents were distributed among her children, Nellie inheriting 'a strong true mezzo-soprano'.[27] The eldest brother, Herbert, was both a singer (as a boy chorister, later a bass, at Ripon Cathedral) and a painter; Fuller remembered 'a respectable oil of his of tall grey tree trunks' in his grandparents' dining-room, 'though Herbert's initials were followed by an acknowledgement to some other painter'[28] – possibly the early, representational Mondrian. Herbert died in the influenza epidemic of 1918. The second child, Edith, initially married a gasworks manager who also died young – 'A somewhat Victorian deathrate persisted in places like Oldham,' Fuller noted drily[29] – and subsequently a trombonist and double-bass player with the splendid name of Archie Gladman, who died of tuberculosis. Nellie was the third child, and after her came John, a celebrated 'female impersonator': Fuller possessed 'a printed postcard of him in drag, signed by him with his sobriquet "Violet"'.[30] Though he had an administrative job in the cotton trade, his acting career flourished and included a long-running BBC radio series with Wilfred Pickles, a meshing of disparate activities somewhat paralleled by the 'spanner and pen' life of his nephew. Small-town Tory though it may have been, the Broadbent family clearly possessed a diverse, even an unconventional range of creative talent, as Fuller implied in a Radio 3 conversation with Anthony Thwaite:

I was interested in my maternal family's doings and what their friends did; and there was this slight ambience of singing, and doing etchings in the kitchen, and that kind of thing, which interested me very much; and they were rather good conversationalists – sort of anecdotal – and my grandfather was mixed up in local politics and so on. So there was a good deal going on which would interest a small boy.[31]

After her husband's death, Nellie moved with her two surviving children, Roy and John, to Blackpool; and there they rented rooms in the house of a Mrs Vero and her son – 'the first I recall of the Dickensian characters encountered in my mother's wanderings during the rest of my life with her'.[32] Willie Vero, who was in his early twenties, might indeed have been invented specifically to complement the Broadbent tradition of creative eccentricity: he interspersed repeated performances of Rachmaninov's C sharp minor Prelude with invented Pinteresque dialogues in alternating bass and falsetto voices. This period was succeeded first by a brief and unsuccessful interlude in Oldham, and then by a return to Blackpool, to different though nearby rooms in the house of Miss Barraclough, 'a gigantically fat woman who slept in the kitchen and never bathed'.[33] This arrangement was to last a couple of years, and by the time restlessness or exasperation with Miss Barraclough's personal hygiene prompted Nellie to move once again, this time to rooms in a private hotel called Seacliffe, Roy had become a boarder at a somewhat undistinguished local independent school. No wonder his happiest early memories – those, at any rate, which most nearly approach the undemonstrative stability of conventional family life – were of his grandparents' house in Hollins Road where, the table cleared after a lunch of hotpot and apple pie, he would paint or draw and inhabit for a while the seldom-attainable condition of 'normal' childhood.

★

'Had my family or school recognized my true bent, or had I been born twenty years later, I would surely have ended teaching English,' wrote Roy Fuller in 1972.[34] If he had been allowed to take his chances in dull though adequate local authority schools, there is every likelihood that he would have won a university scholarship and eventually been able to pursue a career of his own choosing. But his mother had understandable if flawed reasons for sending him off to boarding school: there was the unstable, fatherless home; and she, as a young widow, had her own life to piece together. In deciding between Blackpool's two private boys' schools, and settling on the one which was not destined to grow into a minor public school, she again may have had plausible reasons, no doubt persuading herself that the humbler establishment was the more friendly, less forbidding, and of course cheaper of the two. Nor was Arthur Anderson, the headmaster and proprietor of the grandly-named Blackpool High School – or Seafolde House, as Fuller would call it both in his memoirs and in his novel *The Ruined Boys* – entirely without admirable qualities, at least in retrospect: the memoirist, confessing to his own 'testy reactionariness', had to note that 'The values the Headmaster tried to inculcate and the teaching he so ably undertook have lost some of their hypocritical or irrelevant undertones during the decline in public and private standards since the novel was written in the Fifties.'[35] Nevertheless, the school was pitifully small, academically unambitious, financially unstable, and well on the way downhill into a state of terminal decline (it finally closed in 1937).

In the novel – which carries a queasily convincing sense of adolescent insecurity, period detail and dated schoolboy slang – Fuller is transformed into the central character Gerald Bracher: though one mustn't read *The Ruined Boys* as a mechanically exact *roman-à-clef*, there are numerous points of close correspondence with the memoirs. Taken together, the two sources describe in some detail a kind of school which, as their author put it (with a nice regression to northern idiom), 'will likely be unfamiliar fifty years on'.[36] The most immediately striking aspect of this unfamiliarity is Blackpool High School's modest, and hence impossibly inefficient, size. Although in the novel it is plausibly expanded, using physical details ingeniously borrowed from a prep-school and wartime billet called Seafield Park at Fareham in Hampshire,[37] to include a 'turreted, many-chimneyed mansion and the more regular shapes of the school block',[38] it actually comprised an adjacent pair of semi-detached houses at 17–19 Alexandra Road, South Shore, with classrooms and eventually a laboratory in their former back-gardens.[39] When Roy went there in 1923, at the age of eleven, there were younger boys of nine or ten below him in Form 1, and pupils remained up to the age of sixteen or seventeen in a rudimentary sixth form; yet the total roll numbered only a hundred or so, of whom thirty were boarders, and this decreased during Fuller's time at the school. Writing in 1984 to Kenneth Shenton, a teacher at the ultimately more prosperous Arnold School and author of its history, he offered a telling glimpse of the two establishments' see-sawing fortunes during his own schooldays:

> Yes, the Blackpool High School was in Alexandra Road. When I first went there, I think in 1923, it was still a plausible rival to Arnold House (as Arnold School was then known), though by that time Arnold House had moved to the more suitable site in Lytham Road. The headmaster, Arthur P. Anderson, was an excellent teacher & formidable character, but may not have been as astute (or lucky) on the business side as F.T. Pennington [headmaster of Arnold House]. Anyway, the High School declined & Arnold House flourished; in my day the latter being thought rather ambitiously bumptious in aspiring to Public School status. Rather strangely, the schools had by 1923 stopped playing each other at games: possibly Anderson & Pennington were at daggers drawn, or maybe the High School First Elevens would have been a match only for Arnold House Seconds – & as I write this it comes to me that Arnold House may even at that date have changed from the proletarian soccer to the snobbish (in those parts) rugby union. The contact between the schools was confined to the boarders both attending Matins at the South Shore Parish Church, glaring at one another from widely-spaced pews. We were even then outnumbered, & I rather think Arnold House may have built its own Chapel during my days or soon thereafter.[40]

While Blackpool High School's declining roll certainly resulted in small classes and indivdual attention, it obviously precluded effective academic specialisation of the high-flying sort which requires plenty of bright pupils and a large, well-qualified teaching staff.

To account for his overwhelming feeling of nervous alienation, the fictional Gerald Bracher is given a distant South African background and a motherless home, his mother having gone off with another man in Durban. The analogy between this predicament and Fuller's own rootless and fatherless state is self-evident, the fictional transposition arbitrary and transparent, but the strategy admits levels of emotional resonance which are far beyond the ironic restraint of the memoirs. Near the beginning of the book and suffering from toothache (one of many Graham Greene-ish touches in Fuller's fiction), Bracher reflects: 'A difficult period of his life stretched before him when he would have to discover, through his pain, the unknown procedure for obtaining permission to leave the school premises, for finding the dentist's surgery...'.[41] The matter of a day or two for which the actual toothache may trouble him thus becomes an emblem for the apparently infinite 'difficult *period of his life*' during which he must come painfully to terms with the inscrutable procedures and regulations of the school; and the period may indeed prove to be even longer than that, as the shy and insecure adult discovers that equally problematic negotiations with the society around him persist throughout his life. Throughout *The Ruined Boys*, Bracher repeatedly attempts to unscramble the code and to win the good opinion of Mr Pemberton, the headmaster, a character only loosely and negatively based on Anderson; but he is frustrated both by his naïve overeagerness to do (and be seen to do) the right thing and, more seriously, by his failure to perceive that Pemberton, far from being a figure of exemplary virtue, is an erratic, hypocritical prig.

In a scene of cumulative, multi-layered irony, Bracher is persuaded by Slade (a boy whom he normally regards with contempt) to report to Mr Norfolk, the hearty young games master who has conceived the appalling notion of a compulsory school boxing tournament, the culprit responsible for removing the weights from the school's weighing-machine and thus scuppering the tournament – a fat, unattractive boy called Cole. Bracher has made enemies in the school and is terrified of being legitimately hit by them, so he has no taste for the tournament; but his fear of boxing is overruled by his anxiety to behave correctly. The two set off to find Mr Norfolk, at first failing to do so in a beautifully-evoked, smoke-filled Masters' Common Room before encountering him instead at the foot of a staircase: '"This is very serious," he said and Gerald had a fresh awed sense of the enormity of Cole's action and the importance of his own role in the crisis that was now unfolding.'[42] The trio then proceeds to the Headmaster's study, and the unfortunate Cole is summoned: he explains that, being 'very heavy' but totally unathletic, he has sabotaged the tournament to protect himself from being knocked about in the ring by a proper heavyweight.

The ensuing silence was broken only by a subdued sniff from

Cole. Then the Headmaster said: "'I'm very heavy, sir.'" Gerald saw that his body was shaken by rage and knew that he had sadly underestimated Cole's punishment. But in the same moment his apprehension was turned to astonishment. Mr Pemberton was shaking with laughter, a strange sound that he had never heard before and that he could not have imagined. He stole a glance at Mr Norfolk in case some reaction was demanded of him that he could not visualize from his own understanding of the situation – in case, say, the Headmaster had gone insane. But Mr Norfolk's countenance was still set in the severity of expression which a few moments ago had seemed infinitely appropriate, his bird's eyes half veiled.[43]

Mr Pemberton concludes that Cole's action was 'Very wrong but very resourceful' and urges the other two boys to learn that 'There is nothing wrong in protecting oneself from injustice. Rebellion is often praiseworthy. Our friend here went a little too far, that is all.' And Bracher, reflecting on all this, sees 'how totally he had misjudged the situation: the Headmaster had not only extracted the true meaning from it but put it in proper perspective'.[44] That Mr Pemberton's behaviour may have been either wilfully perverse or informed by dishonourably pragmatic considerations doesn't occur to him.

Later in the same term, Bracher unwittingly puts the Headmaster's commendation of justified rebellion to the test by venturing into the town on a Monday (rather than the prescribed Wednesday or Saturday) to change a book at a commercial lending-library, motivated solely by a commendable enthusiasm for reading. As a result he receives from Mr Pemberton a sarcastic enquiry ("'Have you read all your English set books, then, and the books in the Library?'"), a pompous lecture on responsibility, and a caning. Still Bracher resolves 'never again to offend against the school's morality' and ridiculously begins to question his motives for reading: 'even the excuse he had originally given himself for breaking bounds was tainted, for he now saw that his inordinate desire for books could not be separated from his desire for what he might find in them... the girl with her clothes torn savagely from her.'[45]

Only near the end of the novel, accused of an unmentionable sexual impropriety with Slade, who has rather abruptly been trans-lated into a figure of enviable and eclectic cultural precocity, does he angrily defend himself and finally realise that (in every sense) 'the Headmaster was a small man'.[46] It's not before time. Quite apart from witnessing numerous instances of Mr Pemberton's bombastic folly and flatulent rhetoric, Bracher has also learned that his indulgence towards Cole and indeed towards the whole 'corpulent family' (his mother has presented Sports Day prizes and his father fulfilled a similar function on Speech Day) stems from the fact that the school property is mortgaged to Cole's father. The image of the school fields 'split up into building plots when Alderman Cole exercised his rights as mortgagee'[47] – which accompanies the recognition that the school is a symbol not, after all, of some honourable idealism but of a corrupt real world – seems to echo the 'red rust' of creeping suburban development which E.M. Forster feared would similarly overwhelm Howards End.

Was the young Fuller really as obtuse as his fictional counterpart? He may well have been. His mother's peregrinations and his own helpless sense of responsibility for her, to say nothing of his already introspective character, had led to acute social isolation; apart from his cousins and various children connected with lodgings or hotels, the memoirs provide no evidence of friends among his contemporaries until he went to 'Seafolde House'. There, his fellow-pupils tended to be odd rather than able. One, improbably called Hamlet, treated his adolescent pimples by injecting them with Euthymol toothpaste on a pin. Another, Burt Briggs (he is called Byng in *Souvenirs* and *The Strange and the Good*; Howarth, perhaps also Mountain, in *The Ruined Boys*), was an early audience for Fuller's steadily developing sardonic wit; the two of them were especially fond of teasing an ape-like boy called J.C. Haigh ('Ames') and nicknamed Gorill, whose purloined exercise books provided a rich source of entertainment. One of Haigh's efforts included the 'succinct but mysteriously Joycean' narrative: 'He stooped. He stoped. He stopped.' Another ended: 'All done by kindness. J.C. Haigh.' Fuller noted that these words were 'still useful today, marking completion of some satisfying and satisfactory job'.[48] Also among his 'Seafolde House' contemporaries was the Headmaster's plump son, Ronald Anderson – Kenneth, or Ettaboo, in the memoirs and evidently the model for Cole in *The Ruined Boys*.[49]

It may not have been difficult to shine in this company, but Fuller shone spectacularly, both in academic terms (although 'I wasn't literary at school at all. I was mathematical')[50] and in other, possibly less expected ways. 'We congratulate Fuller,' writes the author of 'School House Notes' in the Winter 1926 *Blackpool High School Magazine*, 'upon his appointment as Prefect and his election as Secretary of Games.'[51] The article is unblushingly signed 'R.B. Fuller (Captain)'. He had, at any rate, the satisfaction of being a very large fish in his tiny pond even if it took him, like Bracher, a long time to realise that the school's smallness extended to its Headmaster:

> One evening, not long after the end of my final term, the door-bell rang and I found the Headmaster standing outside. It was only then, away from the school or school occasions for the first time, that I saw that he was shorter than I... As a matter of fact there had been an affair in my last or penultimate term that had put me in his bad books and it struck me that he had come to report about that to my mother, belatedness not making this dread speculation much less likely to be true having regard to his measured and steadfast character.[52]

In fact, Arthur Anderson had arrived, far more astonishingly, to invite his former pupil to the Palace Varieties, where the music-hall mime Joe Jackson was appearing; while Roy painfully suppressed his laughter, the Headmaster sat mirthlessly through the perfor-mance, only relenting at the end to remark, 'Foolish fellow'.[53] If the school failed to provide Fuller with much in the way of academic qualifications, it nevertheless gave him something more valuable for a writer, a ripe selection of human quirkiness; it also taught him the effectiveness of formal respectability as a mask for his incurable insecurity, a lesson which would develop into a lifelong habit.

Culturally, the most decisive influence of his schooldays – instrumental in shaping both his literary and his musical taste – was the master called Mr Tregenza in the memoirs and Mr Percy in the novel. In this case, the correspondences are exceptionally close. Mr Tregenza lent Fuller books from his own collection, starting with Ian Hay and O. Henry: 'He asked which I'd liked better. I said the Ian Hay (it was *Pip and Pipette*), speaking the truth though conscious that O. Henry was the more considerable literary artist.'[54] Mr Percy also starts by lending Bracher a pair of books: '"Which did you like the better?" "Poe's *Tales of Mystery and Imagination*." "A bit nearer *Fu-Manchu*, eh?" "Not really, sir." "No, not really."'[55] Mr Tregenza played Chopin's *Fantaisie Impromptu* in a classroom after

evening prep; Mr Percy plays a Schubert Impromptu in the school
hall after evening prep, and both Fuller and Bracher overcome their
shyness to listen and learn. The mannerisms and physical characteristics of the two masters are identical:

> He was short, stout, as uncommunicative as I later became,
> possibly in his mid-forties. When accompanying the boarders
> on their Sunday walk he sometimes held his walking stick
> upright behind his back, the crook hooked on to the brim of his
> trilby to stop it being blown off in the stiff wind usually preva-
> lent at Blackpool.[56]

> The duty master took the Sunday afternoon walk… Today the
> master was Mr Percy, who walked alone behind the long straggle
> of boys, his stout form boxed in a loud check overcoat, occa-
> sionally holding his hat on in the stiff sea breeze with the crook
> of his ashplant.[57]

Mr Tregenza was promoted to the post of Senior Master, an unexpected elevation which Fuller suspected was actually a symptom of
the school's decline, like his own inclusion in the cricket team. By
contrast, the unlucky Mr Percy – who shows no respect for his
Headmaster's fatuous formalities, has an affair with Mr Pemberton's
niece, and (his crowning glory) inadvertently contrives to clobber
the strategically vital Cole with a cricket-bat – is forced to resign.

★

On leaving Miss Barraclough's, the Fullers moved to a private hotel
called Seacliffe, run by a resident proprietress with her three daughters, which overlooked both the sea and the Metropole, at that time
Blackpool's leading hotel. It must have been a topsy-turvy milieu for
an adolescent, surrounded by oddly deracinated adults whose lives
had lapsed into a state of permanent holiday, whereas the actual
holiday season would be principally defined by the hectic comings
and goings of others, 'some making departures and reappearances…
reminiscent of Chekhov'.[58] Indeed, Fuller's poem 'Chekhov' might
equally be read as a recollection of Seacliffe:

> Chekhov saw life as a series of departures;
> Its crises blurred by train times, bags, galoshes.
> Instead of saying the important word
> The hurried characters only breathe Farewell.

And what there was of meaning in it all
Is left entirely to the minor figures:
Aged or stupid, across the deserted stage,
They carry, like a tray, the forgotten symbol.[59]

Notable among the place's more or less permanent fixtures was Miss Paine, a domineering white-wigged woman who actually lived at the Metropole, where she would sometimes treat Roy and his brother to an early dinner in the grillroom; there they would choose the cheapest dish on the menu, sausages and chips, 'either at her bidding, or more likely, through some subtle appeal to our consciences (mine at least already tenderized by long knowledge of my mother's limited resources after my father's early death)';[60] such tact, however laudable, is not a universal quality of adolescence, but it is certainly symptomatic of Roy's over-developed feelings of self-consciousness and insecurity.

The regular or semi-permanent visitors at Seacliffe itself included Mr Heaton, 'an elderly valetudenarian' with 'a digestion which incessantly generated wind',[61] and Mr Wheatcroft, 'a stoutish dapper man of late-middle-age',[62] who managed a wine-merchant's and was interested in Mrs Fuller. The private hotel, with its inevitable collection of ageing characters cast adrift, was a quirky choice of habitat for a widow in her late thirties, unless intended to invite the sort of attention which, in Mr Wheatcroft's case, seems not to have been reciprocated. The experience of living in a residential community of eccentrics was not, however, to be wasted on her elder son: the convalescent home for the mentally ill in *Stares*, with its explicitly Chekhovian subtext, is essentially just such a place, although that novel, Fuller's last, would not appear until over sixty years later ('Sometimes,' says one of the characters, 'it seems just a mediocre hotel, such as one used to come across more in the past');[63] while Mr Napur, the Asian lawyer in *The Father's Comedy*, is derived in name at least from a young Indian student who improbably lodged at Seacliffe. After a while, the proprietress, her daughters and the Fullers moved to a smaller though more elegant establishment in Wilton Parade, and there Roy 'passed the holidays of my later schooldays: dim period, scarcely worth trying in the least to depict, as it seems to me now'.[64] That sounds transparently evasive; and so it proves, for a little later in *Souvenirs* Fuller explains his reticence in terms which do, after all, admit that he endured the authentic pangs of adolescent angst:

I remember playing the first movement of Mozart's late G minor symphony, recently acquired, one summer afternoon by the open window... I expect I was also conscious that a few of the holiday-makers perambulating below, including some beautiful and intelligent girl, might well hear the strains and think that in the unusually chic and convenient premises high above dwelt an appropriately lofty intelligence. Insane intellectual and amatory fantasies of adolescence, unspeakable yearnings and frustrations of that epoch, so prolonged, seemingly unassuagable! I would not like to have to write about them again, as either reality or fiction, let alone relive them.[65]

There are of course children of varying ages in Fuller's novels – one of which, *With My Little Eye*, actually has an adolescent first-person narrator – but it is surely significant that in *The Perfect Fool*, the work of fiction most closely modelled on his private growing-up (as opposed to his necessarily more public life at school), he jumps with disruptive abruptness from childhood in Chapter II to employment as a trainee journalist, a wry transmogrification for the solicitor's articled clerk, in Chapter III.[66] This reluctance to deal either in memoir or in novel with the time of emotional turmoil which for many writers provides an important and even an obsessional theme, far from being suggestive of a 'dim period', might more plausibly indicate some intensely painful confusion and unhappiness to which the adult never became fully reconciled.

A distinct but corroborative instance of the self-censorship which Fuller seems to have imposed on his recollections of this period concerns his younger brother John, whose latter schooldays were spent at King William's College on the Isle of Man but who for a while attended Blackpool High School (he went on to a distinguished career in catering education, becoming Professor at the University of Strathclyde). Fuller records that, as head house prefect in his last year at school, he beat his younger brother for eating shrimps at a stall on the promenade, and comments:

The incident encapsulates much of its epoch: the tradition of behaviour for boys wearing the school uniform; my dotty and priggish devotion to authority; my brother's early enterprise and gourmandism, the latter eventually international. It hardly needs saying that in later life I had to have the occasion recalled to me: the censor had expunged the memory.[67]

It hardly needs saying, either, that a different sort of writer would have been haunted by such recollections instead of expunging them from his memory.

By the time Roy left school, his incurably restless mother had decided to move yet again, to a peculiar second-floor flat near Seacliffe – so near, indeed, that it also overlooked the Metropole, though the main entrance rather than the grill-room aspect; it was here that he fruitlessly attempted to impress passers-by with the records of Mozart's Symphony No 40 and here too that Arthur Anderson called on his unlikely theatrical excursion. The flat was oddly organised, with its bathroom and second bedroom across the access staircase, and the cooking area concealed behind a partition in the dining room: Mrs Fuller's domestic arrangements once again seem to have been almost wilfully unconventional, and her son conceded that it was a 'bohemian lay-out'.[68] His literary ambitions were already formed, but his external personality had been still more forcefully shaped – childhood insecurity, financial prudence and the ethos of Blackpool High School all urged him towards reticent respectability – and 'bohemian' would not be, then or later, a term of approbation in his vocabulary.

It would be naïve to suppose that any writer's adolescence need be exceptionally wild or exciting (a withdrawn, bookish existence seems a likelier preparation for the job), but the matter is worth dwelling on in Fuller's case for two reasons. One is that the nomadic, fatherless life would have provided a more extrovert child with an unusual degree of social freedom; Roy, however, was burdened both with an elder son's overwhelming feelings of responsibility and with a sense of his own inadequacy in fulfilling the filial role. The other is that the purportedly 'dim period' of Roy's adolescence was spent not in some remote hamlet nor in a drearily conformist suburbia but in Blackpool, a place which, to the southern English mind, all too easily appears as a kind of joke, the essence of northern seaside vulgarity; and Fuller's memoirs – written, of course, long after he had done his best to assume a southern accent and consciousness – do little to counteract that perception. Part of the problem was that 'in Blackpool I had lost the scenes of early childhood, meaningful however banal... This was a spiritual loss, felt quite early (no doubt subconsciously connected with my lost father), and therefore significant to me as the writer I wanted from the age of fifteen or so to become.'[69] The intellectually ambitious adolescent, unless he grows up in an exceptionally cultivated milieu, invariably views the society around him with contemptuous disdain – the stance is both protective colouring and self-definition – but Fuller's reaction against Blackpool was not only virulent but long-lasting. Revisiting his home town in 1939, admittedly in an ideologically excitable state of mind, he wrote to Julian Symons:

> This is the ideal fascist state – the people are without independent political thought and well disciplined but they are also abundantly fed and amused. The great newspaper here is the *Daily Dispatch* which hides all news of Danzig, etc. in its inner pages and gives prominence to the WEATHER and UNUSUAL items of news from the seaside. Several times a day an aeroplane flies over the town suggesting that one uses a sun tan lotion or purchases a LI-LO. A li-lo is a table-tennis but to which is attached a rubber ball by an elastic thread. The apparatus can be manipulated to bounce the ball on the bat. But the life of the town centres around Epstein's *Adam* which is exhibited in the main street & can be seen for 6d. Everyone has been or is going to see *Adam*. A popular song publisher, Mr Lawrence Wright [who under his alter ego, Horatio Nicholls, was the composer of 'Shepherd of the Hills', a childhood favourite of Fuller's] is showing the sculpture & he has commissioned Epstein to do an *Eve* for £20,000. *Adam* is a most universal topic of conversation & is regarded as *rude*. Most of the visitors here are misshapen and ugly and they are of low intelligence. All London Marxists should spend their holidays here so that they may appreciate better the task which lies ahead of the revolutionary parties.
>
> I cannot conceive how I was able to spend so many years of my life in this dump.[70]

Yet there is another side of Blackpool which Fuller scarcely mentions. It is among the country's more distinguished seaside resorts, even now not altogether devoid of what he refers to as 'tone', and its Tower (reproduced in an elegant sepia photograph on the dust-jacket of *Souvenirs*) is probably the most celebrated coastal monument in Britain. Still more to the point, while Fuller was growing up there, it was a thriving cultural centre. Writing about Blackpool in an enjoyable and instructive anthology called *Beside the*

Seaside, first published in 1934, James Laver praises the beach, the Tower (with grotto and aquarium beneath), and the lately-demolished Big Wheel, before turning his attention to the theatre:

> Blackpool seems to have more theatres than any other place in England, with the exception of London. Theatrical managers discovered long ago the advantages of trying-out plays in the provinces prior to their London production. The problem was to find some place where there was a genuine enthusiasm for the theatre combined with a sound critical sense, and it is significant that both the favourite spots here these conditions are most completely realised are in Lancashire: one being Manchester and the other Blackpool. The Blackpool audience, in summer at any rate, provides a very useful cross-section of the British public... The results are happy enough. The managers are provided with a useful dress rehearsal and a breathing space in which necessary adjustments can be made, and Blackpool has the benefit of a series of productions which are very nearly up to the highest standards of the Metropolis. The actors love it. Manchester, for all its virtues, is not exactly the place one would choose for a holiday, but Blackpool has most of the advantages of Manchester and many of its own besides...
>
> The theatres where the London companies chiefly perform are the Opera House, the Grand and the Winter Garden. The last-named has also a ballroom, a floral hall and a cinema in the same building, while the Palace has a cinema and a Palais-de-Danse. I leave out the cinemas because the fare they offer is the same everywhere. But Blackpool has more than a dozen of them, including one or two large ones, extremely comfortable and up to date.[71]

Very early in his memoirs, Fuller notes that he 'inherited a sufficient taste for the boards from my mother's side'[72] – though how cautious and revealing is the word 'sufficient' in that context – and he also recalls how the advertising billboard displayed in Miss Barraclough's garden entitled her to two free seats at a local cinema, where Roy would accompany her to Monday matinees: 'Thus, and at others of Blackpool's numerous cinemas, was sustained – developed, rather – my passion for that art.'[73] Though there are subsequent references in *Souvenirs* to both theatre (as the venue for variety more often than for serious drama) and cinema, there is little sense of that abundance, surpassed only by London and Manchester, indicated by Laver. The 'passion' for cinema, in particular, remained essentially a private one. No doubt this was partly due to the ambiguous cultural status of film; but it seems more than likely that both theatre and cinema could set up bohemian resonances which the young Roy Fuller would find disturbingly incompatible with his outwardly conventional self. This was certainly to be the case after he had left school, as *The Perfect Fool* implies and as we shall see in due course.

In the latter part of his life, and especially during the period of his Oxford professorship (1968–73), Fuller would argue for 'highbrow' as against 'middlebrow' values in art, with a touch of understandable testiness which may have been misinterpreted by those of his audience who were unacquainted with his style of mischievously self-mocking irony. It was a habit, and an anxiety, which reached back to his childhood:

> I marvel now at the culture with which my mind was stuffed: characters such as Marzipan the Magician from a comic called *The Rainbow*; the vigorous pen and ink illustrations to the serials in *Chums*; silent films with actors now almost forgotten like George K. Arthur and Lya de Putti, the latter, as he confessed, touching even my grandfather's libido; and songs from drawing-rooms.... A wonder that a little later on there was any room for the *Fantaisie Impromptu*, *The Dynasts* and so forth.[74]

The unequal, and of course predetermined, tussle between high and low culture was especially evident in his relationship with music. Despite the enlightening influence of Mr Tregenza, he never quite lost his affection for what he disparagingly called 'pier-end' music – the strongly melodic popular classics which could be readily arranged for limited orchestration while remaining instantly recognisable – or for the dance-band tunes of his childhood, such as Horatio Nicholls' 'Shepherd of the Hills'; his son, John Fuller, remembering his own childhood, commented that his father would take him 'to the Music Hall rather than the ballet'.[75] Yet, about the time he began to listen to Mr Tregenza's piano-playing, Fuller 'was conscious of losing arguments with two day-boy pianists in which I foolishly maintained that compared with "pier-end" music... classical music lacked the essential ingredient of tunes.'[76] One of these pianists, Leslie Toft, on whom Slade in *The*

Ruined Boys is loosely based, was to become a close friend and cultural mentor.

Leslie's taste in music was confident and unambiguous, prompting Roy to feel characteristically insecure about his own:

> Because Leslie greatly admired Cortot he possessed César Franck's *Variations Symphoniques* played by that pianist but his taste was really more severely classical. I nervously revealed to him my purchase of an album of Ignaz Friedman's performance of the Grieg piano concerto on dark-blue label Columbia discs, the work to a tyro of those days seeming almost modern and possibly ephemeral. A little later I was even more nervous about Ravel's *Introduction and Allegro*, on plum label HMV's, the colour again indicating cheapness.[77]

The friendship was to prove momentous, dotted with the kind of mutual cultural discovery which is only ever likely to occur between sympathetic near-contemporaries, in essence very like Philip Larkin and his schoolfriend Jim Sutton discovering American jazz.[78] For instance, when 'we realised that neither of us had ever heard Beethoven's Fifth Symphony', the remedy was instant and, by Roy's cautious standards, startlingly impulsive: he at once asked his mother 'to fund the purchase', after which he and Leslie went off to buy 'the album of four black label HMV records conducted by Sir Landon Ronald, the cost twenty-four shillings, a tidy sum'.[79]

A parallel friendship developed between the two boys' mothers, so that in 1929 they holidayed together in London. Roy and Leslie took themselves off to a Prom at the Queen's Hall, while the two mothers and Roy's brother John sought amusement elsewhere. Fuller's recollection of that evening's end is revealing:

> I cannot remember if Leslie and I glimpsed Sir Henry [Wood] on that first night. When we returned to the Regent Palace Hotel my mother told me that she and Leslie's mother, with my brother, had strolled out after dinner to find a likely cinema, which they did in the Haymarket. The ladies had been baffled by the film on show, though my brother's laughter had dislodged him from his seat. But even he found difficulty in describing what he had seen. Despite the pleasures of the concert I felt jealous, for after a brief spell of resistance to the shocking American voices and general

vulgarity I had succumbed to the talkies as I had to silent pictures. The film had been *The Cocoanuts*.[80]

That familiar, treacherous nostalgia of the self-made intellectual for more demotic forms of art was to become for Fuller an abiding preoccupation; as Noel Coward famously put it, 'Extraordinary how potent cheap music is.'

★

At his 'Seafolde House' interview, Roy Fuller's mother had assured the Headmaster that her son was 'a terrible reader', and the misunderstood colloquialism temporarily consigned him to the ignominious Form 2b: in other words, he was the kind of child who, formal qualifications aside, was always going to provide his own literary education, irrespective of the goodness or badness of his school. When asked by an interviewer, Brian Morton, whether he had received a good literary education at school, he replied in a single decisive word − 'Rotten' − before elaborating somewhat:

> I wasn't literary at school at all. I was mathematical. As for home, my father died when I was very young, but he had read. He had a bookcase full of John Buchan, things like that. So there were books about when I was younger. My mother would borrow books from the twopenny library but not literary stuff. Yet my brother and I both became fanatical readers; he is four years younger than I am and has been a great book-collector all his life. He was reading Dostoyevsky at twelve. It was just some bug we were born with.[81]

'I can't really remember a time when reading or being read to wasn't an indispensable drug,' he told Alan Ross in another interview. Bug or drug, it was certainly an addiction:

> I think I must have been thirteen or fourteen when I began to write in a competitive literary way − minuscule Maeterlinckian plays, as I remember. Then I ploughed through a number of more or less unsuitable influences: G.K. Chesterton, H.G. Wells, Humbert Wolfe, Aldous Huxley, *et al.* − though the last-named has always been behind my prose fiction, particularly his eye for nose-picking and the like. Only at eighteen when I was luckily made aware of Edgell Rickword, Auden, Spender and Empson did I begin to compete in any sensible way...[82]

The theme was constant, though amenable to quite startling variations, such as this one from a lecture delivered to the Royal Society of Literature at much the same time:

> My life was as provincial, my background as non-literary, my schooling as uninspired, my further education as truncated, as Owen's. But at 16 I bought Ezra Pound's *Selected Poems*, then just published, edited and introduced by T.S. Eliot. And I knew the Eliot collected poems of 1925. Needless to say, such poetic education was completely extra-curricular, for at that time the verse anthologies included in the set books for matriculation took one no farther than Margaret L. Woods and John Drinkwater.[83]

The memoirs provide the most considered view of the terrible reader's addiction, charting a progress which begins with Richmal Crompton and moves on to E. Phillips Oppenheim;[84] continues with him writing 'short stories in the manner of H.G. Wells and Aldous Huxley' in 1928 'or possibly earlier';[85] finds him sidetracked by D.H. Lawrence;[86] and eventually arrives at Auden, Rickword, and Spender under the guidance of John Davenport.[87]

Even though Fuller may have regretted the deficiencies in an education which resulted in his being articled to a firm of Blackpool solicitors at the age of sixteen, it would be unwise to accept that regret as unqualified or to share it unreservedly. The very fact that in the late 1950s, when his son had completed an academically more prosperous school career at St Paul's – John was at Oxford and editing *Isis* when *The Ruined Boys* appeared in 1959 – he should have so carefully reworked his own schooldays into fiction is one clear instance of the way in which his life and art were always inseparably entwined: 'I suppose for me everyday life has never ceased to seem poetic life'.[88] To suggest that being forced into an everyday, office-bound career for which he felt he had no particular talent was therefore actually a blessing might represent an over-effortful translation of necessity into virtue, but it unmistakably made him the distinctive writer he was.

Fuller left Blackpool High School at the end of the autumn term in 1928, and the following spring commenced his five years' articles with the firm of T. & F. Wylie Kay. 'The choice that was put to me,' he told Anthony Thwaite, was that there was enough money for me to become qualified in a profession. And in those days, the easiest way and the cheapest way, I think, to become qualified was not to go to university but to go and be articled or apprenticed or whatever it might be. I was literary even at fifteen, sixteen, faintly ambitious in a vague way. The law, being not very far from Victorian days at that time, seemed to have this literary aura: nothing could be further, really, from reality; the ordinary provincial solicitor had absolutely no more literary trimmings than the ordinary provincial butcher. But in my mind was the notion that to study to be a lawyer and qualify would give me a bit of a leg-up in the practice of literature, and that at some suitable day one could glide over as Galsworthy had done and become a successful novelist. Hopeless notion, really.[89]

He was at once immersed in an Arnold Bennett-like provincial business environment which, despite his retrospective grumblings, suited his imagination well; indeed, Bennett and Fuller himself are among the surprisingly few twentieth-century English writers to have seen the endless comic and ironic possibilities of that richly eccentric world. 'T. &. F. Wylie Kay was not the right sort of firm to train me in the practice of the law,' he recalled,[90] but it had other attractions. There were two partners, uncle and nephew, Tom and Eric Wylie Kay; Fuller was articled to Mr Eric. Both were smart dressers, Mr Tom being visited by a tailor from Savile Row to be be measured for his suits, which were rumoured to cost fourteen guineas and which contributed formatively to Fuller's lifelong obsession with sartorial correctness;[91] he himself obtained suits locally, from the ready-to-wear department of Southworth's, where one of the Southworth brothers – a slender man with centre-parted brilliantined hair and a speech impediment – would invariably pronounce them to be 'Very tony, Mr Fuller. Extremely nutty.'[92] Fuller continued to patronise Southworth's, no doubt for satirical as well as sartorial reasons, until he finally left Blackpool in 1936; he was married in one of their suits (it was light brown and, unlike Mr Tom's, cost a mere three guineas), while a very warm and substantial camel-coloured overcoat which he had made by them was subsequently lent to Giles Romilly in 1940 and ended up with him in Colditz, where its nuttiness must have been somewhat compromised.

Fuller had two companions in his upstairs room at Wylie Kay's: G.W. Briggs, a graduate articled clerk (called, with odd literalness, Byng in the memoirs, like his namesake at 'Seafolde House') who possessed an enviable raglan overcoat 'built for Byng by obviously excellent tailors in his university town',[93] and Norman Lees, the engrossing clerk, more impoverished in bowler hat and shabby gabardine raincoat; eventually they were joined by another articled clerk, 'Fatty' Mason, who was notable mainly for his expensive Stetson trilby hat but useful because his arrival made up a bridge four. This required a certain degree of subterfuge, with cards laid out in a desk drawer which could be closed at the sound of the managing clerk's approaching footsteps, and made a restful change from the articled clerks' other regular occupation, which was betting on horses according to an inevitably hopeless system called 'The 220' which Fuller, with a persistence 'typical of my stubborn support in several of life's affairs, of dotty logic over common sense',[94] was the last to abandon, having cashed in his only asset, £10 of National Savings Certificates − not a fortune perhaps, but enough to have bought three suits from Southworth's. He later expressed surprise at the tolerable quality of work done in the office, 'considering the problems of bridge and horses in the background'.[95] Occasionally, the Fuller-Lees-Briggs triumvirate would undertake out-of-office excursions, including visits to Kempton Park races and to the Lake District: 'I remember that Lakes trip,' he told Lees; 'at any rate, I remember swimming in a tarn with GWB − in the nude − to which he may have been accustomed from his Cambridge days (cf Anthony Blunt, etc). As I recall, you were more prudent.'[96]

Of these early colleagues, Norman Lees had talents of observant mimicry and literary parody, as well as 'a deep quirkiness and reticence about him', qualities which neatly matched Fuller's own: 'I remember his once pointing out the grammatical curiousness of the idiom (I think a wholly North of England one) "partly what", and then moving on to a kind of Empsonian discussion (the occasion must have been in a pub) of the difference between saying a glass was "partly what full" and "partly what empty".'[97] Anecdotes like that provide vivid reminders of the way in which life in a provincial solicitor's office had for this young writer distinct similarities with more conventional kinds of further education; in its own way, Wylie Kay's was not unlike the architect's office in Dorchester

where the sixteen-year-old Thomas Hardy served his apprentice-
ship, 'an exceptionally literate place for a young man who already
had a stock of reading in his head'.[98] The parodic humour, too, was
appropriately of the sort usually described as 'undergraduate'. Fifty
years later, Fuller would admiringly recall Lees' version of
Tennyson's 'The Revenge', in which the second line ('And a
pinnace, like a flutter'd bird, came flying from far away') was
emended to 'And a pinnace, like a buttered turd, came sliding from
far away',[99] having first engaged in some scholarly debate with the
author: 'I will brood on "sliding" (apropos buttered turds)...
Tennyson had "flying" and retaining that incongruously I'm not
sure doesn't add to the effect.'[100] Lees, who was to remain a friend
until his death in 1987, later qualified as a solicitor and eventually
set up his own successful practice in Blackpool, acting professionally for Fuller during the latter's war service abroad. (It was
Norman Lees, too, who was able to warn Fuller, when *The Ruined
Boys* was in typescript, that Arthur Anderson, presumed safely
dead, was very much alive and teaching,[101] and indeed attending
church. Fuller gratefully replied: 'Your vivid picture of the aged
A.P.A. & his aged spouse, walking to Holy Trinity tore at my heart
strings, in more senses than one. Plainly, I shall have to remove
from my story any matter that might offend, for there is no doubt
they will go on walking to H.T. for many years.')[102]

To enhance his somewhat restricted legal education, or more
probably to break up the bridge four, Fuller was transferred from
the congenial idleness of his upstairs room to the less colourful
though equally odd litigation department. Here he worked alongside a pallid, funereal individual called Gaggs, whom he renamed
Docking, after the town's leading undertakers, and an elderly solicitor called Harry Ianson who had 'white hair, a red face, big ears, a
scattering of fangs, and a voice so loud that on the telephone some
claimed he could be heard in the back street'.[103] Ianson was friendly
enough, and he had a pungent line in creative vulgarity, but as a
source of legal instruction he was almost completely useless. He
soon left the firm, in any case, during a general upheaval caused by
the death of Mr Tom; this event disclosed a substratum of familial
disharmony which would have delighted Arnold Bennett, an
unsuspected feud between uncle and nephew. Mr Tom left a good
deal of money, but Mr Eric got none of it (although he inherited
the practice), and the administration of the estate was pointedly

passed to a firm in Manchester. Fuller, with his already well-developed sartorial obsession, seems to have been chiefly impressed by the fact that the clerks were to have suits of mourning, though he was less pleased to discover that these would be made by a client, 'a tailor not noted for raglan or ratcatcher or anything to go with a hat by Stetson'.[104]

Mr Eric's tenure as senior partner at Wylie Kay's did not last long. While driving along Blackpool Promenade, he suffered a fatal heart attack and crashed, with an aptness which in fiction might seem thoroughly suspect, into the Hotel Metropole.

★

Fuller's life as an articled clerk may have had an appearance of humdrum confinement, but it was to provide his escape-route from Blackpool and, by a bizarre sequence of chances, his introduction to the literary world. In due course, he would spend time in London preparing for the Law Society's examinations. Meanwhile, there were twice-weekly visits, on Mondays and Thursdays during term time, to the law department at Manchester University. His compulsory lectures were in the afternoons, which left the mornings free for browsing in bookshops, where he acquired among other things the Egoist Press *Dubliners* and wistfully wondered how to obtain the elusive book there tantalisingly described as 'In Preparation *Ulysses*'. It was of course a retrospective journey towards the places of early childhood – on one occasion literally so when, having stayed for a concert and belatedly discovered that the last train to Blackpool didn't run on Mondays, he turned up late in the evening on the doorstep of his surprised grandparents in Hollins Road, Oldham. That Monday concert, one of a popular 'Municipal' series given by the Hallé and doubtless comprising repertoire not far removed from the pier end, was for Fuller something of an aberration; but he devotedly attended the more substantial Thursday programmes, despite his lack of enthusiasm for the permanent conductor, Hamilton Harty.

On one notable occasion, however, Constant Lambert's *The Rio Grande* was conducted by the composer, and the piano part, much to Fuller's surprise, was 'brilliantly played by Harty'.[105] This would have been the work's first concert performance, following its BBC première on 12 December 1929, which was, says Lambert's biographer Andrew Motion, 'more than simply a

success: it was the popular triumph of his career as a composer'.[106]
Lambert was also to prove an enduring influence on Fuller through
his book *Music Ho!*, published in 1934, one theme of which is

> the desirability of a continuous tradition in music of the modern
> epoch – the fingerprinting and almost unconscious changing of
> the old forms being sufficient 'progress' in the art, a notion
> (though I put it crudely) that has always greatly attracted me in
> the arts generally.[107]

Echoes not only of Lambert's cultural bearings but of his critical
style recur in Fuller's work, notably in his Oxford lectures.

It was on the last train back to Blackpool, and therefore after a
Thursday concert, that he met the friend called Bobby in the
memoirs, on whom Jack Burton in *The Perfect Fool* is cautiously
based. Bobby, who was in his mid-thirties, was a dapperly-dressed
regular concert-goer, at whose suggestion Fuller subscribed to the
chamber concerts held in the Metropole lounge; he worked as a
rep for a firm of manufacturing chemists, keeping the corner-shops
of Lancashire stocked up with remedies for common complaints, a
mildly though perhaps enjoyably ludicrous occupation for so
theatrical a character. Fuller rejected with some embarrassment
Bobby's 'rarely and most tactfully indicated' sexual interest,[108]
which seems not to have affected their friendship at the time; after
the war, however, he rather awkwardly avoided a purely social
reunion, and there is an unmistakable shadow of his sense of having
failed his friend in *Fantasy and Fugue*.[109] But Bobby was of even
greater significance in Fuller's life for almost inadvertently introducing him to John Davenport, his first real acquaintance within
the literary world and the most formative single influence on his
adult reading (and, hence, writing). As is often the case, the actual
course of events has a quality of accidental, lop-sided irony which
is quite missing in the fiction derived from it.

In 1930,[110] Muriel George, soon to become a film actress special-
ising in the portrayal of charladies and landladies, was appearing
with her husband Ernest Butcher in what was 'essentially a pierrot
show or concert party, such as my Uncle John had figured in as the
soubrette during the First World War'[111] on Blackpool's Central
Pier. It sounds exactly the kind of entertainment which the culturally aspirant eighteen-year-old Roy Fuller might by then have
treated with some disdain, but he nevertheless allowed himself to be

taken to it by Bobby, who was acquainted with Muriel George. After the show they went backstage to meet her: there, Fuller was presented, doubtless with more than a touch of gently malicious campness, as 'a slavish admirer'. Lurking in the shadows of the dressing-room was a portly young man: this was her son, John Davenport, who had launched his literary career by co-editing and contributing to *Cambridge Poetry 1929* and who had been fore-warned of Fuller's own ambitions as a writer. He would become a famously irascible character as well as a highly influential literary journalist on the *Observer*, and he was impressive even in 1930:

> In later years he put on more weight but even when I first knew him he was notably solid, a stout man of the formidable rather than the genial kind. His brown hair was cut and brushed in schoolboy style... above a flat face. Bulldog Drummond is intro-duced as ugly but attractive, a rather literary concept which John, however, could be said to embody. On me he made an impression hardly to be over-emphasised.[112]

Hitherto, Fuller had been intoxicated by D.H. Lawrence, of whose recent death ('shocking as the death of Byron in a former day')[113] he had learned from another traveller's evening paper on the train back from Manchester; his devotion had an evangelical tinge, and he was fond of commending Lawrence to the typists at Wylie Kay's, who were not greatly impressed. Whatever Lawrence's ideo-logical attractions, later to be dismissed in characteristic phrases such as 'Lawrentian tripe'[114] and 'full of bosh',[115] he was quite the wrong sort of writer, in tone and technique (or lack of it) for Fuller to emulate. Davenport advised his new protégé, with understand-able self-interest, to acquire *Cambridge Poetry 1929* and to read other poems by Auden, Spender, Edgell Rickword. 'He simply,' Fuller told Anthony Thwaite,

> gave me a sort of reading-list: the Auden 1930 *Poems*, which one could buy for two and sixpence; there was no Spender book to buy, but you could buy the *Oxford Poetry* of 1930, which had about half a dozen poems by Spender in. So I was really in at the beginning of that, and most fortunate I count myself in so being, because otherwise it might have taken several years to get to known them, in which case I should have gone on writing like Sir Sacheverell Sitwell.[116]

As Samuel Hynes, identifying the 'characteristic qualities of between-the-wars poetry', has pointed out, 'The tone was ironic, could be bitter or angry, and could hate and condemn, but it avoided the upper register of emotions, the range of nobility and splendour and high tragedy.'[117] Naturally, the patient did not instantly adjust to this more nutritious and, as it were, higher-fibre literary diet: 'The drama of coming across for the first time the work of Rickword, Empson, Spender, Auden, *et al*, though stirring must not be exaggerated. The penny took a little time really to drop.'[118] But drop it did, with decisive and permanent consequences for Fuller's own poetry. Interestingly, it was the more accessible, less abrasive Spender who was at first more influential than Auden:

> I think it was Spender who had more impact: memorability, in the old sense of poetry being memorable, and *like* poetry, and being 'poetic' in inverted commas, was still there in Spender; plus these themes about Marxism, about unemployment, about a future and better life for the mass of mankind – not at all crudely expressed, but mixed up in this really and it seems to me now still excellent and very memorable poetry. The case of Auden I think I got something much cruder from. I very much liked his couplets in Tennyson's 'Loxley Hall' metre, dealing with contemporary things – that struck me as all good stuff.[119]

By this time, the flat overlooking the Metropole had become too much for Mrs Fuller: her worsening though undiagnosed hyperthyroidism was ostensibly the reason for moving but, as her son drily noted, 'My mother's restlessness was not always altogether forced by events and possibly met some inner need.'[120] She was also advised that sea air would be beneficial and took to travelling back and forth from Blackpool to the Isle of Man in order to inhale plenty of it. The young Frank Kermode 'was a purser on the IOM boats at the epoch my mother used to cross regularly for her health,' Fuller would delightedly discover; 'Probably punched her ticket.'[121] The Fullers' new rooms were in the semi-bungalow of a Mrs Sidey, at the southern end of Blackpool and an awkward tram-journey away from Wylie Kay's. They took with them an African grey parrot, a present from Leslie's father; the other residents, already installed, were a an ill-tempered Pekinese bitch called Beauty and Mrs Sidey's sallow son Victor:

He was as taken with the parrot as his zest for life allowed, standing in front of the cage watching the bird preening, juggling a sunflower seed with beak and tongue, clambering laboriously about the wire enclosure, pursuing other psittacine occupations. Sometimes Victor would utter the single syllable 'warks' which more often than not the bird echoed, but whether Victor taught the parrot this enigmatic word or vice versa was uncertain.[122]

As the creative environment of a budding writer who was just discovering the poetry of his major contemporaries, this milieu obviously left much to be desired.

Though Mrs Sidey was unmemorable – at least by comparison with parrot, Pekinese and Victor – 'like some weak monarch she gave her name to the epoch'.[123] Among that epoch's defining moments was Fuller's decision to start smoking cigarettes, less from any particular craving for their taste than from the sense that they were part of his emerging adult personality. It was also momentous, in a perhaps not wholly dissimilar way, as the period during which he first introduced his fiancée, Kathleen Smith, whom he would marry in 1936, to his mother and brother. These two events, however different in scale they may appear to be, have a clear sub-text in common: they are symbols of autonomy, gestures of rejection. It was time for the northern boy to become a southern man.

2: Southern Man

The constantly astonishing feature of central London, as
surprising to those who know it from infancy as to any
outsider, is its compactness: the way that everything in the heart of
the capital, the area loosely comprised by the West End and the
City, is within walking distance of everything else, so that the
streetmaps in the *A–Z* appear fussily over-ambitious as one steps
within minutes from Soho into Covent Garden and from Covent
Garden into Holborn. For Roy Fuller, studying at the law tutors
Gibson and Weldon in Chancery Lane while living in digs in
Guildford Street (between Russell Square and Gray's Inn Road), it
must have seemed smaller than Blackpool, and certainly more
conveniently arranged. 'London,' he recalled, 'had previously been
only the subject of a few brief visits, but I was soon on terms with
it in 1931, at least the Soho, Bloomsbury, Chancery Lane axis;
using the Underground a good deal.'[1]

At least two faces, those of Graham Miller and Eric Ashton,
were familiar from his home town. Miller ('Gilbert Waller' in
Fuller's memoirs) had been a day-boy contemporary at Blackpool
High School, where he distinguished himself by appearing at a
Boarders' Concert to provide, standing on a chair, an impromptu
performance of 'The Lass with a Delicate Air'.[2] Though true to his
owlishly impudent character, this was presumably not the specific
reason why he was later punched by an athletic older boy called
Wetton (who, like Mountain, his fictional counterpart in *The
Ruined Boys*, inspires in Fuller/Bracher a degree of frank hero
worship). Learning of this assault, Miller's father marched into the
playground and in return punched Wetton; then he withdrew his
son and transferred him to the presumably more peaceable environment of a Quaker boarding school, consistent with the whole-
food idealism of Mrs Miller, rather than with her husband's
unreconstructed Old Testament view of justice. Unsurprisingly,
young Graham's flair for subversive impertinence was not at all
dimmed by this experience, and he became a journalist on the *West
Lancashire Evening Gazette*. In 1931 he was taking a year's course in

journalism at London University, on the understanding (not to be fulfilled) that he would thereafter return to his former employment in Blackpool; instead, he worked first on the *Holborn Gazette* and then for the *Daily Express*, initially on lineage though subsequently as a salaried staff reporter:

> With merely a touch or two the boy soprano had transformed himself into a somewhat transatlantic idea of a journalist: a trenchcoat almost invariably worn; either no hat or a trilby with a brim turned down all the way round; cigarette in a holder; a hint of sideburns.[3]

Fuller the memoirist was to find his friendship with Miller 'strange', but to a less subjective eye it seems utterly comprehensible. Miller's lovably roguish qualities of nerve and plausibility were precisely what Fuller felt to be lacking in his own character; Miller, conversely, was quite untouched by the Fuller's rather prissy striving for correctness, respectability and timid good taste. 'Intellectually,' wrote Fuller, 'we had little in common, but he did introduce me to the records of such as Duke Ellington, Louis Armstrong, Joe Venuti, some of which (mainly the more *cantabile*, less frenetic parts) I liked a great deal.'[4] The delicious inappropriateness of '*cantabile*' as a term applicable to jazz is revealing beyond its intended retrospective irony. Always exaggeratedly aware of his own perceived shortcomings, Fuller was as envious of Miller's confidently journalistic grasp of affairs as he had been of Wetton's equally confident athleticism, even though he was amply provided with both these talents himself.

Miller was a compulsive prankster. In its mildest and most innocent manifestation, this enabled him to smuggle his friend into an English Literature lecture at the university after which, with a typical switch from shyness into its combative counterpart, Fuller ended up arguing with the lecturer. A more juvenile and perhaps more characteristic prank entailed sprinkling sneezing-powder on the centre pages of the *Evening Standard* before visiting the pubs of Gray's Inn Road, where one of the pair would open the paper at the bar and with a feigned sneeze disseminate the powder among the customers before retreating to observe its effects. Fuller's digs in Guildford Street had previously been occupied by Miller, who left after quarrelling with the landlady; on the penultimate day of Fuller's two-month spell there, and with his connivance, Miller re-entered the premises and concealed a kipper behind a picture in the dining-room – a stunt presumably imitated from the boarding-house of Beachcomber's Mrs McGurgle.

With impressive consistency, Miller adopted a similar approach to his professional life. By the time of Fuller's second stint in London, he had become a staff reporter on the *Express*, on one occasion in-geniously fabricating an interview with Sarah Churchill from a couple of doorstep 'no comments', and on another contriving to photograph a supposedly murdered corpse through having a chum in the mortuary. Fuller's contribution to the latter prank involved propping up the head, apparently with the help of a hammer. The photograph was printed, the corpse adorned with a fake collar and tie, even though the coroner's verdict of death by natural causes rather spoilt the story. Nevertheless, the mortuary visit would prove useful to Fuller when he turned his hand to crime fiction.

Though his style of journalism would increasingly come to dominate the popular press, Graham Miller was not to enjoy a distinguished career with the Beaverbrook empire. He contracted tuberculosis, nevertheless treating his illness with characteristic panache:

> He said once he woke out of a doze in hospital to find a cler-gyman at his bedside, perhaps even muttering some *nunc dimittis* over him. For the first time, he realized his death was antici-pated, resolved there and the to postpone that fate; as an initial step telling the cleric to bugger off. A quack remedy for consumption called UMKALAOBO had been achieving publicity for its efficiency, perhaps in the *Daily Express*, despite the connotation of witch-doctoring in the name. It was the invention of Major C.H. Stevens, who inspired the creation by H.G. Wells of Tono-Bungay and its originator in the epony-mous novel. Miller commanded his parents to obtain a supply, took it as directed, and was quite rapidly cured.[5]

Later, Miller became English correspondent for the New York *Daily News* and was, according to Fuller, 'fabulously rich on a bottomless expense account';[6] by the early 1950s, he was living with his second wife in Chiswick, near Roy Fuller's brother John. One Guy Fawkes' Night, the various Fullers were invited round; the fireworks were accompanied by traditional Lancashire parkin and treacle toffee. This seemed to Fuller 'somewhat precious', but in a way it was both nostalgic and oddly prescient: soon afterwards Miller's wife ran off with the local vicar, while Miller himself eventually returned to Blackpool, married a third time, and was last seen by the indefatigable Lees 'sitting idly outside an emporium selling (*inter alia*) picture postcards'.[7] It was a ludicrously apt and rather touching end.

Eric Ashton ('Alec Marston' in the memoirs), though outwardly less eccentric than Miller, was the son of a Blackpool councillor who hoarded cartons of Kensitas cigarettes (to accumulate the gift-coupons in advance) and owed his income to the manufacture of a doubtful substance called 'confectioner's egg'. Fuller, who had graduated from his mother's Craven A to Player's Gold Leaf, 'sometimes accepted a Kensitas from Councillor Marston, but marvelled at anyone smoking the things, even allowing for the gifts':[8] the due consideration of smoking habits, minutiae of a subculture now almost wholly extinguished, would remain for Fuller a vital factor in assessing an individual's character, rather as his grandfather had based his deductions on whether or not the rind remained attached to a portion of cheese.

Fuller had known Eric Ashton at kindergarten, 'where he had stood out as a knowing and articulate infant',[9] qualities which he retained as a surprisingly young advertising copy-writer. Ashton, exemplifying what would become a well-documented link between advertising and the murkier corners of the literary world, introduced Fuller to the cafés and characters of Soho, especially the Café Bleu in Old Compton Street and its habitués such as Ironfoot Jack and the poet Paul Potts. It says much for Fuller's youthful perspicacity that he was not remotely taken in by this Bohemian blur:

> Though I liked Soho, I saw that those of its denizens I knew were failures, perhaps permanently in that category... I used to wonder, as the hours slipped away in the Bleu, just when the painters painted and the writers wrote, though the same question applied to me with even greater point.[10]

In a sense, this is true. Like every intelligent young writer, Fuller was frustrated by a feeling of time wasted, and still more dismayed by it in retrospect. Was he himself, after all, so very far from the Bleu category, idly listening to records of Red Nichols or playing the pin-table at Charley's café in Marchmont Street, where Miller, whose favourite haunt it was, would in bad times subsist on a

'Cupper tea and a golden pudding'?[11] If the answer to that question is an unqualified 'yes', it is because Fuller knew beyond doubt that, for him at least, the full-time 'creative' life would have been a dangerous delusion and because Charley's café belonged unmistakably to a recognisable everyday world rather than to some self-insulating artistic enclave. The choice of Marchmont Street rather than Old Compton Street defines Fuller's character better than cigarette-brands or cheese-rinds and clearly indicates the kind of writer he was to become.

Eric Ashton soon returned to Blackpool, eventually succeeding to his father's confectioner's egg business, which flourished during and after the war. A little later, he turned up with a girl at the Fullers' flat in Blackheath and the following evening entertained them to a lavish and somewhat alcoholic dinner at the Gargoyle Club (which appears as the Corydon Club, and its bandleader Buddy Featherstonehaugh as Sonny Frankland, in *Fantasy and Fugue*). However, among the many dubious attributes of confectioner's egg was its provision for Ashton of wealth insufficiently disclosed to the Inland Revenue:

> Most of his acquaintances must have been sympathetic or at least tactful, but when his old friend Waller called on him, the former's opening words, uttered not without relish, were: 'Well, you *are* in the shit, aren't you?' Though the confrontation came to us second-hand, one could visualize Waller on the doorstep, trenchcoat open, carrying a walking-stick, and blinking owlishly – characteristic image from the days when I, too, had helped to waft sneezing-powder into the nostrils of quiet drinkers on the edge of Bloomsbury. The tax fraud earned Ashton a spell in prison, though his prosperity seemed not much affected, and he survived Waller for a good few years in the Channel Isles, where the Inland Revenue's fell hand did not extend.[12]

★

When Fuller spotted Aldous Huxley in St James's Square, he followed him into Straker's, the stationers; Huxley, wearing a tweed suit and an unusual plain orange tie, and for some reason carrying a cheap edition of his own *Crome Yellow*, picked up and examined 'a grotesquely large model of a lead-pencil tip',[13] after which Fuller retreated in embarrassment. On another occasion,

browsing from the pavement, he knocked over a few books in
Charlie Lahr's glassless bookshop in Red Lion Street and imagined
himself 'for ever stigmatized in his view as a careless nitwtit'.[14]
There was nothing unusual about his wish to stare at the famous,
still less about his clumsiness in so precarious an environment as
Lahr's bookshop; the only odd common feature is the painful
intensity of his self-consciousness.

Admissions of shyness and awkwardness, an inability to make
social small-talk or to cope confidently with life's trivial transactions, echo and re-echo through Fuller's work. There is no reason
to doubt their sincerity. At the same time, it is worth insisting that
the cultural ambitions which prompted a young man from
Lancashire to dog Aldous Huxley's footsteps or to browse in
Charlie Lahr's bookshop were rooted in coherent intellectual and
democratic principles. As a regular patron of the fivepenny seats in
the gallery of the Old Vic, Fuller would find himself among 'a fair
proportion of local residents, some regulars, or otherwise known to
each other, a few of proletarian eccentricity – an extension of the
life of the market stalls in The Cut and Lower Marsh'.[15] The significance of this is precisely that it was unsurprising: it confirmed ideas
and ideals, rooted in Fuller's Oldham days, which were to inform
his entire life.

> That the cultural aspirations of the poor, or not over well-off,
> paralleled what came more easily to the affluent seemed to me
> perfectly natural. Questions of elitism, of hating 'bourgeois'
> culture, of a special brand of drama or poetry for the working class
> did not arise; and even in later, Marxist days I imagined culture
> being desirably broadened as much by increased leisure and pros-
> perity as by new forms and attitudes. Cruder (indeed, sillier) art
> for the 'community' would have been a complete puzzlement...
> I never doubted toiling humanity's essential goodness, its innate
> wish for advancement. That the latter was widespread among the
> lower classes was demonstrated, one might add, by conversations
> had and overheard during the ensuing war.[16]

On such generous and provenly workable principles were founded
grammar schools and public libraries, the WEA and the Third
Programme. The future member of the Arts Council and governor
of the BBC would find himself understandably baffled and angered
by their eventual abandonment.

Of course, Fuller's London life in 1931 and 1933 did have its more exclusive aspect, and this — the irony could hardly be lost on him — was one which held little real interest. Still, he did his best. One of the lecturers at Gibson and Weldon, L. Crispin Warmington, was fond of enlivening his discourse on hypothetical land disputes — which seemed typically to occur in Esher — concerning Blackacre and Whiteacre by introducing Greenacre and exceptionally Purpleacre into the argument. Fuller would do without the monochrome names altogether and begin with Puceacre; he would also choose literary rather than litigious pseudonyms, such as Panurge or Stephen Dedalus, to label test papers. It was perhaps as well for his results that he had not at this stage come across the the name of the film actor Edward Everett Horton's estate, which was Belly Acres. The attractions of a knowing, bookish jokiness must have seemed irresistible in student days 'dominated by the common law, the great leading cases about the escape from property of dangerous substances; snails in ginger-beer bottles; advertisements guaranteeing the efficacy of influenza remedies'.[17] The case of Donoghue v. Stevenson (1932) — in which Mrs Donoghue, who had encountered a decomposing snail in her ginger-beer, successfully sued the manufacturer — was topical as well as legally important, though unlikely to prove of consuming interest to an aspiring poet.[18]

However tedious the syllabus may have seemed, the Law Society's examinations were more than just a routine formality. The failure rate could be at least 40 per cent, condemning many to hopeless careers as unqualified legal executives. Fuller had no great enthusiasm for his profession, and he resolved never to study for an examination again, but his abilities were better suited to the Law than he would probably have cared to admit. In both the Intermediate Examination of March 1931 and the Final of November 1933, he passed comfortably.

Thus qualified as a solicitor, he naturally returned to Blackpool, to T. & F. Wylie Kay's, where he was paid £3 a week — *ex gratia*, for he had no formal entitlement to a salary until his articles expired. His restlessness became evident, if not clearly focused, almost immediately; Parker and Parker, a rival firm of solicitors based in Preston, offered him the post of manager at their tiny Blackpool branch — the staff comprised Fuller and the office boy, but business was so slack that the boy had often to be sent home early — and a

salary of £4.10s a week, a figure which Wylie Kay's would almost
certainly have matched with some tactful persuasion. As a kind of
wilful wrong choice, it oddly mirrored his mother's choice of the
declining Blackpool High School over the flourishing Arnold
School; for though as a one-man-band he necessarily learnt a bit
(not least how to fend off impostors such as the inventor of a novel
hospital bed who was subsequently convicted of fraud), within a
year one of the Parker brothers died, the practice was merged with
the firm of W. and B. Blackhurst, whose main office was in
Blackpool, and the branch of Parker's closed down. Fuller might
have expected, and without extraordinary effort obtained, the offer
of a job with Blackhurst's. Interviewed by William Blackhurst ('a
dark, stout, forceful man in his forties'), and asked how he would
have set about building up the practice, Fuller 'said something
about joining a golf club, which I imagined to be received wisdom.
Had I specified the Masons it would have been no farther from my
inclinations or intentions.'[19] However impeccable the wisdom, it
does sound as if he wasn't really trying.

One reason for his lack of keenness about the golf-clubbing
aspect of a solicitor's life was his increasing political engagement.
He was inclined to trace this back to the morning after the General
Election of December 1923, when the boarders of Blackpool High
School encountered, on their way to breakfast, the Headmaster's
plump son displaying the result for the Blackpool constituency – in
which the Liberal candidate had ousted the sitting Conservative
member. During his remaining schooldays, he had become
'convinced of the justice and feasibility of socialism'; at the General
Election of 1927, 'I proclaimed my allegiance to Labour, a position
still highly unrespectable for the provincial middle-classes.'[20] This
allegiance remained essentially unfocused – it was sufficiently
blurred for him to have attended the inaugural meeting of Mosley's
New Party during his first spell in London, and to have been flattered by the attention of Harold Nicolson, whom he met in a train
corridor and who admired his red sweater – until his return to
Blackpool in 1931 when, declaring his readiness to join the
Communist Party of Great Britain, he was introduced by Eric
Ashton to a discussion group which met above a pub.

Prominent among the group's members were Terry Warnock,
'one of the few men I have known whose views and proposals for
action almost invariably seemed correct',[21] and Ben Goodman, the

local leader of the CPGB, at whose behest Fuller occasionally stood on the street selling the *Daily Worker* and even wrote for the paper 'about the problems of the seasonal worker, particularly as to unemployment benefit, law being much involved'.[22] Though initially ignorant about political procedures, resolutions and amendments, and the identities of trades unions known only by initials or acronyms,

> By the time of the General Election of 1935 I was able with outward sangfroid to chair a large meting in the Co-operative Hall under the auspices of the local branch of the 'Peace Council', a popular front organization which might have been invented for a left-winger leading a respectable bourgeois existence; in a sense was![23]

This undertaking, momentous in any case for a shy 23-year-old newly qualified solicitor, was made the more risky by the simultaneous presence on the platform of all three local candidates. The Conservative, a barrister called J. Roland Robinson, brilliantly discomfited the chairman by asking him to lead the meeting in singing the National Anthem, an obviously impossible demand at such an avowedly internationalist gathering. Fuller replied, 'That is not on the meeting's agenda,' but had to stand 'in agonized silent embarrassement' as Robinson 'raised his voice in song, in which he was quickly joined by a sufficient number.'[24] To make matters worse, Robinson was duly elected and remained Blackpool's MP until 1964, when he became Governor of Bermuda and took the wonderfully Audenesque title of Lord Martonmere.

In 1935, then, Fuller found himself qualified but unemployed, with the only entry on his CV, after his articles, a year's terminal managership of a notably unsuccessful solicitor's branch office. Half-heartedly, he attached a sign saying 'R.B. FULLER SOLICITOR' to the gate-post of his mother's latest house: it was hopelessly located from a business point of view, although – if he had chosen to take his own whimsical advice – conveniently close to the North Shore Golf Club. A few passers-by actually dropped in, but there was never going to be a living in it. He applied for various jobs, recognising the unpalatable fact that he might after all have to remain in the North, far from where he supposed the hub of literary life might be. However, early in 1936, he was interviewed for an assistant solicitorship with the firm of Kingsford, Flower and

Pain, at Ashford in Kent: he got the job. No doubt it seemed an ordinarily lucky break, a tolerable stop-gap position in a small, distant, unfamiliar town. But it was much more than that: his war service apart, Fuller would work and live for the rest of his life on the Kentish side of the Thames.

★

During the three years he spent working in Ashford, Fuller became a husband, a father, a respectably published poet and a properly competent solicitor. Of course, on paper he could already lay claim to the last of these qualifications – 'I am accustomed to working without supervision,' he would quite truthfully state in his job applications, omitting to add that he had seldom had any work worth speaking of – but at Kingsford, Flower and Pain, he discovered he still had plenty to learn. His principal teacher was the junior partner, Harold Pain: old-fashioned, in gold-rimmed spectacles, starched collar and clerical grey suit, Pain proved to be benevolent and efficient and, above all, genuinely fond of his work as a country solicitor. Fuller affectionately recalled: 'About the ordinary affairs of humanity (moving house, say, or dying) with which his professional work was pretty well exclusively concerned, he spoke with a committed enjoyment almost gastronomic at moments of greatest enthusiasm, when one detected a faint slushing of saliva under some of his words...'.[25] Harold Pain was precisely the man to demonstrate that conveyancing involved actual properties, with all their obstinate peculiarities, rather than elegant fictions called Purpleacre and Puceacre. Occasionally, the clients themselves might turn out to be equally distinctive: 'As a matter of interest,' Fuller proudly reported to Norman Lees in 1937, 'I've just conveyed a plot of land to Edith Evans – *the* E.E.'[26]

Not that his duties were confined to desk-bound matters: on the contrary, he had been employed mainly to spare Frank Flower, the senior partner, the trouble of appearing in court. Cases he later remembered concerned a First World War pilot on a drugs charge, a dairy farmer alleged to have watered his milk, and a young man accused of raping his sister-in-law: they were not the stuff which would have kept Rumpole well-fed, but they were more than enough to engage an imagination which toyed with the idea of writing crime fiction and a mind more fascinated by the law than its owner usually cared to admit. (There is a charming giveaway

aside in which he describes himself while waiting for his interview
at Kingsford's, 'passing the time by reading a volume of the Law
Reports, always containing something fresh and good',[27] which
hardly seems the attitude of one who still felt he had been
dragooned into his profession.) Often, he would be driven to court
by the articled clerk, Richard Flower, in his father's soft-top
Triumph Roadster; and on one memorable occasion the somewhat
sinister Ashford Superintendent of Police (who was 'fat and jolly
but, as one conceived it, not jolly all through') gave him a lift back
from a magistrates' court, 'at least one stop on the way, at the
premises of an obsequious publican, confirming the view of the
police taken by *State and Revolution*'.[28] Such material would have
needed little more than a nudge to become part of a decidedly *noir*
detective novel: two unpublished works of fiction – *Next Day*
(1939/40) and the interesting but incomplete *The Agents* (begun in
October 1940) – glance in this direction, but the fat, only partially
jolly Ashford Superintendent eventually metamorphoses into
Inspector Toller in *With My Little Eye* ('He was fattish, and his face
was fat... He looked like a once-handsome, once-jolly farmer who
had just come out of jail with jaundice').[29]

Active involvement in left-wing politics was obviously less available to a comfortably employed solicitor in Kent than to an unemployed one in Blackpool, yet – perhaps consequently – Fuller's
political views developed a stridency presumably unsuspected by
Messrs Flower and Pain. On 12 March 1936, he wrote from his
digs at 32 Wellesley Road, Ashford, a letter of corrosive fury to
Derek Savage:

> If you are writing *modern* verse, you must either be reactionary or
> revolutionary i.e. a Fascist or a Communist. Art is conditioned by
> the economic relations of society, and society at the moment is in
> the throes of a change from one set of economic relations to
> another viz. capitalism to communism. If you are not writing
> modern verse you are entirely negligable [*sic*] e.g. W.H.Davies in
> our time, Stephen Phillips *et al* poetasters in former time.
>
> Really, this is all elementary Marxism – but the Poets' Corner
> & *New Verse* have not learnt it yet.
>
> Take war – what's the good of writing (sentimentally) about
> it if you don't know what causes it? That's the weakness of all the
> 1914–18 war poets.[30]

That last paragraph was to prove especially ironic, during the coming decade, for this poet of the Second World War.

Meanwhile, the remaining few years of peace were, in every way, almost too packed. On 25 June 1936, Fuller – wearing, of course, a suit from Southworth's – married Kathleen Smith, whom he had met some seven years earlier and who at that time worked for the *West Lancashire Evening Gazette*. They moved to a flat above a sweet-shop at 227a Faversham Road, Kennington, a village just outside Ashford: the landlord wanted to redecorate it and charge 17s 6d a week, but in a possibly unfamiliar spirit of Northern canniness they beat him down to sixteen shillings by doing without the redecoration. At that price, they had to expect some peculiar feature, and in this flat the drawback was a minute kitchen: 'A good job my mother saw the premises only as a *fait accompli*,' said Fuller, an odd worry in view of her own determinedly eccentric choice of dwellings.[31] To Savage, he described it as 'further into the country – away from this un-English world of civil war, united fronts, anti-Jew baiting, improved workers' conditions, soviets and other continental activities!'[32] In the same letter he wrote, with odd reticence or reluctance: 'I have to say that I have married a wife.' However, he said nothing at all of what must, by mid-December, have been his most pressing concern: on New Year's Day 1937, Kathleen gave birth to a son, John Leopold, named after his uncle and his grandfather, and happily unperturbed by the man in far-away Oldham Market Place with as many noses as there were days in the year. Within a few months, his father could report to Lees: 'The scion of the Fullers grows in wisdom and stature. I now see him on the floor consuming hairs from the carpet.'[33]

While living in Kennington, the Fullers made good friends: Mervyn Bompas, junior partner in Ashford's main firm of solicitors (Hallett, Creery and Co.), from whom Mrs Fuller acquired the permanently-shortened forename 'Kate'; Jack Clark, then at Oxford, whose family lived nearby in the village, and who with a fellow undergraduate called Rodney Philips (founder of the magazine *Polemic*) first met them literally on their doorstep on a summer evening in 1938. The Oxonian pair 'were in some disbelief that close to the Clark family house could actually reside a contributor to *New Writing*, as, in a way that now seems baffling, had been reported to them.'[34] But such was the astonishing case, thanks to a poem in memory of Maurice Stott, a friend from his Blackpool

'loose group' days, called 'To M.S., Killed in Spain'.[35] Not only had
he been published; he had even been heard of.

His earlier published poems – he had unsuccessfully been
sending off work to magazines like *John O'London's Weekly* since his
schooldays – had appeared in the 'Poets' Corner' of the *Sunday
Referee* in 1933 and, more plausibly, in Geoffrey Grigson's *New
Verse* the following year. Payment from the *Sunday Referee* came in
the curious form of a penknife; nevertheless, 'it was a Sunday paper
with a respectable circulation, so one was really rather chuffed
at seeing one's poem there.'[36] These poems were credited to
R.B. Fuller, which was at that time somewhat inauspiciously the
name, attached to a Blackpool gatepost, of an unemployed solicitor. It was Julian Symons, whom he met soon after the start of the
magazine *Twentieth Century Verse* in 1937, who presciently advised:
'Unless it is Reginald, you ought to use your first name.'[37] Initials
had served Yeats, Eliot and Auden well enough, but Symons had
correctly identified the predominant literary style of the future.
'The person I met,' Symons later recalled,

> was a handsome slim figure of medium height, soberly dressed
> yet giving a slightly dandyish impression, with a pleasant voice
> that retained a slight trace of Lancastrian origin, and a manner
> originally cautious but within a few minutes easy, down-to-
> earth, at times sharp or ironic.[38]

Twentieth Century Verse provided both an antidote to the shortcomings of Grigson's magazine, and a focus for writers like Fuller, and
Symons himself, who felt excluded by the public school and
Oxbridge bias of *New Verse* and of John Lehmann's *New Writing*,
founded in 1936. 'I talked to Herbert [Mallalieu] and Derek
[Savage] about my idea of starting a magazine,' wrote Symons. 'No
doubt we had in mind getting our own poems printed, but there
was a real difference of attitude then between poets who had been
to a university, like Auden, Spender, MacNeice, Day Lewis,
Lehmann, and those who hadn't, like Thomas, Barker, Ruthven
[Todd], Roy Fuller, and the three of us';[39] Fuller would in due
course submit a contributor's note for the magazine in which,
somewhat ambiguously, he described himself as 'Handicapped by
attendance at neither Public School or University'.[40] This kind of
negative kinship proved to be a strongly unifying force, as George
Woodcock, another contributor to *Twentieth Century Verse* born in

the same year as Fuller and Symons, has also noted:

> We were all brought up, not without difficulty, by mothers after our fathers had died during our childhood. Unlike the elder poets of the Thirties (Spender only three years older but a real generation gap between), we were not Oxbridge products, nor indeed had we attended any university except for Roy's brief law courses at London [sic]. And none of us belonged to what Julian called the 'homosexual sodality' which so dominated the orthodox avant-gardism of the times.[41]

That the launch of *Twentieth Century Verse* should coincide with Fuller's arrival as a serious poet was a happy chance, as was the fact that Symons was temporarily living with Herbert and Marjorie Mallalieu in Croydon, thus conferring a cultural respectability on suburban South London to which Fuller would shortly add his own presence. They were to remain lifelong friends.

Fuller's poems of the mid-1930s – at first written, and rewritten, in a Kirby Series feint ruled pad but from March 1935 onwards carefully transcribed into a large 'Memoranda or Minute Book' – are seldom altogether successful. Many are in the genre he described as 'proletcult', a difficult mode at the best of times and an impossible one for a young poet, dizzy with the influence of Auden and Spender, uncertain of his own voice or technique:

> The enormous figures of the ancients
> With their incredible achievements
> Block all the doors I open, like
> A nightmare of essayed escape.
> > Their touch and lack of knowledge
> > Impermanence
> > And influence
> Damp down my courage.[42]

But no poet develops in a straight line, however inconvenient that may prove for critics, and the exceptions can seem startlingly ahead of their time both in tone and in subject-matter. An excellent example from the 'Memoranda or Minute Book' is 'Future Fossils', written in February 1937, uncollected until it appeared in the pamphlet *As From The Thirties*, and wryly described by its author as 'from my Kentish rural period':[43]

Our doom a commonplace of history –
The creeping icecap's hunger, plenty's cancers;
Implements lost or broken before the fire
Blackens the soil and scabs a finished epoch.
The seeds of the wild strawberry will show
Among bare ribs, the summer death ordained
By declaration of demented leaders.

But yet on many nights by foothills where
The sky's slack velvet curtain's blown away,
The future fossils walk with prickling skin
To sense their progeny at the start of eras.
Such haunting times, the recompense for failure,
Are evidenced by marks of black and red
That flesh the fragments of extinct hyenas.[44]

The shadow of Auden is self-evident, both in the general tone and
in the particular predilection for cosmic pronouncement which
Auden himself could mysteriously get away with, but which almost
always sounds uncomfortably bombastic in the work of his
admirers. Yet Fuller's readers will be at least as struck by other
aspects of the poem. The notion of a global history, in which
mankind plays only an infinitesimal part, is a recurring one which
informs, for example, a major poem of the mid-1960s, 'Orders';
the elegantly compressed iambic line 'The sky's slack velvet
curtain's blown away' is one which could sit comfortably among
the late sonnets; while the fondness for the words 'epoch' and 'era'
(often used ironically to describe any period longer than a day or
two) was to become a lifelong verbal quirk. Although the older
poet would have avoided both the 'demented leaders' and the
'extinct hyenas' – both of which carry unmistakable 1930s resonances – 'Future Fossils' demonstrates how impressively Fuller was
maturing in his Kentish rural period.

Julian Symons remarks that they 'remained on surname terms
until mid-1938',[45] though this was Fuller's characteristic style, similarly employed in his frank and exasperated letters to D.S. Savage.
'My first Xtian name,' R.B. Fuller finally confessed, 'is Roy – the
other is a family name, repellant & barbaric, & best left in the
shadows.'[46] By this time Symons, who was working as secretary for
Mr Budette of Victoria Lighting and Dynamos and its magnificently improbable subsidiary the Kleenair Toilet Fan Company,

had moved to a basement flat in Pimlico; there, or in convenient pubs, contributors to *Twentieth Century Verse* would meet to debate the literary matters of the moment. Not all those invited met with Fuller's approval; he particularly disliked Ruthven Todd, whose 'parrot and jackdaw ways used to offend my Lancastrian puritanism',[47] and whose physical appearance he recalled with fastidious, fascinated distaste: 'hair by no means short and always ruffled, but black, like plumage, matching the rims of his gig-lamps, big even before the fashion for big spectacles came in'.[48] Julian Maclaren-Ross would recall him in similar terms ('a shock of black hair piled high above a narrow pale wedge shaped face and the side struts of his large square framed spectacles were the thickest I'd yet encountered')[49] but with rather more affection; however, Fuller's view was shared by someone whom he would have liked even less and with whom Symons was to find himself embroiled in a legal scuffle: the extraordinary Count Potocki of Montalk, in whose book *Social Climbers in Bloomsbury* Ruthven Todd appears as Driven Mud.[50] Symons also remembers an evening at the surrealist artist Toni del Renzio's flat in Soho, during which Fuller 'sat completely silent in the midst of what I suppose was distastefully bohemian talk, until I took mercy on him and said we must go'.[51] While such occasions undoubtedly did much to confirm Fuller in the anti-bohemian stance formulated during his law student days, he was perfectly aware that his estranged reticence was at least equally due to mere shyness: 'I enjoyed meeting Mallalieu, Todd & the rest,' he told Symons after he had attended his first literary gathering in Pimlico; 'I may have concealed this, not having many of the social graces. I hope we can meet again pretty soon.'[52]

The suggestion that the Fullers, with their infant son John, should join Julian Symons and the Mallalieus, with their even younger son Paul, in a fortnight's holiday came from Symons. An exchange of letters followed, conducted on Fuller's side with pessimistic relish. Devon he thought 'rather too far': 'A long train journey with infants comes straight out of Dante – and fares, too, are a consideration.'[53] Symons meanwhile was 'worming through Daltons to see what we can find',[54] without success:

From the wastes of St. George's Square comes a silence which is almost audible. The silence of one who has drained the cup of Dalton's to the bitter dregs and has found no health. Can it be that there are no owners of insanitary cottages & victorian furniture left who wish to make a profit of 500% in the month of August out of us?[55]

Symons' next suggestion, the Suffolk coast, found no more favour than Devon with Fuller: 'it sounds flat & bleak & full of chapped girls slitting herrings,' he grumbled. 'Meanwhile FULLER is seen with a chance in the race, moving past the tiring horses in the straight,' he declared with, as it turned out, premature triumphalism: 'What I had in mind was Rye or Winchelsea or thereabouts',[56] and he was making enquiries through agents. Two days later, however, a possibility elsewhere on the Kent coast appeared:

The Old Golf House, St. Margarets-at-Cliff – very genteel & doubtless sporting. "3 bedrooms, bathroom, 2 rec. rooms. Garden $^1/_2$ acre. Water, elec., gas. Summer 2/5 gns." St. Margaret's is about 4 miles the other side of Dover – the "agents" say quiet, pretty, clean beach, hidden in a bay from both Dover and Deal. Shall I make enquiries?

I think the bungalow town should be approached with caution for fear of stockbrokers' clerks etc. lurking, disguised as fathers of families.

I like the plot of Todd's novel. We all ought to write novels. In fact we all ought to give up our jobs & live at The Old Golf House. The more I live in this stinking world the more I realise that the only way to be happy is to do a little thing seriously & narrowly e.g. collect coins or write verse. The ivory tower for me every time.

If we had taken a little more care with this correspondence it would have been good enough for P★★★H.[57]

But the correspondence wasn't quite over yet. On 11 July, Fuller capitulated: 'If we are near the sea & there are no bugs I really don't think it matters much… My Rye Agents,' he conceded, 'have revealed themselves in a shoddy light – they have not even produced an Old Golf House.'[58] So he accepted, with reservations, Symons' final choice of St Mary's Bay: 'My wife, having through long contact with me acquired something of my cautious legal mind, tells me to warn you that St. Mary's Bay is bleak, flat and unromantic: we thus evade any responsibility for Mallalieu putting his head in the cook-an-heat (sic) after a couple of days.'[59] Nevertheless, the holiday was altogether a success, despite the accuracy of Kate's information about the place; for Symons, who lost in the sea a pair of false teeth which Fuller miraculously retrieved a few minutes later, it was invested with almost magical significance.

The Enterprise of St Mary's Bay, as Symons called it, had after-effects of varying significance. The penurious Mallalieu failed for months to settle a debt of £1, infuriating the parsimonious Fuller: 'I am very petty-bourgeois about money,' he admitted.[60] Meanwhile, the owner of the rented bungalow, a Mr Cooper, accused them of having caused some minor damage, inducing in Fuller a degree of cheerfully facetious paranoia: 'Snooper Cooper seen by Kate in Ashford – snooping in a cooping manner. We make it clear that personally we deny liability.'[61] And there was an interestingly troublesome poem, 'August 1938', whose second stanza originally opened with these problematical lines:

> Aeroplanes softly landing
> Beyond the willowed marsh:
> The penis lighthouse standing
> Aloof with rolling eye
> From shingle flat and harsh...

Fuller comments on this, in *Vamp Till Ready*:

I was not happy with penis, though moderately descriptive. For one thing, a George Barker poem had already used the noun adjectivally in the phrase 'the penis waterpistol'; for another, the medical/obscene connotation offended me in the context. Doubtful, moreover if it can be maintained that the organs in question have *rolling* eyes, though that epithet may have been introduced after I had changed the other epithet to 'sexy', the latter word not ideal but better then than after forty years of continuing debasement. What the lighthouse was more like (the one at Dungeness) was a vinegar bottle with a perforated ceramic attachment to its cork, enabling the acetic fluid to be sprinkled over a plate or newspaper of fish-and-chips.[62]

In successive revisions, the offending phrase would become 'sexy lighthouse',[63] 'virile lighthouse',[64] and 'phallic lighthouse',[65] none of them wholly successful: 'A great difference between poetry in St

Mary's Bay times and now would be the present likelihood of the
actual vinegar-bottle being worked in,' Fuller added, neatly indi-
cating a change in general poetic practice between the 1930s and
the 1980s, as well as the development of a quirky, concrete speci-
ficity in his own writing. This point alone makes 'August 1938' a
fascinating piece; but there is something still more striking about it,
which only becomes obvious when one looks at a complete stanza.
Here is the first:

> Mapping this bay and charting
> The water's ribby base
> By individual smarting
> And walks in shifting sand,
> We note the official place;
> Dover with pursed-up lips
> Behind the purple land
> Blowing her little ships
> To danger, large and bland...[66]

Fuller described his nine-line stanza as 'a wrong-headed or cloth-
eared attempt at novelty',[67] but it seems to me a notable success,
anticipating the assymetrically-rhymed stanzas of Philip Larkin; still
more to the point, the three-stress lines snaking, often without
end-stops, through the long verses look back to Yeats' 'Easter 1916'
and, most strikingly of all, forward to Auden's '1 September 1939'.
In 'August 1938', the disciple pulls off the remarkable feat of being
at least one step ahead of his master.

'Do you think the little 6-line thing you wrote at St.M.B. is
good? Or amusing?' asked Julian Symons.[68] This is the poem called
'After the Holiday' – uncollected, like 'Future Fossils' until the *As
from the Thirties* pamphlet – and it finds Fuller writing with taut
confidence, juxtaposing familiar details in the slightly skewed,
disconcerting style which was to become so distinctively his own:

> After the holiday the daws begin
> To bore their holes of sound;
> And on the lawn
> The first brown crumbs of leaf.
> I, looking through my snapshot album, find
> The last a fatal X-ray negative.[69]

And in other respects, too, the Ashford years saw the emergence of enduring characteristics, from an attentive interest in local nature ('the limes of Kennington Lees astonishingly holding their golden leaves far into autumn, utterly unlike Blackpool trees') to

> ...the gramophone records bought then, those of the Busch Quartet playing Beethoven's Opus 131, and the young Ella Fitzgerald singing 'Deep in the Heart of the South', persisting mélange of taste I never thought unusual. The time there, as measured by the calendar several months less than three years, seems, because of personal and public happenings, of huge amplitude, especially compared with the flickering by of seasons in old age.[70]

★

Fuller was inclined to make much of what he presented as the weaker aspects of his personality: shyness, reticence, ineffectuality, a reluctance to seize the golden opportunity. Yet a common, possibly a universal corollary of such characteristics is the capacity for pursuing particular defined goals with great tenacity. An unambitious man, or even an ordinarily ambitious one, would have counted himself lucky to have an interesting job with congenial company in an attractive part of Kent. Fuller, however, had set his heart on London, and after only a year or so with Kingsford's was on the look-out for a post which would not only offer professional advancement but would allow him to live nearer his new literary friends. The advertisement in the *Law Society's Gazette* to which he replied was for an assistant solicitor with what was carefully described as a 'large corporate body' in South-East London. This large corporate body turned out to be the Woolwich Equitable Building Society.

The account in *Vamp Till Ready* of his interview at the Woolwich – or, as it was then and until quite recently known, 'the Equitable' – focuses on the kind of low-key but intensely evocative detail which would always engage his attention. He recalled the train journey from Ashford and his uncertainty about whether to alight at Woolwich Dockyard or (correctly) at Woolwich Arsenal; the market, and in particular the irascible and immovable book-stall-keeper who had 'educated half Woolwich' (a passage unfortunately cut from *The Strange and the Good*);[71] the public lavatory where he had a 'wash and brush up', including liquid soap and a clean towel in a paper sleeve, for 2d; and the suit of brown Manx tweed made for him in homage to Aldous Huxley's by an out-fitter in Ashford. He also recalled the interview itself, with A.E. Shrimpton, who had been responsible for establishing the society's own legal department – by then numbering sixty or so staff – and who 'plainly felt, in some not entirely obscure way, that it would be an advantage to have a fellow at hand used to defending in cases of rape and watered milk'.[72] The Manx tweed suit created a good impression, as did Fuller's cheerful appearance; on his arrival he joked to Shrimpton's secretary about a sound peculiar to solicitors' premises (the nearby drone of someone examining an abstract of title), so both were smiling when they entered the office.

Fred Shrimpton, a mild-mannered but punctilious solicitor then in his mid-forties, was among the small group of senior Woolwich executives with whom Fuller was to enjoy a long and successful if not wholly untroubled professional relationship. On the day of his interview, or soon afterwards, he was introduced to the others over a formal sit-down tea, a regular amenity which greatly impressed him; a somewhat vestigial form of it appears in *Image of a Society*. He especially noted their smoking habits. T.R. Chandler, the General Manager and Secretary, was a formidable figure of immense building society experience, nearing retirement; he liked a pipe, and his tobacco-pouch invariably contained a mixture of Player's Gold Block and Balkan Sobranie. The Assistant General Manager, 'a sweet-natured man called Austin Smith', was a Gold Flake smoker (as was Fred Shrimpton); while Harold Codner, the Agency Manager, preferred Capstan. However, the Assistant Secretary, Alexander Meikle, a young and exceptionally able Scottish accountant, showed a distinctness bordering on the eccentric by smoking Du Maurier. In Sandy Meikle's case, at least, Fuller's notion that an individual's choice of cigarette might provide a key to his character seems to have been well-founded.

This image of a group of men sitting comfortably amidst the light wood panelling of Equitable House, tucking into a substantial tea (comprising bread-and-butter and jam, cakes and biscuits), and then complacently smoking their assorted cigarettes and pipes may suggest a peculiarly cosy approach to the running of a 'large corpo-rate body'. It was certainly, as far as possible, benevolent. The depression of the early 1930s had caused long-term difficulties for mortgage borrowers on a scale which was not to be matched until the early 1990s; F.W. Wellman, a man 'of infinite compassion and patience' in charge of arrears, reported daily to Chandler, and some important cases were doubtless resolved in amiable discussion over the tea-table. Fuller also drew attention to his senior colleagues' 'standards of work and, above all, of personal dignity and integrity',[73] their implicit understanding of the idea of mutuality in a building society – the meaning, indeed, of that cumbersome yet exact word 'Equitable'. By quickly identifying the building society as a positive force for social and moral good, he was able to manage an accommodation between his new employment and his political principles.

He joined the Woolwich Equitable on 1 December 1938, and in the same week the Fullers moved from Kennington to an unlovely maisonette in Blackheath, at 36 Kidbrooke Park Road, SE3 – a thoroughfare principally familiar to generations of Kent motorists as one of the main southern feeder roads to the Blackwall Tunnel. It was also conveniently placed for the air-raids which he already felt certain would eventually occur: 'I rather think our rationalization was that since we were doomed anyway we might as well be doomed at a substantially increased salary in a place we wanted to be in.'[74] His main feeling was of simple pride at having achieved a long-nurtured ambition. 'Perhaps you can call on me next week or the week after – for supper say,' he wrote, with the tragi-comic Victorian formality of Mr Pooter, to Derek Savage;[75] but he was still remarkably naïve about London, as his next letter, after Savage had declined the invitation, shows: 'I had no idea N.21 was so far from S.E.3.'[76] Much later, confirming and perhaps recalling this exchange, he would characterise the move as 'fulfilling after a few bosh shots my wish to get to London – of which, except for the West End, I was quite ignorant.'[77] The Fullers' home comprised the first and second floors of a late Victorian house: it was large, cold, and offensively decorated (they particularly disliked the dark green woodwork); in winter, the pipes froze, and when they thawed they burst. Roy's mother, recuperating after a partial thyroidectomy, came to stay and was suitably dismayed, taking special exception to a disused sink on the top floor which she discovered to be full of back numbers of the *Left Review*. Outside was a derelict car of Jack Clark's, which had chosen the Fullers' front garden as its terminal destination. When in the second year of the war the place was bombed, the elder Mrs Fuller may have felt that was the best thing for it.

In ordinary times, her son would have been similarly dissatisfied
by this ramshackle existence in a style arguably not quite fitting for
a solicitor with the leading local building society, and would have
set about improving things (he did have a go at covering the dark
green woodwork with white paint, and made a poor job of it). But
the times were far from ordinary. During the Munich crisis, Kate
and the infant John had decamped to Blackpool; and at the beginning of September 1939 Roy saw them off at Euston once again, as
for a second time they returned to her parents' home to escape the
all-too-real dangers of war-time life in Kidbrooke Park Road.
Meanwhile, alongside the political upheavals, he was busily consol-
idating his professional position with the Woolwich and developing
his literary friendships. He had, after all, arrived in London.

Then, in the last month of the decade, his first collection –
chastely entitled *Poems*, in admiring and aspiring homage to Auden
– appeared. Later, he liked to think that this chronological near-
miss had saved him from disgrace – 'I was within an ace of
becoming tagged a Forties poet, ghastly fate for one who regarded
Forties poetry as being rather poor compared with the previous
epoch'[78] – though in fact it probably, with more doubtful benefit,
prevented him from 'belonging' to either decade and hence
blurred his subsequent critical reputation. His future publisher,
The Hogarth Press, had rejected the book: 'My poems from
Hogarth were lying on the mat this morning. Even a NICE letter
from Lehmann could not disguise the fact that they had been
REFUSED.'[79] Instead, the book was published by The Fortune
Press, run single-handedly by the remarkable R.A. Caton; by the
mid-1940s his poetry list included titles by Fuller, Gavin Ewart,
Julian Symons, D. S. Savage, Dylan Thomas, Christopher Middle-
ton and Philip Larkin, among numerous and equally varied others.
It takes only a glance to see that Caton's editorial policy was not so
much catholic as random; indeed, his main line of business was in
areas of erotica which for years were the mainstay of dim bookshops off the Charing Cross Road. As A.T. Tolley notes, 'Typical
Fortune Press titles were *Chastisement across the ages* (as late as 1956)
or the series with variations on the title "A Diary of the Teens" by
"A Boy" that appeared from 1937 to 1954.'[80] Perhaps Caton simply
liked short-run, low-cost publishing with distribution via mail-
order or specialist shops, for here his distinct subject-areas had a
good deal in common; he may also have had a gambler's faith that

among all his unknown poets there must be one future bestseller who would make his fortune. That was certainly Fuller's reading of the situation: Caton, he wrote, 'thinks all the Fortune Poets are embryo Kiplings or Wheeler Wilcoxes and that he will cash in on their later successes.'[81]

It says something for Caton's tact (or his business sense) that he kept the advance publicity for different parts of his list scrupulously separate, launching 'The Fortune Poets' with much dignity in the pages of Julian Symons' magazine *Twentieth Century Verse*, from which the books could be ordered. Symons remembers him with amused affection:

> There was, as he said, no money in poetry, but still he printed first volumes by a good many young poets of the time, including Fuller, Ewart, Francis Scarfe, George Woodcock. Apart from one case, that in which he bought the copyright of Thomas's *Eighteen Poems* outright for only £15 according to Thomas's biographer, he paid no money to his authors and even to write of them being 'on his list' would be misleading, because he issued no list. I was never able to find out how many copies he printed of each book he produced, but I suppose several of them are rarities now. Perhaps there was a little money in poetry for Caton after all. I hope so... It was the belief of some writers that he never read their work, although this was rather complicated by his saying to me about Gavin Ewart's *Poems and Songs*: 'This fellow Ewart now, he's rather spicy, eh?'
>
> Apart from his liking for spiciness, Caton had no particular literary tastes or opinions, and he later published *The White Horseman*, the anthology by those Apocalyptic poets who ushered in the woolly 'forties and swamped the commonsensible minor 'thirties writers. He was, I think, a little astonished to find that anybody took his Fortune poets seriously. When Tambimuttu attacked my poems he wrote to me: 'The review of your poems seems rather offensive – is the reviewer the brown fellow?'[82]

This versatile publisher was not, as is sometimes implied, a 'vanity press': as Symons confirms, Fuller neither paid Caton nor was paid by him. Philip Larkin, in the Introduction to the 1966 reissue of his first collection, *The North Ship*, recalled a similar cashless informality in his dealings with Caton six years later;[83] while Julian Maclaren-Ross, having failed to receive any payment for a story in

Fortune Anthology, recorded Bill Makins' suggestion 'that the Anthology should appear in future under its initials only as these seemed appropriate enough.'[84]

When proofs of *Poems* arrived, however, Fuller was put out to find that the poems were run-on rather than each starting on a new page. Worse was to come: 'And when the volume was at last in my hands and I slipped off the dust jacket, I saw to my horror that along the spine, between ROY FULLER and POEMS, was not a dot or asterisk or other printer's device I should have considered satisfactory, but a hyphen.'[85] But perhaps this was of less importance than he thought: it was Caton's cautious practice only to bind up a few copies at a time, storing the rest as loose sheets, and even the modest run of *Poems* appeared in at least two different bindings. 'In either state,' Fuller would later note with glum pleasure, 'it is a satisfactorily rare book.'[86] The dust-jacket which he had been so eager to slip off, incidentally, indicated the limits of Caton's discretion, for its back cover proudly displayed a 'List of Books from The Fortune Press': *Tortures and Torments of the Christian Martyrs*, *Boy Sailors*, *Fourteen: A Diary of the Teens*, *Fifteen*…

The inclusions and exclusions of the book are slightly puzzling: 'August 1938' (at this point simply called 'August'), with its problematical lighthouse, is here; but the much finer 'After the Holiday' is not, and neither is 'Future Fossils'. The opening poem, 'New Year', may have played a rather misleading part in selling the collection to Caton:

> Solace me with your sex that I may not know
> How fast your heart beats on the other side
> To mine; how they will set those boys to kill
> In summer, the most beautiful season for war.[87]

It is, however, sufficiently arresting – and prophetic – on its own somewhat Audenesque terms: *Poems* is, just as Fuller wished, distinctly a book of the thirties, and the little fictional eight-liners later called 'The Rumour'[88] and 'The Visits'[89] glance back to the more grotesque elements of the Auden-Isherwood imaginative world as well as forward to the pathological undertones of Fuller's post-war crime novels. Uneven though the collection certainly is, it has moments of almost unnerving confidence, when the predominant tone of Fuller's apprentice years fuses indivisibly into the emergent texture of his mature verse, as it does in the first stanza of the poem eventually entitled 'End of a City':

> Birds in the pattern of a constellation,
> Blank pale blue sky, white walls of a citadel,
> Silence of country without inhabitants.
> The shining aqueducts, elaborate drains,
> Puffed fountains cleanse a sheeted culture
> Where the greatest movement is the soft
> Wear of stone by water that leaves no trace
> Of green, coming from static glaciers.[90]

Though the examples of watery engineering seem to parody Auden's fondness for the higher plumbing, the unforced descriptive movement here was to serve Fuller well in his East African poems. There is, indeed, another poem in the book ('So many rivers in a land of mountains')[91] which at first glance may look like a premonition of his African travels; perhaps it was this which led Tambimuttu erroneously to include this evidently pre-war poem in his 1942 anthology *Poetry in Wartime*.[92]

Despite its shortcomings, *Poems* served at the time its essentially reputation-building purpose: 'Roy Fuller,' wrote Stephen Spender in the *New Statesman*, 'has a sensitive, delicate and genuine gift which should mature and deserves encouragement.'[93]

Part Two: Writer and Society

1: War Poet

'One of the things I admired most about Roy,' wrote Julian Symons in an affectionate memoir, 'was that as man and poet he knew quite certainly the way he wished to live, and what he hoped to achieve. Life in suburban Blackheath, with the Woolwich office in easy reach, suited him perfectly, and I don't think he ever thought seriously of moving elsewhere...'[1] He had unerringly chosen this domestic location and this permanent career in 1938; between 1940 and 1946, however, his life was to be dominated by locations and events of an entirely different sort.

The outbreak of war caused him inconvenience rather than distress: he would quote with approval Freud's dictum that obsessional people feel better in war-time, when everyone else is more or less in the same state,[2] and he certainly managed to tolerate a disrupted life with good-humoured stoicism. Kate and John spent most of the early war years in Blackpool, so Roy usually had the maisonette to himself; however, his wife was present when he attempted to dig a slit-trench in the pebbly back garden, remarking that he had in fact succeeded in creating a convenient grave. In Kate's enforced absence, he spent a good deal of time with Julian Symons, who now lived in Denmark Hill and was engaged to Jack Clark's sister, Kathleen: they ate together, played snooker in a Temperance Billiards Hall, and sometimes 'dined out' at Bicards on the South Side of Clapham Common: 'The safest dish on offer was baked beans on toast, but those with hardihood might order a pie.'[3]

This shadowy, subfusc world of blackout suited his temperament and his imagination. 'The last trains go earlier, stations are like aquaria, / The mauve-lit carriages are full of lust,' he wrote in 'First Winter of the War', a fine poem which strangely remained uncollected until the 'From an Old File' section of *Tiny Tears*:

> It is dark at four and on the peopled streets,
> The ornamented banks and turreted offices,
> The moon pours out a deathly and powdered grey:
> The city noises come out of a desert.

It is dark at twelve: I walk down the up escalator
And see that hooded figure before me
Ascending motionless upon a certain step.
As I try to pass, it will stab me with a year.[4]

His inner landscape was equally transformed. The pervasive atmosphere of dusky containment enabled him to evolve, for the first
time, that contemplative books-and-music mode which was to
become so characteristic of his much later work:

Sitting at home and reading Julien Benda;
Evening descending in successive gauzes –
Pantomime transformation scene reversed;
A point releasing Haydn from a groove
In waves alternately severe and tender:

A curious way to spend a night of war![5]

Further on in this poem, 'The Phoney War', he notices 'the
martins' squeaking' and confesses his 'increasing fondness for
Henry James'. Nor was this very striking premonition of an older
self the only beneficial effect which the early days of the war had
upon his writing. His previous poems had been frequently marred
by clumsiness, opacity, an apparent uncertainty about what they
were actually *for*. Now, his well-developed powers of observation
could be employed to illuminate a larger theme, as the opening of
'Autumn 1939' (originally entitled 'November 1939', and the first
poem in his second collection, *The Middle of a War*) clearly shows:

Cigar-coloured bracken, the gloom between the trees,
The straight wet by-pass through the shaven clover,
Smell of the war as if already these
    Were salient or cover.[6]

'Much virtue in If', as Touchstone so wisely said; even more in 'as
if'. By moving from a poetry of statement to a poetry of metaphor,
Fuller added both resonance and clarity to his work: the poem
becomes meaningful to the reader as an expression of universal
rather than exclusively personal unease, and is much the richer for
it. As it happens, Fuller was to recall the somewhat prosaic occasion
of the poem: he and Jack Clark had stopped – the car, being
Clark's, had quite possibly stopped of its own volition – on the
Maidstone road near Sidcup. 'Even in November, apparently,' he

added, 'one's nerves were still sensitive about the changed state of the world.'[7] That, of course, is not a bad condition for a writer's nerves to be in.

His nervousness seemed to be abundantly justified. 'I am in the 1912 class,' he glumly reminded Norman Lees in March 1940,

> & due to go in JUNE, probably. I am not exempt, have no influence, no *mechanical* ability: in fine, the ideal infantryman. I hope to be able to spread some *sedition* before I'm blown up, however. I feel commissions are to be avoided. 2nd Lts. are killed off like flies – & think of one's day to day companions – the Fats [i.e. Fatty Mason] of this world. I think you might get a clerking job as a private – I am too big, too deceptively robust. It is all a bugger.[8]

Nevertheless, during that spring and summer, his call-up papers failed to materialise. Instead, early one morning in the autumn of 1940, he was awoken by large pieces of plaster ceiling dropping on top of him, even though he had taken the precaution of sleeping on the half-landing rather than in the top-floor bedroom: a land-mine had fallen across the the road, and the maisonette was effectively ruined. In a spirit of dogged eccentricity reminiscent of his grandfather Fred Broadbent, Fuller set about clearing up the mess, having first donned a suitable hat – or rather, an unsuitable one: it was a fishing-hat he had bought on account of its, and his, resemblance to Van Gogh's *Portrait of a Young Man*. Thus occupied, he worked on through the morning, until he was discovered by a conveyancing managing clerk (and ARP officer), Reg Edwards, who had been sent out from the office to investigate his absence and who was astonished to find him industriously alive and curiously attired amid the ruins of Kidbrooke Park Road. Edwards, quickly persuading him that the place was uninhabitable, suggested that he should collect together a few essential belongings and decamp to Equitable House, where a number of Woolwich employees had already taken refuge in the basement strongroom. This peculiar expedient had been made possible by the society's apparently prudent decision to evacuate its important documents from the strongroom to a tunnel in the North Downs near Westerham. While Equitable House remained virtually unscathed, the papers stored in the tunnel were attacked first by damp and then by an electrical fire in the equipment installed to dry them out. Reconstituting the damaged titles was to prove a formidable task for the Solicitor's Department after the war.

However bizarre a habitat the strongroom may have been, it compared favourably with the alternative solitary existence in a bombed and boarded-up maisonette. Fuller typically spent his evenings playing cards, after which one of the assembled company would undertake an expedition to the nearest fish-and-chip shop, or in the cinema or the billiards saloon. The strongroom residents necessarily formed a chummily egalitarian group, whose exact composition altered with changing individual circumstances: there were oddly distorted echoes of the past – both boarding school and private hotel – and perhaps a hint too of the near future in the navy. His call-up papers arrived at the beginning of April 1941; he was to report to HMS *Ganges* on the twenty-first. He cleared up at the office and at the maisonette, and went off to Blackpool to spend his remaining time with Kate and John.

When the appointed day arrived, it was marked by a typically wry coincidence: for there on the platform at Blackpool station, also waiting for the London train, was possibly the least appropriate of all Fuller's acquaintances, the journalist and prankster Graham Miller, exempted by his history of tuberculosis from war service. The pair shared an otherwise empty third-class compartment into which Miller magically introduced two glasses and a bottle of claret; from Euston they almost inevitably proceeded to Charley's café in Marchmont Street. It was late in the afternoon when Fuller, his nerves and digestion unimproved by the day's entertainment, boarded the train from Liverpool Street to Harwich.

HMS *Ganges* was the Royal Navy's training establishment on the Shotley peninsula in Suffolk, separated from Harwich by the River Stour and from Felixstowe by the River Orwell. Delayed by air-raids, Fuller's train cautiously edged its way through Essex, depositing more and more of its passengers until all who remained were men of his own age, evidently bound for the same destination. By now, of course, they were late: sufficiently late to find themselves joined on Parkeston Quay by a party of far from sober future colleagues returning from an evening 'ashore'. From there they were ferried across the Stour to Shotley, given cocoa (Fuller typically noted both the superior quality of the beverage, though by that hour it was tepid, and the immaculate condition of vat and ladle), and finally directed to a dormitory. The day ended, as it had begun, with a Blackpool coincidence: in the next bed was an old friend, and indeed another journalist, Rod Davies, a colleague of Kate's from her *West Lancashire Evening Gazette* days. For sheer improbability, the small worlds of fiction seldom match those of real life.

Improbable or not, that was a good omen: preposterously, as he pointed out, for 'a non-games-playing solicitor in his thirtieth year',[9] Fuller grudgingly enjoyed his time at HMS *Ganges*, tolerating huge quantities of agreeably stodgy food – half-bricks of 'figgy duff' were manageable though a double portion of corned beef proved troublesome – which were counteracted by squad drill, PT, swimming, gymnastics and football, and for once feeling conscious of physical fitness; with his habitual interest in sartorial matters, he was fascinated by the minutiae of naval uniform, especially the arcanely complicated square rig. All the same, his account of HMS *Ganges* in memoirs written forty years later unsurprisingly softens the detail; a letter to Julian Symons, written a week after his arrival, provides an altogether saltier description of his first impressions. It is worth quoting at some length:

> I am in that first stage of that descent to the Middle Ages you wot of when the faculty of writing is being lost. My speech is becoming brutish, thumbs turning opposite to the fingers, do I imagine it or is there the feel of a stump at the arse when I sit down. This is the 'deadening process' which one undergoes in the Forces, according to a letter from Woodcock which I have at last received, I dare aver. Already I have no fucking patience with French George…
>
> Life in the *Ganges* is pretty boring, as you might guess. Existence is on a low level of pleasure, so that anything remotely pleasing is pleasurable e.g. a *sing-song*. One can't pass judgement after a week, but I should say I'll survive it and change in the process. The prospects of a soft job seem remote, so that I shall become clearly what Marxist literary critics call 'proletarianised' – & no phoney Swingall Randler [Randall Swingler] proletarianism either. At the moment I've little or no desire to write, although I see that being *with* so many people is a good thing thing from the writing point of view. But so far I've still managed to treat people as I always treat them, i.e. almost ignore them, but that cannot go on if I am to survive. I have met a man I knew in B'pool, a journalist, who is in Beatty [Annexe], & he

& I and a little lawyer's clerk have made a little private world of private jokes e.g. to speak like the PO's & to swear in every sentence. The method of inculcating morale is incredibly inept – Hitler *must* win on that alone. The officers make half-hearted appeals to the team spirit – 'A clean mess is a happy mess' – the POs are old, competent, nitwits who advise working hard merely in order to avoid trouble. No one, even in set pep-talks, dare invoke directly 'democracy' or 'loyalty'.

The men being called up seem about 50% middle-class, getting bald, stodgy, nearly all v. nice. In our working party this week there is a lovely Scot, the double of Claude Rains, who can give points, K. my dear, to D. Savage in the matter of looks & intelligence too, if truth be known...

There are no doors on the lavatories & no flies on the trousers, as you probably know. I have so far: cleaned brass-work, washed greasy cloths, served dinners, wheeled carts, polished floors, mended window blinds, had a bilious attack, 2 no. 9s & filled in Income Tax Returns for some PO's. Last week there was the coldest east wind you could imagine, in which we stood about for hours. In the middle of it we marched to the baths, mercifully enclosed & heated, put on wet duck suits & had a swimming test in them. This is all what the Captain calls 'discipline', or 'attention to details', a phrase he got, he says, from his friend a Rear-Admiral. Another sweet pep talk came from the M.O., a young man with a self-consciously man-to-man manner. 'Fellows come & ask me how to avoid getting a dose. There's only one way – don't stick your prick into anything diseased' & so on. Luckily I avoided the Chaplain, being a wicked Atheist.[10]

On 'May the something, 1941', he wrote again, thanking Symons for sending copies of *Poetry* and *Kingdom Come* (which he had nicknamed 'Condom King'): 'Your kind soul shines like a dollar on a sweep's arse, as our drill instructor might say.' By then, he could have cheerfully used the expression himself:

I've heard no more war folk-songs: only two which I think are well known in civvie street. One has 3 nice lines –

> There's no paper in the bogs
> So they wait until it clogs
> Then they saw it off in logs, Imovine

I'm not sure about the last word – it appears to be the name of the patron or deity to whom the poem is addressed. The other begins –

> Bang it into Lulu,
> Bang it good and strong,
> Or what shall we do for a good blow through
> When Lulu's dead and gone.

But you probably know these.

Yes, I suppose you are right about proletarianisation. Already I am appointed one of the mess class leaders – head prefect or *agent provocateur* status – and thus get out of some of the more menial tasks. I make the boys form fours and march them about and am very WEAK. I shall in due course wear a blue arm band with a red crown on it – v. natty. We moved into this little mess last Saturday. Sunday morning on the parade is a tremendous affair lasting an hour, with the Marine Band and a pukka (?) march past the Captain who carries a silver tipped cane and a ton of gold braid. I dodged Church & then played 3 games of snooker – there are 5 nearly new tables. Have I told you all this? Am I turning already into a gun-sight bore?

I haven't, however, told you about Monday – over 5 hours squad drill & Tuesday 4 hours ditto. Or today's PT which started with a ½ mile run, continued with horrible exercises punctuated with ¼ mile runs & finished with a game of hand-ball-cum-rugby in which I sustained two scratched arms, a ditto neck & a bleeding nose. Luckily I skilfully avoided an hour's row on the river tonight by hanging back as class leader until all the boats were filled. I am eating nearly as much as you & look like a character out of, say, *To Have & Have Not*.

I've no desire to write yet, but feel myself *settling down*. I am always fairly tired & short of time. Our mess is v. genteel – the most desperate character is only a little Scot with his master's ticket. There are two more solicitors! And I go drinking in the canteen with a London stockbroker. One of my co-class leaders is a reader of *Scrutiny* with a tendency to talk about Hopkins. But of a mess of 59, 2 have broken their wrists, one collapsed with a heart attack, another is running a high temperature in the Sick Bay & a fifth has broken his head on a tap in the wash-house. This is, I think, naval discipline or something. We have a nice little cissy who gets into trouble with his rifle. Our (above quoted) drill sergeant says to him 'You're a bloody cream-stick' (sic). I forgot: he has contracted a septic ankle or something – 6 down out of 59…

I went to Ipswich the other night & played a nice game of snooker in a nice pub but I. is dead & dull. The thing one hears about it is 'You can get a bit of cunt in the Switch' and that about sums it up. For those who want them French letters can be had of the M.O. on leave nights and they are said to be as thick as hose-pipes.

My brain is becoming as enfeebled as my body & I must stop. I shall read K.C. & Poetry lying on my bed & smoke some of my dinkey home mades. Do dodge the bombs both of you.[11]

Doubtless encouraged by such vividness, Julian Symons asked Fuller to contribute to an anthology of war poetry, which was to be published by Penguin in 1942; recalling 'The Airman's Alphabet' from Auden's The Orators,[12] he provided 'ABC of a Naval Trainee'. The poem tries hard to maintain a degree of sardonic scepticism, but the irrepressible jauntiness of the ballad metre and the slightly naïve excitement of the demotic language give the game away:

> A is the anger we hide with some danger,
> Keeping it down like the thirteenth beer.
> B is the boredom we feel in this bedlam.
> C is the cautious and supervised cheer.
>
> D is the tea dope and E English duping,
> Too feeble for folly, too strong for revolt.
> F is the adjective near every object,
> The chief of desires for both genius and dolt.
>
> G is the gun which can kill at, say, Greenwich
> If fired at St Martin's, and H is our hate
> Non-existent behind it wherever we wind it.
> I is the image of common man's fate.
>
> J is the Joan or the Jill or Joanna,
> Appearing, in dreams, as a just-missed train.
> K is the kindness like Christmas tree candles
> Unexpected and grateful as poppies in grain.[13]

That note – the unexpected discovery of kindness – is one which informs his memories of HMS *Ganges* in *Vamp Till Ready* and a recurring theme in his work. But the poem, which takes another six stanzas to reach Z, is only a qualified success: its studied matey-ness, though honourably and generously meant, rings false from one who never much cared for drunkenness although he did (in a passage of his memoirs cut from *The Strange and the Good*) rather coyly admit to 'a taste for swearing'[14] which is amply confirmed in his less inhibited letters.

Life at Shotley turned out to be educative in unexpected ways, mostly in terms of physical chores: he would later cite, as an instance of the sheltered life led by the pre-war middle-class male, the novelty of grasping a broom for the first time and discovering, with pleased astonishment, how the thing actually worked.[15] Other exertions were more obviously momentous: 'Today I have climbed the mast, a TEST à la Isherwood, & now feel v. tough & pleased with myself.'[16] He was, in fact, so memorably pleased with himself that when, thirty-five years later, the Shotley mast was listed as a monument by the Department of the Environment, he was spurred to epigrammatic recollection:

> Inscribe thereon that in 1941
> I climbed it twice in fright.
> Once as routine but also (to make sure
> I dared) the previous night.[17]

Immersed in so much unfamiliar and in its way invigorating expe-rience, he was frustrated by the relatively sluggish progress of his writing; he knew, all too well, that what he needed was 'some leisure and a little classical music on the gramophone by way of a laxative'[18] – a self-diagnosis which he might have made, in much the same terms, at almost any point in the next fifty years. 'I've not written anything since the Trainee,' he grumbled, three weeks later. 'The *Ganges* gets on my NERVES: it is a most unsuitable place for a minor poet.'[19]

Nor was Fred Shrimpton at the Woolwich happy with the status of his protégé, even though he had progressed from broom-pushing to mast-climbing: 'I must now write to Shrimpton who is displeased about my being Ord. Sea. & who thinks that a niche will soon be found for me in the Admiralty.'[20] Shrimpton, though right about the Admiralty, was wrong about 'soon'; for, towards the end

of Fuller's spell at HMS *Ganges*, an educational opportunity of a
different sort occurred. A notice invited volunteers with School
Certificate credits in Maths and Physics to join a course, the nature
of which was otherwise vague: according to rumour, it would be at
a civilian technical college, and it would certainly delay the ominous
prospect of active service. That was enough to persuade him to sign
up. Afterwards, he would come to reflect 'with a tinge of regret that
I might have had a more satisfactory and less boring war, if a shorter
life, had I let my name be struck off the list.'[21] The name remained;
consequently, he was soon to find himself studying radar in
Aberdeen, as unlikely an occupation for a poet and solicitor as could
be imagined. Before that, however, he had to survive Chatham.

He was only there for three weeks or so – in June and July 1941
– but that was more than enough: 'The discomfort and squalor
were sensational.'[22] When in barracks, he had to sleep in the airless,
overcrowded chalk tunnel; by comparison, the servicemen's
dosshouses in Chatham (described in a slightly later poem,
'Saturday Night in a Sailor's Home')[23] provided amenities which,
however basic, were greatly sought-after. Either way, there was no
escaping what he called 'the obscene realities': the all-night
coughing, 'Sour, damp smells', and 'drummings of fluid on
enamel' – or, as he later paraphrased it, 'peeing in enamel pos'[24] (he
was responding to a 'slipshod and impercipient' essay in which Eric
Homberger criticised the 'generality' of 'obscene realities').[25]
Whereas at its best HMS *Ganges* presented the navy in an affectionate spirit of schoolboyish activity, Chatham imposed tasks of
malevolent and almost surreal pointlessness. One day was spent
chipping rust off a frigate; another in an expedition to the Natural
History Museum, which was being used as a store for semi-perish-
able food. There, trucks were to be loaded with sacks of dried peas,
but the sacks turned out to be overrun with nesting museum mice,
who must formerly have led a decidedly ascetic life; it was altogether a 'disagreeable mission among the pink mouslings and grey
mouse-shit of SW3'.[26] At least Chatham's reasonable proximity to
London meant that Fuller, when off-duty, could go there for more
sociable purposes, such as visiting John Lehmann or Julian and
Kathleen Symons. Though writing little, he assiduously kept up his
literary friendships, demonstrating both personal loyalty and that
clarity of ambition which continually underpinned his sometimes
tactical reticence. Still, such civilised contacts provided small

consolation for the conditions he had to tolerate at Chatham. It was a relief when Fuller, along with some familiar HMS *Ganges* faces and others, found himself packed off to Aberdeen.

★

It could only be an improvement, and it was a striking one:

> I meant to write you a verse epistle about Aberdeen – and indeed started one – but decided the catalogue type of poem in the manner of early Macneice was passée and that's what it would have been. I am surprised that neither Allott nor M. nor Auden ever wrote a poem about Aberdeen: about the birdshit streaked statue of Burns, the enormous ditto of Bruce or some other wild man, the pretty girls with baddish legs & accents as alien as Garbo's, the house where Beattie lived & died (Beattie, whom with Blair & Falconer you so often tried to sell me for threepence), the granite houses of the suburbs which from a slight eminence look like a herd of angular elephants. Byron as a boy spent his holidays here. On lavatory walls is scribbled *Scotland for Ever* & the young wear music-hall kilts. Scotland feels itself to be an oppressed nation: kind but proud; cultured but shabby. You can get six books at a time from the Public Library – I got Landor, Shakespeare, Chapman and Professor Malinovski yesterday. Whether I shall read them or not is another matter – I feel only like snooker & the cinema at the moment & there are dozens of cinemas & across the road from 498 Union St a lovely billiards saloon. Why don't you live in Aberdeen? Why aren't we both here for the duration with great flat feet & £500 a year?[27]

The atmosphere of Aberdeen, Fuller found, 'was not far from that of peacetime summers of the past: modest seaside lodgings occupied by respectable but jolly bachelors, pubs and girls in mind.'[28] He quickly grasped the theoretical possibility – and applied his solicitor's skills to negotiating the reality – of drawing a living-out allowance from the navy, and was thus able to be joined by Kate and John in civilised digs at 142 Osborne Place; they even managed to acquire a portable HMV gramophone and a supply of records (the clarinet trios of Mozart and Brahms remained memorable), which provided a welcome respite from the ubiquitous pap piped over Tannoys in RN bases. Here, too, he was able to view political life with a degree of increasingly sceptical detachment: 'Stalin is

really Ramsay McDonald with a dyed moustache,' he wrote to
Julian Symons:

> Bill [the Communist propagandist William Rust] was here on
> Sunday with a platform of respectable town councillors. My
> reports are that he said support Churchill, but said it with a Left
> accent. It is too much for us parlour revolutionaries, I fear. As an
> antidote to this war stuff I am reading (a) Sir James Frazer & (b)
> Grierson's edition of Donne.[29]

The course itself, in part of Robert Gordon's College requisitioned for the purpose, was taught by able lecturers who were in
turn surprised and delighted by the quality of their students: nevertheless, Fuller, 'who had never in his life filed a piece of metal or
soldered a wire', found the practical side 'infuriating',[30] and his
mastery of it proceeded somewhat erratically. 'I could not
adequately communicate the fantasy & farce of my attempts to
draw the circuits of a 4 valve receiver, file a piece of brass square,
understand the principles of the electric motor,' he wrote on 17
August;[31] a month later, although 'the mystery of electricity &
electro-magnetic waves' continued to deepen, he had 'from
diagrams, constructed in the lab a 3 valve receiver on which I listen
to dance music on the Forces programme when I should be finding
out why the music comes';[32] while in mid-September 'I finished
my 5 valve superhet receiver but it does nothing but oscillate like a
pair of copulating cats.'[33] He subsequently failed and had to retake
the final practical test. Even though a certain mystery surrounded
the course's exact purpose, the theoretical aspects of radar interested him; the formal education whose limitations he would sometimes lament had advantageously failed to instil in him a rigid
arts/science division: 'What a bonus,' he would write, 'that intellectual development never ceases, in the ill-educated at least!'[34]
Meanwhile, his literary self-education continued at its usual hectic
pace, none the worse for a touch of naval down-to-earthness. By
October, he had been reading, among other things, the letters of
Henry James:

> What was the horrid dark *secret* of his life? He drank little,
> smoked less, fucked not at all – there aren't many more things
> that could counterpoise that immense façade of the complex
> literary figure. I think he was really a woman, like George Eliot.

But you can still send me the anecdote of Gladstone on Wordsworth. I've been glancing at Blake – what a crib of old George Barker, eh? ... Some nice remarks, too – 'Art is First in Intellectuals & Ought to be First in Nations.' I've just finished *New Year Letter*, which I thought very good – at least the letter part. The sonnet sequence is awful. Tennyson he is all over again as I've always said. I'd like to have written the passage beginning 'He never won complete support'. All very accomplished, very managed, very nice – like the make-up of a smart woman of 39.[35]

This essentially civilian academic existence could hardly remain permanently undisturbed by naval routine. A harbour defence company was formed and a few elements of service life – PT and church parade – were reinstated; but the familiarity of both the landscape and the faces ('thumbed and known / As a pack of cards') effectively destroyed any sense of military urgency:

> And nothing happens but the passage of time,
> The monotonous wave on which we are borne and hope
> Will never break. But we suspect already
> The constant ache as something malignant and
> Descry unspeakable deeps in the boring sand.
>
> And on the quay, in our imagination,
> The grass of starvation sprouts between the stone,
> And ruins are implicit in every structure.
> Gently we probe the kind and comic faces
> For the strength of heroes and for martyrs' bones.[36]

Low-key and affectionate (the 'comic faces' were originally 'speaking faces', but the change makes them no less likeable), the poem captures almost too successfully a sense of time suspended: in the closing lines of the first stanza quoted above, language and metre seem completely overwhelmed by the pervasive inertia. The paradox, of course, was that while the sojourn in Aberdeen represented a welcome postponement of unpleasantness to come, the relative inactivity might in itself become intolerable. On balance, however, it had been a 'Hibernian idyll':

> Farewell to the excellent lecturer whose 'er' of hesitation was *in excelsis* the characteristic and imitable Aberdeen 'ee', rather saliva-surrounded; to the pubs, unwelcoming to ladies, some-

times confining them with their escorts in waist-high pens,
symbolism never quite fathomed; to the delicious species of *crois-
sant*, 'buttery rowies', always provided fresh for breakfast by our
landlady; to the strong, clean city itself, then supportive of many
arts, not least the 'varieties', where old favourites were still to be
seen. Farewell, above all, to old familiar faces, for at the end of
the course some of us were assigned to the Fleet Air Arm,
changing our home port to the FAA base at Lee-on-the-Solent.[37]

Such fulsome enthusiasm is uncharacteristic; yet it is much in character for Fuller to lavish his praise upon so stern and purposeful a
place as Aberdeen. If it supported the arts, it did so in a thoroughly
unbohemian spirit; while, unlike Blackpool, it was not the kind of
resort at which an unfrocked vicar might exhibit himself in a barrel.[38]

Fuller left Aberdeen in November 1941, and the poem he wrote
to mark the occasion ('November 1941',[39] later retitled 'Autumn
1941')[40] plainly demonstrates an unresolved conflict of styles. It
opens with a magisterially Audenesque passive and a resonant
enigma: 'The objects are disposed: the sky is suitable.' The line's air
of authority effectively disguises its meaninglessness. What objects?
By whom and how were they disposed? For what purpose is the
sky suitable? Fuller provides only a kind of answer by at once
shifting into his own more characteristic mode of well-judged,
unemphatic description: 'Where the coast curves the waves' blown
smoke / Blurs with the city's and the pencilled ships / Lumber like
toys.' That is neatly done, if not strikingly unlike a hundred other
poems, but after another four lines the poet interrupts himself:
'Well then? It is here one asks the question.' The 'one' does
nothing to mitigate the speciousness of the gesture, which seems to
signal a further modulation into some more overtly rhetorical tone.
So it proves, and Fuller himself would later dismiss the rest of the
poem as 'merely... a rhetoric and an attempt at generalisation'.[41]
And yet that isn't quite fair, for the final lines have a spaciousness
and dignity which anticipates his later blank verse:

> How will this end? The answer is not in doubt;
> For the mood at last plunges to earth like a shot airman:
> The only truth is the truth of graves and mirrors.
> And people walk about with death inside them
> Beseeching the poets to make it real. The sea,
> The desolate sea, divides; the heavens are

Perpetual; and the city with its million
Falls to its knees in the sand. O heroes, comrades,
The world is no vision and is devoid of ghosts.

Of course, we might justly have reservations about moods plunging
to earth or the gratuitous repetition in 'The desolate sea', but the
concluding mismatch of heroic vocative with empty vision is brilliantly effective, catching on a grander scale the disconnection
between military ideal and reality already suggested in 'Defending
the Harbour'.

The Royal Naval Air Station, Lee-on-the-Solent (its name,
HMS *Daedalus*, strangely echoing, apart from the not wholly
encouraging classical connotation, Fuller's Joycean law student
pseudonym) marked an unambiguous return to the disciplines and
deprivations of service life. Conspicuous among the latter was the
surrender of his splendid uniform in exchange for plain fore-and-
aft rig – three-buttoned jacket, trousers, small-peaked cap – the
unflattering garb of the unflatteringly-named 'Air Fitters (DF)'.
Fuller was suitably miffed: 'My glamour had gone, not to be
restored until, after years at this dowdy chrysalis stage, sudden
emergence as RNVR officer.'[42] Radar training continued, but
although there were lectures there was no equipment, and the
teachers were not up to Aberdeen standard. When the equipment
finally arrived, it had to be guarded by the class members, the 4
a.m. to 8 a.m. watch, which entailed first sleeping in a cold
wooden hut nearby, proving especially undesirable. There was a
shortage of books and a surfeit of inescapably relayed popular
music. There were 'no electric fires, pubs across the road, boiled
eggs (even 4 minute b.e.), new (to me) Dickson Carrs. Instead I
have to listen, like a man who has just acquired a set of Russian
Linguaphone records, to Bill, and avoid, as far as possible, the
deadly Horace.'[43] In a poem called 'Royal Naval Air Station', Fuller
made the best of it:

> The piano, hollow and sentimental, plays,
> And outside, falling in a moonlit haze,
> The rain is endless as the empty days.
>
> Here in the mess, on beds, on benches, fall
> The blue serge limbs in shapes fantastical:
> The photographs of girls are on the wall.

And the songs of the minute walk into our ears;
Behind the easy words are difficult tears:
The pain which stabs is dragged out over years.[44]

Being separated from Kate and John after the relatively normal
domestic life of Aberdeen was especially irksome, more frustrating
than the indisputable physical distance which would intervene with
service overseas. He returned to the subject, with unusual tenderness, in 'The End of a Leave': 'Suddenly our relation / Is terrify-
ingly simple / Against our wretched times…'[45]

Taking a calculated gamble with his title – one exactly vindicated by events, as it turned out – Fuller wrote at Lee-on-the-
Solent the poem which gave its name to his second collection:

The Middle of a War

My photograph already looks historic.
The promising youthful face, the matelot's collar,
Say 'This one is remembered for a lyric.
His place and period – nothing could be duller.'

Its position is already indicated –
The son or brother in the album; pained
The expression and the garments dated,
His fate so obviously preordained.

The original turns away: as horrible thoughts,
Loud fluttering aircraft slope above his head
At dusk. The ridiculous empires break like biscuits.
Ah, life has been abandoned by the boats –
Only the trodden island and the dead
Remain, and the once inestimable caskets.[46]

The poem is prescient in other ways too. Fuller would always be
drawn to sonnets, both singly and in sequences. This one is notable
for the assurance with which it turns its subject into history, the
first of several occasions on which he would provide himself with
an ironic obituary. The use of time here is particularly subtle,
embracing not only the 'then' of the photograph and the 'now' of
the poet quizzically inspecting it, but the blithely dismissive future;
the complex meshing of perspectives gives the poem an entirely
new authority. Fuller later thought it necessary to provide a somewhat apologetic explanation of 'Loud fluttering aircraft' ('the

The Middle of a War

My photograph already looks historic.
The promising youthful face, the matelot's collar,
Say 'This one is remembered for a lyric.
His place and period — nothing could be fuller!'

Its position is already miscalced —
The son or brother in the album; faded
The expression and the garments dated,
His fate so obviously pre-ordained.

The original turns away: as horrible thoughts,
Loud fluttering aircraft stop above his head
At Musk. The ridiculous empires break like biscuits.
Ah, life has been abandoned by the boats —
Only the trodden island and the dead
Remain, and the once inestimable caskets.

'The Middle of a War':
reproduced from Fuller's letter to Julian Symons,
19 February 1942.

strange aircraft still used by the Navy – the Swordfish and the amphibian Walrus strangest'),[47] though the seemingly paradoxical image works effectively in any case, picking up the insubstantial-ness of 'thoughts' in the preceding line.

'The Middle of a War' seems to have struck everyone who read it as an important poem which exactly captured its moment. On leave in Blackpool, and with the urgency of a writer sensing a winner, he wrote it on the second page of a letter to Julian Symons,[48] for possible inclusion in the issue of *Poetry* which Symons was editing. But a month later John Lehmann had read it too and seen not only a contribution for *Penguin New Writing* but the title-poem for a collection to be published by The Hogarth Press:

> I sent Lehmann my poems (to be considered as a *book*) & he took a fancy to *The Middle of a War* & wants to use it in *P.N.W.* No 13 (along with *The Growth of Crime* & the poem that was broadcast ['Royal Naval Air Station']). I told him I'd given it you but that I thought I could get it back. Can I? Or will it do for *Poetry* in spite of its coming out in *P.N.W.*?[49]

Though Fuller was at this time slightly wary of his future publisher ('he is v. amiable,' he wrote in the same letter, 'but his *taste* I suspect a bit'), Lehmann's judgement would be entirely vindicated. Forty years later, the poem was in a sense reclaimed by its original recip-ient, when Symons chose the author's reading of it as one of his eight records in the BBC radio programme *Desert Island Discs*. Fuller was thrilled: 'We enjoyed DID. Quite a frisson when "The Middle of a War" emerged – though I did recall you'd said some-thing about a poem of mine.'[50] Alan Brownjohn, too, was 'delighted to hear "The Middle of a War" on *Desert Island Discs*.'[51]

In March 1942, Fuller was transferred to HMS *Daedalus*'s over-flow establishment, Seafield Park, near Fareham, and an altogether gentler if somewhat eccentric regime. It was commanded by a retired and recalled Warrant Officer, promoted to Lieutenant-Commander, and duties there might include painting his car, working on his boat, or looking after his two pet monkeys. Such peculiarities were perhaps inspired by the premises, for the place had formerly been a prep school, and many of its physical features were to be overlaid with those of Blackpool High School to create the fictional Seafolde House of *The Ruined Boys*. Its function in 1942 was essentially to provide accommodation for those waiting to be drafted abroad, including not only Fuller but his colleague from Aberdeen, Willie Robertson; though both had initially failed the practical test at the end of the radar course, 'after a severe battle of wits with Horace & Bill I managed to pass the practical test (90% I got, to spite them both) & am now available for draft';[52] he was duly promoted to 'Leading Air Fitter (DF)'.

Encouraged by the comparatively civilised atmosphere of Seafield Park, Fuller installed Kate and John in nearby digs. But time was running out. Within a week of his wife and son arriving in Hampshire came the news that the Ceylon draft, himself included, was to leave within twenty-four hours: Fuller was on watch duty at the time, so the news was delivered to Kate by Willie Robertson, who was bound for the same destination although he 'had actually officially requested to be taken off the Ceylon draft, on the ground that his wife would be upset at his going';[53] in the circumstances, no more sympathetic messenger could have been imagined. The next morning, Kate optimistically cycled over to Seafield Park, in the hope of catching a glimpse of Roy – 'which she did from a distance over the tail of a truck taking the draft and its bags and ammicks [naval slang for hammocks] to RNAS, Lee, to join those on the draft already there.'[54] Soon he would be on the troop train, heading for Liverpool and embarkation, in the middle of a war.

★

> And now I am alone. I am once more
> The far-off boy without a memory,
> Wandering with an empty deadened self.[55]

That was how Fuller saw it when he parted from Kate in April 1942, and in an important sense he was absolutely right: he had always been lonely within a crowd, not only because his background and temperament so disposed him, but above all because intellectually he found himself unable to level with the crowd's compromises – his feelings of exclusion as a schoolboy, his distaste for the vulgar excesses of popular entertainment, the awkwardness of his brief foray into Blackpool politics were all evidence of that. Yet, in the ordinary context of physical solitude, 'alone' was precisely what he would not be for a long time, aboard a troopship bound for Ceylon.

The all-night train journey to Liverpool provided a foretaste of 'a depth of proletarian service existence scarcely plumbed before, not even in Chatham Barracks, where at least frequent escape "ashore" could be envisaged'.[56] From Aintree station, the Fleet Air Arm draft of 125 men were delivered to a nearby transit camp, where they ate an indifferent meal interrupted by an uncouth army detachment 'who burst into the mess and barged about for advantageous places in the food queue';[57] this too was an accurate indication of social conventions to be endured on the troopship. Meanwhile, on Monday 13 April at the transit camp, Fuller wrote the first entry in the detailed journal which he was to keep regularly for the next four months; it would provide a rich source of material for *The Perfect Fool* and *Home and Dry* as well as for poems. Like his war-time letters to Julian Symons, the journal entries are notable for their uninhibited freshness and instructive as evidence of the raw material he so scrupulously refined:

> No 1 Transit Camp near Liverpool. Dust blowing off dried mud of parade ground. Arrived in Army transport after all night journey frm RNB Sta Pompey: all night journey during which I tried to read *The White Cockatoo* (a bad thriller) but mostly dozed or watched game of baccarat at next table – played by 4 Air Macs [mechanics] for high stakes. One red hair, pimples – 'a cock sucking get' his favourite appellation. Another nicknamed *Toscanini* – usually *Toscafuckinini* or *Tosca*, rather dour, rather sad at losing money. Stooge of party small simpler man – *Ivan* or *Ivanskavinski Skavar* – who persisted in betting miserable threepences. We are bored & pessimistic. All chokka [Fuller's own gloss: 'Fed up, browned-off. Sometimes almost to tears'], all hoping some *phenomenon* will prevent us going or at least getting there. "I never did the Japs any harm." Willie's catchword is "Its not fair, its not right. A nigger's left ball."... A sentimental feeling of being in a typical scene or situation – draft to Ceylon – of common fate with these men. I start this journal on principle – I hope it comes to something. Buzz that we go tomorrow on the *Capetown Castle* – rumoured to be luxury, pleasure cruiser boat. Alternative buzz – we go tonight, that RNVR Lt. in/c awaits a signal at seven. Everything is buzzes.[58]

Next day, 14 April, they moved to Liverpool docks and boarded the *Capetown Castle*, a 22,000 ton liner; they sailed at noon on the fifteenth, part of a small convoy which by dusk had swelled to some twenty ships, with an escort of cruisers and destroyers. Fuller's shifting *alter ego*, Alan Percival in *The Perfect Fool*, is at this point in his story virtually indistinguishable from his creator:

> The first-class lounge of the liner had been filled, like a giant egg-box, with close tiers of bunks, but in the entrance lobby from the deck there was room for only two two-bunk tiers. One of these bunks bore the number of the card handed to Alan on embarkation. He contemplated with alarm the crowded alleyways and claustrophobic layers of the main part of the lounge, and to allay the jealousy of others complained about the traffic past his bunk and the draught through the doors.
>
> When they were under way, these disadvantages (which initially he had almost had to exercise his ingenuity to find) became truly nerve-racking.[59]

In his memoirs, Fuller recalled the space thus inhabited as the ballroom, and likened the arrangement of the bunks to a wine-rack rather than a giant egg-box, but in either case the extent of the overpopulation is clear. There were reportedly 4,000 men on board, constantly forming queues and congestion, and even a more easily gregarious man would have found the conditions trying. But, quite apart from the physical discomfort, there was the peculiar sting of destroyed illusions and disappointed ideals, as Alan Percival furiously discovers after his mug has been stolen by some villainous air mechanic:

> He writhed to think of the tripe he had put in his letters, let run through his head, at his initial training establishment – about the virtues of his fellow-conscripts and his indissoluable unity with them... Balls to humanity. It was smelly, ugly, thieving, doomed. It opened its silly mouth and unwilled, loud and meaningless sounds came out. As it passed him it jostled him, as uncontrolled, as careless of its body, as a member of a herd.[60]

Though this passage is closely based on Fuller's journal for Thursday 16 April, the latter conveys an authentic howl of shattered idealism which has been filtered out of Alan Percival's version:

> Fuck all natural objects, love for fellow men – I shrink to think of the bullshit I've written about navy life. I should have waited

for something like this, something which gives you suicidal impulses, an even grey of misery. Sea dead calm yesterday. Slight swell this morning. When it gets rough suicidal impulses should be something more.[61]

His retrospective real-life counterpart was more temperate, but not much:

Vanished my Wordsworthian interest in natural objects, Spenderian love of fellow men: I squirmed to recall the bullshit I had written about naval life, luckily in letters rather than verse. The even blankness of depression by no means excluded suicidal impulses, as in prisons and concentration camps.[62]

He had a point. It was not simply the uncomfortable conditions – no great novelty to one who had survived Blackpool dormitories, the Woolwich strongroom and the Chatham tunnels – but the inescapable sense of a decline from his excellent training in Shotley and Aberdeen. And beyond this there was the appalling discovery that he had been mistaken about the essential nature of human beings: it was the most traumatic moment of his adult life, and it permanently affected his political philosophy. As close and sympathetic a friend as Julian Symons never became fully reconciled to Fuller's damaged social idealism; but Symons never sailed in a troopship. The distinction is made with characteristic tact and generosity in Fuller's late novel *The Carnal Island*. There, the elderly poet Daniel House tries to define the way in which the war affected creative artists, with the exception of his writer friend Bob Calwell, who was unfit for war service:

'Since the General Strike – or slump, if you like – something has taken place in England. Something vague, perhaps not very important. I think it occurred in the ranks during the last war. Bob Calwell missed it. There's been nothing else, unless you count a monotonous series of wrong by-ways taken.'[63]

If it was typical of Fuller to feel oppressed by squalid conditions and dismayed by shattered ideals, it was also typical of him to make the best of things. 'Better today, much better – in both body and soul,' he wrote on Saturday 18 April.[64] A week later: 'Yesterday we started daily lime juice rations & saw the first flying fish. At dusk they looked like dragonflies but this morning in the sun more like swallows.'[65] It sounds almost idyllic; yet in the sonnet 'Troopship', which concludes *The Middle of a War*, this image of the flying-fish is juxtaposed with the loneliness of being, however crowdedly, at sea:

> Now the fish fly, the multiple skies display
> Still more astounding patterns, the colours are
> More brilliant than fluid paint, the grey more grey.
>
> At dawn I saw a solitary star
> Making a wake across the broken sea,
> Against the heavens swayed a sable spar.
>
> The hissing of the deep is silence, the
> Only noise is our memories.
>
>   O far
> From our desires, at every torrid port,
> Between the gem-hung velvet of the waves,
> Our sires and grandsires in their green flesh start,
> Bend skinny elbows, warn: 'We have no graves.
> We passed this way, with good defended ill.
> Our virtue perished, evil is prince there still.'[66]

The opening is wonderfully assured, of course, and yet the assurance seems to derive from the poet's unspoken feeling that this is the sort of thing one ought to write about flying-fish: the gesture is conventional, and for just that reason confident. Fuller's more honest response is the more uncertain one signalled by that uneasily isolated central couplet with its painfully suspended line-ending on a rhymed 'the'. Yet, as in 'Autumn 1941', he attempts to resolve his uncertainties with a universal, rhetorical peroration: when he reprinted the piece in his *New and Collected Poems*, he substituted 'sweaty' for 'torrid', which is a minor improvement, but the real problems are the archaic 'sires and grandsires' and the congested ending. If the point is that even a justifiable war is futile, in moral terms a losing battle, then 'evil is prince there still' is a curiously mannered way of putting it.

Though temporarily cheered by flying-fish, Fuller sought to improve his lot in more permanent and practical ways. The lack of civilised washing facilities – the on-deck 'ablutions' provided for the troops were without water except for two short periods in the morning and early evening – proved especially irksome. Alan

Percival, returning from watch one night, unexpectedly finds himself in 'a corridor into which opened at least two bathrooms, where some Army and Air Force sergeants were cleaning their razors and splashing their bull necks in abundant running water',[67] and accordingly decides to avail himself of this forbidden luxury. Fuller himself was more forthright about his intentions: 'I say "wandering", but it sticks in my mind that the exploration was specifically to discover such a wash-place, probably having observed vestiges of it in the shining faces and and shirt-sleeved state of certain senior NCOs.'[68] He used it regularly, even nodding to a few of the army and air force sergeants, who assumed him to be a Petty Officer, and he soon made a further discovery:

> I found a small room, empty, containing a bath. I slipped in, bolted the door. In the linen dolly-bag issued at *Ganges* for toilet articles I had a cake of salt water soap bought with blind fore-thought from the ship's canteen. The great taps soon filled the commodious bath with sea-water. Lying in it, my nude body seemed already at the mercy of the greater saline element outside the ship. The squeakings and blowings from the timbers and vents round me were far from reassuring; the ambiguous trousers and shirt on the adjacent floor seemed a protection lost.[69]

The anecdote is interesting not only because this was 'the moment of greatest unease of the voyage' (outstripping, that is to say, the occasion on which within an hour and a half two nearby ships exploded), but because it so nicely enshrines apparently contradictory aspects of Fuller's character: obsessive fastidiousness and obstinate recklessness.

On 27 April, the *Capetown Castle* docked at Freetown, Sierra Leone. The heat and light, at first exhilarating, soon became enervating. On Friday 1 May there was an evening concert, after which came speeches by the captain of one of the escorting cruisers and by the captain of the *Capetown Castle* (not recorded in Fuller's memoirs but reproduced almost verbatim from his journal in *The Perfect Fool*). The former begins by telling them 'one thing I do know – you're going to fight the Japs'; their symbol of the rising sun, he says, must be turned into the setting sun, and he continues:

> 'I didn't mean to be theatrical. We English are not given to being theatrical. We take a lot of rousing. But, by God, when we

are roused…! Make no mistake: the Japanese are formidable opponents, ruthless opponents. We English can be just as formidable, just as ruthless. You men have got to learn that there aren't any rules in this game. You've got to shoot even when the Japanese have their hands up.'

Someone shouted out: 'That's right. No prisoners.' There was more crashing applause.

The captain went on: 'I'm glad you agree. I've told my ship's company that there will be no prisoners on my ship. Nor will they be taken prisoner. Thank you.'

The captain of the troopship then came forward to the rail at the side of the dais, resting one foot on it, holding it with his hands and hunching over it, his simian appearance making one expect the extra grasp round it of a prehensile tail. He said: 'I'm only a humble old merchant seaman. But I fly the red ensign. I fly it day and night, so that I can open fire at any time. I don't care who's on board – men, women or children – this ship won't be taken. I'll go down with that red ensign flying.'[70]

Of course, such sentiments shouldn't have been particularly surprising. Bloodthirstily brainless patriotism is a concomitant of any war – even little ones, as the tabloid treatment of the Falklands conflict more recently illustrated. But for Fuller, continually alert to the way in which good causes are wrecked by simplistic jingoism, it was deeply depressing, 'a sharper case of the kind exemplified by the future Lord Martonmere starting to sing the National Anthem at my peace meeting in the Thirties. It seemed as though one forgot, until so reminded, that a great part of mankind was engaged in putting its nationalistic and aggressive feelings into practice.'[71] Yet what plainer instance of just that activity could there be than the spectacle of 4,000 assorted service personnel sailing round the coast of Africa in a troopship? He couldn't avoid the fact that the captains' views, however objectionable, at least provided a coherent *raison d'être* for the mission – something conspicuously absent from his own well-intentioned idealistic muddle. And that, naturally, compounded his misery: 'The evidence of so much hatred appalls me,' he wrote in his journal; 'I went to my gun-post horribly shaken.'[72]

They sailed from Freetown on 3 May and within two days Fuller's gestures at a travel-journal – 'Sun still shines – it is said that sometime today we crossed the Equator' – gave way once again to furious despair: 'I hate the smell of these men, the way they open their uncouth mouths and emit loud meaningless noises – more stupid than animals… I love and pity them less frequently on this fucking troopship than anywhere.'[73] That is partly a transferred frustration: he was missing Kate terribly, dreaming about her vividly, and like many an emotionally reticent man he converted his unhappiness into quite other sorts of anger. When he gave the mildest hint of his mood in letters home, he was summoned to an interview of tragi-comic absurdity:

> Thorley (Lt. RNVR) called me to his cabin about two of my letters – they had been passed on to him by the censoring Capt. of Marines. The objection mainly was to two phrases 'This bloody troopship' and 'the moral objection to war'. We had a long & amiable discussion. I tried to point out that saying one saw the moral objection to war was not a criticism of the Government. He countered by finding in the letter the words 'political' and 'economic'. Damning! He tried to be paternal & point out that to fight a dictatorship one had to become a dictator – but of course it was no use. Then, coming another tack, he said that the *tone* of the letter was depressing. I asked him politely if there was any objection officially to that. So then, to point a moral, he read aloud to me one of the letters he was writing – and in a couple of sentences we came to a description of the lavish menu provided for the officers! It was hopeless & we parted with mutual apologies – he will blue pencil the offending passages – and regard me in the future as a v. doubtful character, I fear.[74]

Typically, Fuller's patient and polite behaviour masks his utter intransigence, a pattern which would recur both in his naval career and throughout his life.

The *Capetown Castle* arrived at Durban on 18 May; Fuller immediately noticed the premises of industrial concerns such as Dunlop, Lever Brothers and Standard Oil, confirming his belief that they were primarily engaged in the defence of capitalist imperialism rather than of any nobler ideal. He was appalled by racial segregation, and throughout his time in Africa in a blunderingly good-natured way 'enjoyed mucking in where possible with non-whites';[75] he rightly noted that the arrival of thousands of white servicemen carrying out menial duties must have been to the non-white population an astonishing spectacle and in its small way a liberalising influence.

Within a couple of hours, they had moved off to a transit camp at Clairwood, six miles out of Durban. 'Everyone is here!' he exclaimed delightedly in his journal,[76] as he re-encountered friends from Shotley and Aberdeen. In a way which would recur as a charming yet highly practical motif in his African travels, he translated the scene into terms of manageably familiar domesticity:

> Clairwood Camp, a town of tents pitched on a gentle hillside, overlooked a landscape through which I might have been driven by Richard Flower on our pre-war circuits of the Kent and East Sussex courts. The first meal eaten was tea: on the tables were newly-broached two-pound tins of preserves. By moving round, in the style of the Mad Hatter's tea-party, it was possible to sample half-a-dozen or so varieties, which I did, greedy after the lousy grub of the *Capetown Castle* – even trying out such dubieties as tomato jam. To South African marmalade, almost invariably excellent, I have stayed faithful to this day.[77]

That his ideological detestation of South Africa should have been overriden – from 1942 'to this day' (1984) – by a preference for her marmalade is characteristic: an instance less of moral hypocrisy than of amiable obduracy about matters of quotidian detail – clothes, hot water, bread.

At Clairwood the company was congenial and the lit alleyways between the tents amazing after blacked-out England; while Durban, abundantly supplied with goods which were rationed or scarce at home (ice-cream, fruit, clothes, cigarettes, chocolate), seemed a city of anachronistic, almost immoral luxury. There was South African brandy at ninepence a nip and concerts by the Durban Symphony Orchestra. The war in Europe seemed less real than ever. Yet there was something wrong with Durban, and of course Fuller worried away at analysing it:

> There is a stink about it all – remittance man luxury or something. All the books & cosmetics, the whisky & gin, the fountain pens watches & cameras are imported – usually of course, british or american. S.A. appears to manufacture fuck all – just a great plantation where the whites live on the backs of the

Indians & natives & drive about in great high powered
American cars. The girls in their summer frocks with italicised
bosoms are v. attractive indeed. The ricksha drivers are Zulus in
shabby native headresses & so on. Skyscraper flats on the front.
A frail & diminutive Indian boy in the pub selling C.P.
pamphlets.[78]

Still, at least he remained alert to, and reassured by, female beauty;
and sometimes, as he noted on 5 June, by male beauty too: 'In the
showers a Javanese boy (Royal Netherlands Navy), beautifully
compact, shaped, muscled, with a body of coffee-cream, and black
nipples & penis.'[79]

On 11 June, the Fleet Air Arm detachment went aboard the
Manela, 'a nasty, rusty, quite small craft, said to have been
condemned before the war';[80] Willie Robertson quickly discovered
a fat Scottish cook, cleaning baking tins allegedly unused for fifteen
years, and enquired about the vessel's seaworthiness. '"Is she a guid
sailing ship?" "Anything but thaat," said the cook. "It's a wonder
she's no moving the noo." We were, of course, still at the quayside.'[81] Next day, they sailed for Mombasa, their subsequent destination undisclosed though by now believed not to be Ceylon. Also
on board were a handsome cat with its kittens, and a few mangy
hens. The vessel rolled like Mae West, Fuller's 'ammick' was on the
wrong side of her permanent list, and her crew seemed 'surly and
villainous'; meanwhile, he tried to read *Henry Esmond*, which
prompted the glum reflection that 'Thackeray was just the sort of
author thrifty patriots took from their shelves to give to the
fighting services and merchant navy.'[82] He had reason for gratitude
to those thrifty patriots, nevertheless, for whenever his sea-borne
misery threatened to become intolerable he could at least take
refuge in reading:

On this ship I have read so far Balzac's *César Birotteau* & *Father
Goriot*, *The Alchemist*, *A New Way to Pay Old Debts*, *Hatter's
Castle*, about half *Esmond*, odd poems & stories in magazines.
This is self-abuse, not reading. *César Birotteau* never gets going –
quite useless to impede what little action it has by laborious
accounts of the origins of the characters. *F. Goriot* v. good, I
think. But there's something horribly vulgar about Balzac...
The spectacular downfall, the ditto revenge, the rise to power –
surely what Balzac was trying to do didn't need these props.[83]

After just over a week's voyage, the *Manela* safely arrived at
Mombasa; and there Fuller and his colleagues discovered to their
astonishment that they were actually bound for the new naval air
station at Nairobi:

> Arr. Mombasa fourish. Green low coast, white red roofed villas,
> a concealed estuary with *Indomitable*, *Royal Sovereign* in it. Bailey
> announced tonight we are going to Nairobi (!) where aero-
> drome is in the course of construction. Everybody is v. pleased
> at prospect of SAFETY − except about 15 hardy folk who are
> said to have volunteered for a carrier. The porthole nearest me
> frames *Indom*.[84]

★

Kenya − or, as it was then still usually called, British East Africa − is
the one country outside England with which Roy Fuller is inex-
tricably associated as a writer. It provides the settings for most of
the poems, including such well-known ones as 'The Green Hills of
Africa' and 'The Giraffes', in his third collection, *A Lost Season*
(1944); for his children's novel, *Savage Gold* (1946); and, as the basis
of an unnamed East African colony, for *The Father's Comedy* (1961),
one of his most successful works of adult fiction. His first impressions of the place, however, were not at all favourable.

> The Splendide Hotel was not splendid. It was a detached, white-
> washed building, two stories high, in a back street. In the hall
> were three old grey dogs, with hairless and distended stomachs,
> which on the entry of Robert and the Count came up panting
> their bad breaths furiously. From the hall one could see the back
> door where a few dusty hens shuffled about. A cloud of flies rose
> from the hotel register as Robert made to sign his name.[85]

This fictional hotel from *Savage Gold* is a none-too-distant relative
of the 'incredibly decrepit' Jaurina Hotel, noticed by Fuller on his
Sunday shore leave in Mombasa. 'A general and profound *malaise*
(or something) hangs over it all,' he recorded in his journal. 'What
remains with me is the *hopeless* air which hung over everything:
what one thinks is let's get out & leave the mess for the natives to
clear up as best they can.'[86] Though he had only learnt of the
Nairobi posting on the previous day, disbelief was already beginning to question such implausible good luck. On the Monday,

however, he found himself one of ten in the advance party due to leave that afternoon for the Nairobi Civil Aerodrome. Seats had been booked on the ordinary train, leaving Mombasa at 4.30 p.m.: after the modes of travel experienced during the preceding weeks, it was disconcerting to be served by stewards in the dining-car, and then to sleep in the fresh linen of a couchette. Even the habitually ironic prose of the memoirs succumbs to the sense of natural luxuriance and enormous space: 'Before the early equatorial night fell the long train could be seen chugging upwards through dramatic forest land; by morning the compartment window framed grassy highland plains with their herds of game and immense skies, soon to become utterly familiar.'[87] And with this familiarity and this landscape a distinct, newly confident note was to enter Fuller's poetry, as the opening stanza of 'The Green Hills of Africa' (here in its original version) clearly shows:

> The green, humped, wrinkled hills: with such a look
> Of age (or is it youth?) as to erect the hair.
> They crouch above the ports or on the plain,
> Under the matchless skies; are like the offered
> Shoulders of a girl you only half know.
> What covers them so softly, vividly?
> They break at the sea in a cliff, a mouth of red:
> Upon the plain they are unapproachable,
> So massive, furrowed, so dramatically lit.[88]

Fuller's first few months in Nairobi were not without their problems. He immediately fell out with several of the ruling clique – not for the first, or the last, time in his service career querying orders and disputing status – and used the episode with very little modification in *The Perfect Fool*.[89] Such work as there was – it involved both repairing aircraft radar sets and modifying airframes to enable these novel devices to be installed – was neither exciting nor exacting, and left plenty of time for such seemingly inessential chores as 'chipping paint off an old car being renovated for the clique to use on shooting trips'.[90] Relief from this pointless drudgery came in mid-August, when Fuller, along with another leading air fitter called Bob Park, was transferred from the main hangar to a separate building reserved for the servicing of IFF (Identification Friend or Foe) radar equipment and known as the 'iffy hut'. Not only did this provide him with a modestly purposeful occupation; it also, out of working hours, gave him a useful refuge – he called it his 'IFFory Tower'[91] – for writing poems or letters.

Those working hours were congenial too, a tropical routine which started early and ended at lunchtime. In the afternoons, while his colleagues slept, Fuller would explore the Athi Plain:

> Under a sun almost too bright and hot for comfort, the blue hills, backed by rotund white clouds, stayed in the far distance; less far, but seemingly not getting much nearer, were a few brown *rondevaals*, each with its small green *shamba*, and mysterious life unexplored. By a still-moist watercourse a secretary bird might be gravely stalking; once I came on a still-recognizable dead hyena.[92]

Then he would catch the 'shore leave' lorry for Nairobi. Once in the city itself, he passed the time wandering, shopping, visiting the library, before going into the lounge of the New Stanley Hotel where he could get on with some writing over an early evening beer or two. More sociably, there was a 'cheap and excellent' servicemen's canteen, run by Lady Delamere, and the scene on 27 July of a misapprehension whose significance was not lost on him:

> Three negroes, in the American Army, came in the canteen in town. Up bustles Lady Delamere & bursts into Swahili telling them they can't be served. 'Excuse me, madam,' says one of them, 'I talk no other language but English.'[93]

Often, however, he dined alone in a small 'quite chic' restaurant and went on to one of the two or three cinemas (whose bars offered escape from any especially dreadful films), at some stage in the evening usually meeting Bob or Willie. As wartime service lives go, it was almost indecently cushy. When *Poetry (Chicago)* asked for a contributor's note, 'I gave some account of these matters, on which they commented that I made darkest Africa sound like Evanston, Illinois.'[94]

His fragile but steadily returning confidence was boosted in September, when his name was put forward for a commission: 'I must record the fact that I'm only allowing myself to be recommended because of the chance of going home!' he wrote,[95] and in *Home and Dry* described this as 'a statement I see no reason to doubt'.[96] He was, as always, genuinely gratified by any recognition of his ability: 'My position has subtly changed, I see – I think I am

becoming a sort of *personage*.'[97] There was satisfaction, too, in news
from England about the remarkable success of *The Middle of a War*.
'I had an airgraph from Lehmann today [1 December 1942] saying
that up to the end of October it had sold 700–800 copies, which to
one hitherto brought out by that masterly *hoarder* of books, Caton,
seems phenomenal.'[98] In November, this success was consolidated
by another favourable review from Stephen Spender:

> Mr Roy Fuller is quite definitely a 'war poet'. He is a member
> of the Fleet Air Arm, and his best and most recent poems
> directly derive from his life as a sailor, and his feelings about the
> war. The war has provided him with an experience which,
> though painful, has immensely sharpened his perceptions,
> which, as the earlier poems in this volume show, have tended
> towards the vague and the general. But now he is the only poet
> who has given us as clear a picture of the life of the Forces as
> some of the war artists have done in painting.[99]

Fuller, as Robert Hewison points out in *Under Siege*, 'probably
saw more violent destruction at first hand while still a civilian during
the Blitz'; and yet, as he rightly adds, the spell in Kenya 'brings out
strongly two further themes of service poetry: the impact of travel,
the loneliness of separation.'[100] There is indeed a sense in which the
most characteristic poetry of the Second World War, unlike that of
the First, is not about war at all but about the interlocked themes of
travel and separation. As he wrote to John Lehmann:

> The trouble is I seem to have escaped the war again – it must be
> fated that there shall be no war-poets. I just have the disadvan-
> tages of noise and gregariousness without the stimulant of
> action. I shall have to do some nature poems – there is certainly
> enough nature.[101]

Thus, *A Lost Season* opens with a poem ('In Africa') in which the
unattainable, almost intolerable *distance* which Fuller noted in his
walks on the Athi Plain becomes an exact metaphor for his inescapable loneliness:

> For those who are in love and are exiled
> Can never discover
> How to be happy: looking upon the wild
> They see for ever

The cultivated acre of their pain;
The clouds like dreams,
Involved, improbable; the endless plain
Precisely as it seems.[102]

The assured directness of those lines, though by no means consistently sustained throughout the book, is the quality which above all distinguishes Fuller's second wartime collection from his earlier work.

The misery of separation from Kate (and John) was sharpened, or at any rate modified, by severely practical considerations. In *Home and Dry*, he records how his wife, not much pleased by her enforced and lengthy return to her parental home in Blackpool, eventually moved to a nearby flat – this rare commodity having been obtained with the assistance of a friend on the local paper, none other than the wife of Rod Davies (last encountered on the coincidence-laden first day at HMS *Ganges*), who alerted Kate to suitable classified ads before publication. The flat, whose rooms were in reality distributed throughout a house inhabited by mild eccentrics, was in the well-established Fuller tradition of dotty accommodation – a tradition which, incidentally, does much to explain why, once happily settled in Blackheath after the war, they stayed firmly put. But this was by no means the only problem, as Fuller's letters to his Blackpool solicitor-friend, Norman Lees, demonstrate. On the day charmingly identified as '5 August (I mean September) 1942 (at least I know the year)', he wrote 'to thank you for all your help to Kate – in almost every letter there is mention of you untangling my affairs which, lawyer-like, I left in disgraceful disorder.'[103] By 13 October, the untangling process had reached Nairobi, there acquiring some fresh tangles:

I engineered into town this morning with my friend Park, armed with the documents and your lucid letter of instructions & made a grand tour of the notaries. Mr A was at court all morning, Mr B would not be back until after lunch (golf?) and Mr Suleeman Kerjee (or something) turned out to be only a commissioner although he had an office smellier than anything formerly in Bisley Street. At length I secured the offices of Mr Barret who did all the necessary & had the affidavit engrossed merely for the price of the stamps ('couldn't charge a professional friend'). His London agents are Gibsons, he told me, which gave us a little topic of conversation. Anyway here is the stuff – hope it doesn't get sunk. The Power I think is v. nicely succinct – I'm infinitely obliged for all your trouble.[104]

And on 13 June 1943: 'How are you faring with my horrible income tax matters? I know Kate must keep worrying you.'[105] Such complications were by no means uncommon, of course; all the same they interestingly confirm that Fuller, like many fastidious and apparently well-organised people, was very far from infallible in dealing with personal concerns ironically quite close to his own sphere of professional competence.

Life in the Kenyan uplands meanwhile retained its outward resemblance to that of Evanston, Illinois. With three friends (Bob, Willie, and Tom Duncan, another member of the Aberdeen course), Fuller spent a drinking and tennis-playing weekend as guests of the manager of East African Breweries; the same Scottish Mafia, with its grateful Sassenach accessory, also managed to acquire honorary membership of a 'working-man's club with large knobs on' which existed for railway employees. Elsewhere, he got to know Stan Martin, who ran the flour mill, and his wife Hilda, becoming a frequent visitor to their relaxed and civilised home, where he could be 'part of ordinary life once more' – a phrase which exactly recalls his childhood affection for his grandparents' house.[106] There were concerts, at which one memorable performer was the pianist Ivor Keys, then in the army and stationed nearby, later Professor of Music at Birmingham; at the theatre, the local amateur operatic society performed Gounod's *Faust*. When some entitlement to leave arose, Willie Robertson proposed that he and Fuller should undertake an excursion to Kampala, returning via Lake Victoria on a steamer belonging to the railway company. In Kampala, they stayed in some luxury at the Imperial Hotel; Fuller failed to entice a giant crocodile called Lutembe from the among the lake reeds in which it was supposed to live, though he was photographed standing by a swimming pool with a man who looked like Alfred Hitchcock. 'Ugandan society,' he noted, 'was immediately detectable as superior to Kenyan':

Absent, the powerful, exploitive, but disgruntled class of white settlers, baronial in a Shakespearean sense; one felt the country was being run entirely for the benefit of the indigenous popula-tion – in Kampala, black, tall and stately, the women headgeared and swathed in bright cloth (carrying off even the banal designs of Lancashire mills), a dramatic change from the scurrying brown Kikuyu women of Nairobi and its environs, shaven heads often bent against a strap bearing some back-breaking load.[107]

The lake steamer was Scottish-built and provided with Scottish officers, so 'Willie was soon on terms, discovering friends, ancestors and tramlines in common'. Otherwise the voyage seemed essentially Conradian, with Graham Greeneish overtones, as when at Bukoba 'a white-habited monk arrived on a motor-cycle and sidecar for supplies from the ship.'[108] On their return to Kenya, they disembarked at Kisumu, where Fuller spent some time with an elderly solicitor in need of a younger partner: would he be interested, after the war? The Asians were litigious, the prospects good.

Fuller's initial training as a radar mechanic had promised (and delivered) promotion to leading hand on completion of the course; further promotion to Petty Officer would come a year after that. The navy honoured its commitment to the day. The tangible benefits of the PO's mess proved to be unspectacular: sauces and pickles on the table, comfortable chairs and spirits (including some dangerous Australian gin) in the bar. The main practical chore was the inspection of guard posts at night, in the company of a black sergeant:

I do not understand
Your language, nor you mine.
If we communicate
It is hardly the word that matters or the sign,
But what I can divine.

Are they in London white
Or black? How do you know,
Not speaking my tongue, the names
Of our tribes? It could be as easily a blow
As a match you give me now.

The very lack of a common language allows Fuller to recognise the deeper bond – somewhat idealised if not actually imaginary – or, as he more sceptically puts it in *Home and Dry*: 'some communication occurred... not least astonishment that I should be able to utter the names of tribes.'[109] But 'The White Conscript and the Black Conscript', like 'In Africa', is a poem dignified by its assured simplicity, one which repudiates as irrelevant literary game-playing, Audenesque or otherwise, at least for the time being. It can hardly be expected to resolve the complex problems of colonialism, race and culture on which it touches, yet it does possess an enviable clarity of statement:

> If only I could tell you
> That in my country there
> Are millions as poor as you
> And almost as unfree: if I could share
> Our burdens of despair.[110]

★

In April 1943, Fuller was sent to RNAS Tanga, on the coast north of Zanzibar, to share some of the expertise he had acquired in the iffy hut by lecturing on IFF to aircrews; he travelled by train to Mombasa, then by truck to Port Reitz, and finally by air to Tanga in a dismayingly damp and rusty Albacore. It was a tedious and disagreeable interlude, marginally redeemed by the sympathetic presence of a regular RAF sergeant called Jack Jolly and of an otherwise unidentified character (his real name, Fuller said, had 'sunk through my porous memory')[111] who appears in *The Perfect Fool* as 'Charlie Fowler'. The latter contrived an elaborate and clearly therapeutic fantasy, which he envisaged in the form of a novel, commencing 'in a naval air station in the tropics. They call it an air station but in fact it is just a clearing of swamp in the palm trees.' Here, the Charlie Fowler character is persecuted by a lazy toffee-nosed journalist-turned-radar-mechanic (Alan Percival, i.e. Fuller) and, more seriously, by the Master-at-Arms or 'joss-man'. Time passes, however: the war ends, Charlie and the journalist are demobbed, the joss-man's time expires. Charlie Fowler continues:

> 'More time passes. The scene is Fowler Grange, and Lord Fowler is there sitting in a coat with an astrakhan collar, stroking his jasper moustaches. A bloke comes in with some jellied eel on a gold plate and puts it in front of Lord Fowler and Lord Fowler sees a bit of old dried jellied eel from a previous occasion adhering to the underneath part of the plate, and he says: "Who washed this plate up?" The major-domo says: "The poor old dishwasher what washes everything up in Fowler Grange." "Well, send the bastard in." The Fleet Street journalist comes in

and Lord Fowler says to him: "You're a worse bastard dishwasher than you was a journalist. I'm giving you the push." The journalist goes down on his knees but it's no go. Then Lord Fowler has a butcher's out of the window and sees a bloke pulling a cart across Fowler Park and says: "Who's that bastard blot on the landscape?" The major-domo says: "The poor shit-shoveller what empties the cess pit." "Bring my binoculars," says Lord Fowler and when he takes a butcher's through them he sees it is the joss-man pulling the cart, so he goes upstairs and has a good shit.'[112]

The schoolboy-subversive tone of this, though amusing enough on its own terms, says a good deal about the atmosphere at RNAS Tanga. Nor was the eponymous town much more encouraging, its houses unsociably turned inward on courtyards away from the deserted streets, its principal source of much-needed refreshment an aerated water factory:

> In the garden of the aerated water factory
> Is an iron fountain and the doves
> Come to its lip to drink.
> Outside the totos are begging for five-cent pieces;
> Boys whose faces are done in sepia, the places
> Round their eyes and the irises still running.[113]

At the base, the Petty Officers' Mess was attended, like the Lieutenant-Commander's quarters at Seafield Park, by pet monkeys:

> Just now I visited the monkeys: they
> Are captive near the mess. And so the day
> Ends simply with a sudden darkness, while
> Again across the palm trees, like a file,
>   The rain swings from the bay.[114]

Caged and frustrated, the monkeys provided apt emblems for the condition of Fuller and his colleagues, many of whom became ill with malaria, dysentery or insect bites. He had been suffering from an ear infection, which during his stay at Tanga so worsened that he decided to consult the Medical Officer. The ensuing dialogue, whose surreal Goon Show logic resembles a conversation between Eccles and Colonel Bloodnock, was incorporated verbatim in *The Perfect Fool*;[115] but it also appears, without the interruptions of fictional narrative, in his memoirs:

'What have I got, sir?'
'Tropical ear.'
'Is it − serious?'
'No, no. All ears are tropical in the tropics.'[116]

Fuller's ear, however, was sufficiently tropical to produce a temperature of 106°. He was transferred to the RN section of the civilian
hospital in Tanga, where his condition was rediagnosed as tropical
throat. In the insomniac nights he would wander out from his ward
onto the cool terracotta tiles of an adjacent veranda, making no
progress towards recovery, until reprimanded by the hospital's
director: 'You must stay in bed... You must not get out of bed for
anything.'[117] Obeying this instruction had the doubly desirable result
of hastening both his release from hospital and his return to Nairobi.

He travelled by rail, with an overnight stop and change of trains
at Moshi, close to the foothills of Kilimanjaro. There he followed
the example set by other passengers and dined at an unattractive
nearby hotel before making his way back to the station − for he
understood that passengers might remain on the Tanga-Moshi train
overnight, and he happily recalled his first journey from Mombasa
to Nairobi with its immaculate couchettes and attentive stewards.
This time, though, the train turned out to be dark and deserted,
parked in a siding; nevertheless, he spent an uncomfortable night in
it, accompanied only by attentive mosquitos. The incident, as he
ruefully admitted, was absolutely in character:

> Later, someone in Nairobi told me I could have claimed, from the
> RPO's office, reimbursement of the cost of a hotel room had I
> produced the bill, but of course my action was not the result of
> poverty or even parsimony, rather arose from too great a respect
> for rules and authority... Shyness, too, played a big part in the
> business; also an unjustified reliance on mankind behaving ratio-
> nally, especially when so instructed. It may seem odd that these
> traits accompany a strong noncomformity of thought, a willing-
> ness to be in a minority of one, but so it has been. From a slightly
> different aspect the persona may be seen as that of the Fool, the
> gormless but intelligent innocent who only learns about life
> through his enormous gaffes, and even then repeats them. Such
> was the representation attempted in *The Perfect Fool*.[118]

Not only is this an abiding theme; it also provides the prototype for one of Fuller's most familiar late self-characterisations: 'I play – I am! – the Shakespearean daft old man.'[119]

The following morning he breakfasted at the hotel and then, before his train left, went for a walk in the forlorn hope that the low cloud would break to allow him a glimpse of Kilimanjaro. The mountain remained completely invisible. Instead, according to the poem 'Today and Tomorrow', he looked across 'the rows of sugar cane' and bade 'good-day to sweet brown boys/Who keep their goats beneath that sheeted peak',[120] though afterwards he wondered whether the sugar cane might not have been maze and the goats sheep.

Back in Nairobi, thanks to the Moshi station mosquitos, he became ill with malaria: 'I moved back here last week and then on Sunday I developed malaria and now it's Thursday in the sick bay,' he told Julian Symons, who was himself recovering from an operation to remove a fibrous tumour from his arm: 'It will be our operations we shall talk about after the war.'[121] He was subsequently sent on recuperative leave – at the charitable expense of the Kenya Women's Volunteer Organisation – to a hotel at Nyeri, adjacent to Mount Kenya. Two prose pieces, 'The Sick Bay' and 'The People Round About', describe these episodes: the first appeared in the short-lived magazine *Equator*, edited by Edward Lowbury (the poet and microbiologist, then with the RAMC in East Africa), and the second in *Penguin New Writing*; both were reprinted as an Appendix to *Home and Dry*.[122] 'The Sick Bay' is a piece of conventional narrative which might without difficulty have been worked into *The Perfect Fool*, but 'The People Round About' is another matter altogether. The narrator, essentially nameless though once passingly referred to as 'Fuller' by another character, purports to be writing in the hotel bar about some of his fellow-residents: 'I become more and more uncertain about the relationship between life and prose fiction. I begin to think that I do not see enough complication in the former to be able to write the latter.' The resulting story is thus a piece of fictionalised reportage, slightly skewed from actual events, almost exactly in the manner of Isherwood's *Goodbye to Berlin*. The style and technique, although clearly derivative, seem precisely suited both to this material and to Fuller himself, who at this stage had published no prose fiction:

> The most delightful character in the hotel is a man who looks very much like the film actor Conrad Veidt. He is an army

officer but wears plain clothes all the time – such things as corduroy trousers, yellow shirts, sports coats slashed with leather, and on Saturday night, when there was a dance in the hotel, a dinner-jacket with black mosquito boots. I have never seen anyone with such a consistently straight back. Eating, drinking or playing the gambling machine in the bar, his back is vertical, as straight as his nose, and his well-shaped nostrils are from time to time slightly dilated. His hair is brilliantined and brushed straight back. This gambling machine is an old-fashioned one, where you catch steel balls between two parallel movable arms: the balls come down between a mesh of pins, so quickly and irregularly that it is very difficult to take any money out of the machine at all, and it is a shilling a go. Nevertheless, the machine is very popular and forms a topic of conversation and a focal point for people in the bar, whose faces light up as soon as anyone puts a shilling in it. Very often it is Conrad Veidt who is sitting in front of it on a high stool, marvellously erect and masterful, his elbows tucked in, his whisky-and-soda and a pile of shillings on top of the machine. 'It's so *frightfully* wearing,' he says. 'It makes me boss-eyed.' But he goes on playing. His young, dark and decorative wife, who wears trousers and drinks beer, stands by his side.

The nicest man is about forty-five and rather shaky, having been blown up in some part of the war. He totters about ready to be amiable, with a book under his arm, which he reads over his solitary meals. At the bar one night he and the Captain and I played the golf game with the poker dice which are always on the bar counter. When he was throwing for the last of his five knaves, he kept turning out a queen. 'Here's that dreadful woman again!' he cried, with his mouth twitching under his moustache. He encourages Conrad Veidt at the gambling machines and some-times self-deprecatingly plays a game himself. I wonder whether perhaps he is not *rather* complicated.[123]

The careful description of clothes and hair is characteristic, but other features of this passage are a little more surprising: the buttonholing, conversational present tense, reminiscent of Isherwood's 'A Berlin Diary'; the consciously poised blend of narrative involvement and ironic detachment; the archness of that italicised '*rather*' in the final sentence. Auden had obviously been a major influence on Fuller's early poetry; yet here it suddenly becomes clear that his literary habits were more broadly formed by the writers of the 1930s. He was wholly conscious of this, for when he wrote to Julian Symons about 'the pre-war booze in the posh hotel... and the pre-war people and how I played Russian Pool with an army captain and an oil man from Persia,' he added: 'But only a pre-war Isherwood could do justice to it all.'[124] Something of this Isherwood tone resurfaces much later on, in *The Carnal Island*.

The original publication of 'The People Round About' had one slightly bizarre consequence. Later in the story, a Petty Officer, who is known to 'Fuller' and who has been accidentally shot while hunting, dies. After its appearance in *Penguin New Writing*, the real PO's parents wrote to the real Roy Fuller, requesting an interview which might help to clarify the circumstances of their son's death: 'In vain in my reply did I emphasise that my knowledge was entirely hearsay, and that the "I" of the piece knowing the deceased was a fictional twist.'[125] How right the story's 'I' had been to confess his uncertainty 'about the relationship between life and prose fiction'.

Soon after returning to Nairobi from Nyeri, Fuller learnt that he was being sent to start a Radar – or 'Special W/T' – Section at Port Reitz, hitherto memorable mainly for its rusty Albacore. While recognising the comparative cushiness of the assignment, he was unenthusiastic. While he was slowly reconciling himself to the idea, news reached the iffy hut that he was to be commissioned and that he would therefore be travelling not to Port Reitz but back to the UK: 'That the frustration of marital and paternal love was to be ended gave a physical shock the like of which I had never experienced before, nor have since.'[126] His journal, which for the previous year had been intermittent and sketchy, has an almost disbelievingly laconic entry for 27 July 1943: 'It looks as though I really go tomorrow.'[127] At last he was on his way home.

★

On 29 July 1943, PO FULLER FAA – thus self-described in red lettering on a japanned tin box acquired during his travels – noted in his journal: 'Left Nairobi 5 o'clock train yesterday and landed up here in Mombasa at English Point – tents, flies on the food, forgotten men – a transit camp.'[128] It was the first leg of another frustratingly complicated journey: by troopship from Mombasa to Durban; by slow, stopping train to Cape Town, followed by weeks in transit camp; by another troopship, joining a convoy at Gibraltar, bound for Glasgow; and finally docking on a wet, cold, Scottish November day, further tempered by the compulsory return to home base – Lee-on-the-Solent – before going on leave back up to Blackpool. Among his companions was a fellow Lancastrian, Petty Officer Fred Bridle, similarly homeward-bound, who thus accompanied him throughout the journey – even on the last lap, which consisted of a nostalgic dinner at the Regent Palace Grillroom followed by the overnight train from Euston to Blackpool: they requisitioned an empty first-class compartment for themselves and secured the centre-opening doors onto the corridor with a scarf, as well as they might. Reaching Blackpool early next mornng (Bridle had alighted a couple of stations before), Fuller caught a workman's tram, thereafter lugging his baggage on foot from the stop to the house in Seafield Road, overlooking Happy Valley: 'My mother-in-law, not yet dressed, let me in. Kate and Johnny were still in their beds, so I went up to them.'[129] Next day, he wrote to Julian Symons: 'Arrived here yesterday morning after a journey devised by The Admiralty in association with Kafka. But ARRIVED, anyway – it is all slightly unbelievable and most NICE.'[130]

At Durban, Fuller had completed what he would call 'the best poem I wrote during the war, or at any rate the least spoiled'.[131] That judgement is revealing; the poem, 'The Statue', is confident and quite successful, but in a somewhat grandiose rhetorical manner which is not wholly characteristic of its author:

The noises of the harbour die, the smoke is petrified
Against the thick but vacant, fading light, and shadows slide
From under stone and iron, darkest now. The last birds glide.

Upon this black-boned, white-splashed, far receding vista of grey
Is an equestrian statue, by the ocean, trampling the day,
Its green bronze flaked like petals, catching night before the bay.

This heroic object, commemorating some South African pioneer or warrior (Fuller couldn't remember precisely who, but that perhaps adds to the image's generalising force) is ironically contrasted with a quite different sort of statuesque figure:

Last night between the crowded, stifling decks I saw a man,
Smoking a big curved pipe, who contemplated his great wan
And dirty feet while minute after tedious minute ran –

This in the city now, whose floor is permanent and still,
Among the news of history and sense of an obscure will,
Is all the image I can summon up, my thought's rank kill;

As though there dominated this sea's threshold and this night
Not the raised hooves, the thick snake neck, the profile, and the
    might,
The wrought, eternal bronze, the dead protagonist, the fight,

But that unmoving, pale but living shape that drops no tears,
Ridiculous and haunting, which each epoch reappears,
And is what history is not. O love, O human fears![132]

The poem risks investing everything in its last three lines. Though
perilously close to sententiousness and sentimentality, it is largely
vindicated by a sense of moral authority: Fuller is surely right to
commemorate the image of everyman rather than that of the
nameless hero. The biographical context, too, helps to explain and
to authenticate that yearning for the human in the notably
eloquent final stanza. 'The Statue' is an impeccably worthy piece,
built round a neat juxtaposition of images and decently written.
But as a candidate for 'the best poem I wrote during the war' it is
an unlikely choice.

It is not, however, an inexplicable one. Despite the good friendships, the amusing interludes and the comparatively easy life, Fuller
had detested the preceding two and a half years, and that detestation had, for him, tainted many of the poems written then. Nor
was it just the separation from his wife and son, the unattractive
aspects of troopship humanity, the shortages and occasional
discomforts (which he seems to have not much minded): he
disliked the life precisely *because* it was easy. He hated being
'excluded from real work':

> Moreover, I was unused to lavish manpower supply, the Great
> Pyramid Syndrome it might be named, despite my bridge-
> playing articled clerk days, and a season of office-cricket as an
> assistant solicitor. The leisurely pace of proletarian work, when
> continuously available, was also something impossible to
> become accustomed to. I am apt to say, with truth, that I am
> never bored... But I was bored during the war.[133]

Perhaps he would have found it galling to admit that some of his finest war-time poems were products of that boredom, though the proposition doesn't seem a particularly startling one. The most successful pieces from his time in Kenya – 'In Africa', 'The Green Hills of Africa', 'The Giraffes', 'The Plains', 'Sadness, Glass, Theory', for instance – possess the controlled fluency, emotional restraint and, at best, the ironic poise which would come to characterise his more mature writing. Their recurrent weakness – a hint of dutifulness, of poetry written partly out of a feeling that while he was there he *ought* to be writing a poem or two – is readily understandable in the work of a young writer who finds himself far from home, in unfamiliar places under extraordinary circumstances. Alternatively, a decent case could be made for the view that Fuller's most impressive war-time poems belong to the period 1939-41, when he was in London, before his call-up.

But a third possibility exists, one partially obscured by Fuller's subsequent revision of his early work. At the end of the three weeks' leave in which he was reunited with Kate and John, he returned not to Lee itself, nor to Seafield Park, but to a further overflow establishment at Bedhampton: 'Submerged again! I had forgotten, or almost, this dreamlike world of huts and empty fields, cold air and warm stoves, and ridiculous duties.'[134] There, free from both the dangers (in his case fairly marginal ones) and the travelogue-inducing locations of foreign service, he was able to reflect more soberly on the four-year-old war and its human consequences. Despite such experiences as his encounter at Cape Town with a group of Commandos ('lumpen-proletarian barbarians' with 'great boots, and loud voices, and red, boily faces'),

> I suppose I never entirely lost the sense that the frightful transit camp at Liverpool, troopships themselves, mines, killing and maiming one's fellow men, were aberrations: that the war could be won or outlasted simply through endurance. Of course, my verse reflects the hopelessness and horrors of armed conflict: the nine sonnets I wrote in that December of 1943 at Bedhampton – a new camp of Nissen huts along a bleak road out of Portsmouth – are still evidence of that, perhaps too much so. When I reprinted the sonnets in my *Collected Poems* of 1962 I made some revisions that I see now are not at all beneficial...[135]

He went on to say that he found the sonnet sequence, 'Winter in England' 'difficult to judge'. He had always found it so: writing in

1944 to Julian Symons, he was 'particularly glad you like "Winter
in England" which I like myself now more than when I wrote it –
I had ma doots then.'[136] But the reader is likely to be struck by the
resurgence of what Fuller, in the second of the sonnets, calls 'a
huge, authentic feeling': concerns which had necessarily been held
in abeyance while he was in Africa – the essentially English context
of his central and unresolved socialist/élitist tension, for instance –
emerge in grainy, grimy details of almost cinematic *verité*; by
comparison, 'The Statue', appearing only two pages earlier in *A
Lost Season*, looks remote and flounderingly rhapsodic. The setting
of that second sonnet could hardly be more apt:

> The music and the shadows in the dark
> Cinema stir a huge, authentic feeling,
> And, when the lights come on, the shabby ceiling,
> The scarred green walls and seats confirm the stark
> Contrast between the crust and infinite deeps.
> I go to the canteen, ramshackle, warm,
> And move among the poor anonymous swarm;
> I am awake but everybody sleeps.
>
> Outside: the moonlit fields, the cruel blue –
> Which box another world; as that absurd,
> Frail and material life of Keats contained
> A second, utterly unlike, self-made,
> And contradicting all experience
> Except this rarest, fearfullest, most true.[137]

As usual with Fuller's earlier poetry, it's easy to seize on the technical awkwardnesses: rhymes which creakily announce their own
expedience (notably that plural 'deeps') and, in the sestet, half-
rhymes so tenuous that it's momentarily hard to see which is
which; the lumbering entry of Keats, later revised to 'Material life
of sonneteers contains', which helps the half-rhyme stagger to its
feet but is scarcely any other kind of improvement. Yet these
imperfections are outweighed by decisive gains: the appropriately
plain, understated description of the cinema; the melancholic
sense, here quite free from self-dramatisation, of a lonely man
within a crowd; and, best of all, the compact, perhaps even briefly
puzzling, image which opens the sestet. Instead of presenting us
with the conventional, and thus relatively comfortable, notion of a

spherical world surrounded by limitless space, Fuller imagines 'the moonlit fields' as the base and 'the cruel blue' as the lid of a rectangular box – something like a shoe-box, no doubt, with proportions similar to those of a cinema auditorium. Outside that first shabby box, there is merely another larger one.

An acute feeling of claustrophobia informs the entire sequence. It begins in an unlikeable pub:

> A three badge killick in the public bar
> Voluptuously lips his beer. The girl
> Behind the counter reads an early *Star*.
> Suddenly from the radio is a whirl
> Of classical emotion, and the drums
> Precisely mark despair, the violin
> Unending ferment. Some chrysanthemums
> Outside the window, yellow, pale, burn thin.[138]

Revising this later, Fuller altered the odd but effective 'lips' to Northern-demotic 'sups', which in war-time Hampshire would probably have sounded even odder; but, either way, the opening instantly creates a convincingly tawdry atmosphere. The background music, perceived in deliberately devalued emotional terms, only makes matters worse – an almost intolerably brutal irony for a writer whose love of music is so deep-rooted. The chrysanthemums, however, are not a great success, wrong-footing the metre, straining the rhyme-scheme, and producing that anomalous-sounding 'burn thin': presumably their pallid yellow reminds him of a feeble flame, but to describe so rotund a flower as in any sense 'thin' seems absurd (the phrase remained unaltered in both editions of the *Collected*, however, so Fuller must have thought better of it than I do). In the next line he calls them 'strange winter flowers'. Perhaps they are dead, though in that case they would be brown rather than yellow; like everything else in the poem they become subsumed

> Into the littoral which borders death.
> The ancient sailor holds an unplumbed glass;
> The girl is instantly a sculptured mass.

This transition from naturalism to symbolism is over-abrupt and the control of diction not quite secure – 'unplumbed glass' seems too literary, 'sculptured mass' too prosaic – but the poem has the unmistakable advantage of evolving meditatively from an appar-

ently unremarkable, local scene; and that, of course, is the characteristic method of Fuller's later poetry.

Images of claustrophobic containment and futility recur
throughout the sequence: the camp is a place 'Where uniforms and
rain make thick the night' (4) and where 'My working-party hacks
the grass, the tall / Tubers of summer rusty as the sickle' (9). In the
fifth sonnet, the image of men parading 'Day after day upon the
concrete square' (another rectangular world, like the box-within-
a-box of the cinema) leads into this generalisation:

> Now man must be political or die;
> Nor is there really that alternative.
> Correctly to be dedicated and to live
> By chance, is what the kind implores. The sky
> Is smutted with migrating birds or ships;
> The kiss of winter is with cracking lips.[139]

One can see why Fuller found the sequence 'difficult to judge': these
are lines whose virtues of directness and sincerity are almost insepa-
rable from their vices. 'Now man must be political or die' echoes
Auden's 'We must love one another or die', sharing its infamous
problem (there is, as the next line concedes, no 'or' about it: we must
do both) and adding another of its own (why now? why not always?).
The conclusion takes the splendidly vivid idea of the sky being
'smutted', and then proceeds to confuse it with 'ships': unless they
are airships, they must be on the horizon, which is only marginally
in the sky, rather than up there with the migrating birds. (In the
revised version, 'By chance, is what the kind implores' becomes 'By
chance, is what the species asks': an improvement, for once.)

The snag with politically committed writing – and this is as true
of Auden's political poems as it is of Fuller's – is that the passionate
urgency of utterance is so easily transformed into excruciating
banality. In the sixth sonnet, three men are chatting round a stove:

> 'The strikers should be shot,' one says: his hand
> A craftsman's, capable and rough. The second:
> 'Niggers and Jews I hate.' It is the squawking
> Of an obscene and guiltless bird. They sit,
> Free men, in prison. And the third: 'I hate
> Nobody' – raising, to gesticulate,
> His arm in navy with a gun upon it.[140]

We shall almost certainly share Fuller's helpless anger, his appalled recognition that these men, with whom he finds himself serving in defence of 'freedom', are doubly imprisoned – both by the physical limits of the camp, reiterated throughout the sequence, and more fundamentally by their reductive bigotries. But stridency is infectious: the 'obscene and guiltless bird' does nothing to assist the case and seems logically questionable, since the meaninglessness of a parrot's squawked language, which exempts it from guilt, must also temper its obscenity.

'Winter in England', then, is probably too seriously flawed to qualify as 'the best poem I wrote during the war'; but it is of enormous interest, establishing Fuller in his most characteristic future role as a compassionate yet critical observer of the society around him. For once, 'agenda-setting' seems exactly the appropriate phrase.

★

After Bedhampton, Fuller was packed off on a course to HMS *Ariel* – a vilely punning name for a radar training establishment – near Warrington. He noted wryly that since he had sat idly in a Nissen hut at HMS *Daedalus* two years earlier, waiting for the novel and top-secret radar equipment to arrive, an establishment entirely devoted to disseminating knowledge of the subject had been created. He was not at all impressed:

> Swarms of young PO instructors, by appearance all grammar school swots, had been bred to train the greater swarms of erks, from whose ranks most of the POs had emerged without setting a foot outside *Ariel*. Above the POs were numbers of 'schoolies', RN schoolmasters, who had got up the theory of radio and radar equipment as though it were some traditional intellectual discipline.[141]

Alan Percival, in *The Perfect Fool*, is more scathing still. In the novel Fuller ingeniously substitutes for the Admiralty's dreadful joke a worse one of his own:

> A race had sprung up of instructor petty officers – mainly men whose experience of the Navy had been restricted to passing through *Resistance*; clever, comfort-loving, ex-grammar-school boys whose destiny since call-up had been the radio and radar world and had never lived in the slums and dangers outside it.

There was a smug atmosphere at *Resistance* – even its name was twee, with the heroic play on the word for a common radio component.[142]

Both accounts strike a note of embittered shrillness, an almost hysterical detestation of these featherbedded instructors; for this, the experiences underlying 'Winter in England' perhaps provide some explanation. But Fuller's sense of discontent was more deep-rooted than that: it was 1944; he was fed up with the war, fed up with the random shunting-about of naval life; and the fact that HMS *Ariel* was sufficiently close to Blackpool for him to snatch the odd Saturday night with his wife and son at a dismal unlicensed hotel in suburban Warrington – linoleum on the dining-room floor and spam for high tea – only served to emphasise the unsatisfactory nature of this existence. 'The course is v. wearing,' he told Julian Symons, 'and so, I think, is THE STATE OF THE WORLD. What one needs is to be permanently pickled.'[143]

He was some way into the PO's course at *Ariel* before his promotion to Sub-Lieutenant arrived: this entailed travelling to Portsmouth and, naturaly, a good deal of formal dressing-up, which as usual he relished. After that, it was back to Warrington to start, from scratch, the even longer officers' course, which covered every radio and radar set used in the FAA. By April, he was 'in a fit of literary constipation, spiritual depression and so forth, & spend the nights drinking mild beer & playing bridge.'[144] A week later: 'The course is driving me dotty.'[145] And at the end of the month he reported:

I am well, too, but my nerves are in shreds consequent on this ere radio. I joined The Warrington Public Library last week as a partial antidote & have borrowed all sorts of fat, readable books. *The Heritage of Symbolism* for one thing, which I think extremely good, though not up your street I fear. But there are clear and stimulating accounts of Blok and Rilke and Valéry that you'd find valuable, I think. Certainly one realises, reading the book, how much influence one has got second hand which one should have got first hand – alas, we have been too efficient as company secretaries and solicitors to find the time for these foreign languages. Now I'm reading *To the Finland Station* which the Lt-Cdr thinks, no doubt, to be an improving work on the development of European railways, little knowing etc. etc.[146]

Still, promotion had brought some perks: a cabin of his own, though it did nothing for his insomnia; and, since he could now pass freely in and out of the place, a more elastic interpretation of his weekend leaves.

When the course ended in June, Fuller applied for a post at the Admiralty: this would at least enable him to pick up the threads of a London life into which he had hardly settled before the war. As soon as he learned that his application had been successful, his mood was transformed. 'I have been *translated*,' he told Symons, in a letter from Blackpool. 'On Friday afternoon I was taken off course & appointed to, believe it or not, the Admiralty. On Saty morning I came here on leave, dizzy with what certainly seems at the moment extreme good fortune.'[147] He would travel down to London on 6 July, he said, and would 'stay at some officers' club until I get settled in, as they say'. When he arrived at his shared room in the temporary officers' club in Piccadilly, he immediately noticed that his fellow-occupant, installed but absent, was someone of distinct literary taste, for among the books on his bedside locker were copies of *Penguin New Writing*. They retired for the night at different times, and did not actually speak until the following morning, although 'I actually divined in a matter of moments who he must be, so rigorous were the sieves of literary sophistication and the Andrew.'[148] He could not, however, have been expected to divine that his room-mate was to become a lifelong friend, editor of the magazine with which he would become most closely associated, and the first publisher of his memoirs: for the empty bed's missing tenant, already making his name as a poet, was the 22-year-old Alan Ross.

In 'Reading *The Bostonians* in Algeciras Bay', written twenty years later and dedicated to Ross, Fuller would affectionately recall 'that room of our chance meeting / Over the crumby Piccadilly / Of 1944'.[149] For his part, Ross, soon to take up an Admiralty post but at that time an Assistant Intelligence Officer based at Harwich – where his 'congenial home' was aboard 'HMS *Badger*, a pre-war floating brothel which used to anchor outside limits and doubled up as a Casino' – already knew 'nearly all Roy Fuller's poems by heart... reading admiringly on my bunk in *Badger* before whisky took its toll or the padre hauled me out for a nightcap.'[150]

Fuller's longer-term temporary accommodation was in the doubtful-sounding Paddington Grande Hotel (he would shortly borrow that superfluous 'e' for the equally inappropriately-named Hotel Splendide in *Savage Gold*). Its grandeur, indeed, did not stretch to the provision of meals, so he would breakfast in the Coventry Street Corner House on his way to Rex House in Lower Regent Street, home of the Directorate of Naval Air Radio (DNAR) and of the Directorate of Air Equipment (DAE), to which he was initially appointed. This mildly surreal organisation closely resembled the War Office setting of Dennis Potter's *Lipstick on Your Collar*, for which it might indeed have provided the model:

> I was in a not-large room with four other officers, initially five, for I had a brief overlapping period with the officer I was to succeed. We sat at tables, three facing three, nearness to the window depending on seniority. Diagonally opposite me, by the window, only partly visible behind accumulated files, volumes of Admiralty Fleet Orders (AFOs) and other technical works, sat Cornish-Bowden, a Commander in the Supply Branch. Above a dark-eyed, sallow face, his thin black hair was brillianted close to his head. I would sometimes out of earshot refer to him as Cornish-Pasty, the puerile vulgarism not unapt having regard to his complexion.[151]

They each had a number, and the Lieutenant whose desk and title he would shortly inherit was called E5, 'a cheerful, extravert young man, with pilot's wings' who 'had crashed an aircraft, I think in the course of some ferrying job; perhaps he had displayed other less sensational disadvantages for the pilot's profession, and been sent to DAE to be "lost".'[152] He was certainly lost in terms of competence or even of the most elementary common-sense. One of the first matters E5 and his successor had jointly to deal with – 'reminiscent of those tricky ones about water running into cisterns with outlets, encountered at school' – was the provision of flying helmets for the Fleet Air Arm. E5 displayed the reckless confidence which had earned him his wings or perhaps lost him his plane. '"Let's put 30,000," he said, as I momentarily sat next to him, the better to observe his craft.'[153]

Naturally, this affronted both Fuller's thrifty disposition and his solicitorial accuracy. Once the deficient E5 was out of the way, he set about remedying the affair and soon discovered that a similar vagueness afflicted the closely-related provision of the FAA's earphones and microphones; furthermore, the 'massive loose-leaf catalogue of Fleet Air Arm stores (borrowed from the barricade round Cornish-Bowden)'[154] disclosed numerous types of the things, without giving any indication of their compatibility or obsolescence. He found that the FAA had a professional statistician – Mr R.E. Beard of Prudential Assurance, a man of reassuring ability – whom he was able to consult on such arcane matters as the rate of wastage of flying helmets. In the end it became obvious that the stores book 'required drastic emendation', and when Fuller drafted the relevant AFO 'even Cornish-Pasty found little wrong with it'. As he sardonically and not untruthfully noted, 'it was my greatest contribution to what was commonly called "the war effort".'[155]

Early in 1945, he was transferred from DAE to DNAR – geographically simply to a different floor in Rex House, a larger office with a better view – where he became Technical Assistant to Basil Willett, the Director of Naval Air Radio. Willett was fifty-ish, weatherbeaten, extremely able and unselfconsciously charming: altogether a more impressive sort of boss than Cornish-Pasty. In practice, Fuller's main role was to sift through the enormous amount of paper which arrived in the Director's office – 'dockets for his attention, and appreciations, studies and periodicals of diverse kind, some from the United States, some Secret and Most Secret, most Confidential'[156] – sorting out the relatively few items which were worth Willett's attention: ironically, in the closing months of the war, he was at last employed on a task for which his legal training precisely fitted him. And already something of an end-of-term feeling was beginning to assert itself. Fuller had always assumed that he would return to his pre-war employment ('Did you see that the Woolwich Equitable is amalgamating with another big Society?' he had asked Symons, with undisguised excitement, while still at HMS *Ariel*: 'Total capital will be 86 millions. You see the Wallace Stevensish position that lies ahead for me!');[157] so he was unsurprised when Fred Shrimpton from the Woolwich, anxious to reassemble his peace-time team, took him to lunch at Scotts. At about the same time, Captain Willett was offered a managing directorship by Marconi's and enlisted Fuller's literary help to compose the letter which successfully secured his premature release from the Navy. Yet not everyone in DNAR was so keen to return to civilian life:

One day in Rex House, a skirl of bag-pipes was heard echoing along the carpetless corridors, and soon, at the open door of the office I was then in, Commander Crichton appeared, playing the Scottish instrument, a talent never before suspected. He was in normal naval uniform except that on his head was a bowler hat to which had been affixed a pair of wings, cut out of stiff white paper, presumably symbolic of transference to a different sphere. The Commander was in charge of appointments, had been in fact the man from the Admiralty who had visited *Ariel* at the end of the course. He had been 'bowler-hatted', unwillingly retired, no post at Marconi's or anywhere else, and the quite prolonged musical marching was his protest, as out of character as his mastery of wild laments: it brought his displeasure shockingly home, though unfortunately out of earshot of their Lordships.[158]

After months of dwindling employment at DNAR, Fuller was released from the Navy on 3 December 1945; with demobilization leave, his service just extended into 1946. Unlike Commander Crichton, he knew where he was going next.

★

Indeed, in a sense he had already gone there. Having no desire to prolong his period of residence at the Paddington Grande Hotel, in the summer of 1944 he set about finding a flat in Blackheath. It was a move which typically combined prudence with recklessness: on the one hand, since accommodation would be in short supply after the war, it made good practical sense to put down roots in advance; on the other, there was no certainty that the war *would* end soon, or that Fuller wouldn't find himself shipped off to the Far East, or even that the Woolwich would definitely offer him his old job (Fred Shrimpton's lunch invitation was still the best part of a year away). He chose the spacious ground-floor flat of a grey brick mid-nineteenth century house in St John's Park, a peaceful tree-lined road on the Woolwich side of the heath. It was evidently the right choice, for it would remain the Fullers' home for over a decade, and when they eventually moved it was a distance only of yards, to the house they had built for them in Langton Way, at the end of the St John's Park gardens. If there is something faintly comic about such monumental caution, there is also a clear-headed sense of purpose which many a less securely-based writer might envy:

...we've come to realize that we like it here. The antique and junk shop, the tea shops – even the excellent fish shop – of the Village are pleasures not yet exhausted. Though whenever I go into the country or the metropolis I am creatively stimulated, I am temperamentally in tune with suburbia, which I suppose is London's counterpart of provincial life. Possibly this is the indolent or reactionary way out of abrasive existence but finally one is the person one is.[159]

There were good reasons, too, for their extended tenancy at 16 St John's Park. The flat itself was agreeable and eccentric: a notable feature was an extraordinary conservatory, which the Fullers nick-named the Reptile House, in which the one solid wall comprised a floor-to-ceiling rockery with waterfall; from this an elegant iron staircase led to the huge overgrown garden. Furthermore, their old friends Julian and Kathleen Symons moved into the top flat after the war, adding to a loose though steadily evolving circle of Blackheath writers. An unwritten condition of the lease was the continued employment of a charlady, Mrs Lewisham, whose most memorable remark to Kate Fuller – 'Mrs Symons's Hoover's an Electrolux'[160] – deserves a place in English textbooks, as an unbeatably succinct illustration of the danger of misappropriating proper nouns.

Settling on a permanent home was not Fuller's only act of self-definition in the summer of 1944: for this was the time when his literary career – tentative before the war and, despite Kate's unflagging work as secretary and agent, necessarily inhibited during his time in Africa – began to take shape. He had delivered the type-script of *A Lost Season* to John Lehmann in December 1943, as soon as practicable after his return to England; he was, Lehmann remembered, 'happy indeed to be at home with Kate and his young son John but indefinably suggesting that some inspirational ghost of himself had been left behind'[161] – a judgement which finds some support in the unevenness of Fuller's next collection, *Epitaphs and Occasions*. To mark this occasion, Lehmann gave a party at his flat in Shepherd's Market: the other guests included Stephen Spender and Philip Toynbee; Kate and John had travelled down from Blackpool, 'the latter making a quiet hit'.[162] He liked Spender and got on well with him, in later life regretting that despite a long and amiable acquaintance they never really became close friends. About Toynbee he was much more wary:

My relationship with him was fairly typical of relations with a good few whose background and *modus vivendi* were on a higher social (and intellectual, come to that) level than my own, though shyness and my indolence about personal relations (and much else in life) enter the matter just as much. In one sense, the situation was not unlike the difficulties I found in getting on with the working class in political days of the early Thirties, and, in fact, in the Andrew... Between more or less high falutin small talk and the expletive-studded account of mere events, there is (or at any rate used to be) an area of communication occupied by the lower middle classes characterized by irony, decency and unpretentiousness, and that was what I was used to by birth and upbringing.[163]

This passage is less interesting for restating Fuller's feelings of social and intellectual inadequacy (the latter, at least, surely unwarranted in this company) than for making a more than compensatory positive claim: a mode of discourse 'characterized by irony, decency and unpretentiousness', perhaps less narrowly class-based than he for polemical reasons suggests here, but nevertheless clearly differentiated from the unserviceable dialects which he accurately identifies on either side of it, is the dominant mode of Fuller's writing, in poetry and prose, and arguably of nineteenth and twentieth century English literature as a whole.

It is certainly the mode of *A Lost Season*, which was published on 28 June 1944, a few days after Fuller's appointment to the Admiralty; the title, appropriately enough for poems written during his absence in East Africa, is from Donne's twelfth elegy, 'His Parting from Her':

> Time shall not lose our passages; the spring
> Shall tell how fresh our love was in beginning;
> The summer how it ripened in the ear;
> And autumn, what our golden harvests were.
> The winter I'll not think on to spite thee,
> But count it a lost season, so shall she.

The collection was generally well-received, though often reviewed in tandem with Laurie Lee's *The Sun My Monument*, published simultaneously by the Hogarth Press and preferred by some reviewers – including, rather surprisingly, C. Day Lewis, who found Lee 'the fresher voice of the two'. His decidedly lukewarm review is perceptive in its grudging way, for Day Lewis detects an essential mismatch between Fuller's literary disposition and his African material:

> *A Lost Season* is less successful than Mr Fuller's last book, *The Middle of a War*. East Africa is probably not the easiest place for writing poetry at the best of times: it is to Mr Fuller's credit that he has tried to make use of his experience there, but I do not feel the experience has been thoroughly assimilated. The African poems are an album of snapshots none of which, except 'The Giraffes', seems quite satisfactorily composed. They show an alert, individual response to the unfamiliar (compare MacNeice's 'journalistic' poems), but they do not get inside its skin. The versificaton is, for so promising a technician, rather jaded at times... However, Mr Fuller has already shown himself so proficient and interesting a poet that no one need be distressed by a temporary falling off...[164]

A Lost Season has retained a considerable, though one suspects somewhat ghostly, reputation: readers who can never have seen a copy, and who know the poems only vaguely from anthologies or from the two *Collecteds*, are still apt to utter a grotesquely simplified version of Lehmann's opinion, speaking wistfully of Fuller as a poet whose best work was set in war-time Africa (rather as if they wish he had could have stayed there, like some deluded soldier lost in remote terrain). But to entertain such a view is to offer him up as a sacrificial victim in the foredoomed attempt to identify 'war poets' of the Second World War corresponding to those of the First. Such creatures do not exist: it was a different sort of war and a different sort of poetry. Those differences were most acutely (if rather severely) described, in an Oxford lecture twenty-five years later, by Fuller himself:

> ...when one comes to the English poetry of the Second War one must admit that the personal response was inadequate, and not so much because no Owen was thrown up as because the event was generally understood, civilians and soldiers alike suffered and were without illusion; patriotism and human sacrifice needed no puncturing or illumination; and the longing for peace was present as the first air-raid siren sounded. The 'I' in

the poetry of the Second War is too often simply one suffering nostalgia for a happy personal life that was interrupted or made impossible of achievement by the war.[165]

That retrospective view is unfairly dismissive, of course, but it lends some support to the suggestion that Fuller's most successful war-time poems, those in which nostalgia is checked by a semblance or proximity of ordinary life, were written before his departure from England and after his return.

His African experiences informed another project on which he began work in 1945, writing in a Stationery Office notebook while Cornish-Bowden was either absent or safely incommunicado beyond his monstrous barricade of paperwork: the children's novel set in Kenya, at first called *The Veins of Gold*, and published in 1946, with a jacket and illustrations by Robert Medley, as *Savage Gold*. It bears an ironic relation to the traditional adventure story, as of course does William Golding's *Lord of the Flies*; however, while it is possible to read or to mis-read *Lord of the Flies* pleasurably but in ignorance of the tradition which it subverts, the flavour of Fuller's novel is likely to be entirely lost on children who would probably take *Treasure Island* to be a kind of computer game. In fact, its tone may have been dated even by the mid-1940s − the original jacket winsomely, or warningly, tells us that the author 'was brought up on Frank Richards, E. Phillips Oppenheim and H.G. Wells' − and its ironies too languidly Jamesian for ordinary schoolboys; it is dedicated, of course, to his own extraordinary son. Like his next novel, *With My Little Eye*, it admirably seeks to address a young audience with an adult voice, but there is obviously some truth in his self-deprecating admission that 'I felt my fictive powers were not up to the adult novel' and that 'even as I embarked on *Savage Gold* I envisaged gradually easing myself into fully-felt, and technically flexible, adult fiction.'[166] That, of course, is exactly what he did.

He had already contributed poems to *The Listener*, and in the autumn of 1944 began reviewing regularly for the paper. While at Rex House, he would lunch at least once a week with its Literary Editor, J.R. Ackerley, and William Plomer, then a temporary civil servant in the Admiralty's Naval Intelligence Division, at a vegetarian restaurant called Shearn's, a long-vanished predecessor of Cranks, in Tottenham Court Road: Plomer immortalised this establishment in his poem 'The Flying Bum: 1944', where a nearby flying bomb causes 'A lightly roasted rump of horse' to land among the discomfited vegetarian diners.[167] Fuller liked Joe Ackerley, though regretted that by this time, when Ackerley was forty-eight, 'he wore very ordinary spectacles, and tweed-jacket-grey-slacks sort of clothes, with a beret in inclement weather: these contributed to the lack of distinction that had crept over him.'[168]

Writing unsigned reviews for *The Listener* soon confirmed Fuller's worst fears about the literary aristocracy. His review, in November 1944, of Edith Sitwell's *Green Song and Other Poems* spoke of 'a life-time's work which can hardly be said to be other than minor verse of a limited kind';[169] the following month, reviewing an issue of John Lehmann's *New Writing and Daylight* and faithfully observing Ackerley's instruction to 'please give it its due, without fear or favour',[170] he wrote that Sitwell's contribution to a memorial sympo-sium on Demetrios Capetanakis, the Greek poet and critic who had died at the age of thirty-two, was 'quite remarkable for its overstate-ment, and rather predisposes one against the other essays'.[171] Capetanakis had been a close friend of Ackerley's as well as of Lehmann's, and this, as much as Fuller's author-publisher relationship with Lehmann, would have prompted the scrupulous insistence on objectivity: 'Personal relationships cannot enter into these matters,' Ackerley added.[172] Sitwell, however, perceived only the slight to herself: 'The dregs of the literary population have risen as one worm to insult me,' she told Lehmann,[173] while Ackerley's name was puni-tively deleted from the list of house-guests for the Sitwells' country mansion near Sheffield, Renishaw Hall, 'a huge and gloomy place set on a coalfield'.[174] He was stoical, perhaps not much minding this deprivation, but Lehmann – when Fuller revealed himself as the offending reviewer – was thoroughly miffed: for some months after-wards, fortunately in the fallow period between books, publisher and author were not on speaking terms. Edith Sitwell either never knew or quickly forgot who had written so slightingly of her, for when Fuller was later introduced to her at one of Lehmann's parties, she was civil enough; William Plomer, on the same occasion, observed that she looked 'exactly like Max Miller'.[175]

Living in London, on friendly terms with two of the period's most distinguished editors, it was almost inevitable that Fuller would encounter the great and the good: John and Myfanwy Piper – 'he with premature white hair and bright blue shirt, she with uncurled

hair and no make-up' – joining the Shearn's trio for lunch; or
E.M.Forster, in his 'brown-suited insignificance, inclining to the
shabby', lunching with them at their Akropolis or the White
Tower.[176] During 1945, he continued to write for *The Listener*, but
also contributed to *Tribune*, where he met T.R. Fyvel and his assistant, Bruce Bain (who eventually metamorphosed into his *alter ego*
Richard Findlater), and to a distinguished though more short-lived
left-wing literary magazine, *Our Time*, edited by a 'poetic hero of my
youth and ever after',[177] Edgell Rickword, and his assistant, Arnold
Rattenbury. In an article on 'Poetry and this War', Fuller identified
the 'most important factors determining the character of English
poetry during the late war' as 'the absence of a clear and consistent
political attitude towards the War from English intellectuals as a
whole' and 'the mass withdrawal of poets from active participation in
the War'.[178] With such an excellent network of cultural and political
connections, he was ideally placed to renounce the spanner and live
by the pen: if ever there was a moment to strike out for a freelance
literary career, this was surely it. Yet he chose the flat in Blackheath,
the safe job with the Woolwich. Why?

Because, in a word, it suited him. He had seen the patina of
failure clinging to Bohemian London when he was a law student at
Gibson and Weldon, and he had not changed his mind about that:
the literary pub life of Fitzrovia and Soho in the immediate post-
war years, with its company of boozy eccentrics so memorably
recalled by John Heath-Stubbs in his autobiography, *Hindsights*, was
not for him; with a few notable exceptions (such as Heath-Stubbs
himself), they were in any case not a conspicuously talented bunch.
At the same time, his peripatetic growing-up and pillar-to-post
shunting about by the Navy not unnaturally disposed him to a
domestically settled existence, and not only for his own sake: there
was Kate, of course, and the overriding need to provide for John a
more stable home and a more adequate education than his father
had enjoyed. And, despite his early reservations about a legal career,
he had become good at his job; before the end of the decade the
young poet and novelist's *oeuvre* would have been astonishingly
broadened to include *Questions and Answers in Building Society Law
and Practice* (1949). Beyond all this, and still less predictably, the
suburban-professional perspective would make a distinctive contribution to the continuing development of so ironically-tempered a
writer. But that development was to take some time yet.

2: Images of a Society

➤➤ ➤➤ • ◄◄ ◄◄

As a vulnerable and moving poem entitled 'During a Bombardment by V-Weapons' plainly shows, the Blackheath house-warming was a distinctly ambiguous affair:

> The little noises of the house:
> Drippings between the slates and ceiling;
> From the electric fire's cooling
> Tickings; the dry feet of a mouse:
>
> These at the ending of a war
> Have power to alarm me more
> Than the ridiculous detonations
> Outside the gently coughing curtains.
>
> And, love, I see your pallor bears
> A far more pointed threat than steel.
> Now all the permanent and real
> Furies are settling in upstairs.[1]

With devastating clarity and candour, Fuller here formulates an apparently paradoxical proposition which was to underlie so much of his later poetry and almost all his fiction: the true dangers and ultimate terrors of human experience do not occur in great public events like world wars – which, after all, copiously provide the reassuring security of roles, uniforms, common objectives and patriotic simplicities – but in the minutiae of domestic, suburban life. After quoting the first stanza in *Home and Dry*, Fuller comments: 'The poem goes on to claim that these alarm the poet more than the "ridiculous detonations" produced by the ingenious German rocket-scientists, and that his loved one's pallor poses a worse threat than bombs and bullets.'[2] But 'claim' suggests a degree of dishonesty or evasion, and the passage was dropped from *The Strange and the Good*: the poem seems more deeply unsettled, and unsettling, than its author liked to admit.

'During a Bombardment by V-Weapons' is one of a pair dated 1945 in *Epitaphs and Occasions* (no other poem in the book bears such information, and in *New and Collected Poems* these two are moved back into the second, war-time section); the other, 'Winter Night', in its final lines strikes the same note of neurotic alienation:

> Even the road conveys the sense
> Of being outside experience;
> As though, this winter night of war,
> The world we made were mine no more.[3]

The date is not only there for historical information: it also attempts, in a deliberately half-hearted way, to drive a wedge of distance between the 1945 Roy Fuller and the improved model of 1949 (when *Epitaphs and Occasions* appeared), altogether a more balanced sort of chap who writes historical-geographical pieces ('Knole'), allusive tributes to Dorothy Wordsworth and Emily Dickinson, pleasant light verse about the family cat. The attempt is half-hearted both because Fuller expects us to recognise the truth when we see it and because a similar point is made, with stronger if subtler force, much later in the collection, in one of his most-quoted and least-understood poems, 'Obituary of R. Fuller':

> If any bit of him survives
> It will be that verse which contrives
> To speak in private symbols for
> The peaceful caught in public war.[4]

It looks like little more than a restatement of the by now familiar theme of the individual in wartime, but that would be to underestimate the force of the private/public dichotomy, the clear implication that his primary concern is with 'private symbols' rather than with public statements. For such a writer, suburban peace brought no security.

The middle years of Fuller's literary career largely comprise a series of strategies designed to make creative sense of these tensions, and the first of these is *With My Little Eye* (1948): an ingenious novel which, though it purports to be a successor to *Savage Gold*, intended for a somewhat older but nevertheless non-adult audience, is an altogether different kind of project. Its manuscript title was *De'Ath: A Murder Story for Children and Parents*, and on first publication it was quaintly subtitled 'A Mystery Story for Teen Agers'; however, when it reappeared in 1988 as part of his *Crime Omnibus*, Fuller was 'especially pleased it has now found what I am sure is its rightful level.'[5] Much of the book is set in South London, in the 'decayed Victorian suburb'[6] of Heathstead, with excursions to the coastal resort of Westsea, which is conveniently reached by train from Charing Cross, and to the less readily-identifiable town of Checklock. The adolescent narrator, Frederick French, is the son of a County Court judge, a prosperous widower living in Chelsea: this provides him both with a legal framework and with a characteristically incomplete family background (Bracher, in *The Ruined Boys*, is likewise motherless). His age is uncertain: he teasingly refuses to disclose it at the very start of the novel, adopting a perkily precocious narrative tone which might rapidly have become insufferable but in practice proves surprisingly effective. This fruitful confusion is skilfully compounded by early references to Frederick's literary knowledge: though confidently able to note a court official's resemblance to Caliban,[7] he is daunted by his set holiday reading of Sir Walter Scott's *The Black Dwarf,*[8] and happy to console himself after a hectic day with 'a book by H.G. Wells, called *The First Men in the Moon*';[9] this helps Fuller to create a character who usefully combines disparate elements of sophistication and naïvety. Mildly irritated by his son's spasmodic precocity, the judge worries 'that the school I chose for you is somewhat too advanced. Perhaps you should have gone to Wellington.'[10] Witnessing – and correctly reckoning he can solve – a murder which takes place in a crowded courtroom, Frederick decides: 'Already I saw my future profession, not as hitherto, that of a novelist of genius, but as private detective.'[11] But it as the future 'novelist of genius' that he tells his story.

With My Little Eye romps delightfully through a sequence of incompatible genres which can only be excused by this indulgently unstable adolescent viewpoint. The episode at Westsea races, when the young detective in pursuit of a dubious solicitor (and, as it turns out, banknote-forger) loses all his money on a horse called Murder Most Foul, seems conspicuously indebted to *Brighton Rock.* Thereafter the novel returns more confidently to its South London terrain, before being even more fancifully sidetracked by Rhoda Savage's preposterous mock-Gothic story of the grotesque Dr De'ath, whom she is supposed to marry, and his secretary Mr Brilliant, with whom she is helplessly in love: this is the stuff of fairy-tale or pantomime, but Frederick, abruptly lurching back from sophisticated sleuth to naïve child, swallows it and sets off in pursuit of the villain. In doing so, he manages to get kidnapped by

Oscar Brilliant, the hunchback poet otherwise known (in ironic homage to Scott) as 'Elshie' and last seen scuttling away from the scene of the murder, who is holed up in a Hitchcockian house called Grangemere, 'detached and set among trees'[12] outside Checklock: Fuller's youthful addiction to the cinema (an enthusiasm shared with Greene and partly responsible for the similarities in their novels) is much in evidence here. In his Introduction to the *Crime Omnibus*, Fuller mentions the specific influence of Hitchcock, 'whose films of the 1930s often contained that potent ingredient – the sinister in banal surroundings.' He added, with characteristically acute wryness: '*With My Little Eye* in particular owes much to what might be called the nun in high heels or gun in the chapel collecting-box syndrome.'[13]

Yet, in the midst of this scene, the tone shifts again – this time into unexpectedly acidic literary parody: for Oscar Brilliant is a new-apocalyptic sort of poet, closely associated with a magazine called *The New Revelation* and anxious to praise the work of his friend Gryfydd Jones ('O consultations of fishes in the ocean's blue / Tabernacles and my heart still swimming over / The lucent fathoms of my youth...').[14] And when Frederick in an epilogue recounts his exploits over crumpets and chocolate cake to his foolishly agog housemaster, the narrative style returns comfortingly to that of the boys' adventure story, but the literary joke receives an oblique reprise: 'Toller [the detective in charge of the inquiry] thinks the defence will be able to show that Elshie is insane – he is simple as well as depraved.'[15]

Where With My Little Eye transcends all its variations of genre and parody is in the ironic poise of its descriptive detail. Frederick's age, unspecified but adolescent, turns out to be a distinct advantage: an adult's description of a room as 'panelled in what appeared to be treacle pudding'[16] might seem impossibly winsome, yet here it illuminates both place and character. His public school priggishness is undercut and largely redeemed by vulnerable self-knowledge:

> When I got into the street, Toller's car had gone. The disgusting children played and screamed. The smell from the gasworks was abominable. A man leaning against the wall of the public-house spat richly. I felt very disheartened.[17]

Having tracked down and 'rather implausibly quizzed the Dickensian, Inspector Bucket-like Toller about the investigation

(the readiness of almost everyone to disclose confidential information to a schoolboy, even if he happens to a judge's son, is a flaw in
the book), Frederick lunches at 'the Cottage Restaurant, where,
among chintz curtains and brass pots, I had toad-in-the-hole and
fruit salad served by quavering genteel ladies in smocks matching the
curtains.'[18] That evening, assembling a 'List of Suspects', he leans out
of his bedroom window to watch his father's dinner-guest depart:

> The air was so still that the aroma of their cigars floated up to
> me. The Admiral's foreshortened figure, shaped like a dinghy,
> rowed itself off, and my father looked up and saw me.
> 'What are you doing?' he called.
> 'Making a list of suspects. Shall I add you?'
> My father tore his imaginary hair. 'Go to bed. Go to bed.'[19]

It is moments like these – and they mostly occur in the first half of
the book, before the plot runs away with itself, although there is a
marvellous subway-under-the-Thames chase near the end – that
Fuller seems most at ease with his fiction, because this is where his
fiction is closest to home.

For the grown-up writer and his adolescent narrator do have a
good deal in common: Frederick's wry observation of middle-class
life's quirkier aspects – treacle-pudding panelling, curtain-smocked
ladies, dinghy-shaped admirals – is precisely the poet's, liberated from
the sterner constraints of serious adult verse; the inquisitive legal
mind, with its propensity to poke about in the grubbier corners of
human existence and to discover grotesque fantasy beneath suburban
reality, is his creator's too. Aldous Huxley, he told Alan Ross, 'has
always been behind my prose fiction, particularly his eye for nose-
picking and the like',[20] and he returned to the same image in *Vamp
Till Ready*: 'The minutiae of life, often of what I have called the
nose-picking variety, and later crime, absorbed me.'[21] Beyond that
lies the possibly disturbing implication that this legal-literary cast of
mind shared by character and author is in some respects by definition
immature, adolescent – or, in the Freudian jargon often adopted by
Fuller himself, anal-erotic.[22] Yet this may seem unhelpfully reductive:
another way of viewing *With My Little Eye* is as conclusive evidence
that Fuller's temperament, however one cares to describe it,
equipped him equally well for both main strands of his career.

★

Epitaphs and Occasions wears the somewhat dispiriting air of a book which cannot have been easy to fill, a half-emptiness characteristic of poets' second collections, in which the need to confirm a reputation is so often unmatched by creative urgency; and this becomes less surprising when we recall that, excluding two books written in the exceptional circumstances of war, it was indeed his second collection. It is not just that there are too many thin and repetitive pieces of unfocused introspection, though that is certainly part of the trouble; some of the poems are simply astonishingly bad, and it is hard to feel sure that they are conscious parodies, like the work of Gryfydd Jones in *With My Little Eye*. In 'Schwere Gustav', for instance, we seem to revisiting, intentionally or not, Wordsworth's infamous pond:

> Schwere Gustav, built by Krupps,
> Was the largest of all guns;
> Of thirty-one-inch calibre,
> It fired a shell of seven tons.[23]

The bathetic note is recurrent. 'Winter Night', already quoted for its memorable ending, begins far less promisingly: 'An owl is hooting in the grove, / The moonlight makes the night air mauve...'.[24] In 'Song', wit and sprightly rhyming soon give way to excruciating mock-demotic:

> The psychopathic leader,
> The laisser-faire of God
> The parent who's a bleeder,
> The sergeant who's a sod...[25]

In 'Epitaphs for Soldiers', Fuller writes: 'Incredibly I lasted out a war, / Survived the unnatural, enormous danger';[26] and we may feel, a little unkindly, that given the cushy good-fortune of his war-time career his survival was really not incredible at all, the danger indisputable but rather less than 'enormous'.

Something has plainly gone wrong with the register of these poems, and it is essentially the failure of the pre-war Audenesque tone (as, for instance, in that 'psychopathic leader') to match up with the frustrating drabness of post-war experience. In the book's 'Dedicatory Poem' (to Jack Clark and Alan Ross), Fuller admits as much:

Even between the wars I might
With luck have written something bright.
But now, I feel, the thirties gone,
The dim light's out that could have shone.
My richest ambiguity
Is nightmares now, not poetry.[27]

Nightmares again: at the very point when his life appeared
outwardly to have settled into agreeable stability – pleasant home
with wife and son, secure job, growing literary reputation – Fuller
was having a terrible time. He was always a much more ambitious
man than he generally chose to admit, and would certainly have
felt constrained by the very stability he had so carefully achieved. It
is no accident that *With My Little Eye* should contain in quite
specific ways an upgraded version of his own life: the solicitor has
become a judge who lives in Chelsea, not Blackheath, while the
author's ten-year-old son is translated into a precocious adolescent
whose relationship with his impeccably genteel father is at once
idealised and ironic. Meanwhile, the twin burdens of insomnia and
nightmare, though in a sense put to good use by the nocturnal
reader and writer, were inevitably draining; and his health was not
good in other, more specific ways. He suffered, like his mother,
from thyroid problems, and also from peptic ulcers. His memoirs
make light of this, but Julian Symons recalls:

> ...when, not long after the War's end, Roy's health collapsed,
> Kate cooked special foods for him with unwearying patience.
> Without her constant help, emotional as well as practical, Roy
> would have found it an ever greater struggle to get through the
> worst times. He recovered, although never able to eat and drink
> with complete freedom as he had done when young, and all
> sorts of health problems manifested themselves over the years.[28]

In a curious way – curious, that is, for someone who looked like
a straightforwardly successful professional man – Fuller was experiencing a dilemma which more obviously afflicts the creative free-
lancer: by the time he had positioned himself so that he could do
what he wanted, what he wanted to do had altered beyond recognition or become impossible. He had long been preoccupied with
the idea of the double man, the divided self; and, in 'The Divided
Life Re-lived', he reflected both on the opposition between the

man of action and the man of letters and on his sense of disillusionment with the immediately post-war world. The first three stanzas, describing his view of the garden at dusk, call up images – blackbirds, sparrows, bats, 'the mower furred with grass like filings round a magnet's pole, / Teacups left for ants...' – of exactly the sort which would later prove so consolatory but which here suggest the limitations of the late bourgeois world, for the fourth stanza recalls, with apparently cheerful simplicity, the more democratic and more 'real' society of war:

Once and only once we were in touch with brutal, bloody life
When we got in or kept out of global strife;
And in desert or in dockyard met our coarser fellow men,
Wielding friendly gun or scrubber, not our pen.[29]

But such simplicity is deceptive, of course: for one thing, there is no point, except an empty rhetorical one, in a writer even pretending to prefer the 'friendly gun' to his pen; for another, Fuller had in reality loathed the 'brutal, bloody life' of dockyard and troopship. Yet there was a still greater deception:

How we innocently thought that we should be alone no more,
Linked in death or revolution as in war.
How completely we have slipped into the same old world of cod,
Our companions Henry James or cats or God.

Did 'we' ever innocently believe that? Not for long, surely, is the answer provided by Fuller's war-time journals, with their explicit evidence of social idealism rapidly disintegrating under the pressure of cramped humanity. And what on earth are we to make of his curious codly trinity? After all, he cared a good deal for Henry James and for cats, though rather less for God. Not yet forty, he was understandably unwilling to accept as sufficient the domestic pleasures which would sustain him in later years, though grudgingly prepared to acknowledge their existence (Henry James had already made his appearance as long ago as 'The Phoney War'[30] and 'Reading Henry James',[31] while 'The Family Cat' is in *Epitaphs and Occasions*).[32]

Reviews of *Epitaphs and Occasions*, though appreciative of the book's virtues, struggled to describe its interim quality. The *TLS*, noting that 'Mr Fuller's latest manner is perhaps over-reminiscent of the early Auden, possibly also of the colloquial Byron', concluded:

Epitaphs and Occasions, as its title hints, is not ambitiously creative writing at full stretch; but its best poems are minor verse at its most accomplished. There is no other contemporary poet who reduces so much thought, socially or politically crucial in the widest sense, to so small a space as Mr Fuller has done in this book. The form of the poems may make them seem, at first glance, rather slight, but their content is highly condensed, varied, often both moving and witty. Beneath Mr Fuller's rather fusty cloaks of minor, saddened distemper a major poet is waiting to be revealed. Of his importance there is no question.[33]

The *Manchester Guardian*'s reviewer, identifying exactly the same influences, judged the book altogether more sternly:

He is almost too careworn. As a Marxist, or near-Marxist, he is pardonably unhappy about the nature of Western society. This pessimism he expresses in a manner both classical and loose, slightly Byronic, slightly Audenesque, for

'Feeling and no style is vile.'

He has a wry humour and much intelligence. But one is disappointed that he has merely continued, without developing, his inspiration. Though he writes in our time, he belongs to the last decade.[34]

He had, of course, in the 'Dedicatory Poem', said much the same thing himself.

But what sort of post-war social revolution had Fuller expected or hoped for? His self-contradictory – or perhaps merely confused – ideological position at this time was obvious not just to himself but to his less sympathetic readers. G.S. Fraser, writing in 1949, hit the point with painful accuracy when he complained of 'Mr Roy Fuller, hammering away at his pet word, "*bourgeois*", at a time when most sane people are probably profoundly grateful for the liberal, the rational, the sensitive and the humane elements in the middle-class tradition.'[35] Those are so exactly the qualities exemplified by Fuller both in his professional and in his literary life that it is a little difficult to see how he imagined that a revolution of any sort would enhance them. Was he, as Fraser suggests elsewhere in his essay, simply clinging in a spirit of misplaced nostalgia to the obsolete ideological baggage of the 1930s?

The problem rattles around in an unsatisfactory way from that announcement of the 1923 General Election result, displayed by the recumbent Ettaboo, and his participation a decade later in Blackpool's 'Loose Group' to echoes stretching into the late 1960s: Sandy Meikle, when Chairman of the Woolwich (and himself no less paradoxically an autocratic Liberal), would reflect with puzzled admiration on the astonishing fact that one of his senior executive colleagues was not only a distinguished poet but also a lifelong socialist. Yet, after all, Fuller's socialism was of a kind once utterly familiar in English cultural life, perhaps especially associated with self-made Northern intellectuals; despite his amiable disagreements with Richard Hoggart, he would have entirely assented to the latter's insistence 'that ethical, moral, humanist socialism is an English tradition of long standing and I'm not willing to lose it... I'm a socialist who recognizes first and always that the world is muddy and qualified, and that we're all fallible.'[36]

Soon after the war, Fuller's mother, following a quarter-century of widowhood, rather surprisingly remarried 'a widower somewhat younger than herself, of modest status, and went to live in the cottage he rented in a village outside Huddersfield'.[37] It is hard to tell whether the tone there is one of actual disapproval or merely of habitual irony – certainly the emphasis on the modest status and the rented cottage reads oddly – but possibly it is neither of these: even when he came to write *Spanner and Pen*, he had plainly not shaken off a residual guilt about his emotional reticence towards his mother and, in particular, his inadequate response to her final illness. She died of cancer in 1949, aged sixty-one: still carless, Roy travelled up to Yorkshire by train and bus to visit her on her deathbed, and remembered going downstairs to eat a high-tea of steamed fish which her elder sister Edith, helping out, thought suitable for one who suffered from peptic ulcers. 'I have never thought of it till this moment,' he wrote, forty years later,

> but my mother's death marked the end of the Forties – strange decade, which began, as it were, in the Thirties; actualizing the long-dreaded war, and the conflict with fascism, and ending, so it proved, with a dud social revolution, and the start for me of a fairly steady and greatly more productive life of writing verse, and, indeed, prose.[38]

★

'For the novelist,' Fuller wrote in his contribution to the 'Living in London' series of essays, 'nothing can be better than provincial youth followed by metropolitan manhood.' If his own life had not quite ideally conformed to this scheme (he had left Oldham too early, disliked Blackpool too much, and anyway had come to London as much a solicitor as a writer), nevertheless:

> In fiction I think I've been most successful with the London that unfolds within walking distance of Charing Cross Station (the terminus which is nineteen minutes on the Southern Region line from Blackheath). For this milieu I've retained a provincial's fascinated affection, but of course it is mainly a matter of objects – shops, pubs, clubs, restaurants, theatres, galleries, offices.[39]

He was to put this 'fascinated affection' to good use in his next two works of fiction.

The Second Curtain, his first published novel for adults, was brought out in 1953 by Derek Verschoyle – a former literary editor of *The Spectator* who, following all too closely the example set by John Lehmann, renounced salaried editorship, founded his own eponymous firm, published a few books by Fuller (among others), and soon went out of business: he 'rather sadly ended his days as editor of *The Grower*'.[40] The book had actually been written at the request of Lehmann who, in August 1952, had agreed to publish *Counterparts*,

> but only if there is a saleable book in the offing. So I am uneasily typing out a few chapters of a lousy old thing I have abandoned twice – a sort of thriller that has got wound up in the highbrow entrails of its hero – to see if that will do.[41]

But by December Lehmann had decided to cease trading, and Fuller was left with 'two little orphan books'. 'I am thinking of going to Ian Parsons at Chatto,' he told Symons, 'but will he (or anyone else) want a *poetic* author for their list; even one who occasionally produces a 60,000 word novel?'[42] That was a more prescient question than he could have guessed, and one which would recur several times towards the end of his life. It was Alan Ross who 'luckily, in a way'[43] introduced Fuller to Derek Verschoyle.

Of course, besides the boys' adventure story *Savage Gold* and the far more ambiguously-placed *With My Little Eye*, Fuller had already written a good deal of adult fiction, which included the unpublished novel *Next Day* and the unfinished draft of *The Agents* as well as a few published and at least a dozen unpublished stories; while through the central part of his literary career, up to 1970, poetry and fiction would run so much in parallel that the general perception of him as a 'poet' rather than less narrowly a 'writer' is really an instance of skewed literary perspective, a trick of the critical light. Sardonically aware of this imbalance, in 1960 he went so far as to assert that poetry took 'third place to writing novels and being a solicitor';[44] the overlap between those two favoured activities was sometimes greater than he cared to admit.

So while *The Second Curtain* has a particular strategic importance, it is certainly not the work of a novice. The book concerns a writer and editor, George Garner, who unwittingly becomes embroiled in a tangle of industrial espionage, sexual duplicity and pursuit-induced paranoia: the influences of Greene (who, coincidentally or not, shares the protagonist's initials) and Hitchcock are again much in evidence, above all in the scene where Garner, escaping from a somewhat improbable pursuer, finds himself helplessly trapped among the crowd at a football match. The events are seen entirely from Garner's point of view, although the book is narrated in the third person: 'I should think I was never in doubt that George Garner in *The Second Curtain* was so unlike the author as to make it simpler to depict him in the third person,' said Fuller.[45] And certainly in one respect we will be obliged to agree. Garner has an unkempt, 'artistic' beard, which more conventional characters find off-putting and on which he too frequently ruminates; as well he might, for it is essentially a false beard, and the man beneath it is remarkably like Roy Fuller.

Or rather, to continue in a mode which seems appropriate to this particular fiction, he is remarkably like that *other* Roy Fuller – the one who did not in 1945 rent the flat in Blackheath and resume his job with the Woolwich but accepted the beckoning invitation of a full-time literary career. Their backgrounds are similar, their temperaments identical. Fuller, Garner: as with Bracher in *The Ruined Boys*, the consonance of names signals a consonance of personality. It was a trick to be recycled in the memoirs, where Graham Miller becomes Gilbert Waller, while Fuller's odd pleasure in that -er rhyme stretched back to his schooldays: 'The chiming of his [Miller's] surname with my own struck me, at the age of eleven, as of significance in some mystico-coincidental way.'[46] And though the book's title embodies a specific, ingenious allusiveness (also reaching back to school, to Mr Tregenza's admiration of Busoni), it cannot fail to strike once again that obsessional note of the double, divided self: this is one of several ways in which *The Second Curtain* explores its author's alternative lives.

We first meet Garner while he is lunching with Fox, a purely functional invention who, like a cipher in Dickens, has only to resemble his name: a businessman called 'P' has quixotically proposed to fund a literary magazine, and Fox's purpose is to be the intermediary who offers the editorship to Garner. It is the latter we are meant to observe: a man who is not 'on easy terms with anyone, except those slight acquaintances like his tobacconist who had never tried to penetrate the formidable exterior and found the bog of shyness inside'[47] and who, after the meal, is left standing on the pavement, 'wondering why he had felt a fool in his hat because Fox was not wearing one, and knowing that he would have felt an equal fool if the roles had been reversed'.[48] Beneath the beard – or the hat – the shyness and the lack of self-confidence already seem remarkably familiar.

Garner inhabits a dingy first-floor flat in Bayswater, where his only regular visitors are the blind girl from downstairs who cleans the place (a neat Hitchcockian touch) and her cat; it is socially some way below Fuller's Blackheath and altogether in a different world from Judge French's Chelsea, but its quirkily compact self-sufficiency is affectionately, perhaps almost enviously portrayed. Garner and his wife have parted some years previously – she is barely mentioned, and it is not easy to imagine him married – so much of his leisure time is devoted to correspondence, carefully stored in box files, with old friends: an apt form of intimacy for someone both highly literate and deeply shy (the book's working title was *The Lonely Man*). The most voluminous correspondence is that with the oldest of his friends, William Widgery:

> They had been to the same private school – a ramshackle school for boys of uninterested parents. They had not been precisely friends – Widgery was the younger by a a couple of years – but in their penultimate year they had been thrown together as, in the school's decline, some of Garner's contemporaries had left in a body.[49]

Only the coastline has been changed, so slightly that it might

almost pass for a misprint, from Lancashire to Lincolnshire, while
the schoolboy relationship parallels that between Fuller and Leslie
Toft. In another way, however, Widgery more resembles Eric
Ashton, for he has succeeded to his father's manufacturing business
(electrical components rather than the more fanciful confectioner's
egg) in the bleak Lancashire town of Askington. This apparently
prosaic adult existence is among his assets as a correspondent: he is
a sounding-board unlikely to utter anything more threatening than
a muffled echo.

Next morning, having 'slept – he calculated – five hours', for
insomnia is yet another trait shared with his creator, Garner awakes
to a full dose of Fulleresque angst, as he attempts to switch on his
bedside lamp:

> There was no answering light. He joggled the switch several times
> without result. He heaved himself out of bed, groped to the
> curtains, and drew them back to reveal a newspaper-coloured day.
> He went to the memorandum pad on the mantelpiece and wrote
> on it 'Fri. Buy 60-watt bulb.' Then he looked at his face in the
> mirror and took the crumbs of sleep out of his eyes.[50]

In this unpromising mood he contemplates his post: two cuttings –
one of his article on Wilkie Collins, the other a dismissive sentence
about his own work from a weekly magazine – and a letter from
Viola Widgery informing him that her brother has vanished, and
adding, in an irresistibly ironic postscript: 'Of course, there is much
that cannot be said in a letter.'[51] His duty is plainly to go at once to
Askington, but it is true to his character that he should postpone it
and spend an irresolute morning in the West End, lingering over
records of Bartok in Harridge's before being drawn to Zwemmer's
window by the colourful art books: his personal emotional feelings, he reflects, have 'shrivelled away with disuse' to be replaced
by 'an elaborate system of ersatz and lonely enjoyment – the music
of the gramophone, evenings of intense reading, the breakfast tins
of pilchards and sardines'.[52]

To supplement his meagre income from royalties and reviewing,
Garner works as a reader for publishers called Cuffs, whose offices
are in Long Acre; this is where he goes after a most unFullerish pub
lunch of mild beer and sausage rolls, clearly designed to match the
beard and hairy jacket and to distance him from his author. His
afternoon perusal of dreadful manuscripts is interrupted by Alastair

Cuff and an unwelcome dinner invitation: it is a nice touch which transforms Garner's automatic gesture of avoidance – he pleads the urgent excuse of an old friend's family trouble 'up north' – into his involvement with circumstances far more disturbing than dinner with the boss. He has already reflected that his domestic and professional environment, though perhaps suitable for a poet, is no good for a novelist, who ought to live in 'Lewisham – or Askington',[53] and on the northbound train next morning this ironic spiral receives a further twist. Unable to imagine satisfactorily the scene which will greet his arrival, he

> comforted himself with the thought that whatever happens to oneself, however extraordinary or painful, becomes eventually commonplace and bearable. The empire of self constantly added to itself new wild tracts of territory which it was able to drain, plough, populate, and thus become once again an ordered, homogeneous entity.[54]

It's an idea which has relevance for Fuller's work as a whole, where it applies equally in reverse, so that the 'commonplace and bearable' becomes 'extraordinary and painful'; and, coincidentally, it resembles a point often made by Graham Greene – for instance, when he writes in his autobiography of 'a desire to reduce a chaos of experience to some sort of order, and a hungry curiosity'.[55]

Askington – and the nearby village of Bell, where Widgery and his sister live at Brick House, the name borrowed from A.J.A. Symons' home at Finchingfield, Essex – proves to possess an almost parodic degree of Northernness, all high teas and amateur dramatics. Garner observes this with a certain wry metropolitan superiority, but Fuller's childhood knowledge of the region provides him with a sure-footed feeling for appropriately dated detail which is incorporated into the brother-and-sister household's essentially unchanged domestic arrangements inherited from their parents. That in turn authenticates Viola Widgery's hesitant unfolding of the relationship between her vanished brother and a young man from London called Philip Rogers whom he had recently employed at the mill: Rogers, we learn over the course of two pages, was 'quite cultured', had 'lemon-coloured' hair, 'ran a car' and was 'well dressed – in an artistic sort of way'. Eventually the penny drops. Garner 'felt as though he had been given the key to a code which ran through the long series of Widgery's letters to him – an easy code which he had been a simpleton not to have guessed from the start.'[56] For all his apparent sophistication, he has been shown to be absurdly naïve.

In the evening, he is taken to an amateur performance of *The Years Between*, in order to meet Mr Kershaw, the secretary at the mill, who is performing in it, and also to allow Garner to toy with 'the idea of an essay on popular "serious" art – *The Years Between* and the Warsaw Concerto – how it emerged from popular art *simpliciter* and shaded into the plays of Terence Rattigan and the music of Rachmaninov',[57] not to mention the crime novel shading into the serious literary one. The whole device creaks, but stagyness is to be expected in a book called *The Second Curtain*. Kershaw, playing the minor part of Venning, steals the show – a performance he will repeat in the novel's approximation of 'real life' – and afterwards becomes comically indignant at the suggestion that Willie Widgery might be a 'nancy': his stereotypical small-town conservatism is doubtless borrowed, like his name, from Corny Kershaw, a bridge-playing acquaintance of Alderman Broadbent's – 'He always liked to say the name of a friend of his, Corny (short for Cornelius) Kershaw.'[58] Understandably wearied by the whole business, Garner eventually retires to bed to read *Our Mutual Friend*, which is not a randomly chosen title.

On his return to London he learns of Widgery's death by drowning and has to identify the body – an episode which recalls Fuller's own mortuary visit with Graham Miller twenty years earlier – before going off to lunch with the mysterious benefactor who is to finance *Light*. This is a densely allusive scene. The punningly-named Power House, which has passing resemblances to Equitable House in Woolwich, is an imposing office block on the Embankment, with 'a hall of marble veneering' – Fuller is not letting go of his Dickensian joke – 'and glossy mahogany';[59] the Chairman of Power Manufacturing Corporation Limited (in itself an interesting concept), Claude Perrott, turns out to be a sinister manipulative clown, a combination of the Pierrot suggested by his name and, more specifically, Mr Punch; while his secretary, Sarah Freeman, will prove to be one of two candidates for the title of 'our mutual friend'. There is even a discussion of Perrott's art collection which includes the percipient advice, irrelevant to the novel but in the context of the author's life intriguing, to 'Buy Vaughans'.[60] (Keith Vaughan, born in the same year as Fuller, was the contemporary painter he most admired; both contributed to *Penguin New Writing*; both were advisers as well as regular contributors to John Lehmann's and to Alan Ross's *London Magazine*. Curiously, however, Fuller is mentioned only once in Vaughan's published *Journals*, while Vaughan is entirely excluded from Fuller's memoirs; according to Alan Ross, 'I don't think Roy and Keith ever met except at other people's houses.')[61]

Next day – Wednesday – Kershaw turns up in London, at Cuff's: he says he is going to the police, by whom he thinks he is already being followed. Garner, glad to be rid of him, retreats to the Café Royal for an early evening drink and, perhaps, something to eat:

> He finished his drink and beckoned. 'Another Guinness?' asked the waiter, in his old man's, middle-European voice.
> 'Please,' said Garner. 'Is there anything worth eating tonight?'
> The waiter shrugged his shoulders. 'The ushual things. There iss some game pie – not baad.'
> 'Game pie,' said Garner, dubiously.
> 'Pigeon, you know. But not baad.'
> 'I'll think about it.'[62]

That vignette reminds us of Fuller's debt to the cinema and of his humour. Over his second Guinness, Garner thinks about the troublesome novel based on the early life of Alexander Pope on which he is working, and writes in his notebook: 'A novel is only able to grow through the nourishment provided by the life of the novelist while he is writing it.'[63] He looks up and finds himself being watched by Perrott's secretary. Fuller carefully puts it that way round: Garner merely bumping into her would be an unacceptable coincidence; she pursuing him is a legitimate artifice of plot. Nevertheless, the plot – here as in *With My Little Eye* – does seem to advance with a kind of frenetic implausibility in the centre of this novel.

Eschewing the game pie, the two of them eat at Vittoria's in Dean Street, where the beef escalope may (according to Garner) be horse but where the atmosphere is more authentically bohemian. Garner finds Sarah enchanting, for reasons which should ring alarm bells in our minds if not in his:

> She lived in Chelsea. She liked the ballet, the novels of Graham Greene, the poetry of Cecil Day Lewis. She used a perfume called Arpège by Lanvin. For her last summer holiday she had

been to Rapallo. It was all as he might have invented it for a novel, but the statue was breathing, warm, and not boring.[64]

He proposes a visit to (where else?) the cinema, but Sarah suddenly recalls her promised appearance at a party being given by some impeccably qualified friends – she paints, he works for the British Council, they live in Highgate – to which she invites him. It turns out to be a gathering of second-rate intellectuals, one of whom goes on about his ulcers, which he thinks are caused by the problematical world outside: 'No,' Garner tells him, 'wars are caused by conscious acts, ulcers come from the subconscious. There is a conflict inside you that you haven't told me about or that you're ignorant of. Almost certainly a sexual conflict.'[65] A little later he finds himself talking to a man with a crew-cut:

> 'Take drowning, for instance,' said Garner. 'A man slips on some canine nastiness, and falls into the river. Violent death?'
> 'Oh yes,' said crew-cut. 'Allee samee man steps off pavement and gets knocked down by a truck. So your man was drowned?'
> 'Yes, drowned,' said Garner.
> 'Perhaps you can speak as to street accidents as well?'
> 'No,' said Garner. 'Just drowning.'
> 'Now, our friend here,' said crew-cut, indicating the man with sidewhiskers, 'writes detective stories and simply ignores the fundamentals. What the English detective story lacks is realism – realism about death.'
> 'Realism about everything,' said Garner.
> 'No,' said crew-cut. 'Too much realism and it would cease to be the detective story.'[66]

If Garner were writing a detective novel – rather than a recalcitrant book about Pope which his own life fails to nourish – he might by now begin to wonder about the odd logic of the events surrounding him. But he doesn't, of course: not even when, through his hangover next morning, he reads in the paper that Kershaw has been killed by a lorry in Covent Garden, minutes after leaving Cuffs' office. He has already shown himself, over Widgery's homosexuality, to be hopelessly inept at decoding the significance of matters close to him. Summoned by a telegram (Brick House, Bell, seems not to possess a telephone), he inevitably make his way once more to Askington.

When he gets there, things have changed: he feels 'curiously at home, ready to pick up a book or to eat or to discuss some domestic triviality',[67] and this for Garner is a less familiar, and thus paradoxically more unsettling, feeling than his habitual estrangement. After a visit to the mill, during which he at last discovers that the firm makes radio components, he and Viola Widgery spend an uncharacteristically relaxed evening over a simple meal in a pub:

> He felt a ridiculous urge to talk about himself. 'I'm far from inwardly calm. It's just that I don't show, perhaps, the quaking bog beneath the featureless exterior.' Why shouldn't he talk about himself for a change? Normally he never had the chance. 'But I certainly judge everything in the light of common sense – which few people do, even those who think they have common sense. And why I can do that is because I am emotionally constipated. I feel things, but the feeling doesn't come out. Except when I'm writing.'[68]

The writer talking about himself here is so manifestly Fuller that Garner's reference to his infamous beard, a couple of pages later, as 'an image to block out any other'[69] is clearly meant as a rueful joke on a level quite outside fiction. Back at Brick House, he discovers a book on Tennyson, mysteriously borrowed from the London Library, and promises to return it in the vague hope that it might lead him to Philip Rogers.

When he calls at the London Library on Friday afternoon, however, convinced that now *he* is being followed, he is unable to extract the borrower's name from the lady at the desk and he has (before retreating to the lavatory) to make up a lame excuse about writing a murder story. This little episode had its origins in an incident involving Julian Symons, who now lived at Badlesmere Lees (near Faversham in Kent):

> Blythe on Poisons has led to a slight contretemps at the L.L. It was taken out in the name of R.*B.* Fuller (I was told y'day when I called) & therefore it was thought a *forger* (not a poisoner, as yet) was at work. When I told them Mr Symons often got books for me as I lived in a remote suburb (you must obviously keep BADLESMERE dark) & was aiming to do in his wife, all was explained. But the lady at the receiving counter said wd. Mr S. in future sign his *own* initials when having the books entered.[70]

Garner's explanation at the London Library has an additional
aptness since that evening he must give a talk on 'Godwin to
Greene: the Novel of Pursuit' at the Centre of Contemporary
Culture: though he is better prepared than Holly Martins for his
impromptu lecture in *The Third Man*, the allusion is clear enough.
There is even a distant, waffly chairman called Professor Pedley,
whom we might easily imagine played, like his screen counterpart,
by Wilfrid Hyde-White:

> 'Perhaps I'm old fashioned, but when I read Graham Greene I
> can't help saying to myself "Life simply isn't like this". Now I
> don't say that when I read Trollope, though you and I know
> how much Trollope leaves out.'
>
> Garner quickly adapted himself to the level and said: 'Yes, I
> see what you mean. The Greenish things just don't happen to
> one, do they? The terror in the public lavatory, the spiritual
> crisis on Clapham Common – it's too much.'
>
> 'Too much,' said Professor Pedley. 'We *are* civilized, you
> know: there *is* an order in human affairs...'[71]

It seems hardly too much to suggest that, by this point, irony is not
only the controlling tone but is becoming the actual subject of *The
Second Curtain*.

Garner returns home at last, to read Widgery's will (in which he
has been left £500), listen to a late Beethoven quartet, and contem-
plate the essay on Busoni which he is planning to write and perhaps
to publish in *Light*. We may assume that the work which especially
preoccupies him is *Arlecchino* (1914–16), described by its composer
as 'a dramatic capriccio'; though Fuller could not have seen the
opera which was, coincidentally, first staged in England at
Glyndebourne a year later, in 1954, he could have heard it in a BBC
broadcast in 1939 – for he and Kate had spent most of their 'meagre
pre-marriage savings' on a 'substantial radiogramophone'[72] – and
would have known of the performances at the Venice Festival in
1940 and, especially, at Carnegie Hall, New York, in 1951:

> When the curtain rose on the Busoni opera, he thought, it
> revealed another curtain. The second curtain rose on a puppet
> show. It was the grotesqueness and cruelty of puppets that
> Busoni saw as final reality: as well (Garner guessed) as their raw
> simplicity and symbolism which had fascinated him throughout

his life. And yet (or, rather, because of that) Busoni's masterpiece lacked genius: it was merely *about* genius.

Artists of the second class knew all the rules for being a genius, but missed the final absorption in, acceptance of, life: they preferred art. Busoni once said about Beethoven: one would often like to ask why you are in a bad temper. That was to see things too clearly, just as he saw too clearly to be able to compose the kind of music the times required. And then Busoni really despised the means of music – he wanted a piano with eight octaves or two manuals, and wrote a set of fugues for no particular instrument. Beethoven came to reject all means except the string quartet but he exploited that vehicle, respected it, and made even its elementary resources serve his advanced purposes.[73]

These insights with their barely-disguised authorial self-analysis seem almost too profound to be given to so determinedly second-rate a figure as Garner; characteristically, of course, he doesn't know what to do with them, but blunders on in his perilously innocent way. It is only next day – when, through a childish ruse he has traced the London Library book to a Peter Rackham and discovered at his Chelsea home none other than Sarah Freeman – that the penny even begins to drop: "'The trouble with you,'" she said savagely, "is that you've never lived.'" Like Busoni, he knows all about genius but is unable to surrender himself to life. Peter Rackham, of course, is the man with the crew-cut from the party, who knew all about street accidents, whose hair before it was cut would have been lemon-coloured, who is also Philip Rogers. Perrott's henchman, Sarah's lover, Widgery's seducer: he is truly our mutual friend.

The remaining pages of *The Second Curtain* complete a progress which seems inevitable to the reader if not to Garner. In a manner befitting a man who the previous evening lectured on 'The Novel of Pursuit', he is followed from Rackham's house by an ex-boxer called Forbes Trimmer and only escapes by becoming entangled with a football crowd, though it then proves almost impossible to get out of the stadium: the scene proclaims its Greene-Hitchcock ancestry with shameless delight, and is none the worse for that. In the evening he has been summoned to dine with his sinister bene-factor, Perrott: here the plot-motivation – industrial espionage arising from Widgery's invention of an everlasting lamp filament, an unacceptable notion in Power House – is rather cursorily disclosed, claiming no more attention than it deserves. It makes sense, but only just. Fuller's interest, and ours, since this has all along been a novel of ideas masquerading as a detective fiction, is elsewhere – in the effect of the encounter with an unscrupulous capitalist world upon its irritatingly naïve though not unsympathetic literary protagonist. He throws Perrott's cheque back at him, of course, refuses the bribe and resigns the editorship; and he is beaten up for his trouble on his way home. In the end he writes to Viola Widgery with a fudged, evasive story: at least he is free of emotional responsibility to her as well as released from his editorial chore and all its dubious ramifications. 'The alien machine into which he had accidentally dropped from his own harmless world had thrown him out again, broken, with scarcely any damage or interruption to its purposive wheels.'[75]

We leave Garner talking 'in a voice loaded with tenderness' to the cat from from downstairs. It is almost a moment of the most appalling sentimentality; but triumphantly, and precisely because Fuller has throughout the novel sustained a level of intellectual argument far beyond the demands of his rather mechanical plot, it is more complex than that. Garner is injured and alone, with only the blind girl and the cat left for company in his contracted world; yet he also has Beethoven and Busoni, Pope and Dickens, consolations denied to Perrott (who has to rely on his son at Cambridge for cultural information) and his wealthy but impoverished existence. There is, after all, more than one way of living. Given the choice between those two worlds, Garner is better off as he is.

★

The Second Curtain raises – and seems teasingly intended to raise – a number of important questions about its author; but before coming to them it will be worth glancing more briefly at Fuller's next novel, *Fantasy and Fugue*, published in the following year. In film-making, a useful and economical procedure is sometimes employed in which a pair of movies are made 'back to back': shot over the same period of time, sharing overheads, technical resources, and to some extent even sets and actors. That is very much the relationship between these two novels.

The principal difference is one of perspective: *The Second Curtain*, though narrated from George Garner's viewpoint, ranges

widely across English society and (appropriately, given the protagonist's surname) gathers to itself a varied harvest of social, cultural
and psychological preoccupations; *Fantasy and Fugue*, by contrast, is
a single-track first-person narrative of claustrophobic introspection,
during which we are as trapped inside Harry Sinton's head as he is
– Fuller called it 'a clotted psychological thing, alas'.[76] Yet there is a
catalogue of parallels. Both books explore the idea of doubleness:
Harry, who believes himself to be a murderer, has a brother called
Laurence, who is. Both are set in the London literary world of
around 1950: the brothers are directors of a small publishing house.
Both reinforce their themes by introducing, as fictions within
fiction, theatrical performances: in *Fantasy and Fugue*, it is with
monstrous irony a dramatisation of *The Possessed*. Both have plots
which turn, topically for their time, on the threatened public
disclosure of homosexual affairs. Both end with their central characters isolated from a hostile external reality with which they can
no longer cope. Both are versions of Garner's favourite theme, 'the
novel of pursuit'.

The form of *Fantasy and Fugue* might be described as a single arc
constructed between the pair of double images which opens and
closes the book. In the first of these, Harry Sinton, waking to a
morning consciousness even more pessimistic than George
Garner's, inspects himself in the mirror:

> I got out of bed, drew the curtains and opened the window.
> Light and the noise of traffic drenched the room. I looked in the
> wardrobe mirror as though at the portrait of a stranger whose
> deeply interesting reputation had preceded it. The light-blue
> eyes were set in a skin the colour of a cream rose: the rest of the
> face had a glassy pallor, the dark hair tousled, the jaw already
> becoming formidably bearded. I took off my pyjama jacket and
> found my body oddly unchanged. The invalid's face owned an
> athlete's biceps, marked pectorals, flat belly. This was indeed
> Harry Sinton who regarded me, however damaged, however
> deranged. I stood there in the indecisive mood which I recog-
> nized had become habitual.[77]

The man who here contemplates his double is thus divided within
himself; and he finds his physical image attractive in terms which
are strikingly narcissistic or indeed homoerotic. Furthermore, we
soon discover that he is not only mentally self-imprisoned; he has

entrusted the key to his flat to his housekeeper, Mrs Giddy, with instructions that he is not to be let out (Fuller's crime novels contain an intriguing sequence of solitary male characters – Judge French, George Garner, Harry Sinton and his brother Laurence – attended by female housekeepers of distinctly cinematic ancestry). This voluntary incarceration has been prompted by Harry's compulsive urge to murder; when he reads in the morning's *Times* that a literary acquaintance called Max Callis has died, he rapidly concludes that he has somehow escaped from the flat and killed him. Consequently, he engineers his actual escape from the flat to establish the facts concerning Callis's death and, if possible, an alibi. For most of the book, as he scampers between friends who might help him, Harry Sinton behaves like a man on the run, even though he is being pursued principally by his own fantasy: while Fuller the Freudian plainly intends us to pick up the psychoanalytical sense of that word (and refers us in his *Crime Omnibus* Introduction to *The Interpretation of Dreams*),[78] Fuller the music-lover equally firmly implies that the novel's construction should be viewed as a *fantasia* followed by a fugal finale.

And the finale, with its echoing and answering symmetries, is indeed a fugue (Barbara Gabriel, whose discussion of these novels contains several errors, invokes the wrong art-form when she writes of 'the homoerotic choreography of the ending').[79] One of its interlocking themes is first voiced by another cnveniently-placed housekeeper, Laurence Sinton's Miss Hind, who tells Harry that his brother, not he, was in possession of the murder weapon: '"You left your revolver here when you moved to Luxor Street," she said.'[80] Harry, of course, at first tries to invent some way in which he could have retrieved the gun and carried out the murder, but the idea steadily grows to its inevitable conclusion, a deliberately melodramatic roof-top scene during which he confronts his brother, finally realising that he is responsible for their father's death as well as for Max Callis's (and would cheerfully murder him too), and which ends with Laurence, not Harry, falling to his death. Alongside, or beneath, this fairly mechanical plot is the fugue's other theme, the one which had been ironically suggested at the novel's outset: for, entering what was once his own bedroom in the family home, Harry encounters 'a figure, not myself, who lowered the evening paper and said petulantly: "Who are you?"'[81] It is, of course, a good question, made the more poignant by that insistent 'not myself'. For Harry, it seems 'a logical extension of the night-mare, but that last twist that cannot be borne. "Who the hell are you?" I asked.'[82]

He is Adrian Rossiter, also on the run (but, ignominiously, from National Service), and 'Laurie's' lover: Harry seems to have been as innocent of his brother's sexuality as George Garner was of his oldest friend's. Yet the literary echo primarily suggested is not, as Barbara Gabriel suggests (and despite *fin-de-siècle* echoes such as the description of Laurence's magazine Pavilion as 'only *The Yellow Book* and bile'),[83] Wilde's *The Picture of Dorian Gray*, but the story which is perhaps the most concentrated exploration of the *doppel-gänger* theme in English fiction, Conrad's *The Secret Sharer*. Adrian, like the double concealed in the captain's cabin, will escape to freedom – though only after Fuller, ever the fictional ventriloquist, has given the novel's tone a wrench into pure 1950s campness on its penultimate page:

> Adrian Rossiter's fingers went to his bad teeth. 'Christ!' he said. And then: 'You've a nerve. I'm ringing up for no bloody police. What d'you take me for?'
>
> I brushed past him and started down the stairs. He followed me like a cowed domestic animal. 'Is he dead?' he asked. I felt him pluck at my jacket. 'Are *you* going to get the coppers here?' he said. 'What's going to happen to little me.'
>
> 'Oh flick off,' I said.
>
> 'You're a very rude man,' he said. 'I certainly won't bother to stay here now.'[84]

The note is a familiar and exactly contemporary one, reminiscent of early Angus Wilson: *Hemlock and After* had been published in 1952, the year before *The Second Curtain*, while *Anglo-Saxon Attitudes* would appear in 1956 – and one could easily imagine Adrian Rossiter ending up at Frank Rammage's house in Earl's Court, along with the likes of Vin Salad.

The point is interesting because the homosexual as outsider, a subject of intense topicality in England in the early 1950s, forms a recurrent sub-text in *The Second Curtain* and *Fantasy and Fugue*. When Fuller had chosen his settled domestic existence – the family, the flat in Blackheath, the job with the Woolwich – he had distanced himself from a literary world in which many of his friends happened to be homosexual: John Lehmann, Joe Ackerley,

William Plomer, Keith Vaughan. Although it seems inescapable that Fuller's preoccupation with the *doppelgänger* and its internalised counterpart, the divided self, was among other things a matter of sexuality – of which, if George Garner is to be believed, his ulcers were a symptom: 'There is a conflict inside you... Almost certainly a sexual conflict'[85] – it is equally clear that he used sexuality as a potent image for other kinds of psychlogical pressure. At this stage the homosexual men in the novels are lightly sketched, yet they may nevertheless be given traits possessed by their author, such as the adolescent Laurence's habit of keeping 'methodical and meticulous little books of receipts and expenditure',[86] as if perfecting solicitorial orderliness. More startling – both because it echoes Garner's remarks about sexual conflict and because it has the unmistakable air of an author thinking through his character – is Harry Sinton's meditation while seated in a barber's chair:

> 'The hallmark of the psychopath is homosexuality' – the phrase, recalled suddenly from some book I had read, took on a fresh and personal meaning... I remembered at school, in my sixteenth year, a master called Kevill who taught my set English Literature – an enlightened man who had shown me that poetry meant not 'A thing of beauty is a joy for ever' but 'In my veins there is a wish, And a memory of fish'. I comprehended clearly how I had always thwarted Kevill's personal approaches to me, keeping our relationship on the basis of others' follies, not my own. Kevill must have been homosexual, and now, as I saw the lather brush poised over me again, I regretted with all my heart that I had not surrendered to his affection and protection, had missed the initiation into true feeling that he might have given me, just as he had initiated me into proper intellectual pleasure. It did not disgust me that that surrender might have involved acts in which I had never participated and which were contrary to my whole orientation.[87]

This of course glances back to Fuller's friendship with 'Bobby', yet his sympathetic interest in homosexual characters, as evidenced by the fiction, actually deepened with passing time: Robert Calwell and his boyfriend Billy are arguably the most stable and balanced couple in *The Carnal Island*, while *Stares*, his final novel, is actually narrated by a gay actor.

A related motif in both *The Second Curtain* and *Fantasy and Fugue*

is the unsettling eruption into the present of incidents from the
protagonist's past; and although it might with some justice be said
that there is scarcely a fictional hero of whom this isn't to some
degree true, in Fuller's novels the familiar pattern has a special
poignancy. George Garner's is apparently the more straightforward
of these two cases: the past which returns is, after all, merely a
schoolboy friendship with no hint of later complications. Yet the
importance of such friendships to Fuller is indicated both by the
warm recollection of Leslie Toft in his memoirs and by the intensity of the Bracher/Slade relationship in *The Ruined Boys*: in both,
the keynote is a degree of cultural empathy which is less readily
found in adult life. Garner, on his second visit to Askington, is
moved to learn that 'William was immensely proud of your
letters'[88] and to be reminded of an occasion when, at the age of
thirteen, he joined the two Widgery children and their father for
lunch at the Seaborough Arms. Afterwards, to show off, he bought
cockles from a stall near the harbour, because it was out of bounds:
'He thought that all through life one acted asininely, trying to
impress one's character on the world'. And that evening, in the
school dormitory, he recalled accidentally touching Viola's hands as
'a lost opportunity and pleasure which he had felt would never
come again'.[89] These are crucial points: Garner is someone simultaneously aware of his own painful gaucheness and of his inability
to learn from experience, who typically sees his past in terms of
misunderstood occasions and missed opportunities; in this he
equally resembles the young Fuller fleeing from Aldous Huxley in
Straker's or upsetting books in Charlie Lahr's shop and the elderly
memoirist wryly reflecting on a lifetime's 'gormlessness'.

In Harry Sinton's case, it is the quite recent past which inter-
venes even more disturbingly than the school memory which he
has used to reinforce his sense of guilt. Sitting alone in a Corner
House with an impossible tray of food, a predicament utterly characteristic of Fuller's protagonists, Harry recalls the 'other trauma of
the past – as hurting and revolutionary as your father's death'[90]
which, according to his friend Rimmer, must be buried in his
consciousness. It concerns a man called Fraser whom Harry had
known in the Navy, at first disliking him during training but re-
encountering him more amicably in East Africa, at Port Reitz in
1942:

I found his mind sharp and intelligent about our situation, our companions, the service. We quickly created a private mythology of jokes against our superiors, the food, the climate, the aircraft we had to fly in, our slightly absurd present role in the war.

Our afternoons were usually free. Some of us would drive a truck out of the oppressive clearing in the palm trees which was the airfield, and along the coast to a gently curving bay. In peacetime this had evidently been a recognized bathing place: there was a large but ruined reed hut and, about fifty yards from the shore, a concrete pillar projecting from the water. At the side of the pillar an iron ladder enabled one to climb to the top and dive. The sand of the bay was nearly white, moving with innumerable crabs: the water almost too warm for swimming.[91]

The place and time are only slightly adapted from Fuller's own war experience, for the scene is derived from his spell at RNAS Tanga in 1943:

It was possible to get a lift in a regular truck to Tanga, or slightly beyond to a small bay of silver sand where a diving platform had been erected by some club in the bygone days of peace, an apparatus I brought into a crime novel called *Fantasy and Fugue* after the war. Sometimes I was there alone save for fiddler-crabs and the shoals of tiny coloured fish, the shallower water at the bay's edge almost too warm, bathing of a luxuriousness excelling even Durban's.[92]

The transposition of reminiscence into fiction seems perfectly straightforward; and, the initial dislike apart, we might even tentatively identify the presumably Scottish Fraser (also the surname of Fuller's 'Uncle Alf') with Willie Robertson. However, the subsequent disaster in which Fraser is trapped at the foot of the ladder and, despite Sinton's hopeless attempt to rescue him, drowns ('It all happened quickly and, like so many tragedies, had strong elements of the ludicrous and avoidable'),[93] appears to have no direct biographical parallel. But it does have a parallel which is all the more intriguing for being indirect: for there was of course an accidental death, though by shooting rather than drowning, which made a deep impression on Fuller during his time in Kenya – deep enough, at least, for him to have incorporated it in his story 'The People Round About', with somewhat awkward consequence.[94]

Although he did not personally know the man on whom he based 'Petty Officer Marshall', his subsequent encounter with the bereaved parents left a residue of guilt:

> They suspected negligence in the medical treatment of their son, even something unstraightforward about the accident itself: being put on to my piece had renewed their painful and frustrated quest for the truth. Of course, one knew of the force of love, but perhaps the episode betrays a congenital lack in oneself, some unadmirable trait of the unregenerate *litterateur*, imaginative in the wrong way.[95]

Despite the different circumstances, this experience clearly provided the psychological foundation for Harry Sinton's sense of guilty inadequacy:

> At the inquiry I was commended for the efforts I had made to save Fraser, and I had much public and private sympathy for what was called the ordeal I had been through. But the stupidity of his death haunted me for months, years; and all that time contained deep fissures of misery in which I imagined that it would have been easy for me to have dived again, to have moved more skilfully that trapped, pathetic leg, to have rescued a being more courageous and accomplished than myself.[96]

It's an extreme variation on Fuller's recurrent theme of the failure to make sense of events, though the self-deprecatory 'being more courageous and accomplished than myself' strikes on this occasion a slightly false note, as if tacitly inviting the reader's disagreement. Of course, the paradoxical truth is that the steady accumulation of such self-perceived failures leads to a distinctively rueful kind of wisdom; but that, for both character and author, must come later.

★

Recognising the significance of *The Second Curtain* and *Fantasy and Fugue* – that, besides being accomplished crime novels, they are also complex analyses of his deepest personal preoccupations – gives some coherent shape to what may otherwise seem a blurred episode in Fuller's literary career. Until the triumphant appearance of *Brutus's Orchard* in 1957, his post-war poetic output was notable more for its sustained negotiations with a tone of voice than for memorable individual poems; on the other hand, during the 1950s he published the two adult crime novels, as well as *Image of a Society* and *The Ruined Boys*. The relationship between poetic self and fictive self troubled and puzzled him, as he explained to Norman Lees:

> I've never really accepted myself as a novelist & I get very depressed as I'm writing the things, feeling that I don't now anything about people – what they think, how they behave. But I keep trying again. If a poem goes wrong you can scrap it with equanimity, but with 70 or 80 thousand words of prose – churned out laboriously in one's spare time – one can't help feeling an undying affection for [them], however inadequate they are.[97]

'I'm sure,' he later said, 'that by and large the two things [poems and novels] proceed from different layers of experience so far as content is concerned, and consciousness so far as the composition is concerned.' And he added, in a characteristic image, that 'the process is analogous to the inhibited state of one excretory sphincter when the other is relaxed.'[98] Though this is largely true in terms of his literary practice, the distinction serves equally to emphasise underlying similarities between his creative impulses. Apart from the recurrent, even obsessive thematic links, we might also note here the intriguing congruence of Auden and Greene as major formative influences on his poetry and fiction. For consider the following piece of evidently sub-Auden poetry – the tone and details also reminiscent of Fuller's pre-war suburban work, though the versification is too slack for him – cited by Bernard Bergonzi in *Reading the Thirties*:

> The advertisements trailed along the arterial road:
> Bungalows and a broken farm, short chalky grass
> Where a hoarding had been pulled down,
> A windmill offering tea and lemonade,
> The great ruined sails gaping.

This, as readers of Bergonzi's book will recall, is a trick, and an instructive one. The lines – not from a poem at all, but a versified extract from Graham Greene's *Brighton Rock* – 'reveal not just Greene's capacity to pick up a prevalent tone and mode of observation, but the extent to which his fictional prose was affected by Auden.' Bergonzi adds: 'For novelists to be influenced by other novelists is commonplace; but for a novelist to be influenced by a

poet is, on the face of it, rare.'[99] Not, however, if novelist and poet
are, as in Fuller's case, the same writer – and one, moreover, who
seems to have assimilated the composite Auden/Greene influence
in a way which uncannily confirms Bergonzi's hypothesis.

In the early 1950s, however, Fuller was acutely conscious of new
obstacles to any sort of creative energy: 'When I think back to that
decade following the war, a sense of arduousness and discomfort
comes to me.'[100] The understatement is, as usual, shrewdly judged.
Part of this sense undoubtedly sprang from the profound, and
wholly unexpected, sense of inertia which afflicted British literary
life at this time: it ought to have been a period of idealism and optimism, and yet, as Peter Hennessy says, 'almost everywhere you
touch the written remains of late Forties cultural life a whinge
comes up to greet you.'[101] Paper rationing, tightened rather than
relaxed as a result of the fuel crisis of 1947, made post-war England
an inhospitable place for writers in general and, as Robin Skelton
suggests, for poets in particular:

> The last years of the forties were... difficult for poetry. The
> publishers lost their enthusiasm for it, and the new magazines
> had short lives, while the established ones began to peter out.
> The early fifties saw the death of *Poetry Quarterly*, *Poetry
> (London)*, *Horizon* and *Penguin New Writing*. In 1951 the Festival
> of Britain Poetry Competition was a pathetic failure.[102]

The mood of literary pessimism reached its low point, after the
closure of *Penguin New Writing* and *Horizon*, in 1950. This condition is well summed up by Ian Hamilton:

> Halfway through 1950, the *TLS* set itself the gloomy task of
> describing the English literary situation for the benefit of its
> readers 'oversea'. Poised on the brink of a new half-century, it
> shuffled through the available names, listed the best of the new
> books, and tried to spot some hopeful guide-lines for the future.
> The message came back loud and clear: there weren't any.
> 'Looking back over the novels published during the last 18
> months, it is not easy to discern any marked school of young
> writers coming to the fore.' 'The only alternative that has so far
> presented itself to the younger generation' of poets has been
> whether 'to follow in the wake of Mr Auden or of Mr Thomas'.
> Readers oversea were also warned of the 'gentle dullness that plays

over biography today', of 'the conspicuous dearth of the literature of wit and humour', and of the 'crying need for a magazine that will devote itself to the furtherance of new writers'. And they were offered too a poem by Roy Fuller, called 'The Fifties', which began: 'The wretched summers start again.'[103]

But for Fuller, the summers were 'wretched', and the winters too, in a more personal way. The stoical briskness with which, in *Spanner and Pen*, he treats his post-war health problems – duodenal and gastric ulcers, thyrotoxicosis – can hardly disguise the extent to which he found them wearying and depressing. His physical appearance, a concern as vital to his self-consciousness as to his vanity, altered drastically: in his early thirties, having dispensed with his pre-war moustache, he looked younger than his age; in his early forties, older. Anthony and Ann Thwaite, then students at Oxford, remember being struck by his formal, middle-aged manner when he read to the university's Poetry Society, of which Ann Thwaite was Secretary: 'Being a *respectable* poet,' he warned her, 'I shall be travelling first class.'[104] Alan Brownjohn, also at Oxford in the early 1950s, remembers him on the same occasion as a 'neat, no-nonsense, even dapper figure'.[105] The strikingly handsome, clean-shaven lad in naval uniform in *Penguin New Writing's* photogravure supplement of 1943 had metamorphosed into a severely mous-tached and suited middle-aged solicitor: a natural transformation enough, perhaps, but a disarmingly rapid one.

At the same time, the ground-floor flat in St John's Park, with its virtues of spaciousness, convenience and cheapness (he claimed that parsimony was inherited, like hyperthyroidism, from his mother), became in the early 1950s a rather less desirable habitat:

> Through the entropic principle, applicable to many areas of human life, the flat above fell into the hands first, of representa-tives of the *lumpen-proletariat* who made noise and floods; then, of the cocky and quarrelsome side of the working class, who hung washing out in the garden but declined to help work at its upkeep. How the basement flat came to be occupied by foreign students, some of the Muslim persuasion, who during Ramadhan kept us awake even longer than the Christians above, would be too tedious to recount. In short, as we moved into middle-age we longed for a detached house, centrally heated...[106]

Though this is presented in Fuller's most curmudgeonly old-bufferish style, he clearly had a point; it is revealing, too, and not merely a matter of hindsight, that he should have viewed middle-age as something like a distinct psychological state or a geographical region, to be 'moved into'. Interestingly, this defined territory of middle-age is a place his fictional protagonists are more reluctant to occupy: those variously-distanced alter-egos remain resolutely youthful until the appearance of Harold Colmore in *The Father's Comedy* (1961), as if their parallel lives are also, on a modified Dorian Gray principle, a charm against ageing. As for the Fullers themselves, in 1954 they 'bought part of the garden of a Victorian house in the very road where our flat was, and caused a modest bungalow to be built on it.'[107]

While it was not so modest a bungalow as William Plomer's in Rustington, it was nevertheless a self-effacing and determinedly unmodish place for a highly-regarded writer and successful professional man to live: Brownjohn recalls it as 'that very neat, slightly austere one-storey house'.[108] But like many writers approaching the amorphous stage of mid-career, he had little idea (and even less confidence) about his literary reputation. When he was invited to co-edit the PEN anthology *New Poems 1952* with Clifford Dyment and Montagu Slater, he felt it was 'one of the earliest general recognitions (modest enough) of my presence on the literary scene'.[109] Even at the time, this would have been an absurd piece of self-underestimation: his presence as a poet had been established a decade earlier, he had contributed to the only literary magazine in England to reach a huge popular readership, and his novels – particularly *Savage Gold* – had been respectable successes (*The Second Curtain*, then imminent, would do better still). Compared with him, Dyment and Slater, despite his distinction as Britten's librettist, were minor figures.

His 1954 collection, *Counterparts*, has still something of an interim air, an impression reinforced by the cramped, almost hymnbook-like format of Derek Verschoyle's poetry volumes. It does, however, contain what Alan Brownjohn has usefully described as 'the first wholly successful poems in the "high" Fuller manner':[110] interestingly, this 'high' style will eventually turn out, in a neatly dialectical fashion, to be the antithesis which leads in turn to an effective synthesis of high and low in the late poems. Brownjohn feels that 'Rhetoric of a Journey' – which, like 'Ten

Memorial Poems', concerns the illness and death of Fuller's mother in 1949 – 'is perhaps too slow and solemn', but it is an important if ungainly part of the poet's sustained self-negotiation: 'after the war,' as he himself said, 'following an awkward period of adjustment, I was able to write verse of rather wider scope.'[111] Like George Garner, he travels by train with a nineteenth-century novel (*The Eustace Diamonds* rather than *Our Mutual Friend*) for company, reflecting how, in Trollope's world, 'something is always missing' and 'life is made tolerable' by processes of distancing and omission which are paralleled in his own writing:

> I think of the poem I wrote on another visit –
> A list of the poet's hoarded perceptions:
> The net of walls thrown over waves of green,
> The valleys clogged with villages, the cattle
> Pink against the smoking mills – and only now
> Experience what was delayed and omitted.[112]

This, we discover, was 'each other's load of emotion', a phrase whose very awkwardness aptly indicates the trouble which it caused the emotionally reticent Fuller. He turns from it to what may at first glance seem to be an astonishingly uncharacteristic resolution:

> I would like to renounce the waking rational life,
> The neat completed work, as being quite
> Absurd and cowardly; and leave to posterity
> The words on book-marks, enigmatic notes,
> Thoughts before sleep, the vague unwritten verse
> On people, on the city to which I travel.
> I would like to resolve to live fully
> In the barbarous world of sympathy and fear.

But of course it is no such thing. This is the divided self's wishful thinking, inventing a purely hypothetical alter ego: 'I would like to renounce' or 'I would like to resolve' is not at all the same as renouncing or resolving. It is intellectual man's pointless wish to be intuitive man once again: like Garner – and like Garner's analysis of Busoni, which is essentially self-analysis – Fuller sees himself as someone who knows too much about genius ever to achieve it. Yet at the same time this ideal of the 'irrational' artist is plainly an undesirable as well as an unattainable one; after all, we know what Fuller thought of D.H. Lawrence.

And indeed, in the ensuing brief dialogue between 'life' and 'poet', the poet insists that 'it is your limitations / That enable me to get you down at all': since those fully engaged in a life of heroic or revolutionary proportions will be too caught up in it to trouble themselves with literature, the poet's life will be by definition a partial, limited one. This proposition, which is central to Fuller's work, only seems to be modest or evasive: for, paradoxically, it is the poet's consequent task of creating first-rate work out of a second-rate life which is in its own way heroic. Here, of course, that dichotomy is superimposed upon the more personal sense of alienation inherent in the distance between the intuitive values of the Northern child and the intellectual values of the Southern adult:

> Sometimes I find it possible to feign
> The accent of the past, the vulgar speech
> Which snobbery and art have iced; but feel no longer
> The compulsion of hills, the eternal interests
> Which made my fathers understand each other.

Those fathers would have to be Broadbents rather than Fullers, of course; his abrupt invention of a dynastic past is as touching as it is unconvincing. But it is more than a genealogy that he is claiming here. The rhetoric, the 'high' manner, proclaims this as a deliberate contribution to the tradition of the great meditative Romantic lyric – the 'conversation poems' of Coleridge, Wordsworth's 'Immortality Ode' and, especially, 'Tintern Abbey' with its parallel revisitation of a remembered place. Ironically, however, and although Coleridge or Wordsworth would have understood the force behind 'I can speak easily only to myself', Fuller uses the Romantic form to state an essentially anti-Romantic position. For him, the 'compulsion of hills' is no longer felt and soon too the 'valleys disappear', leaving him to console himself by discovering 'Whether Lizzie Eustace retained her diamonds' and to return to 'the life of omission'. His conclusion – 'Behind me will lie the sad and convulsive events / As narrative art, and as fated, immortal and false' – is in its own hedged-in way an affirmative one, evincing at least a determination to make sense of the life he has, but it is exactly the reverse of that ecstatic reunification of poet and land-scape which ends 'Tintern Abbey':

> Nor wilt thou then forget,
> That after many wanderings, many years
> Of absence, these steep woods and lofty cliffs,
> And this green pastoral landscape, were to me
> More dear, both for themselves, and for thy sake.

Wordsworth, on whom Fuller had both written and broadcast (he took part, with J. Bronowski and Herbert Read, in a discussion called 'New Judgement on Wordsworth' for the BBC Home Service in April 1950), was much on his mind. If 'Tintern Abbey' is a ghostly presence in 'Rhetoric of a Journey', it is commanding one in 'Youth Revisited', in which Fuller returns with his adolescent son to Eastwell Park (where Anne Finch, Countess of Winchilsea, once lived), near his pre-war home in Kent. Wordsworth's 'Five years have passed…' and 'Once again I see / These hedge-rows…' becomes: 'A dozen years have gone since last I saw / This tiny church set on the parkland's edge…'[113] The church has meanwhile become a roofless ruin: as with the abruptly-invoked ancestry in 'Rhetoric of a Journey', the Wordsworthian echoes are overlaid with distant but decisive hints of Yeats. This is a poet very deliberately invoking, and manoeuvring himself into, the Romantic tradition at the moment in his life, after his mother's death and with a now-adolescent son, when he feels the need to redefine himself in relation to the past:

> I wonder if my son completely fails
> To grasp my halting reconstruction of
> My youth. Here, where we brought him in our arms
> Was neat then, facing time with fortitude.
> The statues in the gloom stood for their moral,
> The wicked viscount's smoke rose from the house,
> The evils of the epoch had not quite
> Made rational the artist's accidie.[114]

Romantic rhetoric, at least in this essentially Wordsworthian meditative blank-verse form, was eventually to prove something of a blind alley for Fuller; but the 'evils of the epoch' and 'the artist's accidie' remained abiding preoccupations. In 'Translation', he assumes – in the most cursory and transparent way – the persona of the poet Cinna from *Julius Caesar*, to record his political and cultural disillusionment: 'I will stop expressing my belief in the rosy

/ Future of man', he resolves; and, as for the slaves with whom in the past he has tried to sympathise, 'they are enemies to culture, / Advancement and cleanliness'. He even ventures this not wholly inaccurate prediction:

> When they call me reactionary I shall smile,
> Secure in another dimension. When they say
> 'Cinna has ceased to matter', I shall know
> How well I reflect the times.[115]

The poem cited earlier by Ian Hamilton, 'The Fifties', infinitely removed from the Festival of Britain spirit, gives a global context to helpless political dismay, in the form of a compressed villanelle:

> The wretched summers start again
> With lies and armies ready for
> Advancing on that fast terrain.
>
> Like those of China, Poland, Spain,
> With twenty territories more,
> The wretched summers start again.
>
> The rumours and betrayals stain
> The helpless millions of the poor
> Advancing on that fast terrain.[116]

Another poem in *Counterparts* is actually called 'Inaction'; Brownjohn views this as 'a fine example of his "low" style',[117] but it seems to me rather to be one of those poems, scattered throughout his career, in which two modes are disconcertingly juxtaposed, as they would be in ruminative late sequences such as *From the Joke Shop* and *Available for Dreams*:

> A strange dog trots into the drive, sniffs, turns
> And pees against a mudguard of my car.
> I see this through the window, past *The Times*,
> And drop my toast and impotently glare.[118]

The tone is ridiculously dignified – the outraged *Times*-reading solicitor dropping his toast at the sight of a peeing dog is a character worthy of an H.M. Bateman cartoon – and thus it explodes its own dignity; but the effect is not merely that of a lampoon, partly because of the author's wry self-awareness and partly because of the one brilliantly acute detail which makes the poem funny in a much more complicated way: 'A *strange* dog', Fuller writes, as if a familiar dog peeing on his car would be somehow more acceptable, and we recognise the ludicrous truth in that, and laugh at ourselves instead.

In *Counterparts*, the 'low' style is perhaps more obviously characterised by a poem like 'Necrophagy', a species of sinister nursery-rhyme about eating jelly-babies:

> Some eat the jelly baby whole but most
> Dismember it at leisure,
> For, headless, there is no doubt that it gives
> A reasonable measure
> Of unexampled pleasure.[119]

It also, Fuller adds, 'brings back the feelings of / Our infancy': another method, like those attempted in 'Rhetoric of a Journey' and 'Youth Revisited', of relocating and coming to terms with the lost childhood. That too is a theme which nagged at him through the 1950s, culminating at the end of the decade in what might be seen as his sustained attempt to exorcise it, *The Ruined Boys*.

★

On 10 September 1954, Robert Graves, having read *Counterparts* (he liked the book, and perceptively summed it up as 'oppressed, stoical, humorous, on the whole very well written indeed'), wrote to Fuller: 'But what a world you live in! Stoicism seems the only possible attitude. The word "love" does not occur even to be saluted with a witty Bronx cheer... Your solicitor's job doesn't sound very thrilling...'[120] This letter, Fuller admitted, 'impressed me greatly': in fact, its blend of mischievous provocation and qualified praise got thoroughly under his skin. Recognising that 'quite unconsciously I had been excluding too much from my verse, and that accordingly (or in addition) it lacked ambition',[121] he resolved to do something about it, with the poetic results collected in *Brutus's Orchard* (1957). But in the meantime that other jibe about his unexciting job struck home too: Fuller's next novel, *Image of a Society* (1956), seems designed to prove that the life of a building society solicitor – at any rate, if he worked for the insufficiently fictional Saddleford Building Society – might be very much more thrilling than Graves, or anyone else, had previously imagined.

Image of a Society turns the successful procedures of *The Second Curtain* and *Fantasy and Fugue* inside-out. Their claustrophobic

single-character perspectives are replaced by a rather blurry authorial omniscience which often seems in danger of retreating to the
viewpoint of Philip Witt, the building society solicitor who,
despite his resemblances to Fuller, is by no means the central character in the narrative. At the same time, the pathological extremi-
ties of the earlier novels give way to an essentially humdrum surface
in which the plot-mechanism turns upon nothing more extraordinary than the overvaluing of a property and the careless drawing-
up of a mortgage document. Of course, the point is that in reality
such things can profoundly destabilise both professional and
personal lives, as they do here; but it is immediately clear that we
are concerned with a kind of fiction which differs fundamentally
from the crime novels, a book whose shaping spirit is Arnold
Bennett rather than Graham Greene. Nor can one readily imagine
much in *Image of a Society* featuring in a film by Hitchcock –
although it was, perhaps surprisingly, adapted for television, not
wholly to its author's liking ('...when my novel *Image of a Society*
was dramatised for TV I was pained to see the second or third
executive in a large provincial building society washing the dishes,
and in an apron').[122]

The most important character – one might almost say tragic
hero, for he has the required attributes of ambition, hubris, and a
catastrophic downfall – is Stuart Blackledge, the Mortgage
Manager of the Saddleford Building Society, eager for promotion
to the General Managership, which is soon to become vacant on
the retirement of Herbert Matheson, a benign but ineffectual
figure given to sentimental reminiscence and to immoderate enjoyment of such delicacies as sugared almonds. Blackledge's only
potential competitor for the job is the Accounts Manager, Arnold
Gerson, a fastidious, almost comically unambitious accountant
who drives an old Morris and doesn't play golf. The car, as it
happens, is of more than incidental relevance, for at the start of the
novel Blackledge is preccupied with renumbering the spaces in the
basement car-park so that he gets the heir-apparent's appropriate
No 2 position: the device, for all its apparent banality, is a useful
one which enables Fuller both to illustrate Blackledge's machiavel-
lian tactics and to instruct the reader fairly painlessly in the hier-
archy of building society management. It has to be admitted,
however, that this educational aspect is overdone and tends to sap
the novel's energy: Blackledge is made to address an audience of

schoolchildren – and us – about the society's organisation, yet soon after he asks Witt to give him 'a child's guide to this business of lending on separate flats.'[123] 'My God, Philip, you make it sound complicated!' he complains wearily,[124] in response to a point – that freehold flats are problematical because the building supporting them may fall into disrepair and collapse – which must strike most readers as the merest common-sense and could hardly be news to the Mortgage Manager of a major building society.

One difficulty with Blackledge, which Fuller must have foreseen and to which I shall return, lay quite outside the book itself; but he is, even in strictly literary terms, an awkward character to manage. He is so insistently defined by his obsessive scheming, which is in itself convincing and carefully detailed, that all his actions are called into question: the psychological complexity which Fuller clearly intends is always in danger of slipping into stereotypical villainy. The manipulative note is struck repeatedly in the first part of the book. Ramsden, the House Manager, wonders 'whether Blackledge's questions were not the feint before the smashing blow – a typical Blackledge tactic'.[125] Joining the General Manager for tea, Blackledge contemplates the timing of Matheson's retirement, sees himself 'fated now, after the long years of planning and propaganda, to become in a little while the society's chief executive', and looks forward to 'the new era stretching ahead of reforms and power and increased income'.[126] Having carefully primed a committee to elect him as its chairman, Blackledge feels 'a slight rise in the temperature of the skin under his jaw at the knowledge that one of these nine persons present had preferred Gerson to him'[127] and, having decided (without evidence) who the dissenter must be, makes 'a mental note to have Crump transferred to another department; better still, to one of the branches'.[128] He so relishes the machinery of power that 'even the buying of a packet of cigarettes could involve his secretary, the society's telephone exchange, Ramsden and one of Ramsden's minions'.[129] Only when the renumbered garage spaces percipiently put him in third place, after Gerson, does his public façade begin to crack.

Philip Witt, the solicitor who is the narrative's other focal point, is no less of a problem. Fuller has described him as 'Kafkaesque',[130] and it is true that we glimpse him writing, among other wayward literary endeavours, a story plainly inspired by 'In the Penal Colony', but otherwise the resemblance to Kafka is as implausible

a disguise as George Garner's beard. Fuller has loaded Witt with
some of the least endearing aspects of his own character: debili-
tating insomnia; a digestion which will tolerate neither alcohol nor
fish-and-chips; a self divided between a career which he despises
and a literary ambition in which he lacks confidence. There is even
a strong physical resemblance: 'His face was very smooth, his pallor
had an olive tinge: against it the moustache seemed incongruously
luxuriant and brown.'[131] Allegedly because of his delicate health,
though equally on account of his indecisive nature, he still lives, at
the age of thirty-three, with his parents in a stuccoed, bay-
windowed house which 'stood by itself behind blackened trees, in
a district no longer fashionable':[132] the claustrophobic lower-
middle-class decencies of Fuller's Oldham childhood are recalled,
as they are by the Widgery household in *The Second Curtain*.
Trapped between his sarcastic bullying father and his neurotic
wheedling mother, Philip escapes into the arms of dimly bourgeois
Christine, whose principle concern is to get herself respectably
married before it's too late.

Christine is too conventional and unintellectual for Philip; Rose
Blackledge, on the other hand, is much more cultured and sensitive
than her boorish husband; when Philip and Rose meet at a social
occasion designed primarily to engineer a business coup for Stuart
Blackledge, the preconditions for an affair between them creak into
place. It is a manoeuvre which would embarrass a soap-opera
script-writer: the trouble is not with the social awkwardness, the
misfiring conversational gestures − Fuller has an excellent ear for
these − but with the fact that nothing we have so far learned about
these two people makes their mutual attraction remotely plausible.
That is what love is like, of course; nevertheless the novelist has
somehow to remind and convince us of the fact. Philip must travel
to London to try and unravel the problems of the mortgaged property, West End House (it is in Paddington, but the ex-provincial
Fuller allows his Saddleford executives to be deluded by the name
and postal area, a naivety which seems not so much Northern as
extra-terrestrial); Rose conveniently has a mother in London to
visit. The scene in which they go shopping for clothes before
returning to his hotel has a repressed neurotic intensity which
could have succeeded within the obsessive first-person narrative of
Fantasy and Fugue, but which here collapses into bathos:

'I can never think that anyone can love me,' he said, and saw his hand, with a skill that it did not seem he could own, begin to undo her dress. An absurd compulsion made him go on talking until at last she half sat up and, moving a little away from him, freed herself from the dress, and he saw with, as it were a sense of *déjà vu*, the brassiere and the little drawers. Behind the desire his fear mounted, now that she lay so vulnerably unclothed, that someone in authority would come rapping at the door, challenging with undeniable justice his right to have her with him.[133]

Immediately after this, we find ourselves at a meeting in an accountant's office in Victoria Street, where Philip is representing the Society: no setting in Fuller's novels can have been more familiar to him from his professional life than this, yet the scene, though important in revealing Philip's own share of negligence in drawing up the mortgage, lacks conviction and vitality; the newly-introduced minor characters, including the West End House directors Mr Black and Mr Silowski (the latter a pastiche East European, a less excusable version of the waiter in *The Second Curtain*), are stereotypes. In his fiction, Fuller is often least at ease when too close to home.

And yet, for all its faults, *Image of a Society* has at least two strongly redeeming features. One is that command of detail to reinforce character or atmosphere which distinguishes almost all Fuller's novels: here, this ranges from his customary attention to mannerisms of the nose-picking sort (such as Ramsden 'cleaning his earhole with a paper clip' in the very first sentence)[134] through the cinematic evocations of Saddleford House and its surroundings (Blackledge surveys the scene from his office window: the statue of John Bright in the square outside; a pigeon deposits 'a dropping on the lime-streaked plinth', an image hoarded from wartime Aberdeen; and soon 'A few exclamation marks of rain' appear on the window)[135] to the sustained image of predatory ill-health, running beneath the entire novel, provided by the Blackledges' cat, which early in the book catches a bird trapped in the conservatory and at the end dies of gastro-enteritis. The other is the arguably perverse but nevertheless unquestionable ambition of the book: Arnold Bennett had made novels out of commercial life half a century earlier, but *Image of a Society* both anticipates the naturalistic provincial fiction of the late 1950s (for instance, John Braine's

Room at the Top, about another ambitious Northerner, which appeared in the following year, 1957) and, as Jeremy Lewis puts it, 're-enfranchises the world of nine-to-five as a legitimate subject for the novelist'.[136]

The careful neutrality of 're-enfranchises' and 'legitimate' is much to the point, for the novel's affections are sharply divided. On the one hand, there is Fuller's attentive regard for the minutiae of office-life and his admiration for the values of Herbert Matheson or the vice-chairman, Sir Harold Ashton – men who see the role of the building society as primarily moral rather than commercial but whose standards are in danger of vanishing in a haze of sentimental reminiscence. On the other, there is his detestation of the 'new men' – people like Blackledge and his friend, the speculator Cecil Hepworth – who place financial ambition above principle. In apportioning a share of the blame for the West End House fiasco to Philip Witt, he makes a gesture of even-handedness, but his position is more truthfully if punningly expressed in his 'realization that the writer – all artists – in our society must be dissident'.[137] *Image of a Society* is so permeated with distaste for the emerging managerial style which was to become characteristic of post-war Britain that it seems astonishing that a building society solicitor could publish it and hope to keep his job.

He almost didn't. Naturally, the novel is prefaced with a disclaimer which asserts the fictional status of the Saddleford Building Society and 'its directors, staff and affairs', yet even this seems inescapably tinged with irony: 'Because of my regard for building societies and for my friends who work for them...'[138] Quite apart from the details he had borrowed and modified for the West End House case – in *Spanner and Pen* he records that after the war the Woolwich indeed made substantial, retrospectively ill-judged advances on commercial properties and that 'when the Society had to exercise its power of sale or receivership the position was far from straightforward'[139] – three other aspects of the novel seemed not quite far enough from Woolwich. Firstly, there was the battle for the General Managership. It had no exact parallel in reality, but Alexander Meikle, who had become sole General Manager of the Woolwich in 1946, was said to have manoeuvred Austin E. Smith, with whom he had shared the post for three years, into premature retirement, 'his ancient ambition being to succeed to an unshared General Managership';[140] furthermore, he seems to have methodically obstructed the promotion and influence of another senior colleague, Jack Lindsay, who 'was subject to the unrelenting edge of Sandy's sharp side'.[141] Though the exact circumstances differed, the idea of a power struggle for the senior position involving three distinct personalities – in the novel, Matheson and his potential successors Blackledge and Gerson – had an all too clearly recognisable origin.

Secondly, while Fuller's Saddleford House overlooks the square of a notional Northern town, Equitable House similarly overlooks the market square in Woolwich. Many of the fictional building's internal features, including the boardroom and the room in which the executives take their leisurely afternoon tea, also derive from its southern counterpart. Equitable House even has the model for the subterranean car park whose reorganisation so preoccupies Blackledge. Its practical usefulness and symbolic significance were such that, as late as *Spanner and Pen*, Fuller would recall: 'When I stopped being the Woolwich's solicitor and went on the Board, I lost my space in the basement car-park in Equitable House.'[142] No one reading *Image of a Society* in Woolwich can have failed the iden- tify the book's essential geography.

Thirdly, there is the characterisation. 'To anyone in the society at the time,' recalls Fuller's long-serving Assistant Solicitor, John Dyer, 'the book was a gem. Even the most insignificant characters could be identified around the place, as, indeed, could the ambi- tious protagonists.'[143] Chief among these, inescapably, is Stuart Blackledge. True, he smokes a pipe rather than Du Maurier ciga- rettes; and, of course, he meets an appalling self-inflicted end, while Sandy Meikle would go on triumphantly to become Chairman of the Woolwich. But the style, the speech and the tactics of the two men are often uncannily close. Blackledge, when thwarted, resolves to have the unfortunate Crump transferred to another department or branch; Meikle famously dissolved an entire head office department, dispatching some of its members to remote provincial branches, because someone had the temerity to ask for a pay-rise. As Fuller makes clear in *Spanner and Pen*, Sandy Meikle was capable of enormous kindness and generosity, particu- larly to those whose circumstances most deserved it. However, his management of the Woolwich was characterised by impatient, ruthless ambition; he was among the first to see the building society in national, business-oriented terms rather than as a regional benevolent institution, a point of view which would be entirely vindicated commercially but which was wholly at odds with Fuller's moral position. Meikle was infuriated by *Image of a Society*: Fuller was formally warned that publishing such material was incompatible with his position at the Woolwich (there are no more building societies or mortgage solicitors in his fiction). Thereafter, the relationship between the two ablest men in the society would be one of genuine but cool mutual respect rather than warm friendship.

1 Roy Fuller with younger brother John, Christmas 1924

2(a) Nellie Fuller and her sons

2(b) Timson Street, Failsworth, as it is today

3(a) Hotel Metropole, Blackpool, early twentieth century

3(b) RF (extreme left) and friends, Blackpool High School

4 RF in naval uniform, 1941: 'My photograph already looks historic…'

5(a) 'Willie, Edward, the author – Nairobi, 1942' (RF's annotation)

5(b) 'On the way up – Uganda somewhere' (RF's annotation)

6 RF: 'Part managerial, part poetic…'

7(a) RF, with portrait by June Mendoza

7(b) RF, with BBC colleagues (Sir Michael Swann, second from right), Cardiff, 1973

8 RF, in his 1964 Daimler V8

3: The Middle of a Career

For Fuller, the mid-1950s was a period of consolidation and evolution. The most loyal and perceptive of his literary friends, Julian Symons, feels that 'Roy underwent an emotional crisis at the end of the 40s or in the very early 50s... when it was settled he became another and rather different poet. And person, I suppose.' For Symons, the development was understandably less than welcome: 'He certainly relinquished almost all the social hopes and beliefs of his early poems, something I regretted more than most no doubt.'[1] Yet, as always with Fuller, the underlying consistencies are more striking than the superficial changes. His social ideals had always been firmly rooted in cultural values, and these did not alter. Nor had there ever been much doubt about his need for a stable, orthodox professional life: if, in *Image of a Society*, he teasingly discovered just how far he could go in tickling the Woolwich's more sensitive nerves, he still quietly assumed that he would succeed Fred Shrimpton as the Society's Solicitor, which he duly did in 1958.

But his poetry was changing in an evolutionary and, despite Symons' reservations, beneficial way. While a poem such as 'Rhetoric of a Journey' in *Counterparts* finds him embracing the discursive Romanticism of Wordsworth and Coleridge, his next collection, *Brutus's Orchard*, logically extends this process to include strong hints of Yeats − by no means a new enthusiasm ('Old Yeats knew a thing or two as I've always said')[2] but, perhaps surprisingly, a new influence. It says much for Fuller's sense of poetic discretion that he should have held this grave and ruminative note in reserve until his mid-forties, by which time it had been properly earned, not only by the poet's own experience but also by the social context in which he was now writing. For the tyrannical, conspiratorial Rome of 'The Ides of March' we must, as Alan Brownjohn says, 'read the post-war world − or perhaps even post-Suez Britain, with its conviction of a noble past and its dismal sense of impending menace or chaos in the present';[3] while Fuller himself suggested, in conversation with Anthony Thwaite, a number of parallels: 'rulers being incompetent or corrupt or simply, like Caligula, insane... politicians and high-ups relying on sooth-sayers... popular singers gaining a very large following... people concentrating on the surfaces... chaps being killed – and all this seemed to be like our own age.'[4] In *Brutus's Orchard*, Fuller once more finds an authentic voice for the social moment, just as he had done fifteen years earlier in *The Middle of a War*.

That voice is unmistakably Fuller's own even when it seems at first glance to be most flagrantly Yeatsian:

> Birds on the lake; a distant waterfall:
> Surrounded by its lawns, a vandyke shawl
> Of woods, against the washed-in sky of March,
> The abbey with its broken wall and arch,
> Its scoured and yellow look, has power still
> To move.[5]

The sub-text in these opening lines of 'Newstead Abbey' – more in the nature of a ground-bass than an echo – is plainly 'The Wild Swans at Coole', with overtones of the other two Coole Park poems and of later Yeats generally (the shawl and the 'broken wall and arch' both utterly characteristic images). It is worth recalling that Yeats's great reflective poems were – as one of the finest of them is entitled – 'Meditations in Time of Civil War', while Brutus's meditation in 'The Ides of March' serves as the catalyst for civil war in Rome: the dichotomy of 'noble past' and 'impending menace' in post-Suez Britain identified by Brownjohn, though far from civil war, prompted in Fuller similar symptoms of social dislo-cation. However, again as in Yeats, these coincided precisely with the achievement of a confidently mature poetic style. While Fuller's early poems understandably take their bearings from near-contemporaries such as Auden, those in *Brutus's Orchard* are consciously sited in a much more expansive literary landscape. Indeed, if there is a presence in the book even more powerful than that of Yeats and the Romantic tradition which preceded him, it is Shakespeare's.

At the heart of the book is 'The Ides of March', a poem of auda-cious grandeur and simplicity. It is, simply, a 55-line blank verse meditation spoken or thought to himself by Brutus at the moment before the conspirators enter his orchard in *Julius Caesar*, at II:i:85. Part of Fuller's audacity lies in his use of so mercilessly plain a form to treat a subject which is at once massively heroic and utterly familiar. Yet within three lines he has made it his own:

> Fireballs and thunder augment the wailing wind:
> A vulgar score, but not inappropriate
> To my romantic, classic situation.[6]

The musical analogy is characteristic, the worry that the 'score' might be 'vulgar' still more so; but what brilliantly wrong-foots the reader and stamps the poet's authority on the poem is that subversive wrench of both 'romantic' *and* 'classic' to serve his own purposes. Each is denied its expected literary connotation: 'romantic' here has nothing to do with Wordsworth and everything to do with the vulgar score, as in the 'romantic hero' of a film; while 'classic', through a similar process of wilful misappropriation, is given its loose colloquial sense (as in 'classic car') instead of the cultural-historical meaning which the context seems to propose. This is fair warning that we are entering a world in which the time is doubly out of joint and in which Fuller's ironic-dystopic vision of 1950s England is to be exactly superimposed on the familiar matrix of Shakespeare's tragedy.

Characteristically – recalling 'During a Bombardment by V-Weapons' or the claustrophobic domesticities of the crime novels – Brutus's personal life provides neither sanctuary nor consolation, but a parallel hell:

> Within the house my wife is asleep and dreaming
> That I, too, am cocooned inside the world
> Of love whose fear is that the other world
> Will end it.

Though 'cocooned' has a short-lived ambivalence which simultaneously suggests safety and imprisonment, the following line shows how ineffectual a protection this cocoon actually affords, for the world of love has been corrupted by fear: Brutus is, in fact, Fuller's most intense representative of 'The peaceful caught in public war'.[7] Equally, this other sanctuary, this garden 'Where I come, in better weather, with a book / Or pen and paper', is confounded by 'the creaking trees, the low dark sky', the imminent conspirators. The divided self's main problem is not its division – which might be tolerable and even useful if only it could be adequately managed – but the tendency of its two worlds to spill over and mesh into each other:

> Love and letters:
> One ought to be content – would, if the times
> Were different; if state and man were free,
> The slaves fed well, and wars hung over us
> Not with death's certainty but with the odds
> Merely of dying a not too painful death.
> Yes, I have caught the times like a disease
> Whose remedy is still experimental;
> And felt the times as some enormous gaffe
> I cannot forget.

These lines make a crucial and complex point which is both interestingly interpretative of *Julius Caesar* and essential for the understanding of Fuller's own social or socialist viewpoint. For if it is clear that in bad times the intellectual has a special obligation to exercise his civic responsibility, it is equally clear that once he has 'caught the times like a disease' his capacity for responsible action will be impaired. He is forced to make his civic decision at the very moment – and for the very reason – that he has ceased to trust his own judgement. The conflation of private and public worlds is caught in that extraordinarily impacted syntax: '...the times as some enormous gaffe / I cannot forget'. Again there is a clash of registers, the imperiously historical 'times' against the footlingly colloquial 'gaffe'; and we know, of course, just what sort of man uses words like 'gaffe'. This is the vocabulary of the self-conscious, insecure anti-hero of a Fuller novel, here transformed into a Brutus who will

> select from several complex panaceas,
> Like a shy man confronted with a box
> Of chocolates, the plainest after all.

Interestingly, these anti-heroic characteristics do not at all diminish Brutus; on the contrary, they seem distinctly to enhance this blandest of Shakespeare's tragic heroes by drawing our attention to his peculiarly sympathetic qualities – bookish sensitivity, philosophical gravitas. He is someone, Fuller implies, very like ourselves.

In this, too, the poem is exactly of its moment: it takes the reader's identification with the speaker's predicament for granted. Statements like 'I shall become a traitor, / Technically, to my class, my friend, my country' and 'the important thing is to remove /

Guilt from this orchard' demand our recognition and assent; so too does the undisguised intellectual superiority which describes the conspirators as 'those men of action with / Their simpler motives and their naked knives'. In the terms of that earlier, crucially vulnerable poem 'The Divided Life Re-Lived',[8] Brutus/Fuller here confirms his preference for 'Henry James or cats or God' rather than 'brutal, bloody life', while conceding that it is the intellectual's duty to support action of some sort and the nature of action (for all its 'simpler motives' and 'naked knives') to be fudged, unsatisfactory, provisional. Of course, the cautious, introspective intellectual will to some extent envy the man of action's reckless spontaneity – this is perhaps the most powerfully recurrent of all the many tensions in Fuller's writing – and may even feel that his apparent superiority is a kind of indefensible sham. Fuller's Brutus feels this and for what might justly be called an awful moment wishes the sham to be exposed:

> I hope my wife will walk out of the house
> While I am in their compromising presence,
> And know that what we built had no foundation
> Other than luck and my false privileged role
> In a society that I despised.

While this makes perfect sense in terms of Brutus's psychology as developed in the poem, it is still more persuasive as a description of the socialist poet-solicitor's dark night of the soul.

But Portia does not emerge from the house and neither, for that matter, does Kate. Fuller, ever alert to the ironic juxtapositions of the domestic and the literary, is writing soon after they had acquired their own house and garden in Langton Way, Blackheath, and it is not at all fanciful to suggest that the more deeply-rooted feeling of the poetry from *Brutus's Orchard* onwards is connected with this. Brutus/Fuller attempts a self-reconciliation which is inescapably paradoxical: no passionate man of action himself, not even the 'affable Irregular' of Yeats's 'Meditations in Time of Civil War', 'I merely choose what history foretells.' This elegant and knowing self-delusion, almost a definition of Sartrean bad faith, enables him to proceed to a conclusion of uneasy, half-resolved calm:

> The dawn comes moonlike now between the trees
> And silhouettes some rather muffled figures.

> It is embarrassing to find oneself
> Involved in this clumsy masquerade. There still
> Is time to send a servant with a message:
> 'Brutus is not at home'; time to postpone
> Relief and fear. Yet, plucking nervously
> The pregnant twigs, I stay. Good morning, comrades.

'Fireballs and thunder' have modulated to this 'moonlike' dawn, and the 'vulgar score' of the opening lines to the suspended, imperfect cadence so characteristic of Fuller's later poems.

'The Ides of March' deserves careful attention both as a culmination of the 'divided self' theme and as an outstanding example of Fuller's mature plain style: in choosing it to provide the title for *Brutus's Orchard*, he knew exactly what he was doing. Ideas and images from the poem recur throughout this remarkably coherent collection. The Shakespearian metaphor of illness as a political condition, for instance, underlies a group of poems early in the book[9] and returns at the end in the 'Mythological Sonnets':[10] 'The Day' compares being 'In bed, off work, with a sudden pain' to the terminal condition of 'idle Byzantium' (another glance in the direction of Yeats); while in the fifth mythological sonnet, set in doomed Troy, 'The whole realm is sick'. In one poem, Shakespeare is directly addressed and thanked for his 'marvellous pages';[11] in another, 'The Perturbations of Uranus',[12] both of the book's great literary influences are invoked in successive stanzas – first Yeats ('Our art is the expression of desire, / Yeats said'), then Shakespeare, for the phrase 'through young generations still unborn' is a further echo from *Julius Caesar*.[13]

'The Perturbations of Uranus' is also notable for introducing a subject which will become prominent in Fuller's later poetry and fiction – the ageing writer's speculative interest in younger women – and for reasserting the poet's concern with his self-image:

> Such fame as I have drops from me in a flash
> When the girl behind the café bar sends back
> A candid gaze.

The invisibility of a famous writer – as opposed to a sportsman or an actor or even a musician – is of course compounded when the writer's double self and visible persona is that of a building society solicitor. In 'Amateur Film-Making', he is in a grey, empty park, making a film intended to 'show the poet posed on various backgrounds';[14] but he is excruciatingly aware that the attempt visually to represent 'the poet' is an impossible or at best a mildly ludicrous enterprise:

> I feel
> The initial cobwebs of the rain, and think
> What jam I shall choose for tea, and of a book
> I am reading on psychiatric art, and then
> Of myself, the poet.[15]

Fuller turns respectable domesticity into artful subversion: after all, 'the poet' – if he were to behave in a suitably bohemian fashion and wear a beard like George Garner's – might not take afternoon tea, nor have jam with it, let alone have the luxury of choosing between jams. For Fuller, this juxtaposition of selves is constantly fruitful, constantly infuriating; or, as he puts it in 'At a Warwickshire Mansion': 'Cycles of ulcers, insomnia, poetry – / Badges of office; wished, detested tensions.'[16]

The themes of divided self and sick state are brought together in 'Ambiguities', a somewhat flawed piece dropped from *New and Collected Poems*. It opens with the image of a grotesquely diseased blackbird nevertheless successfully prising a caterpillar from the lawn – this close-up natural observation directly resulting from the Fullers' move to Langton Way, which 'served to funnel some nature into my verse'[17] – but is spoiled by a banal, hectoring conclusion. At the heart of the poem, however, is a particularly eloquent statement of mid-1950s disillusionment:

> The age regards me from the summer sky
> Where aircraft slowly chalk the blue with frost,
> Upon the ageless fire. And while I try
> To balance barren anger and despair
> The creamy smoke boils upright in the air,
>
> And drifts away above the trees and streets,
> And mingles with the haze from factories –
> Organs that raised us, now monstrosities –
> That lies along the river bank like fleets.[18]

Although there are occasional recurrences of Fuller's earlier Audenesque mode in *Brutus's Orchard* (in 'Summer'[19] or 'Pleasure

Drive'),[20] 'Ambiguities', like most of the collection, is both timeless and precisely of its time.

It seems odd, therefore, that *Brutus's Orchard* is not more gener-ally recognised as one of the major books of the 1950s, and its comparative neglect lends weight to Fuller's frequent, ironic-rueful complaint that he was a poet who never quite caught on. Though there is generally little to be said for the 'What if?' variety of literary history, it may seem that on this occasion Fuller was simply unlucky: *Brutus's Orchard* appeared in 1957, the year after Robert Conquest's anthology *New Lines*, by which time the poets of The Movement had essentially claimed the decade as their own. If the sequence of publication had been reversed, things might have looked very different; if Fuller had been slightly younger, he would probably have been in the anthology himself. This hypothesis is made the more persuasive by the reflection that some poems in *Brutus's Orchard* would not only have fitted very happily into *New Lines* but would no doubt have been widely acclaimed as among the best in the book.

All the same, it won't quite do. Fuller not only had twenty years of published work already behind him; he was also incapable of subscribing happily to the poetics of any clique or movement – his relationship with literary history was, in its deceptively quiet way, too ambitious and inclusive for that. Though he admired the 'intel-lectualism and sanity' of the *New Lines* poets as a welcome, neces-sary contrast to the 'deplorable critical standards' and 'slapdash poetic practice' of the 1940s, he was from the start undeceived by their limitations, as he recalled a decade later:

> But as early as 1956 I find I was expressing reservations about the then younger poets. They were, I said (in *The London Magazine*, April 1956) themselves 'a little to blame for not becoming firmly identifiable. If conviction and experimentation are lacking, if there is a general consensus about form and subject, then one needs to have a first name like Kingsley to be easily distinguishable from the ruck.' The occasion for this facetious-ness was a review of *The Less Deceived* by Philip Larkin, a poet I was then apt to confuse with Philip Oakes. It never occurred to me that this extremely well-written book, with it youthful charm and faint sentimentalities, would become the bible of the period and that one of the pieces in it, 'Church Going', would

be quoted, analysed, and anthologized almost as though it were 'Gerontion' or 'Sailing to Byzantium'.[21]

Fuller's judgement of The Movement was acute: the point about the poets' lack of individual distinctiveness would be more laboriously made, and acclaimed as controversially original, by A. Alvarez in his Introduction to *The New Poetry* in 1962; while the 'youthful charm and faint sentimentalities' of *The Less Deceived* are characteristics somewhat obscured by Larkin's subsequent celebrity. (There was nothing sentimental, however, about Larkin's indignant reaction to Fuller's 1956 review, which suggests a man more stung by just criticism than he cared to admit: 'Wouldn't you say, off-hand,' he asked John Wain, 'that if he didn't know the difference between Philip Larkin and Philip Oakes HE SHOULDN'T BE REVIEWING POETRY FOR THE BLOODY SCHOOL MAGAZINE? Well, well. But when I saw what he'd said about E.J. and R.S. [Elizabeth Jennings and R.S. Thomas] I felt relieved I'd got off so lightly.')[22]

In his 1968 lecture on 'Poetry in my Time', Fuller had one further point to make about the poets of *New Lines*: 'the neatness of their verse and the domesticity of their subjects – by no means evils in themselves – intensified the need to break away from the tyranny of the iambic line. In the end,' he felt, 'the very measure seemed to hold the threat of yet another poem about a small dead animal or the poet's infant offspring.'[23] Again, the observation is perfectly valid; but this time Fuller knew that he was also talking about himself.

★

After *Image of a Society* in 1956, Fuller published four further novels within the following decade: *The Ruined Boys* (1959), *The Father's Comedy* (1961), *The Perfect Fool* (1963), and *My Child, My Sister* (1965). That would be a more than respectable tally for a full-time novelist, let alone for a man who now occupied a senior position in his profession as well as writing poems and literary journalism. How on earth did he manage it? Partly by making a virtue of necessity: sleeping little, and reading or writing when he couldn't sleep. But that alone fails to account for the suddenly dominant role of fiction, rather than poetry, during these years. The deeper clue is in the *kind* of fiction these novels – or some of them – are.

The Ruined Boys and *The Perfect Fool* use material closely drawn from Fuller's own early life. Despite their markedly different tones, the two books are complementary: one is a story of childhood set entirely in a boarding school, the other a narrative of growing-up from which school has been completely excluded (and which reads rather oddly as a result). They seem to me to spring from a specific impulse: the perceived need of a middle-aged writer to get his past down on paper in some creative form. Of course, almost all Fuller's fiction contains autobiographical elements; the problem with these two books, even more acutely than with *Image of a Society*, is that the experiences are insufficiently transformed and shaped into fiction. Precisely because their Fullerish central characters so accurately embody aspects of his younger self, they – and the novels they inhabit – seem inhibited by his own shyness and reticence. Despite their qualities, *The Ruined Boys* and *The Perfect Fool* are essentially the Mark I versions of his memoirs, which to a considerable extent supersede them; consequently, the two books have been treated here as parts of the biographical context. In his memoirs Fuller was gently disparaging about both novels; he especially regretted the negative portrait of Arthur Anderson in *The Ruined Boys*, and judged – justly enough – that *The Perfect Fool* was his least successful work of fiction.

The Father's Comedy is another matter altogether. This is not to say that it lacks an autobiographical dimension: on the contrary, it is in some ways the most personally revealing of all Fuller's novels, but this congruence is deeply rooted in psychological insight rather than surface action. Nevertheless, its central character, Harold Colmore, holds a senior executive position in a large organisation and lives in a comfortable South London suburb; he and his wife, Dorothy, have a nineteen-year-old son, Giles, who is away from home (there is also an invisible younger daughter at boarding-school); meanwhile, Harold takes more than a passing interest in one of Giles's girlfriends. To this extent, it seems to be another novel in which Fuller's own life in the 1950s has been gently nudged sideways into fiction. Giles, however, is in the army, doing his National Service, and has been dispatched to a turbulent, tactfully unnamed East African colony in which much of the book is set; John Fuller had recently spent two years in the RAF, and his father's choice of the service with which neither he nor his son were connected is a displacement characteristic of his fictional strategy.

So the novel's opening signals – office-life and adultery in middle-class London – are deliberately misleading. Perhaps for just this reason, knowing that the over-familiar territory of the early pages need not be sustained for the novel's length, Fuller finds even here a fluency which is very different from the often impoverished prose of *Image of a Society*. The leisurely account of Colmore's drive home from the office, stretching over four pages, provides a good example:

> He did not mind the delays and concentration imposed by the rush-hour traffic. Halted behind a long stream of cars at traffic lights, he was completely relaxed, his hands light on the wheel, his eyes taking in the nuances of his situation, ready but not eager to start the familiar action of moving through the gears. The dashboard light shone for him alone, and illuminated the reassuring figures: the ample petrol, with the mileage which he himself had totted up. He looked across with interest but inexplicable superiority at the drivers of other cars – as though their machines were easier to drive, less warm, fast, beautiful. He turned at last on to the bridge and sensed the sudden empty sky above him, glimpsing the lights and reflected lights of the river on his left as it curved through its world of concert halls, hotels, stations, and wharves.[24]

This is an ambitious man, fresh from a fawning interview with his boss, Lord Groves (a Lancastrian with imperfectly assimilated Southern vowels whom Colmore now complacently imagines eating fried plaice and drinking tea), who is heading for a fall of some sort. Fuller sets up, in order to demolish, various possibilities. On reaching home, Colmore finds Dorothy drinking sherry with the doctor's wife, whom he detests: there is a hint of marital tension, or at least imperfect understanding. More disturbingly, there is his affair with Judy Preston, whom we meet in a beautifully-constructed scene interrupted by a mannerless youth: we are likely simultaneously to share Colmore's irritation and to be aware that it is misplaced, that he is actually the social intruder – a neat foretaste of his position later in the book. Thirdly, there is the possible impact of his indiscretions on his career: he is, he thinks, in line for imminent promotion and a knighthood. Up to this point, *The Father's Comedy* exactly if more stylishly retreads ground already covered in *Image of a Society*.

The bombshell takes the unwelcome form of a phone call from an importunate newspaper reporter from whom Colmore eventually learns that his son has been arrested for assaulting an officer in East Africa. Obviously, he must fly out immediately, thus disrupting the delicate fabric of his personal and professional life; less obviously, the experience will radically alter his relationship both with Giles and with his own past. When he arrives in the colony, he encounters a sequence of individuals who seem designed to mislead him and throw him off course, like tests confronting a mythological hero: Hamilton, an amiably bigoted tea-growing 'old settler man';[25] Napur, an Indian solicitor who wants to turn Giles's case into a political *cause célèbre* by briefing 'the great Oldham, Q.C.',[26] a famously irascible left-wing advocate; and Corporal Hare, who tempts both Colmore and Hamilton into an evening of drunken brothel-visiting in which Colmore, ever the outsider, is amazed that 'Hamilton and the girl had actually entered into a sexual commerce, mysterious, sordid – and wounding to him because he had been excluded from it.'[27] Though these three characters are variously disagreeable and ridiculous, they are treated with a sympathetic tolerance which does much to increase our regard for Colmore.

The heart of the book, however, lies in a revelatory series of interviews between father and son (a pattern to be repeated on a smaller scale in *My Child, My Sister*): the progress from estrangement to empathy is developed through an almost balletic sequence of moves and counter-moves, so it seems appropriate that it should begin with an exact physical image of disconnection:

> Colmore went towards him, and saw the simultaneously strange and familiar flesh, the full lower lip cracked and neglected, the shirt held by half a button, an expression of complete neutrality – the expression of an earlier age, almost, reflecting an uncertainty as to the world's view of its possessor's conduct. The proper feeling flooded into his throat and he made for the boy as though to embrace him as he had been used to doing not many years ago. But Giles, imagining that the gesture was intended for the handshake of more recent times, made an inappropriate response, so that father and son were left for a second clutching at portions of each other's garments like ju-jitsu wrestlers.[28]

Wrong-footed from the start, Colmore retreats into helpless clichés – 'It simply isn't like you', 'You've never caused us a moment's anxiety before' – before softening into 'sudden tenderness' as he realises 'that however involved one may be with another's fate, there is a deeper order of reality for the fated.'[29] He also gradually realises that the case has unsuspected moral and political dimensions: he discovers that Lieutenant Andrews, who had been ill-treating a prisoner before Giles's intervention, 'pulled out his revolver' and pointed it at Giles, who hit him with a panga ('a sort of Bronze Age sword');[30] subsequently, from the Commanding Officer, he learns that a copy of Marx's *The German Ideology* has been found in Giles's billet — required reading for the boy who plans to study History at university, but a text to provoke a McCarthyesque reaction in an unintellectual army colonel dealing with rebellious African communists in the late 1950s.

Here it becomes clear that *The Father's Comedy* engages far more profoundly with Fuller's underlying ideological concerns than his more obviously autobiographical novels. When Colmore mentally rehearses the replies he might have made to the C.O. — 'One would, for example, like to have known what other books Giles had had: Kant, Nietzsche, Spengler? But could one have conducted a conversation with Colonel Syrett on this level?'[31] — we can scarcely fail to notice how just that sort of dilemma might occur in his own professional life, or in Fuller's. In Colmore's second conversation with his son, during which Giles speaks with 'a frankness and directness that would have been astonishing to Colmore had it been uttered in his suburban house, but which here was nullified by its outrageous setting',[32] the matter of *The German Ideology* becomes explicit. Colmore's worldly, pragmatic argument is that it is simply unwise and tactless to possess such books in such circumstances: thus, ironically, he adopts a level of discourse as reductive as that he despises in Colonel Syrett. It is left to Giles to raise the stakes by recalling his own upbringing and his father's ideological past:

'So I am to blame for their finding you in possession of the book.'
'If you like to put it that way.'
There was a silence of such depth that it seemed impossible for the conversation to go on. Colmore could hear, no doubt from the grass outside the open window, the continuous high sound of crickets, like an escape of gas. Then Giles said witheringly: 'When did you relegate your own copies of Marx from your study shelves to the loft?'[33]

It is a fair question; and the answer, which has to do with a successful young accountant's professional caution during the war, is timid and muddled if not actually dishonourable. For Colmore, the reminiscence is tinged with affectionate nostalgia, but for Giles, the conflict between the intellectual self and the barbarian world is articulated in more starkly immediate terms: '...we play at being ourselves – at being cultured, liberal, progressive. They believe unquestionably in their ideas – and they're organized to defend them.'[34]

Back at his hotel, Colmore writes to his son a long, autobiographical letter: the device is awkward, but his urgent need to reappraise his own past makes it seem plausible enough. He also reflects inwardly on his pre-war life; here, character and author slide together like a pair of superimposed images and fuse into one:

> When he had qualified he had moved up to town, to a room of his own, and there, in the Gray's Inn Road, his friends had been wage-earners, medical students, journalists on lineage, arty or over-serious girls who were shop-assistants, nurses, waitresses, for whom the world of accountancy did not exist. And this double life, whose purpose and richness was all in its leisure hours – so that he gave to his office at Aubry and Fletcher and to the rooms at the firms where he carried out his audits only a grudging and impoverished talent – was based on an illusion he now found impossible to understand: the illusion that by political action he could change the course of events.[35]

Though this is an undeniably fascinating moment for readers interested in Fuller himself, it is a tricky one for the novel, which might have been sabotaged by a surfeit of introspective apologia. That danger is averted by the scene in which Corporal Hare escorts Colmore and Hamilton for their somewhat bizarre night on the town, and which in turn finally establishes a sense of man-to-man equality in the third and last encounter between father and son before Giles's court-martial:

> Giles grinned. 'Did you really have a night out with him?'
> 'You could call it that.' For a moment Colmore was confused: it seemed as though the girl in the hut were like Judith, some prerogative of his son's on which his desire unlawfully impinged.
> 'What happened?'
> Suddenly Colmore realized the spirituality of his relationship

with Giles. He had to make the same order of effort to speak lightly and without embarrassment as if some searching question had been put to him by the acutest member of the Authority's Board. 'Nothing,' he said. And then he added: 'I regret to say.' The words seemed enormously daring.[36]

Of course, that enormity resides not just in his frankness with his son but in his honesty with himself. Yet Fuller shrewdly resists the temptation to allow Giles an uncomplicated table-turning victory: he is still young, after all. However well-meant his assertion that one shouldn't worry 'if one year you believe in Marx and the next year Gandhi and the next year Roman Catholicism', it founders on what for Fuller, with his preoccupation with the divided self, is an almost unbearable irony: 'You've just got to be yourself. Don't knuckle under to anyone – or any set of beliefs.'[37] Colmore will, in fact, eventually act on just this principle, though at a cost which must be all but unimaginable to his son. For the moment he is overwhelmed by the astonishing discovery 'that he loved his son, as though this were a talent, like playing the violin, that he had never in all his life thought to possess.'[38]

When Colmore discloses, at Giles's trial, his former membership of the Communist Party and his subsequent estrangement from politics, the attempt at self-reconciliation is his author's too. Though his political convictions may have failed to survive the 1930s, they nevertheless had 'certain lasting effects': 'A progressive outlook in the realm of education. Both my children have gone to slightly unconventional schools. And my son particularly has read widely, whatever he wished, including the books I accumulated during the thirties.'[39] Colmore is making a virtue of necessity, obviously, but the case he states has its own awkward authenticity, touching as it does on one of Fuller's central dilemmas: faith in a culturally enabling socialism giving way to a politically uncommitted faith in culture. However, Colmore's statement has a further momentous aspect. Fuller's past political views were a matter of public record – it was assumed within the family that they accounted for his son, having been allotted the 'trade' of interpreter after basic training, being sent to Gloucestershire as a pay clerk rather than assigned to the Russian course at Bodmin – but they seemed not to excite much anxiety among the Woolwich's senior management. Colmore, on the other hand, risks his career (and, we are to assume, loses his chance of a knighthood) by revealing the private rather than the public self.

Giles is acquitted, of course: 'The court find that the accused 2600161 Private Giles Ellis Colmore, Royal Musketry Regiment, is not guilty of the charge.'[40] Even the number is typically allusive: Fuller's in the navy was JX 260161. And even the verdict is typically ironic, for almost immediately Colmore hears Shaw, Giles's solicitor, say to him: 'It never does to be optimistic in litigious matters, otherwise we could have set our minds at rest as soon as your boy had told his story of the gun.' It was, he adds, 'A classic self-defence case.'[41] But if Colmore's vulnerable self-revelation has proved to be in a strictly practical sense unnecessary, that only emphasises its moral and spiritual dimensions. In his post-verdict chat with his son, he even manages to mention his affair with Judith Preston. Then he sends a cable to Dorothy – 'GILES ACQUITTED VERY WELL AND HAPPY MAY BE POSTED HOME SOON' – to which he after a moment's thought adds the postscript: 'ALL OUR LOVE – HAROLD.'[42] The openness of the sentiment seems out of character, an escape from habitual reticence. He feels 'an anxiety to return, to show himself to the Authority and to Dorothy, to find out what his character and career had become, to know the worst.'[43] That feeling, we know, will not remain untarnished – indeed, it receives a slight symbolic check on the book's last page – but it is a potent, necessary one, and it is not the least of Fuller's achievements that for a moment we seem to share it.

★

No doubt there is something wrong with all of us, who practise the arts: whether or not it shows in our work is irrelevant to that.[44]

That is not Fuller himself, but Albert Shore, novelist and narrator of *My Child, My Sister:* a decade older than his creator, he is nevertheless unmistakably a version of the now-familiar Fulleresque hero. In one respect, he takes us back to George Garner in *The Second Curtain*, for he lives by the spannerless pen, as a full-time writer; but Shore, like his father before him, has been an Oxford don, and in his most self-consciously donnish moments his style brilliantly parodies that of an actual Oxonian novelist, J.I.M. Stewart. In other respects – for instance, the extended symbolic retrospect about his nurturing of an abandoned starling chick which deserts him, in 1944, at the same time as his wife – he has much in common with the Fuller of the later poetry (the symbol recurs too, of course, in the title of *Stares*). But essentially the book is a companion-piece to *The Father's Comedy*: there is a similar process of mutual discovery between father and son, and a relationship between the older man and a younger girl (thanks to some tortuously zigzag consanguinity, she is both the daughter of Shore's ex-wife and the half-sister of his son's fiancée); these elements provide the framework for a searching exploration of that 'something wrong' with all creative artists, set against fears of global annihilation prompted by the Cuba crisis of 1961–2.

These are serious matters to be accommodated in a meandering, anecdotal first-person narrative. Fuller – like Yeats, for instance, or Robert Frost – had come to recognise, in fiction and well as in poetry, the tactical benefits to be gained from gently advancing one's age: Albert Shore's ruminations would seem intolerably mannered in a younger narrator, and his relationship with Flip would become cornily, unambiguously sexual. Instead, he aspires to the condition of 'the Shakespearian daft old man', part Prospero, part Lear. The daftness is rather over-insisted upon in the book's opening pages, when he mistakes the sound of his wheezing chest for that of a crying baby and a piece of broken tooth for a fragment of mouse's skull, but subsequently it is a stance which serves him well, excusing his foibles while enabling him eventually to acquire an autumnal wisdom. When we first encounter him, he is in London to visit first the dentist and then his son, Fabian, who works for a modish architect called Shafran and has just been beaten up by the police during a demonstration over the 'Persian' crisis: it is another father's comedy, to the extent that Fabian – as his name suggests – is enacting principles which were once more timidly espoused by the youthful Albert; there are some tantalisingly underwritten vignettes of early 1960s London in these pages. (Fabian, incidentally, not only carries a political resonance but reflects Fuller's enduring fascination with *Twelfth Night* and with this character in particular.)[45]

Back in North Oxford, Albert reflects ruefully on the portrait of himself and his surroundings to be found in a book by Bernard Buckley, a younger, Movementish novelist not unlike John Wain (Alfred, the donnish if unOxonian father in *Strike the Father Dead*, comes irresistibly to mind, and the similar name strongly suggests

an intended allusion): this is doubly ironic, because later he will
learn of the hurt caused by *his* 'fictional' version of his ex-wife's
second husband, Christopher Leaf, and because Buckley's exact
image of a pair of tits flitting across the garden will recur at the very
end of the novel, as 'life' imitates 'art'. When Fabian arrives for
lunch accompanied by a young woman, Albert is initially 'excited
– it is hardly too strong a word – by the opportunity of meeting a
female of his generation',[46] then appalled to discover that she is
Frances Leaf, Christopher's daughter by his first marriage. He
behaves badly, but this is a version of the paternally protective
anxiety Prospero displays towards Miranda and Ferdinand: 'On
analysis I am surprised to find how much of my fear consists of a
concern for others, as one might worry about the effects of one's
fatal disease on the affection and even the daily routine of one's
family.'[47] Like Prospero, too (the chapter closes with a quotation
from *The Tempest*, so the comparison is absolutely explicit), he is
afflicted with mental weariness: 'It strikes me that intellectual
excitement, as though it were a physiological function, has become
dead in me.'[48] It will take someone along the lines of Ariel to
reawaken it.

   This Ariel-figure turns out to be Flip, Christopher and Eve
Leaf's anorexic daughter. She is an extraordinary invention: while
Albert's erotic interest in her is perfectly clear, it is equally obvious
that her deeper fascination lies in the misfit, changeling-like quality
which in this novel is so closely linked with creativity. Significantly,
Albert's positive, stimulating encounters with her – when he drives
her to the life class or meets her at a Tate Gallery private view –
take place within the context of art, whereas the subsequent cata-
strophes (her self-injury on the day of Fabian's and Frances's
marriage, her mental and physical deterioration thereafter) occur in
a world progressively emptied of any creative impulse. Their first
meeting immediately follows and exactly counterpoints Albert's
unsatisfactory visit to Eve, 'an almost strange woman';[49] for the girl
he is to drop off in Brunswick Square is strange in a more
profoundly unsettling way:

> She said to the windscreen: 'It sounds appropriate, doesn't it?'
> 'What does?'
> 'Life class. A class for learning about life.'
> 'Unfortunately there aren't any such.' How had we suddenly

got on terms of these quite intimately foolish generalizations?

'No. I'd like to be taught how to be a real person.'

'Most people are content not to be.'

'I don't mean that. I mean I haven't any identity. Everything you see now – isn't me.'

'Well, I wouldn't like you to think you were seeing the real me, either.'[50]

Albert can pass off his side of this conversation as 'avuncular donnishness', while we may be inclined to feel that Flip's is nothing more than a typical instance of adolescent insecurity. But that would be to underestimate the skill with which Fuller has woven this cat's cradle of relationships: it is precisely because Frances and Fabian are so emphatically Christopher's daughter and Eve's son that she, the child of both parents, feels paradoxically deprived. She is a variation on the theme of the divided self in which a minus sign has somehow insinuated itself into the equation. Albert's temporary error is to assume that her lack of 'identity' renders her a *tabula rasa*, whereas it in fact masks a ferment of conflicts.

He discovers this on the evening of their visit to the Tate. His clandestine letter of invitation, her equally secretive reply, and the fact that her parents happen to be away from home all point to a somewhat different kind of assignation – the kind perceived by one of several tiresome fellow-guests, Edward Pollen: '"That's a nice young girl you've brought with you." The adjectives and noun came from him as though denoting an item of butcher's meat.'[51] Albert tells Pollen that Flip is his step-daughter, a deception which seems half-excusable since he has already told her 'You could have been my daughter',[52] but the relationship is complicated by factors quite apart from her parentage. For one thing, it is here set against the abrasive context of the exhibition itself. Arriving at Millbank, Albert has despondently viewed the altered London skyline as a symptom of terminal cultural decay – 'how can it be that other reasons operated in other cultures at parallel stages to ours to produce the same staggeringly large and elementary shapes?'[53] – and he likes the pictures no better:

> Like the new buildings outside, many of the paintings had been seized by the impulse to elephantine size and staggering simplicity: geometrical shapes of colour confronted us, the painter's

subtlety and invention being confined to his treatment of their borders and his contrast of colour with colour... In the next room were canvases of a somewhat more modest size, some incompletely covered with paint, others filled to the edges with minute scribble. Occasionally a mark of style seemed elusively familiar – where, say, some crudely realistic element could be discerned or the painter had made a savage hook in the paint with the heel of his brush – and one eventually recalled the figurative art of lavatories, and water-colours by infants.[54]

We may suspect, incidentally, that Fuller has some specific infantile water-colours more affectionately in mind, for the same idea occurs in 'Homage to Dr Arnold Gesell and to my Grand-Daughter Sophie' (from *Buff*, published in the same year as *My Child, My Sister*):

> Odd, all the same, that we find her genius
> In doing badly what we all do pretty well.
> The noseless, crop-eared, mad-wigged sketch of 'ba-ba',
> The circular automobiles and circular horses,
> For instance, are measured by us indulgently
> Against a tradition of naturalistic art
> (Which nonetheless expired prior to her).[55]

With Fullerish, only half-serious self-deprecation, Albert tries to dismiss his response as part of 'the commonplace process of becoming reactionary with age', yet he wonders why, unlike the paintings around him, his 'own art is comparatively sane and naturalistic', and even asks the girl: 'Is this your style?'[56] The distinction between an art which seeks to make sense of the world and one which presents a vision of unresolved chaos is crucial: Albert's allegiance to the former is synonymous with his inability to understand or to save Flip, who seems to be an embodiment of the latter. He finds her unfathomable, but in a typically self-conscious way he regards this as a failure of his own perception rather than as a measure of her enigmatic complexity: 'Sometimes in recent years I have sat in front of a blank page and realized that I knew nothing of human character.'[57] His problem is not that he knows nothing but that he misinterprets what he does know.

Thus, when he takes Flip back to her home after the exhibition, his ability to observe is constantly unmatched by his ability to interpret. Her inclusion of a brandy bottle on the coffee tray strikes him as 'touchingly precocious'; while the sight of her sitting, one leg drawn up under her, prompts him to aesthetic contemplation 'only modestly connected with the erotic' and to the arch conclusion: 'Inconceivable that art should have abandoned the figurative.'[58] When, following directly from this reflection, he persuades her to show him some of her own work, all the neat dichotomies which were so carefully formulated during the previous scene are destroyed: for her own paintings and drawings of tiny human figures overwhelmed by their context – 'there were several sketches in which the figure had been reproduced on a disconcertingly small scale and in the sheet's blank rectangle seemed lost or displaced'[59] – are as representational as he could wish though very far from sane or reassuring. Albert responds as best he can, by praising her skill and tactfully evading the perceived cry for help, yet (to his credit) he recognises the inadequacy of his praise: 'It seemed impossible to discard the tone of patronage, or bogusly sagacious age.'[60] After he has left her in inexplicable tears (she says she has 'Just enjoyed the evening, that's all'), he drives away 'with a gnawing conscience, to which was intolerably added the knowledge, as of the deficiencies of my own art, of my unsatisfactoriness at any action arising out of the emotions'.[61] This inability to react to Flip in terms of life rather than of art takes us back to the first of Fuller's inhibited heroes, George Garner, and his version of the same problem: 'Artists of the second class knew all the rules for being a genius, but missed the final absorption in, acceptance of, life: they preferred art.'[62] Albert Shore, too, is – at least at this stage in the book – at best an artist of the second class.

But *My Child, My Sister* is a more generous novel than *The Second Curtain* in allowing its central character greater growth and unambiguous redemption. In a cunning juxtaposition, Fuller takes Albert in the next chapter to a meeting of the Literature Committee of the Larrabeiti Fund, which is considering its grant to James Blagden, a poet who – drunk, lazy and inept, the very model of Bohemian failure detested by Fuller – is plainly unlikely ever to complete his commissioned verse play: of all the committee, only Albert feels inclined to give the benefit of the doubt to a writer so entirely unlike himself. After the meeting he tells himself 'that after all James was very far from the best poet in England and the Bohemian life was stupidly anachronistic',[63] yet his attempt to override his own prejudices, and to repair his damaged conscience, is telling. (There is, incidentally, a prescient note in this former Oxford don's membership of a literature committee: the novel's publication anticipated Fuller's election as Oxford Professor of Poetry by three years, and his chairmanship of the Arts Council's Literature Panel by eleven – though he had already served on its Poetry Panel.)

After the Tate evening Flip writes, but for a fortnight omits to post, an odd and fulsome thank-you letter to Albert. In his reply, he vulnerably confronts the gulf between his art and hers, and obliquely explains his support for Blagden:

> Yes, we must meet again. In fact I was in London the other day and nearly rang you. The 'nearly' is not an indication of the faintness of my wish but of a reluctance to foist my elderly presence on you again. Next time I think I'll be more unscrupulous. Part of my visit was to deal with a difficult poet and that was a hopeless failure. Don't be frightened to be difficult. My own work has always been, like my life, too rational. There is another approach, more daring, hazardous, and in the end more likely to bring success – to go straight for what the work is fundamentally about, regardless of sense, propriety, obligation. Anybody reading this would think I was being hypocritical, since I've always represented the opposite. But reconciliation is the lesson one learns at last.[64]

This reply, however, is still on his desk when Flip herself turns up in Oxford as an unannounced lunch guest with the expected Fabian and Frances. The visit marks the beginning of Flip's eclipse. An after-lunch walk ends at a rural pub which, with a fine disregard for the licensing laws of the time, is open and serving tea: there Albert learns that Frances is pregnant and will marry Fabian as soon as possible. Such a momentous event in her half-siblings' lives can only confirm Flip's sense of her own invisibility, non-existence.

The day of the marriage, switched into a present tense which aptly resembles a slightly disarranged sequence of snapshots, is rich in tragi-comic detail though dominated by Albert's increasing concern about Flip, who is regarded as a peripheral nuisance by everyone else: 'Someone ought to be particularly kind to poor Flip,' he tells Fabian,[65] but it is not enough. Enacting the cry for help which he had perceived in her pictures, she stubs a cigarette out on her hand. Fuller sensibly recesses this potentially melodramatic incident in the mêlée of the occasion, so that the details filter only gradually through the crowd. Standing on the pavement after the newlyweds' departure, her father tells Albert: 'It's difficult to understand. She used to be so good, a model child, never the slightest trouble.'[66] The words, with mischievous irony, are almost exactly those uttered by Colmore to his son in *The Father's Comedy*.[67] Albert recognises and responds to their helpless honesty:

> 'This has been an upsetting time for her like everyone else – the marriage... the pregnancy.' Curious to find oneself tempering reality to him by using so mild and undescriptive an epithet. 'Her painting – girl of deep feeling.'[68]

That halting inarticulacy is all the more touching in a professionally articulate man.

When Albert visits Flip at a nursing home in St John's Wood, he connives at her parents' optimistic fiction that she is somehow getting better, whereas the reverse is clearly the case: she remains haunted by the possibility of nuclear extinction and by the more specific notion that her father, who holds conservative views on the matter, wants it to kill her off. Outside the nursing home, Albert notices 'a pigeon that had been pinkly squashed by a passing car (one wing stamp on the macadam like a diagram in a book on flight) and from which a few feathers were still blowing';[69] as with the infantile water-colours earlier, the image suggests an unusually close correlation between Fuller's fictive and poetic imaginations, for its 'real life' source occurs in the poem called 'In Lambeth Palace Road':

> Not far, as the pigeon flies, from Waterloo,
> Where droppings are thick under glass awnings,
> To the roadway outside St Thomas' Hospital
> On which a pigeon is smeared as on a slide,
> To patients a supererogatory reminder.[70]

To Flip's mother, Albert blandly suggests that she is 'Going on all right, I should say',[71] but privately he feels 'that if Flip prolonged her illness she would find herself in some National Health institution',[72] as eventually she does. The novel's resolution, in fact, exactly parallels that of *The Tempest*: Flip's, or Ariel's, vanishing from the scene is the price of reconciliation between the exiled

Albert/Prospero and his rival, sealed by the marriage of their offspring. It is Eve who, with a frankness which disturbs Albert, explicitly defines the crucial part played by Flip's illness in achieving this: 'The only good thing in it is that it seems to have brought us together again, which I doubt even Fabian and Fanny getting married would have done.'[73] Yet it is not merely that frankness which must prevent an Albert (or a Prospero) ever being wholly assimilated by the quotidian world; he has reflected, much earlier, on the 'something wrong' with all creative people, and now he returns to an idea which has haunted the entire novel:

> I think of the Persian world in Flip's brain whose existence she had so alarmingly hinted on the day of the wedding. Could one say anything of this to Eve; could one ever have said it, even in those long past moments of ecstatic love and admiration for her physical being? And it dauntingly strikes me how imperfectly the healthy understand us, though some actually buy our books, give us honours from their world.[74]

There is, as one might expect from the Shakespearian parallel, an epilogue; but this triumphantly – and unexpectedly – owes more to a quite different book, *Howards End*. Forster's redemptive conclusion finds Helen's child, free but lovingly watched over by her mother and aunt, in the summer garden at Howards End; Fuller's has Freda, the child of Fabian and Frances, with her mellowed if no less ruminative grandfather, in his Oxford garden in September. In each case time has passed, and healed. Albert and Freda play an invented game called 'not very well today', and then he tells her a rather good moral fable about Bear and Snake. The novel ends with a lovely image of seasonal decay and regeneration, but before it does so Albert arrives at his own moment of unsentimental, earned redemption:

> I see that the mere fact of still not being destroyed represents a human triumph. One forgets how short a time needs to be rescued from the odds for happiness to reconstitute itself – for a new generation to establish itself in the very arena where its parents quarrelled.[75]

★

That book's hard-won affirmative ending has a resonance which echoes well beyond the novel itself: for Fuller, the years of prolific

fiction-writing had coincided with – had indeed been the necessary response to – a period of personal crisis and poetic unproduc-
tivity. Stephen Wall, in his review of *My Child, My Sister*,
commented: '...if it seems to have in the context of his career an
unusual significance, it has in itself a distilled quality, as of a work
that has confronted its own limitations and has refused to be belit-
tled by them.'[76] He was right in more than one respect.

My Child, My Sister bears no explicit dedication, though its
closing pages may serve in place of one; its companion-piece, *The
Father's Comedy*, prefiguring the later book's *Tempest*-allusions, is
dedicated as follows:

TO PRUE
The King of Naples, searching by the magic water
That had his son transported, also found a daughter.

'Prue' is Cicely Prudence Martin, whom John Fuller married on 20
July 1960, a month after graduating from New College, Oxford.
The irony of his son's rapid and successful achievement – in which
he took immense pride – of exactly the life his younger self would
have envied was not lost on Fuller: marriage and a degree in 1960,
a first child and a first book of poems in 1961, a visiting lectureship
at Buffalo, New York, in 1962. It was a sequence of events to
remind him of his own youthful missed opportunities and to make
a middle-aged father feel suddenly old – as is similarly the case with
both Harold Colmore and Albert Shore. For Kate Fuller, her only
son's marriage was devastating: 'Her devotion to John approached
adoration, and for years she was not reconciled to the idea that he
could have got married at all.'[77] If *The Father's Comedy* and *My Child,
My Sister* present their respective central characters as rebuilders of
relationships and peacemakers between estranged generations, there
is some reason to suppose that Fuller knew what he was talking
about. The unstated dedication of *My Child, My Sister*, incidentally,
is surely to Sophie, the first of his three granddaughters: they would
also renew his interest in writing for children – later on in verse, but
initially in the Swiftian allegory *Catspaw* (1966), in which the
debate about political ideology is transferred to the cats and dogs of
Pussia and Dogland.

During this period, Fuller seems to have written fewer poems
than at any other time in his adult life. The *Collected Poems* of 1962,
published to mark his fiftieth birthday, contains a mere thirty-five

pages of work uncollected since the publication of *Brutus's Orchard* in 1957, a respectable but slender harvest for so productive a writer; moreover, his next separate collection, *Buff* (1965), seems comparatively thin too. Recognising the ways in which his creative energy was diverted into fiction does not, however, fully explain why it was diverted away from poetry. One inhibiting factor was the very existence of that *Collected Poems*, a book he came quickly to dislike, regarding it as both too interim and too inclusive: for years afterwards, he would alert other writers to the perils of producing such volumes, for example advising Alan Brownjohn in the late 1970s 'not to hurry with a Collected – so often a premature demise.'[78] He also disliked the thoughtful yet grudging treatment given to *Collected Poems* by Graham Martin, who discussed it in the third number of *the Review*. Martin's inability to identify the albatross in 'The Emotion of Fiction' would later be mockingly paraded in an Oxford lecture, 'The Filthy Aunt and the Anonymous Seabird'.[79] All the same, Martin's observation that 'though Fuller is to me a more interesting poet than, say, Graves, it's not easy to forget that he seems to lack Graves' faith that poems are worth writing'[80] was – in 1962 – a telling one.

With the hindsight afforded by *New Poems* (1968), it becomes obvious that Fuller was coming to the end of one poetic seam and was looking for a fresh, unmined one; yet something of the sort might have been deduced from his own comments at the time. When Alan Ross took over *The London Magazine* from John Lehmann and launched his 'New Series' in April 1961, Fuller became one of the 'Editorial Advisers': modestly effacing himself from the all-star cast announced on the cover of its 'Poetry 1962' special number, he nevertheless responded to its questionnaire in a typically dry and quietly mischievous manner. One question – about 'poeticization' of language versus 'natural' diction – elicited a cryptic hint about his own imminent change of style and a wonderfully undeceived piece of self-parody:

> Of course, one isn't aware that diction *has* become artificial until the new diction comes along. There is much 'poeticization' even in the plain diction used currently by many poets – in the very convention of the sort of poem that starts 'I remember my accountant father' or 'I see an earwig cross the path'. Perhaps this is 'undue impoverishment' enough.[81]

Even if the connection between accountant father and solicitor poet seems a little tenuous, the similarity between the earwig on the path and the spider in the bath[82] is plain enough. Despite his triumphantly extended range in *Brutus's Orchard*, Fuller still felt trapped by the quotidian world – apt background for his fiction, but a constraint on his poetry – and its increasingly predictable embodiment in the iambic-lined lyric. A potential remedy lay in the creation of dense, semi-fictive sonnet sequences which could develop beyond the modest scope of his self-contained lyric pieces. The first of these, 'Mythological Sonnets', comes at the end of *Brutus's Orchard*;[83] 'Meredithian Sonnets' form the most substantial group added to the 1962 *Collected Poems*;[84] while *Buff* is framed by 'To X'[85] and 'The Historian'[86] (the non-sonnet sequence 'Off Course',[87] though not published until 1969, is also related to these poems). These sequences, anticipating though quite different in tone from the sonnets of Fuller's last years, have been rightly admired; yet they seem to me to represent both a strategic evasion and a deliberate biographical conundrum.

The set of sixteen-line 'Meredithian Sonnets' is best regarded as a technical adventure in which fragments of the author's own life appear only obliquely. Though the sonnets may be Meredithian in form and theme (recalling Meredith's best-known book, *Modern Love*), the voice which informs them is that of Wallace Stevens, a perilous influence for a poet of altogether leaner diction: for this is the Stevens of 'Sunday Morning' – plum-pudding poetry which seems impressively rich and nutritious until, quite suddenly, it becomes intolerably dull. And that is rather the effect here. The protagonist, Donald E. Stanford confidently states, 'is not Fuller, he is not even a poet though perhaps a poet manqué...';[88] but this is to substitute a certainty for an intended ambiguity (and, if not a poet, what is he doing 'Racking his memory for a useless rhyme'[89] at the end of Sonnet XII?). We know that he cannot 'create', which may mean, more poignantly, that his creativity is inhibited or stifled rather than non-existent. Certainly he is middle-aged, unhappily married, obsessed with unfulfilled dreams of affairs with younger women; but he is not (as Stanford asserts) 'a post-war Prufrock', for where Prufrock lacked emotional experience, this protagonist is cursed with the memory of 'that foul spell cast long ago / By some malicious uninvited elf / Who ordered him to love a purple flower.'[90] The bitterness is the more pungent for poisoning a benignly familiar allusion: though Puck's mischief-making is not in doubt, *A Midsummer Night's Dream* is, after all, a comedy which ends with the promise of *happy* marriage.

The husband padding upstairs in Sonnet XVI, away from his sleeping wife to the maid in the attic, plainly does not live in Langton Way, Blackeath; but it is equally plain that the insomniac reading at night about the owl and contemplating its habits in Sonnet XVII does. This blurry moving in and out of character, though wonderfully convenient for Fuller, does tend to reduce the power of the sequence: both the protagonist and his context lack the carefully crafted detail which makes the fictional heroes convincing in their own right, even though they so frequently resemble to their author.

The chief exhibit here is, of course, 'To X', which in describing an affair between a middle-aged man and a younger woman links even more closely with the novels. It is notoriously difficult to read first-person poems entirely as 'fiction', and only an improbably incurious reader could fail to wonder what Fuller is up to here. Either he is writing about an actual affair; or the affair is a fantasy based on real people, an imagined office romance perhaps; or the whole thing is an invention. His own straightforward-looking explanation teasingly fails to distinguish between the two latter alternatives: 'To X', he said, consisted of 'twenty-one rondels about an imaginary love affair – the precise number and form of the sequence called *Pierrot Lunaire* which Schoenberg once set to music'.[91] Nevertheless, 'What close friends have wondered chiefly is whether the 13-line sonnets for X were an account of an actual love affair,' writes Julian Symons. 'I've no idea, nor have others who've asked me about it... Roy,' he adds, 'was not a confiding man.'[92] One might have thought that Symons would have known, if anyone did, for the sequence's title is an allusion to his own first book of poems, *Confusions About 'X'* (1939). It also obliquely refers, again, to Stevens: 'In a big, boring Yankee biography of Wallace Stevens, it is recorded that he possessed *Confusions About 'X'*. Do you think he pinched the X idea from that? Though I haven't checked, I think the poems of his in which X appears are after 1938.'[93]

Like the Meredithian sequence, 'To X' is an exercise in sonnet-mutation: 'love poems by a kind of sonnet out of a kind of villanelle,' as Alan Brownjohn puts it.[94] It was a notion which would continue to fascinate Fuller. 'Many poets,' he wrote in a review of Edmond Leo Wright's *The Horwich Hennets*, 'must have wanted to write a sequence that would avoid the awesome responsibility of the sonnet sequence yet give a chance of some development in the individual unit'.[95] Here, each poem is of thirteen lines, of which two groups (1, 7 and 13, 2 and 8) are identical apart from adjustments of punctuation, and each contains only two rhymes: as an attempt to create a new diction, the strategy is the polar opposite of the unrhymed syllabics to come in *New Poems*. The rhymes soon make their presence felt:

> The car arrived that brought you to the place:
> As you got out I saw your very groin.
> Thus goddesses, nude, upon a distant quoin
> Reveal their chaste religion to the race.[96]

The three remaining rhymes for 'groin' are 'join', 'loin', and 'macedoine'; so there is more than a little piquancy in Fuller's suggestion, just two years after *Buff* (but by then completing his unrhymed *New Poems*) that Arnold Rattenbury should discard from *his* forthcoming collection 'those poems... where the meaning has to struggle too violently with the rhymes.'[97] Yet, even apart from the rhymes, the diction is outrageously stilted – presumably not by accident but as a way of distancing the subject. This interposition of wilfully baroque language between a writer and material which might otherwise seem uncomfortably close-up owes much to the author who recurs above all in Fuller's reading but who is not a poet, Henry James. James and Stevens – an intriguing pair, both highly-wrought stylists and in their literary procedures conspicuously unAmerican Americans – are the most powerful, and the most perceptible, of the literary ghosts who haunt Fuller at this time. Their presence suggests that he was experiencing a mid-career crisis and that, like many middle-aged writers disenchanted with the contemporary cultural worlds around them, he turned for reassurance to self-consciously mandarin literary figures.

The oddest consequence of this can be seen in the slighter anecdotal pieces in *Buff* – poems more obviously suited to an earlier demotic mode or, of course, to that triumphant fusion of 'high' and 'low' styles which was to come later on. In 'Bagatelles', Fuller's characteristically quirky and accurate observation is deployed in a way which anticipates *From the Joke Shop* but is tripped up by his over-insistent if ironic worries about the mismatching of real life and high art:

> I stop my car to let a girl,
> Carrying a dog, cross the road;
> And think 'Girl with a Dog', but wonder
> If in fact art is better than life.[98]

Or:

> Does a big nose go with playing Bach?
> No more than a collection of Van Gogh
> Postcards with the breasts of fourteen.[99]

The touches of wilful dodderiness and queasy voyeurism in these strange squibs amply confirm Fuller's wisdom in making Albert Shore somewhat older than himself: the stance when adopted by a poet merely in his early fifties seems uncomfortably arch.

The 'Bagatelles' are the work of a writer caught between incompatible stances and modes, and the same feeling of betwixt-and-betweenness is teasingly contained in *Buff*'s epigraph: "'Methinks Buff smiles.' 'Buff neither laughs nor smiles.'" This tension, resulting from a particularly complicated sort of middle-aged crisis, reappears in other poems of this period. In 'Versions of Love', for example, he imagines a textual crux in Shakespeare – it should presumably be in *Hamlet* – in which the Bad Quarto's 'My love for you has faded' and the Folio's 'My love for you was fated' are emended in scholarly if unmetrical fashion to 'My love for you fast endured':

> But this conjecture cannot quite destroy
> The question of what the poet really wrote
> In the glum middle reaches of his life:
> Too sage, too bald, too fearful of fiasco
> To hope beyond his wife,
> Yet aching almost as promptly as a boy.[100]

Shakespeare's baldness, like George Garner's beard, has an air of clownish disguise about it, imposing a degree of distance hardly intended to convince. Meanwhile, if emotional life could be troublesome in Fuller's 'middle reaches', the relationship between art and professional life was proving no less tricky. In 'The Zouave', he considers a reproduction of Van Gogh's painting on an office wall and glumly concludes:

> Art serves the social man, who at this moment
> Writes a report on how a certain law
> Affects the being of the corporation
> (Which hired the office and the reproduction)
> In the world of its rivals and its profitable
> Scope.[101]

For Fuller in the early 1960s – emotionally restless, professionally disillusioned, and deeply dispirited by much of the society around him – the providential intervention of an entirely new and rejuvenating poetic style swiftly followed by his election to an ancient university's most prestigious literary chair would no doubt have seemed the stuff of dreams. Yet that was precisely what would happen in the late 1960s. Not all crises of middle-age are so benignly resolved: if there is a recurrent note of gratitude and even serenity in the final third of Fuller's literary career, it had been well-earned.

Part Three: Blackbirds and Debussy

1: The Double Nature of Nature

❧❧ ❧❧ • ❧❧ ❧❧

The disarmingly plain title Roy Fuller gave to his 1968 collection, *New Poems*, is in fact full of resonance. His first book, published almost thirty years earlier, had been called simply *Poems*, so the intended fresh start couldn't have been more clearly or confidently signalled. Technically, the poems are 'new' – and not just recently-written – because they mark two departures from Fuller's previous practice: he uses syllabic rather than accentual metres, and he avoids end-rhymes. 'The springs of verse are flowing,' he writes, 'after a long / Spell of being bunged up',[1] and his readers seem generally to have welcomed the book as an effective solution to the problems posed by an increasingly congested and constrained style: '...he doesn't exactly break free,' said Ian Hamilton in the *Observer*, 'but he does manage to loosen a few screws.'[2] Flowing springs, loosened screws: the chief effect of the syllabics – often denigrated as an impossibly artificial form – is to unclog Fuller's diction so that his cadences become not only more natural but also more memorable than in much of his earlier work; and this is all the more significant since, having successfully achieved an unforced meditative speaking voice in *New Poems*, he was able to transfer so much of the benefit back to his subsequent metrical writing.

In two of his Oxford lectures ('An Artifice of Versification'[3] and 'Fascinating Rhythm'[4]) and two equally interesting later essays ('Boos of Different Durations'[5] and 'The Bum-Bum Game'[6]) Fuller would investigate the matter of syllabic and accentual metre in some detail. His syllabic practice in *New Poems*, influenced mainly by Auden and by Marianne Moore, was of a straightforwardly pragmatic sort, as he explained in a lecture to the Royal Society of Literature in February 1968:

> Indeed, when one comes to employ it one sees that its apparent arbitrariness and faint absurdity are really not so, for since one works in lines of an odd number of syllables one is working at what seems to be a logical extension of the problems of the normal

English metrical line. Behind the eleven-syllable line, for example, is the ghost of the iambic pentameter, but the constant intrusion of just one extra syllable removes the sense there is about blank verse that its possibilities of variation have already been exhausted, or at any rate discovered, by the great practitioners of the past. Nor is one worried that the iambic may accidentally occur... It has other incidental advantages – for instance, quotations from prose writers can be worked into the fabric of the poem.[7]

That is the refreshingly businesslike voice, infuriating though it may be to more theoretically-inclined critics, of the poet with his sleeves rolled up – and, moreover, thoroughly relishing the practice of his craft. 'An Artifice of Versification', his third Oxford lecture, also shows how practically invigorating syllabics had proved to be for Fuller in his own work:

The use of the technique, if not dictated by mere fashion, must reside in providing an escape from iambic clichés, a chance of making a fresh music. From the poet's point of view, as I can testify, the technique can provide a way into the composition of a poem, particularly at the dry start of a period of poetic productiveness, by freeing him from the preliminary need to hear his subject, his *donnée*, his initial observation or image, as song – or at least the often elusive song of traditional stress metre.[8]

In choosing the title of *New Poems* he may have had Rilke's example (*Neue Gedichte*) in mind, though his epigraph – as slyly ironic as *Buff's* – is taken from Michael Hamburger's translation of Hölderlin:

A mystery are those of pure origin.
Even song may hardly unveil it.
For as you began, so you will remain.[9]

Later in the book he describes the phrase 'those of pure origin' as untranslatable;[10] and the original text, also quoted on the title page, gave him some trouble too. Suspecting an error in his transcription of the German, he wrote to Michael Hamburger; the letter is worth quoting for its remarkable, utterly characteristic combination of extreme scrupulousness and engaging lightness:

Can you solve a textual crux anent my epigraph? As I think I said to you once, my German is totally non-existent, & to my dismay a friend told me that she thought in line 3 it could not possibly be 'anfiengst'. So I have checked the quotation against the text in your big Hölderlin – to find that 'anfiengst' is OK but that apparently 'Reinentsprunges' should be 'Reinentsprungenes! Consternation! I hied myself to the London Library but with limited time between legal chores could not find the poem in the enormous Stuttgart edition, though in an earlier edition (which looked respectable) it was certainly 'Reinentsprungenes'. However, this *could* be an error or misreading carried into the German side of your edition.

What does Stuttgart say? What do *you* say? André Deutsch says it can't be 'Reinentsprung*enes*', but after all he is Hungarian! If there is a second impression I want to make any necessary correction – that is why André has come into it.[11]

Fuller's anxiety in the latter case, seemingly as unspellable as it was untranslatable, proved justified: the misprint was duly corrected in *New and Collected Poems*, where the epigraph is transferred to the head of the poem 'Those of Pure Origin'.[12]

However, 'as you began, so you will remain.' The truly astonishing, and for Fuller desperately welcome, aspect of *New Poems* is the way in which they enable ideas which had bubbled away in his poetry for years to achieve at last their properly fluent expression. Even the unexpected intervention in several poems of plural, uncapitalised gods is not so much an indication of a new self as a relaxed restatement of the old one – or, typically, of old *selves*:

> No one could be more suspicious than I of
> The sudden appearance of divinities
> In middle-aged verses, but how else to describe
> The double nature of nature in epochs
>   Of creative happiness?[13]

The notion of the double self, which torments so many of the novels' central characters and which appears to be painfully irreconcilable in a poems like 'The Divided Life Re-Lived', at last settles into this extraordinarily harmonised consonance: 'The double nature of nature'. He makes a similarly optimistic point in the Oxford lecture 'Professors and Gods', where an assortment of double selves – 'the savant and the layman, the professor and the god, paleface and redskin, Apollo and Dionysus' – is resolved into art:

Truly civilized man has to play both roles but, as Benda asser-
vates, in the one person. And art should be a reflection of that
tricky unity – a unity not of opposites but of the potentials in
human nature and human society.[14]

At the heart of *New Poems* is a complex, ruminative piece called
'Orders', as centrally important a poem in Fuller's work of the late
1960s as 'The Ides of March' had been a decade earlier. It opens in
the deceptively, almost dangerously relaxed mode so typical of his
later poetry, with lines which on the surface seem merely descriptive of suburban wildlife:

> All through the summer a visiting quartet –
> Father and daughter blackbird, pigeon, squirrel.
> Soft cluckings in the tree announce the blackbirds:
> First it was him, daring the dangerous sill;
> Later brought his Cordelia of the brood –
> She pouting and shivering, rather remote.
> Now in her nature like all other daughters
> She drives him off the grapes and bread I scatter.
> Slate-flat, slate-blue taffeta tail embraced by
> Matronly wings, gray marbled evenly gray,
> The pigeon drops draughtsmen on the terrace squares,
> Patrolling ceaselessly. And in the mornings,
> Anxious at the window, one hand clutched at heart,
> My chinless friend, with soil-crumbed neurotic nose,
> And tail a brush for cleaning babies' bottles –
> Disconcertingly like Sam or Sue Squirrel.[15]

It takes a moment to recognise that this is not the soft-centred stuff
it appears to be. Of course, there is the title, with its suggestion that
these orders, natural or otherwise, are to be in some sense exemplary. Then there is the way in which the natural description is
modified, on two distinct flanks, by allusions to art ('quartet',
'Cordelia') and to specifically human life ('like all other daughters',
'cleaning babies' bottles'). But it is the bridging idea of the blackbird Cordelia, mischievously described as 'Now in her *nature* like
all other daughters', which hints at a subtext lurking behind these
and many other lines in *New Poems*:

> The word 'Nature', as is well known, has several meanings.
> Romantic Nature, for example, is an invisible energy behind the

things we see. For some of the Elizabethans, on the other hand,
Nature means the visible creation regarded as an orderly
arrangement. In the course of time 'Nature' changes its
meaning. Furthermore, in any single period more than one
meaning for the word may be current. And, most significant
thing of all, some of these meanings will quarrel.[16]

Those words are from the opening chapter of John F. Danby's study
of *King Lear, Shakespeare's Doctrine of Nature* (1958); the chapter is
called 'The Two Natures'. So devoted a Shakespearian as Fuller
would certainly have read the book, perhaps after it appeared as a
paperback in 1961, and it is not surprising to detect its influence in
poems written during the 1960s: while 'The double nature of
nature' in 'The Visitors' transfers Danby's idea to a different
context, 'Orders' provides the reference back to *King Lear*. That, of
course, is why 'in her nature' is so knowingly disingenuous:
natures, like orders, are plural.

Bearing this in mind, it comes as no surprise either to discover
Fuller, immediately after those opening lines, reading J.B. Bury and
puzzling over 'That mysterious prae-Aryan foreworld':

> Not really understanding the phrase, dimly
> Conceiving a life before the oil-nurtured
> Legions, before the language of short, hard words,
> Before the death ships, the bronze, the chalk horses,
> Which now survives only as our consciousness
> Of the dotty element in our natures...

What Bury's phrase has prompted – though the transition seems so
inevitable that Fuller himself may not have been fully conscious of
it – is a modulation from one Shakespearian debate about nature to
another. For it was Caliban, after all, who found in language 'short,
hard words' – 'You taught me language; and my profit on't / Is, I
know how to curse'[17] – and who, according to Prospero, was 'a
born devil, on whose nature / Nurture can never stick';[18] and these
are precisely the terms Fuller chooses. He goes on to consider
briefly an alternative image of 'the prae-Aryan foreworld' – 'a tiny,
round, thinly black-haired head / Called to the colours from a
cretin valley' – before reaching the still more unsettling idea of an
'unmemorialed existence / To which we may be doomed' after the
(possibly imminent) end of civilisation; this conjecture leads, via a

paragraph-break badly misprinted in *New and Collected Poems*, to
reflections on a deliberately unspecific war:

> The quite senseless war
> Through summer days will run into winter days,
> The war that during my life has scarcely stopped.
> And the government that I elected, like
> All governments, whether elected by me
> Or not, will be powerless or uncaring.
> How strange that in this sphere my desire should be
> Always so different from the general will!

These lines will sharply remind us that the 1960s was the decade of
Vietnam, the India-Pakistan war, the Arab-Israeli Six Day War and
the Nigerian civil war, among others (Fuller's concerns are also
voiced through the character of Albert Shore's son Fabian in *My
Child, My Sister*). They indicate, too, how far we have come from
the wildlife quartet on the lawn; yet there is a sense in which the
progression has been seamless – nothing as unfocused as a stream of
consciousness, but a sequence of associatively linked meditations
well-served by the quietness of the syllabic form. And, thirdly, they
reaffirm some of the enduring qualities of Fuller's poetic character –
humaneness and intelligence allied to a persistent sense of exclusion.

There is one more player, as it were, to be introduced into the
poem, and that is Goethe:

> 'There is no bridge between directional time
> And timeless eternity,' wrote the gloomy
> German; 'between the course of history and
> The existence of a divine world order.'

The quotation is so elliptical and so lacking an obvious context that
we might momentarily wonder whether Fuller's fondness for
incorporating quoted prose in syllabic verse isn't misplaced (we
might also regret 'gloomy / German', a mannerism somewhat akin
to his habit of calling Americans 'Yankees', though perhaps not as
regrettable as 'the Kraut' for Heine in 'On His Sixty-Fifth
Birthday').[19] It proves, however, to be the unifying thought behind
the entire piece; and here, exactly at the centre of the poem, Fuller
begins to draw his own apparently disparate images together
around it. For, as he says, 'the principles ruling / The stuff that
surrounds us' – a homelier formulation than 'timeless eternity' or

'divine world order' – have no connection with 'bird-song, bird-love, the propulsion of metal / Into men'; the gulf between orders, and natures, is greater even than that conceived by Shakespeare or by John F. Danby. Characteristically, the agnostic Fuller is not altogether displeased by this absence of an eternal order in the things around him: worldly time, which 'will change my egotistic young blackbird / Next year to a care-worn mother' is enough to be going on with. And if, as Goethe insists, the 'Idea and common actuality / Must be kept strictly separate', then:

> Very well:
> Assign the business of being a poet
> To an order of things entirely divine,
> And the anguish to its historical material;
> And accept the consolation (in Kafka's terms)
> Of a wound that precisely fits the arrow.[20]

The resigned tone effectively tempers the sententiousness of an idea which might have seemed absurdly grandiose if less judiciously put. Here at last is the key to the writer's inescapably divided self, to the double nature of nature: the divine vocation in constant creative tension with its temporal subject-matter.

It is a brilliant formulation, not least because Fuller recognises that a scheme in which the divine accorded with the worldly would be 'even more frightening'. And in an elegant coda to the poem – lines which represent his syllabic writing at its most fluent and refreshed – he obliquely recalls the mythical consequences of just such an accord:

> And what if ourselves became divine, and fell
> On the pitiful but attractive human,
> Taking the temporary guise of a swan
> Or a serpent: could we return to our more
> Abstract designs untouched by the temporal;
> Would we not afterwards try to get back those
> Beautiful offspring, so mortal, so fated?

The implication that the temporal world is beautiful *because* it is mortal and fated is, like all Fuller's reaffirmations of faith in humanity, the more affecting for being won somewhat against the odds, by a writer who can sometimes seem embattled or alienated. Reaching the end of the poem, we may also notice that its casually ruminative structure is carefully designed: it consists of successive movements, of unequal length, comprising expositions and developments; the second of these introduces, at its internal paragraph-break, a quite specific second subject. The form is, in fact, deliberately symphonic; and that conclusion, its 'Beautiful offspring' returning us to a modified version of the opening theme, is very typical of late romantic – Mahlerian, say, or Elgarian – symphonic writing. In this it implicitly echoes themes from elsewhere in the volume: for instance, 'Sinfonia a Gran Orquesta', where the Ariaga [sic] symphony is juxtaposed with 'Feeling my heart about to accelerate, / I swallow a pill of phenobarbitone';[21] or 'The Symphonist' ('Is it the Sixth were the initial / Largo is chased by two raspberry- / Blowing rondos?').[22]

Though none of the other *New Poems* quite matches the balance of intellectual scope and fine detail in 'Orders', the sense of relaxed movement between meditation and observation distinguishes several of them. 'Windows' is a closely-related example, with the unobtrusively precise description so typical of Fuller at this point ('Sometimes the sky has a ghostly lampshade or / Countenance watermarked in it') leading into the contemplation of a bird beyond the glass:

> And one's fingers against the pane are stopped, by
> A force that whitens the nails, from seizing the
> Dove in their grasp. How tender the world outside
> Seems to be, how full of things one could adore –
> Were it removed, then, this manner of vision,
> Should I fall in the wings of a vast embrace?[23]

Asked which, if any, creatures he preferred to human beings, Fuller once replied 'All.'[24] He told Jonathan Barker 'that Naomi Lewis went right up in his estimation when he heard of her work in attempting to help wounded pigeons in the streets of London';[25] and, in 'To an Unknown Reader', he writes: 'It's part of the character we share to fret / About the animals we've condemned.'[26] Yet his tenderness is continually self-aware and undeceived, grounded in his perception of human shortcomings rather than in anthropomorphic invention. This is especially striking in the poem 'In Memory of my Cat, Domino', where a perilous subject is treated with exemplary honesty:

Rising at dawn to pee, I thought I saw you
Curved in a chair, with head raised to look at me,
As you did at such hours. But the next moment,
More used to the gloom, there was only a jar
And a face-cloth. Time enough, nonetheless,
For love's responsibilities to return
To me.[27]

The poem starts not from the cat's putative qualities but from the human's foolish susceptibility to delusion; it is this frank self-knowledge which immediately validates 'love's responsibilities'. And by continuing to focus on his own strategy for dealing with his 'mourning and loss', Fuller achieves an effect which is at once touching and tough-minded.

When *New Poems* appeared, Fuller was fifty-six: by no means old, yet old enough to have constructed his own imaginative and intellectual world. It is in many ways the book in which he at last seems to feel at home; and in the final poem, 'Last Sheet', he wryly notes some of that world's consolatory furnishings:

...Suddenly it's autumn, I think, as I look in the garden –
A gloomy dripping world, tree-tops lost in cloud.
Is it possible anyone so silly can
Write anything good? I don't hear, like poor Virginia,
The birds outside the window talking Greek. I see
My blackbird visitor and wonder where he sleeps,
As sleep he must. And catch my face in the pane,
Becoming ancestral, a cartoon of the mask
To which I've always been indulgent. And turn
To put a disc of Debussy on the machine:
This is what I'd have written had I had genius.[28]

Blackbirds and Debussy: one could, after all, do a lot worse.

★

Fuller, of course, had no more legitimate claim to be an 'Oggsford man' than the great Jay Gatsby himself, since he was 'not actually a graduate of any school except life';[29] nevertheless, with his son a serving Oxford don and one of his fictional heroes (Albert Shore in *My Child, My Sister*) a retired one, he had both actual and imaginative affinities with the place. His election in 1968 as Oxford Professor of Poetry – he succeeded Edmund Blunden, who had resigned the post without completing his five-year term – thus brought him into an environment of agreeably tempered unfamiliarity. When Blunden was appointed, few people outside the relatively contained worlds of Oxford and literary gossip had taken a great deal of notice; two years later, however, universities and poetry had both become more newsworthy topics, and this combination of the two proved irresistible to the media. Bookmakers offered odds, while the press (as would subsequently become the custom with other literary appointments and awards) treated the occasion as a combination of publicity-stunt and horse-race; the *New Statesman*, meanwhile, ran a mock-election of its own, soliticiting the views of well-known literary Oxford graduates, from which Fuller emerged as clear favourite (to the paper's literary editor, Anthony Thwaite, he sent a grateful note 'from your Conservative candidate, with thanks'). The other candidates – who included Yevgeny Yevtushenko and Adrian Mitchell – were a colourfully ill-assorted bunch. Some of them, or their sponsors, played up to the media; but John Fuller, in a well-judged piece of insider dealing, merely ensured that a copy of his father's *New Poems* was placed in each Senior Common Room.

In the event, Fuller's runner-up was Oxford's own resident contender, Enid Starkie, who had organised the successful campaigns of Day Lewis in 1951, Auden in 1956 and Blunden in 1966. The latter success was at the expense of the Maurice Bowra-backed Robert Lowell, so her own defeat by Bowra's preferred candidate on this occasion settled an old Oxonian score and embodied more than one sort of poetic justice: Blunden's resounding victory over Lowell had been widely condemned as an appalling instance of literary xenophobia.[30] Fuller would later say that had he known in advance of Starkie's 'perfectly sensible' candidature 'I may well have declined to stand myself',[31] but the remark represents the triumph of chivalry over judgement: in 1968 she was already eccentric and ill, and she died early in 1970. The victorious candidate, finding that this anachronistic and somewhat dotty contest had brought the fame that thirty years of publishing actual books had failed to bestow on him, reported back to Norman Lees in Blackpool with irony-tinged pride:

> I actually won th'election and since then chaos has descended in the shape of the mass media and a hundred or two letters –

including one from a lady who nursed me as a baby and one from a Supply Petty Officer in charge of the rum in a troop ship I once voyaged in! As to the mass media, at one stage a chap called, I think, Whittaker, from the Lancashire Daily Post telephoned and I rashly mentioned your name as one of my few remaining contacts with those parts. He claimed to know you well and perhaps he has subsequently pestered you. Hard to be both discreet and amiable on such occasions.[32]

Two months later, Fuller's evident pleasure in his new-found celebrity had been outweighed by irritation at its irrational cause:

Katharine [Lees' daughter, Katharine Cooke] is right when she says that the publicity has probably boosted my sales – my new books of poems is actually sold out & has been re-printed & it looks as though my *Collected Poems* will have to be re-printed as well. Ludicrous state of affairs, for I'm just the same writer I was before the election! Many importunate editors, lecture-arrangers & lunatics have written to me & indeed still write.[33]

Meanwhile, Oxford's academic establishment breathed an almost unanimous sigh of relief on finding that its most public literary honour had landed in such capably safe hands: Fuller was greeted with a 'uniformly generous' welcome which recognised him as the saviour who had rescued the university from variously inappropriate, if potentially comical, alternatives. The drinks and dinners with distinguished elderly dons, who once would have intimidated or infuriated him, now flattered his increasingly conservative persona. And Oxford's lucky escape was also, in a different sense, his own: still a full-time employee of the Woolwich as its senior solicitor, he had sought and obtained the consent of his chairman, Sandy Meikle (who was shrewd enough to see that any inconvenience to the society would be immeasurably outweighed by the prestige of the appointment), before standing. Implicit in this was the assumption that Fuller would in future be less concerned with the Woolwich's day-to-day legal work; he was appointed to the society's board in the following year and succeeded as solicitor by his assistant, Mark Preston, who recalls the election as 'some sort of catalyst... an event which very strongly prompted Roy in his late 50s at last to take the decision to leave the law and concentrate on writing'.[34]

Nevertheless, his triumphant election to the Oxford chair –
which seemed, in one simple move, to liberate him from total
commitment to the Woolwich, provide regular excursions to a
congenial place, and vastly enhance his literary standing – was more
complicated than it seemed. Even though English students in 1968
were, with the exception of those at Essex or the LSE, less excitable
than their Parisian counterparts, it was inescapably, in Stephen
Spender's phrase, 'The year of the young rebels'. At first, in
February 1968, this seemed to Fuller a cause for guarded optimism:

> ...as the sixties end, though the response of the young is not yet
> political to a situation which above all else is political (as it has
> been throughout my lifetime) it is nearer so than at any moment
> since the war – and therefore, it seems to me, the more capable
> of requiring and initiating poetic order.[35]

One unexpected consequence of the militant mood, clearly
evident in the somewhat embattled tone of his Oxford lectures,
was that the ideals to which he had remained loyal, of a culturally
enabling socialism, suddenly seemed to bounce wrongly, like
mysteriously defective tennis balls. Instead of appearing civilised
yet teasingly subversive, he struck many of his audience as merely
reactionary; while the fact that he had forged a literary career out
of an ordinary rather than a specially privileged life, working for an
ideologically defensible mutual institution rather than for a frankly
capitalist corporation, considerations which ought to have
endeared him to left-wing students, perversely led him to appear
insufficiently exotic. Of course, the cussedness which made him
such an invaluably awkward member of boards and committees
played its part: in his very first lecture, 'Philistines and Jacobins', he
took delightedly mischievous swipes at The Beatles and other pop
musicians (dismissed, in a word calculated to cause maximum irritation, as 'kitsch') as well as 'the James Bond and Liverpool poets
cults';[36] he lamented the confusion of highbrow and lowbrow
culture, just as Constant Lambert had done in *Music Ho!*;[37] and he
mischievously cited Matthew Arnold's view that 'As for rioting,
the old Roman way of dealing with *that* is always the right one;
flog the rank and file, and fling the ring-leaders from the Tarpeian
Rock.'[38]

But his Oxford audience should have had wit enough to see
what he was up to. 'I think my only virtues,' he told Alan Ross, 'are

(a) a nose for the phoney and (b) a continuing reliance on things I became convinced of in my youth';[39] while an interview he gave to the *Guardian* in 1970 shows how he envisaged his professorial role beyond the lecture theatre and how doggedly consistent his literary stance had remained since the 1930s:

> The young man at Oxford who hasn't made up his mind what to do but feels he has literary and academic leanings has actually no conception of the strategy of his life. He thinks vaguely of a job with a publisher or in the BBC but he cannot conceive a sort of humdrum life which produces creative work as well. The fact that someone is on hand who has done this may be a kind of reassurance that there is some kind of life to be made without dotty bohemianism or perennial studentship.[40]

Those final coat-trailing words, though they form part of a tenaciously held view, are not wholly uncomplicated either: readers who suspected Fuller of unconsidered anti-student hostility both missed the point and fell into the trap he had mischievously sprung for them. In one of his most wide-ranging and deeply engaged lectures, 'The Radical Skinhead', he slyly accused 'the young' of lacking 'literary discrimination', choosing favourites as if 'picking the coconut wheels from a bag of liquorice allsorts';[41] renewed his assaults on middlebrow culture, media vulgarisation and (not for the last time) Arts Council support for trendy 'events'; and then assured his presumably astonished audience:

> My two years in Oxford have confirmed what I previously conceived, that the best minds of the rising generation are not only not inferior to those of past generations but also possess special qualities of seriousness, gentleness and compassion, no doubt stemming particularly from the post-War reduction in educational exclusiveness and from better teaching and, above all, from the sense of appalling danger and unrivalled opportunity rising from the contemporary situation of mankind.[42]

As ever, he was the double man, negotiating his own self-contradictions. For instance, in February 1970, he wrote to Arnold Rattenbury about the troubles at the University of Warwick, where a sit-in had been provoked by the interference of powerful business interests in university affairs, unequivocally siding with the students:

Saw copies of the Warwick documents while I was in Oxford, through a couple of left-wing undergraduates, friends of John's. Though one *knows* such things go on, that doesn't make them less blankly stupid & sinister when one sees the evidence.[43]

Encouraged, Rattenbury urged him to send a message of support to E.P. Thompson, who was to provide in a Penguin Education Special called *Warwick University Ltd* a well-documented account of the affair. Thompson had told Rattenbury that such messages, 'the eminenter the better', would be useful and that 'the floors were cold and uncomfortable and that poems to read would help! Not poems about Work-Ins, not poems by Adrian Mitchell, just poems. He is a cultured man.'[44] Fuller's response is revealing and endearing, a masterly balancing-act:

I didn't send a message to Warwick. Mainly it was that I've evolved a fairly rigid rule not to sign things (and so forth) unless the impulse is already there, comes from my own volition. But also my sense is that protest on matters of this sort is more effective on a more considered occasion: in fact, I was working on an Oxford lecture for next Hilary Term which had to do with this topic when Warwick broke; and I shall risk the whole thing being out of date by then (but I don't think it will be). Moreover, I'm not convinced that Sit-ins, Work-ins and the like don't confuse the important issues with the stupid ones – and mix up the real radicals with the merely gormless. Did you see that cartoon in *Private Eye*? Two students, one long-locked and bearded, opening files. The other student: 'It says you're a hairy twit.'[45]

It is a cautious, discriminating response – as ever, Fuller is at pains to disentangle the worthwhile from the bogus – but it is certainly not an unsympathetic one. For a contrasting, truly splenetic view of student unrest, one has only to turn to the letters written in the same period by Philip Larkin: 'Did you see that poncing student of ours shooting off his mouth to the Press Association... Fuck the whole lot of them.'[46]

All the same, the experience of Oxford – where, according to Anthony Thwaite, Fuller 'to some extent found himself ignored' and 'where at the moment of writing [1973] many students... are distrustful of what they regard as arid reasonableness'[47] – certainly nudged him towards a more cautious conservatism. Replying to the *London Magazine* questionnaire in 1962, he had boldly declared: 'I just wish English poets would be less cosy and self-satisfied and inbred as a group, and that their poems would take imaginative flight from the first person.'[48] But when he came to answer a similar question for the magazine *Tracks* in 1970, the combination of Sixties populism and professorial disenchantment prompted a rather different line: 'My hope is, and I don't think it an entirely idle one, that the greater interest in poetry will ally itself to better taste and skill. Particularly, I hope English poetry will extend the *English* tradition, not follow some bastard mid-Atlantic mode.'[49]

Among the people Fuller met for the first time through his Oxford professorship were an elderly poet and a young editor. In working with syllabic metres, and in preparing both the FRSL lecture 'Poetry in my Time' and the Oxford lecture 'An Artifice of Versification', he had come across the syllabic poetry of Elizabeth Daryush, Robert Bridges' daughter. She had been born in 1887, a year before Fuller's mother and 'early enough for her arrival to have been commented on by Gerard Manley Hopkins',[50] so he was understandably if irrationally surprised to discover that she was still living at Boar's Hill, outside Oxford, where she invited him to visit her after an exchange of letters in October 1969. Her father had been a celebrated prosodist, of course, while Daryush had explained her own use of syllabics as long ago as 1934; her work was championed – in his typically grudging, Jaques-like way – by another great poetic professor, Yvor Winters, who thought her 'a very minor poet but at her best a fine one... Her technical virtuosity within very short poems is sometimes brilliant.'[51] Stockwell, Boar's Hill lived up to its literary ghosts, for there Fuller found himself 'in the vanished world of Bridges, Masefield, the young Robert Graves – a large house but rather spartan; a courteous reception from the owners; provision of good coffee; literary talk'.[52] In her letter of invitation, Daryush had promised to show him her recent, unpublished work. She was as good as her word: he left with the manuscript of a new collection of poems.

In an optimistic spirit of Oxonian loyalty, he took the book to Jon Stallworthy at Oxford University Press; they had published Daryush in the 1930s but were disinclined to renew the association. Fuller consequently offered the manuscript which became *Verses: Seventh Book* to a new small publisher based just outside Oxford – at Pin Farm, South Hinksey – which had grown out of the undergraduate poetry magazine *Carcanet* and was run by the President of the university Poetry Society, Michael Schmidt, whom he met in February 1970. After reading it, Schmidt told Fuller: 'I have read the book closely now, and can say frankly that I don't like it at all. But I see the point of publishing it as an historical piece.'[53] The collection duly appeared in 1971, with an introduction by Fuller (a selection from Daryush's earlier work appeared in 1972 and a *Collected Poems*, introduced by Donald Davie, in 1976). In *Spanner and Pen*, Fuller would recall how 'even then Michael was practical and enthusiastic about bringing into print (or back into print) the unfashionable (as well as promoting new authors), though one had no conception of the substantial and remarkable publisher he would become'.[54] His association with Carcanet, and with Schmidt's subsequent magazines *Poetry Nation* and *PN Review*, was to continue for the rest of his life. Fuller advised the firm on possible solutions to its not infrequent crises of under-capitalisation, suggesting as early as 1973 that 'may be there is no real alternative to becoming part of a larger body, not necessarily a publishing firm – perhaps a printer who wanted to diversify';[55] he nagged editors, such as John Gross of the *TLS*, when they were slow or reluctant to print reviews of particularly worthy Carcanet books; he was responsible for arranging Carcanet's publication of Allen Tate's *Memories and Essays*; and, after leaving the Arts Council, he wryly admitted that 'when I was Chmn of the Lit Panel shunting money to the Corn Exchange was one of the very few things I did with a clear conscience.'[56]

★

In the New Year's Honours for 1970, Fuller was awarded the CBE; the timing of the ceremony made it almost a birthday present for him. 'I collected my bauble from the Palace this week,' he told Norman Lees on 12 February:

> As I said to Kate thereafter, the Empire is now in safe hands. I've worked fairly hard since I retired, and so have two short books coming out one at the end of this year and the other at the beginning of next. But the Profship or impending old age or both brings [*sic*] a great many unwanted chores in the literary and academic worlds which seem to keep me from actual *writing* almost as much as did the dear old law – or at any rate writing

what I really want to write. One of the books referred to above is in fact my first six lectures at Oxford, so there is an element of cheating about that.[57]

The other book, published in the autumn of 1970, was his novel, *The Carnal Island*: its central characters are, as it happens, an elderly poet and a young editor. In distinct if oblique ways it seems to develop themes brought sharply into focus by Oxford – the relationships between youth and age, art and life, culture and history – yet these were, after all, matters which had always concerned him. Equally, like so much of his later work, the book is nourished by his wide and varied reading: 'When I was thinking about the novel,' he told Raymond Gardner, 'I read about an old love affair Hardy was supposed to have had which resulted in an illegitimate child.'[58] This was the remarkable theory, propounded by Lois Deacon and Terry Coleman in *Providence and Mr Hardy* (1966) – and carefully demolished by Robert Gittings in a *TLS* article reprinted as the appendix to his *Young Thomas Hardy* – that 'The young Thomas Hardy... had a child by a very young girl [Tryphena Sparks], ostensibly his cousin, but really his niece.'[59]

Another perceptible though transposed influence is Christopher Isherwood's *A Meeting by the River*, which had been published in 1967 and which would, indeed, have provided an equally apt title for Fuller's book: Isherwood's reunion of two brothers – an exact parallel for Fuller's double life or divided self – is transformed into the no less revelatory encounter between young and old writer, while the opening exchange of letters hints that this book also may have been planned as an epistolary novel. Isherwood, an early and enduring influence on Fuller's prose, is a ghostly presence in other ways too: *The Carnal Island*, like *The World in the Evening*, is a novel which takes its title from a fictional literary work within it; while the fictional writer Bob Calwell is an ingenious composite character in which Isherwood (along with Auden, Spender and Plomer) is certainly an ingredient.

The Carnal Island is the most subtly-written of all Fuller's novels – it was the only one he redrafted, and he thought the others 'suffered from not having more drafts'[60] – as well as the most compact. It is set in a single weekend, almost entirely between the afternoons of Saturday and Sunday, and its preliminary business is briskly dispatched in brief flashbacks and a series of letters between

James Ross, a young poet who works as a publisher's editor, and
Daniel House, born in 1890 and widely regarded as 'the most
distinguished living English poet'.[61] They have already met once, at
L'Escargot, during one of House's rare visits to London on literary
business. House, as Ross then discovers, exactly resembles his
familiar book-jacket image: 'a photograph, much reproduced
presumably through lack of choice, of an elderly man with bulging
forehead and noticeable moustache, dated in the history of fashion
by a double-breasted jacket in herring-bone tweed'.[62] Here, not for
the last time in the novel, Fuller is making deft creative use of an
occasion from his earlier in his own life – in this case, from 1944:

> I admit to being awed when the party joining us was E.M.
> Forster... what enured was the incongruous, the potentially
> comic – the eminent novelist's brown-suited insignificance,
> inclining to the shabby. I used elements of the occasion more
> than twenty-five years later for the first meeting of the old and
> young poets in my novel *The Carnal Island*.[63]

Since James Ross narrates the novel in the first person, it is almost
inevitable that Fuller should have recycled autobigraphical material
into his life as well as into House's, but the choice of viewpoint is
significant, and not merely for practical reasons: after all, Fuller's
own date of birth, 1912, puts him chronologically closer to the old
poet than to the young one. In *My Child, My Sister*, he had created
a narrator older than himself; five years later, in *The Carnal Island*,
he needed to make the opposite adjustment (and the same would
be true of *Stares*). The point is reinforced by some pleasingly elliptical jokes. At the very start of the book, House apologies for refer-
ring to Wallace Stevens' essay 'The Figure of the Youth as Virile
Poet' as 'The Figure of the Poet as Virile Youth'; 'I prefer your
title!' says Ross.[64] Later, he recalls a story purportedly by Calwell,
which precisely parallels the ageing novelist's predicament:

> I thought of Calwell's story – it was in his second book – of the
> vaudeville artist whose 'act' is his impersonation of an old man.
> As his career goes on he needs to use less and less make-up, until,
> indeed, vanity and the fear of appearing to theatre managements
> to be too decrepit to fulfil his engagements compels him actu-
> ally to make up to look younger. Long before the end he has to
> drop the dénouement of the act, which was the snatching off of

the 'bald' wig and the nose wax just before the final curtain; while the point of the act, the phenomenal acrobatic agility of the 'old' man, becomes more agonizingly effortful to achieve.[65]

Of course, there is also a great deal of Fuller's background in House: Northern childhood, legal training, affectionately knowing asides about Rent Acts (House troubled by the clash of ideologies, like Fuller over Mrs Borders).[66] Above all, they have in common a wryness of literary temperament: 'The poetic character,' House observes early in the book, 'is one of constant feigning';[67] and, later, 'If only one's art hadn't always to be ironical.'[68] Nevertheless, Ross's is the mind we are asked sympathetically to inhabit – with its youthful enthusiasms, nervous hesitations and sudden blundering confidences – and among the book's many qualities is the skill with which Fuller creates and sustains his tone of voice, even if there are disconcerting moments at which James Ross seems a prematurely middle-aged young man, as when he has to sit on his bed 'the more safely to take off my pants'[69] or is assumed to worry about getting his hair wet, 'an insight not far from the mark'.[70]

Ross has arranged to visit House at his coastal home, which is carefully unidentified, to try to talk him into editing an anthology: the location bears some resemblance to the Isle of Purbeck but seems to be sited further west, and Fuller has superimposed wartime memories of the Shotley peninsula in Suffolk as well as 'the dark shape of a lighthouse or other phallic monument'[71] from St Mary's Bay in Kent. Ross has the feeble, imperfectly worked-out ulterior motive of planning an unannounced visit to an old flame whose parental home is *en route*. She, of course, is elsewhere: the consolation for the reader, if not for the narrator, is a slight but perfect vignette of the residents' lounge in a country hotel where Ross is obliged to spend Friday night. On reaching his destination, he is promptly bitten in the ankle by House's dog, perhaps the best of several excellent animals in Fuller's fiction, who is called Prince or Rascal:

'He answers to both names,' said House, as though this denoted unusual talent. 'Rascal got abbreviated to Ras, and that naturally became Prince Monolulu which in its turn became shortened to Prince. Typical linguistic evolution.' He was about to walk on but changed his mind and added, after a moment's thought: 'I say "naturally" but of course you're too young to remember the famous racecourse tipster Ras, Prince Monolulu.'[72]

People not only talk to animals but through them: the dog –
elderly, irascible and eccentric, his master's familiar – enables House
to reveal an unfeigned, affectionate generosity which is not otherwise easily accommodated in his life. Yvonne, his second wife, a
former publisher's secretary and much younger than himself, is
solicitous but detached: one peculiarity of their relationship,
borrowed from Kate Fuller's war-time fellow-tenants Mr and Mrs
Denton, finds House 'scrabbling gently on the door' of her
bedroom in the early hours;[73] when he 'wanted in *The Carnal Island*
to suggest marriage's hidden strangeness,' he 'remembered the
Dentons' bedroom door.'[74] It is strangeness, not unkindness: as in
My Child, My Sister, Fuller's attitude to human oddity is one of
mellow yet unsentimental benevolence.

The Carnal Island is of course an autumnal novel, both in
House's personal chronology and in its seasonal setting. The note is
struck, with almost outrageous archetypal symbolism, early on, just
after House and Ross (and indeed Rascal) have finished their tea in
the garden:

> He might very well not see another summer. One realized
> why all his recent verse recorded so scrupulously skies, birds,
> light, flora. He poked with his walking-stick into a cavity at the
> base of the apple tree and succeeded in bringing out several
> squarish lumps of rotten wood, like bad teeth, from which a few
> earwigs crawled. 'Do you think if I squirted some wood preser-
> vative down here it would help?' he said. 'I filled the hole with
> cement a few years ago, but the bloody parasites seem to have
> eaten that as well. Very sad. The old tree seems doomed.'[75]

Within the limpid simplicity of this passage is a vital clue to the
nature of *The Carnal Island*: for the book should be read partly as a
codicil and a counterbalance to the Oxford lectures, to which it
adds quite different kinds of perception about literary creativity.
The recognition here of the way in which the likelihood of imminent mortality sharpens one's appreciation of recurring seasonal
phenomena is of course made all the more acute by its perfect
fulfilment in Fuller's own poems.

Indoors, after tea, shown to his room by Mrs House with her
'severe bun'[76] and 'evidently unabundant favour',[77] Ross reflects
that 'A guest room is a museum, illustrative of past epochs of the
host's life.'[78] This is true both of the objects (a bed formerly slept in

by its owner; 'superannuated paperbacks', including *The Portable Nietzsche*, conveniently book-marked) to be found in the room and of the significant view from its window of the 'island' which is really a peninsula, 'the locale of House's erotic poems of the late twenties';[79] there is also, of course, the punning sense of House having become his house. That pun's more serious implication – the consonance of man, place and past – is a motif which recurs throughout the novel. Downstairs, Ross discovers House now dressed in maroon velvet jacket, bow tie, and felt slippers: the effect is quirky yet coherent, unmistakably literary but a far cry from the dubious bohemianism of Garner's beard and hairy jacket. He is recharging an ancient soda-siphon: his neighbour, Colonel Dodd, who is to join them after dinner, likes soda in his whisky, which is decidedly not to his credit; it is the kind of detail, like the smoking-habits of the Woolwich board, which Fuller always found, and was able to make, telling. Meanwhile, the other guests at dinner are to be Bob Calwell and his boyfriend, 'Billy something', who 'owns a snack-bar, perhaps two or three. Bob's very lucky to have found him.'[80]

This gathering is artfully constructed. The absence of any heterosexual erotic distraction – remedied later in the book – prompts conversation in which irony shades towards campness; Bob and Billy, whose culinary interests stretch well beyond snack-bar sophistication, seem to represent a successful marriage of art with life; yet Bob is a writer who has fallen silent in the post-war era, a failure which House (before Calwell's arrival) interestingly ascribes to the state of England itself. The voice is unmistakably Fuller's – or, more precisely, it is *one* voice of Fuller's divided self, and Ross tentatively articulates another:

'Since the General Strike – or slump, if you like – something has taken place in England. Something vague, perhaps not very important. I think it occurred in the ranks during the last war. Bob Calwell missed it. There's been nothing else, unless you count a monotonous series of wrong by-ways taken.'

'Are you saying that artists have therefore been *ipso facto* condemned to failure?'

'To insignificant status.'

'I should want to think that out.'

'Imagine a writer,' said House, 'overwhelmingly possessed of the only important notion of our time – that every action must be devoted to the correct changing of society – passing his productive years in the England that's existed since 1945.'

'But there are other important notions. Death. Love. And so on and so forth.'

'They sound daft as soon as you mention them,' said House, in what might be imagined to be his Leeds manner.[81]

Ross's more affirmative, and equally Fullerish, response to this dilemma of the writer in an indifferent society is to propose that there is 'always a margin for the artist to work in'. It is a notion somewhat redefined over dinner itself, when House gives an account of his hernia operation ('the ideal trauma for the ancient poet') and the incidental pleasure of 'a young nurse pressing a suppository up one's backside': 'It was part of the artist's working margin, though as originally propounded I'd had something rather different in mind.'[82] The point has an importance beyond the anecdotal: so much of Fuller's late poetry attempts to redefine, and rehabilitate, material which might have been considered marginal in this sense.

The Dodds, making their appearance after dinner, serve mainly to confirm House's susceptibility to hopeless desire – Ross overhears Colonel Dodd rebuking him for his indiscretions with field-glasses, which appear to be trained on 'Angie', presumably a daughter or even granddaughter – and to unsuspected conventional dullnesses such as playing bridge. Ross's reflection on this, though reasonable as far as it goes, for once betrays his youthful naïvety:

> Of course, it was absurd to imagine the celebrated poet by virtue of his status immune from the trivialities of existence as from frustrated lusts. A glimmer came to me of the desolation of his life, not only in the exacerbations of its day to day grind but also in its absence of expectancy, of future change – though no doubt all was redeemed by creativity, the prospect and achievements of creativity.[83]

This is of course only partly true; yet, in reformulating Albert Shore's perception that creativity fills a void which would otherwise be occupied by intolerable despair, Ross is made to re-state a point which goes to the heart of Fuller's own creative life and explains the poetic fecundity of his later years – for which, in retrospect, *The Carnal Island* may serve as prologue or manifesto.

However, the most engrossing part of the evening is still to come. After his other guests have left, House takes Ross into his study, pours two large whiskies, and talks about names:

'John House is a more plausible name for an English poet than Daniel House. I couldn't have thought so in 1917 or whenever it was. Or perhaps I had the idea that a poetic reputation might damage my name as a barrister. Then when they asked me about it before painting my name at the entrance to chambers, I said, "Put J.D. House". It never struck me that I could have published under that cognomen. But later on two initials became very fashionable…'[84]

And later on again, of course, when Julian Symons advised R.B. Fuller to call himself Roy in 1937, they would become unfashionable once more; while in 'Chinoiserie' Fuller records how 'eventually' his own poetic reputation 'Actually incremented my income / And stopped hurting my respectability.'[85] Such chronological cross-references seem exactly right for the occasion: the late-night conversation in House's study with its uncurtained French windows overlooking the estuary. As Fulke Greville so marvellously put it: 'The present time upon time passed striketh.'[86] When House puts on a record of Jimmy Guiffre, 'actually pronouncing it right', Ross thinks: 'That House's out-of-dateness should be so nearly up to date was touching as well as surprising.'[87] The creative moment is not so much outside time as the sum of different times perfectly superimposed, like congruent images on overlaid transparent sheets. When House leaves the room ('Old codger's weakness'), Ross has his moment of epiphany:

Left alone in the semi-darkness, the whisky-glass preternaturally hard in my fingers, a slight air creaking the french windows, I felt as thought I could write down some hitherto unimagined words — as though, indeed, the actual writing of the words would be superfluous, since the insight they would show would always be with me, communicable at will.[88]

The insight may be treacherous, as much to do with whisky as with creativity, but it is no less necessary for that. Ross seems to compromise the privileged moment, however, by failing to resist the temptation to glance at House's diary, finding himself unmentioned on the day of their meeting in London. Yet that too is salutary and instructive: he is only just earning his place in House's life, though House may already have come to occupy the imaginative centre of his.

While, according to House, the truth can never be told, 'a better version of it can be established';[89] he seems to be paraphrasing Charles Tomlinson's 'The artist lies / For the improvement of truth. Believe him',[90] though a poet so elderly as to appear at one point unfamiliar with Auden is perhaps unlikely to have come across Tomlinson. But it is fair warning that the confidences he imparts to Ross – about his affair with a woman who lived on the peninsula and his fathering of an illegitimate daughter, born in 1924, who still lives there and whom he proposes to visit next day – may not be uncomplicated. The peninsula, the carnal island, is perhaps the place where life and art most closely intersect, where truth is improved by symbolism and myth.

When they set off next morning, the expedition does seem in some way fated. They travel to the river in House's 'small elderly Austin' which, not at all to Ross's surprise, he admits to having put 'upside down in a ditch';[91] they cross the river on a still more decrepit ferry, whose boatman we shall later discover is called Charlie (almost, as Ross reflects, a familiarisation of Charon). While they wait on the quay, another of Fuller's law-defying pubs, for it is Sunday and surely not yet midday, provides drinks. Ross, we feel, has been admitted to House's book of life – he would certainly by now desrve a mention in the diary – by being precisely the kind of young writer of whom *Fuller* would approve, someone over whom the *zeitgeist* 'had only wafted superficially':

> I was touched. 'I believe you're trying to flatter in your clumsy old-fashioned way. What do you want?'
> 'You're giving it,' he said. 'You know in L'Escargot I was quite on tenterhooks that eventually you'd say something foolish. Or, rather, something that would show we weren't on the same beam after all. Not that I agreed with everything you said. By no means. But you never peeled off a layer that revealed a soft centre. How rare that is. Think of that ass Rupert Doings.'[92]

If literary activity involves improving the truth, then it also demands concealment and a particular sort of toughness: House's formulation is stringent as well as generous. The 'ass', incidentally, is Rupert Dalton, organiser of a festival in which House has declined to take part, and very much the type of modish littérateur who would cause Fuller intense irritation in his later years.

The first person met on the peninsula proves to be Jan, House's granddaughter, previously unmentioned and immediately attractive, her father a long-vanished feckless deckhand; her mother, Margaret, though the 'inheritance of House's noses prevented her from having any good looks', has grey hair which 'had been dark, the hair of the girl in *The Carnal Island*'.[93] They, and Jan's friend Linda, lunch at the kitchen table in the house once tenanted by Margaret's grandfather, latterly bought by House, in which this chain of illegitimate, alternative lives had begun. Once again, as in Greville's memorable image, past and present seem to strike against each other. For House, approaching his eighty-fifth birthday, the occasion prompts him to reflect on the repetitious habits of the elderly writer, and to reformulate an idea touched on the previous evening and crucial to Fuller's own career:

> 'The poetic persona I used to assume was always much older than my real age,' House was saying. 'Though one completely failed to understand the deficiencies and disasters that would actually arrive with the years. Even now I could present myself as wholly decrepit instead of partially so.'
>
> 'Rather like that story of Calwell's about the music-hall impersonator.'
>
> 'Yes, yes.' He did his imitation of a Shakespearean actor laughing like an old man.[94]

Fuller, voicing through House with prescient exactness the concerns of his own last years, was not yet sixty when he wrote *The Carnal Island*.

After lunch the girls, egged on by House, decide to go swimming, and it is then that Ross, feeling 'curiously cheated, like the reader of a detective fiction who finds the solution depending on a clue unfairly withheld by the author',[95] discovers that Jan has a partially withered leg. For Ross, the revelation suggests 'Ibsenesque symbolism'; the reader, however, will more immediately recall the psychological illness of Flip in *My Child, My Sister*. In each case, the desired and idealised girl proves to be incurably blemished: it is partly that the ideal cannot be allowed to survive unchallenged, partly that the older man (though in Ross's cases he is not that much older) must be punished for his lascivious intent. And if that implies a sternly conventional moral perspective, it also confirms each book in its transcendental, symbolic ambitions. When, after the swim, House and Linda absent themselves in a rather implausible search for fossils, Ross at least manages to hold Jan in a brief embrace which is all the more touching for its decorous hesitancy; if the restraint seems uncharacteristic of the late 1960s, it is consistent with Ross's other unyouthful traits and with House's opinion of him as 'a sagacious young man'.[96] The moment passes, the others return, and the four of them go off for tea in the garden of an establishment which House grandly describes as 'Mrs Walton's emporium'.[97] It is a late afternoon in autumn; and the novel, like the day and the season, begins to turn towards its inevitable conclusion:

> Jan proffered the cake. A small leaf drifted down and actually settled on it. I tried to track down my sudden sense of unlightened melancholy, at first ascribing it to the season and then realizing it resided in this last dish on the table. Only a few mouthfuls separated me from the totally unsatisfactory state of Jan's absence.[98]

Alone once again on the quay, waiting for Charlie to cross from the opposite shore, the two poets return to the theme of art's ability to improve on the truth while remaining true to itself. Art, argues House, can eventually almost ennoble our deficiencies through what he calls its 'consolations' and Ross its 'transforming power' (Fuller astutely gives the more modest but serviceable term to the more experienced writer), though a note of caution also follows from this: 'After all, life's something other than art, even in the latter's naturalistic manifestations – even for the artist.'[99] When the boat arrives, Charlie proves to be a dourly alcoholic Scot, doubtless recalled, like the vessel itself, from Fuller's days in the navy; he claims to have had two vessels torpedoed under him in the war, though House suspects that he probably spent his time hiring out rowing-boats at Oban: 'Everyone lies about the past.'[100] This distinction between such lying and the improvement of truth which turns a peninsula into a carnal island is of course a fine but important one. On the borderline stand those works which engage with both life and art: obituaries, biographies. 'Autobiographies also lie,' says Ross, and House adds: 'So do biographies.'[101] He wonders whether Ross will now attempt to unravel the secrets of his life, the Jamesian figure in the carpet:

'If it were feasible,' House said, 'I'd like to prevent any biography.'

It struck me with alarm, with an awed sense of possibilities, that perhaps seeing the non-feasibility he'd chosen me for the task: wanting in particular a sympathizer to spill the beans that were undoubtedly going to be discovered by anyone rooting about in the past.[102]

The catastrophe is Forsterian. In its abrupt extinction of the novel's spiritual centre, it recalls the death of Mrs Wilcox in *Howards End*; in its shocking physical suddenness, it is more like the death of the child in the overturned coach at the end of *Where Angels Fear to Tread*. Typically, Fuller has reached deeply into the past, to the drowning incident at the Kenyan bathing-place, to authenticate his emotional and psychological grasp of the moment. When the bows seem about to crash into the quayside, the disaster is briefly averted; then the stern hits a pile, and the vessel sinks within three minutes. Labouring in the water with his 'old man of the sea', Ross is 'struck more than anything by the sense of the world's unfairness in assuming that I was capable of saving him':

> Then both House and I were being supported by strong arms from a rowing-boat. It seemed typical of my *ex post facto* nature that when rescue was certain I should yield him up reluctantly. How curious our physical intimacy in the sea, unparalleled by anything else in the close contacts of the weekend![103]

Despite Ross's efforts, House has died of heart failure by the time they have been brought on to the quay.

There is a brief epilogue, in which the capable and considerate Yvonne visits Ross in his hospital bed: it is appropriately low-key, a reaffirmation of quotidian decencies which are as valued in this book as they were in Fuller's life. But the reader will rightly feel that the novel's consuming interest dies with House, and that the few pages following it must have something of the obituary tone so recently diagnosed by House himself. 'Like ordinary people,' Fuller wrote elsewhere, 'poets long to be loved. But all that is necessary is that they should be understood.'[104] By the end of *The Carnal Island*, we may astonishingly feel that we have come both to love and to understand House; and, through him, his author too.

2: Part Managerial, Part Poetic

The Oxford chair and CBE were honours enough to crown any poet's life, and they might have been followed by another slim volume or two, and an updated *Collected*; but Fuller's later years were not to be at all like that. Quite apart from his much more considerable literary productivity, in the 1970s he would be greatly in demand as a respected member of cultural committees – at the BBC, the Arts Council, and the Library Advisory Council – for which his unusual blend of legal and literary expertise precisely suited him. As Jonathan Barker, who worked with him closely at the Arts Council and Poetry Book Society, rightly observes, Fuller's 'quality of getting to the heart of an institution and serving it effectively was a lifelong thing'.[1] He could also be an effective institutional saboteur, which may on occasion be at least as valuable.

As a prelude to all this, however, he received a second and more prestigious honour later in 1970, when he was awarded the Queen's Gold Medal for Poetry. 'Just heard this morning I go to Buck House on December 2,' he told Julian Symons; 'lucky my interest in racing is not yet dimmed.'[2] These two occasions, and subsequent meetings with Her Majesty, both at Buckingham Palace and at the Royal Society of Literature, turned him into an unexpectedly devoted monarchist, even though he kept all the paperwork connected with royalty in a file labelled 'ALF GARNETT'.[3] At the RSL 150th anniversary poetry reading in 1975, the Queen asked his opinion of Ted Hughes: 'Well,' Fuller replied, 'he certainly looks like a poet.'[4] Naturally, he was unsurprised by Hughes's appointment as Poet Laureate nine years later, though he over-scrupulously failed to make use of his insider knowledge when he could have placed a substantial bet on this outcome with William Hill at odds of 5-1. Perhaps the formative experience of regularly losing with Briggs and Lees on 'The 220' had left him with an enduring sense that actually winning money by gambling was a notion scarcely to be contemplated. Gambler or not, his interest in racing remained, as he said, undimmed, and so did his enthusiasm for football. Indeed, the crucial matter in that

letter to Symons of 11 November 1970 is not his impending visit
to 'Buck House' but a jauntily perceptive match report:

> Fired by that pleasant outing to Stamford Bridge, I went to the
> Valley last Saturday. Nearly another neurotic fiasco, but the boys
> rallied nobly in the last quart d'heure, and Kenning equalised with
> a fine shot. Plumb and Went not bad... but Bond too intellectual
> for the particular brand of Div. football played that afternoon.[5]

His allegiance to Charlton Athletic presumably played no part in
securing his invitation to join the BBC's Board of Governors,
though in a sense it ought to have done – for it neatly reaffirmed the
congruence between his own wide-ranging cultural interests and the
concerns of public service broadcasting. Taking up his appointment
on 1 January 1972, just over a month before his sixtieth birthday, he
must have been inescapably reminded both of his own earlier self-
definition as 'Part managerial, part poetic'[6] and of Yeats's description
of himself in 'Among School Children' as 'A sixty-year-old smiling
public man'.[7] And, indeed, the BBC provided a good deal for him to
smile about: of all the organisations with which he was associated, it
was the one which received – for a time, at any rate – his warmest,
least qualified approval. His age and his lack of a university education
made him unusually appreciative of the corporation's high cultural
role – particularly as exemplified by the Third Programme, *The
Listener*, and BBC-2 – but he had also retained a quirkily various
interest in more demotic cultural forms: John Dyer, one of his
Woolwich colleagues, remembers his enthusiasm for Sergeant Bilko[8]
while Julian Symons recalls his liking for 'comics from Sid Field to
Tony Hancock',[9] and Alan Brownjohn his even more improbable
enjoyment of Paul Daniels.[10] He was well aware of his excellent
credentials for membership of BOG (as the BBC's Board of
Governors was informally known), and uncharacteristically
immodest about them: 'If I may say so,' he wrote,

> I was an ideal governor: familiar with the arts; liking discrimi-
> natingly a good few popular entertainments, such as jazz and
> stand-up comedians; experienced in the law and the workings
> of a large corporation; and with a fair knowledge of the world
> of real property.[11]

As for those running the corporation, 'I doubt if any British organization, including universities and Civil Service, contained a

greater percentage of able brains and fluent tongues':[12] prominent among these were the Director-General, Charles Curran, and the 'truly excellent'[13] Chairman, Lord Hill, whom Fuller quickly came to admire despite the eccentricities of a past career which he lightly sketched in verses read at the dinner to mark Hill's retirement, on 13 December 1972:

> He in the past ('twas very odd)
> Had served first Mammon and then God
> In this same field of broadcasting,
> Yet managed to advance the thing.
> And prior to that he did not shirk
> Making the nation's bowels work.[14]

Hill was succeeded by 'another outstanding Chairman', Sir Michael Swann, formerly Vice-Chancellor at Edinburgh, with whom he shared a habit of tactful indiscretion noted in a later commemorative poem:

> Charles Hill was our dear Chairman then,
> Most openly devious of men,
> Whose love of letting gossip out
> (Before executives were about)
> Was hardly much improved upon
> By his successor, Michael Swann.[15]

'In appointing him to the BBC (Michael said), Edward Heath told him he thought of it as a university',[16] a view enthusiastically endorsed by Fuller. For him, it was 'a university open to all; an island of culture in the very areas where philistinism might be especially rampant'.[17] Though the island had already been eroded – for instance, by the introduction in 1967 of 'frightful' Radio 1 – that underlying notion of a modified Reithianism still seemed, in the early 1970s, largely unassailable. As late as 1982, he was staunchly (and optimistically) defending it:

> I would think of the BBC as something with cultural traditions and the ability to survive awful periods: I would put that with universities as things that might endure during some frightful dark age – dark age financially, dark age culturally. The Arts Council I would be inclined not to put in that category. But although I'm gloomy about the curve history has taken in my

time, which does seem to be, in Leonard Woolf's phrase, downhill all the way... I always have been aware of, to use a high-
faluting term, human spirit, which renews itself in the most
remarkable way.[18]

At the same time, the BBC also seemed to resemble another
institution with which he was much more familiar. 'Like building
societies,' he would write, 'the BBC is an admirable *echt*-British
creation which the rot of modern times does its best to ruin.'[19] He
was pleased by the symmetry as well as the convenience of the
Woolwich's board meeting on Tuesdays and the BBC's on
Thursdays, and liked to see himself as similarly indispensable to
each: 'battling all week with 'flu' in February 1972, he was nevertheless 'rising from my sick bed to go to the Boards of the
Woolwich & the BBC, wrongly feeling that neither organization
could carry on without my meddling';[20] two years later, he was
suffering from a 'devastating flu-y cold all week, during which,
with great nobility, went to my BBC & WEBS board meetings
(couldn't bear to let either organization get away with anything
without putting my oar in!)'.[21] Despite the characteristic self-
deprecation, the value he seriously attached to his attendance at
such meetings is plain enough.

Nor is there any reason to think him misguided: he was, as he
(again characteristically) put it, 'quite a good trooper, normally
giving decent value',[22] and he was an inspired choice even among
an evidently talented group of BBC Governors. Where his judgement was to prove least secure was, interestingly, not in the field of
popular entertainment (for which he had a genuine if nostalgic
affection) nor in matters of high culture (where his taste, as his later
poems amply suggest, was both wide and discriminating), but in
borderline areas where he perceived the latter to have been damag-
ingly tainted by the former. He cites one instance of this, minor in
itself but potent as an emblem of cultural misunderstanding, in
Spanner and Pen. He had been persuaded by the Head of Television
Music and Arts, Humphrey Burton, to address a meeting of his
department's staff about the role of the Governors, and he must
have seemed the ideal person to do so: however, rather as with the
Oxford professorship, there was a mischievous ingredient of
cultural mismatch in the air. Dennis Potter's play *Brimstone and
Treacle* had recently been withdrawn before transmission, and

Fuller found himself with a hostile audience keen to attack what they saw as gubernatorial censorship. Worse, his own appearance was followed by that of Potter himself, whose 'reception by the assembled staff was like that of a well-loved comic; his least observation received with warmth, often with laughter'.[23] It was an intolerable position, and a less civil man would have loudly said so; Fuller, however, politely sat through the proceedings until he had to leave to keep another engagement. Nevertheless, he could not quite forgive Potter:

> Middlebrow, but sexually and (to an extent) politically probing the limits of programming, Dennis Potter's art is regarded as high art within television. So much tripe is purveyed by the medium that this attitude seems plausible to many outside.[24]

Two points spice this occasion with retrospective irony. One is the reflection that, had he not been so discomfited by the *Brimstone and Treacle* affair, Fuller might have found much to like in works such as *Pennies from Heaven* or *The Singing Detective*, which had a good deal in common with his own fictions. The other is the fact that, in his 1993 James McTaggart lecture, Potter was to accuse the BBC of cultural dereliction in terms which Fuller would certainly, if perhaps a little grudgingly, applauded. By this time – with the intellectual downgrading of Radio 3, the steady transformation of BBC-2 into a channel not noticeably less populist than BBC-1, and the closure of *The Listener* – most of the principles tenaciously defended by Fuller during the 1970s had been surrendered.

Indeed, as he remarked in *Spanner and Pen*, 'even in my time a war had to be waged against degenerating standards in speech and decorum in BBC programmes'.[25] Some of his complaints seem exaggerated or priggish: he came increasingly to dislike coarse humour, dirty jokes, and an ever-expanding area of art which he dismissed as 'pornography'. His protests about the 'vulgar, even outrageous' nature of broadcast comedy and its 'sexual *double entendres*'[26] conveniently ignore the rougher side of the music-hall tradition, the obscene jokes and songs he cheerfully learnt in the navy, and even so relatively recent a phenomenon as the radio programme *Round the Horne* in the 1950s. Yet he was surely right to deplore the steady spread of mispronunciations, clichés and inaccurate grammar in BBC English – really examples of the mistaken belief that cultural institutions should be representative rather than exemplary – and to cite convincing instances (concerning the composer Sir Thomas Armstrong and the poet Arthur Waley) of Radio 3's reluctance to broadcast material which would once have found its natural home on the Third Programme. In his poem to mark the retirement of Lord [George] Howard in 1983, he offered a not wholly fanciful prophecy of the state of BBC radio a decade later:

> Or we could try perhaps to show
> Him tuned to Nineties Radio
> (Which some of us now here may miss,
> Reconciled thus to death's harsh kiss).
> On Radio 4, the news, then – news:
> Even on a news-fan the common views
> And common voices pall. George whisks
> To 3 for Desert Island Discs,
> Passing the local wavelength where
> Specially-blended rubbish blares.[27]

★

Reviewing Elizabeth Jennings's *Growing-Points* in 1975, and noting her change of publisher, Roy Fuller commented: 'the emphemerality of poetry lists and poets' publication difficulties are an unpublicized evil of stagflation.'[28] His own publishing arrangements, at any rate, seemed secure: *Tiny Tears*, which appeared in 1973, is dedicated 'For André, Diana and Nick commemorating twenty-one years of André Deutsch Limited', the firm whose list he had gratefully joined following Derek Verschoyle's failure in 1954; and it was swiftly followed by a further collection, *From the Joke Shop*, in 1975. After that, however, his relationship with Deutsch was to come to a surprisingly acrimonious end.

The two books are in several respects complementary. The first, which contains a wide-ranging assortment of forms and themes, stretches back to include occasional poems from the 1960s and, in the section called 'From an Old File', even earlier pieces; while the second consists of sixty-three poems in 'Iambics that keep falling in in threes'[29] which 'are almost all rooted in personal life and run chronologically from the Summer of 1973 to the Spring of 1974.'[30] The central images of their title-poems – a crying doll from a toy shop, false ears from a joke shop – indicate a shared ironic register whose lightness is always threatened by the grotesque. They indicate, too, the characteristic method of Fuller's late poems: after his larger-scale historical, mythological and philosophical projects, from *Brutus's Orchard* to *New Poems*, he turns to a mode in which the 'high' and 'low' styles combine as intellectual and cultural life is continually juxtaposed with quotidian oddities.

This mode is not yet quite as secure as it would eventually, and triumphantly, become: the somersaults of irony may seem over-insistent, the intended nudges of self-deprecation uncomfortably close to prods. When in 'To an Unknown Reader' he tries to assure the would-be or unpublished 'bathroom vocalist' of a poet that he or she is better off without 'a whole lifetime's remorseful exposure / Of a talent falling short of its vision',[31] that 'whole' seems dangerously over-emphatic, supporting a proposition which is simply untrue. The following piece of self-advice (from 'Diary Entries'), which he has no intention of taking, fails to convince in much the same way:

> A good thing on waking to drink cold water
> Through the nose (I read in some Yogi handbook).
> A good thing also to stop writing verses
> About one's ailments and daydreams of romance.[32]

Nevertheless, such self-conscious ruminations about the 'literary life in late middle-age'[33] become more touchingly effective in a trio of poems about his Oxonian connections. In the first, 'Mothy Invocation', which has clear echoes of Hardy's 'An August Midnight', he asks the moth to

> Fly westwards where the Thames divides
> And round the tawny city glides
> Whose name by luck enlaurelled mine.[34]

In the second, he reflects on the toothless Edmond Halley, his own unexpected election to an Oxford chair, and his increasing proximity to Halley's 'fish and pudding stage'.[35] And in the third, 'To my Grand-Daughters', he imagines with gleeful satisfaction the time when, at John Fuller's home in North Oxford,

> Your suitors will wait for you uneasily,
> Caught in the hall by the expert on Auden
>   And invited to join him
>   In some devilish word-game...[36]

These are poems validated by their author's straightforwardly honest pride in his own and his son's achievements; they also share a tone of rueful lightness with the poems for children which he was writing in the early 1970s, an overlap wryly acknowledged in 'The Poet: His Public' from *Poor Roy*:

> I wrote a book for girls and boys –
> *Seen Grandpa Lately?*
> I doubt if any child enjoys
> It greatly.
>
> But several grown-ups said to me:
> 'It's rather good –
> The first lot of your poetry
> We've understood.'[37]

All the same, *Tiny Tears* is inescapably, and in a mildly pejorative sense, a very literary book – the only one of Fuller's in which material drawn explicitly from the world of literature seems to overwhelm the quotidian world with which it is typically so well harmonised. This impression is confirmed by the poems on literary occasions (T.S. Eliot's memorial service, Auden's birthday), the homages and memorials (Kafka, Randall Swingler), and the allusive sonnets ('Sonnet 155' and the necessarily unrhymed 'No Rhymes'). The slightly unsettling new tone is plainly a spin-off from Fuller's Oxford years, during which many of these poems were written. The most successful are those which provide foretastes of the creative Indian summer still to come, a phenomenon quite recklessly prognosticated in 'Magnolia':

> My study has been repainted 'Magnolia'.
> Before, it was a sombre reddish brown.
> Surely a fresh creative period
> Opens, perhaps of spirituality.[38]

Yet the qualities of this 'fresh creative period' are much more accurately hinted at in another poem:

> After a few laps my old cat walks away
> From the saucer with an irritable jerk of tail:
> Five minutes later is back to try the stuff
> Again. And well I know the mood myself.

> How long shall I settle to these discs of Brahms'
> Late keyboard pieces? Yet what else but art
> Could I hope now might echo and assuage
> The tenderness and sadness of keeping house?[39]

Those first two stanzas of 'Late Period' precisely illustrate the intimate transactions between everyday life and high culture which
characterise the poetry of Fuller's last years; while the complex
emotion of the final sentence – with its discreet references to his
own retirement and to Kate's poor health, and its subtle echo of
Albert Shore's ruminations on the necessity of art in *My Child, My
Sister* – is handled with extraordinary delicacy.

Though it may be mildly anachronistic to speak of a poet in his
sixties 'finding his voice', that is exactly what seems to be happening
both here and in a wonderful poem called 'The Unremarkable
Year'. With its wry catalogue of things not happening, this resembles a distant, grown-up relation of Larkin's 'I Remember, I
Remember'. Typically, it begins by ruminating on the garden's bird-
life – 'The great thrushes have not appeared this year', unlike the
year in which they 'fell like a camouflaged platoon' – before gently
celebrating the virtues of unremarkableness:

> But there is much to be said for a summer
> Without alarms. The plum crop is modest,
> The monarch has remained unchanged,
> Small differences only in one's teeth and hair and verse-forms.[40]

The deliberately ludicrous juxtaposition of modest plum crop,
unchanged monarch and 'teeth and hair and verse-forms' turns out
to be, far from ludicrously, an instance of apparently unrelated ideas
brought into harmony, as the poem's final stanza elegantly
confirms:

> So that the year of painting the shed,
> Of missing strange calls, deep dappled breasts,
> Is also that of harmonies
> That have made one's life and art for evermore off-key.

The paradox of *harmonies* making 'one's life and art for evermore
off-key' is all the more disturbing for being quietly stated; yet it
amounts to nothing less than a reformulation of Hamlet's 'The
time is out of joint...'.[41]

Three subsequent collections – *From the Joke Shop*, *Subsequent to Summer*, and *Available for Dreams* – are explicit attempts to find coherent, unifying forms for such journal-like material. The first of these, with its relaxed iambic triplets charting a notebooky progress through the seasons, might seem almost too easy a solution, as Fuller frankly admits when he observes (after poems called 'Insomnia' and 'In Praise of Wakefulness'), 'The bedside notebook yields its gibberish';[42] and any reader intent on extracting a selection of duff lines from this book would have no trouble. Such a reader would be utterly missing the point, however, for the low-key or self-deprecating interventions always serve some counter-pointing purpose. This is made clear early on, in the poem 'Orphans', ostensibly about a fledgling pigeon, which turns first into a meditation on the conflicting notes of 'cosiness' and 'remorse' in his work and then abruptly into a more searching explanation of his interest in the subject:

> Calamitous, a bird's abandonment:
> But what about my own young orphancy?
> The unreachable corner where I hid or died?[43]

That sudden reaching-back to childhood, with its enormous implication about the effect on his own character of his father's death, leads naturally into the next poem, 'The Card Table' – the table in question being that at which his father, Issy Gotcliffe [*sic*] and the Weinbergs played – and thence, indeed, to the autobiographical article 'Long Time a Child' and to *Souvenirs*. To notice this is to recognise not only the intermingling of different kinds of creative material in the poetry but also the new fluidity of movement between verse and autobiographical prose, a medium he had not explored at any length since his war-time journal; understandably, the sense of the literary life as a single full-time occupation occurs at the point when, after his retirement from the Woolwich and with his Oxford stint complete, he found himself with an unfamiliar degree of freedom.

This leisure provides an abundance of absurdity. Sunning himself in the garden, he wonders whether he wouldn't make 'quite good material for compost';[44] reading the newspaper, he tears out a coupon for a strange device called a Spatter Guard, although the Fullers already have two;[45] shopping in Marks and Spencer, he decides that the revolution-triggering intolerable state might be defined as 'The prospect of not affording sausages';[46] while in Boots the Chemists, the 'oldish fellow' obstructing him proves to be his own image in a mirrored wall.[47] Such whimsical incidents are actually essential to the texture of a sequence whose mode is equally often elegiac: those commemorated include his uncle John Broadbent, Kenneth Allott and W.H. Auden, and there are also birthday tributes, not dissimilar in tone, to friends such as John Lehmann and Huw Weldon. The turning of the year through its autumn and winter quarters, the meditations on illness and ageing, and the consolatory invocations of music all reinforce this note.

Because of its complex, mutually enriching interactions, *From the Joke Shop* is best read as a single work; yet within it the most striking poems are perhaps those, like 'Orphans', in which Fuller writes about himself with an unusual degree of candour, which become more profound as the seasons darken and the sequence develops. In recalling his Uncle John, who died on 3 September 1973 and whose parallel careers as actor and administrator are memorably sketched in *Souvenirs*, he feels, suddenly and incongruously, almost homesick:

> A mile from here one might, if one so wished,
> Into the urban Thames expectorate.
> It strikes me that I'm very far from home;
>
> Yet this is where I've lived most of my life.
> A sorrowing infant on the Pennine moors,
> The borderer became a natural exile.[48]

This authentic vulnerability is all the more touching in an often somewhat guarded poet, and it is a recurrent motif. Indeed, once that mood had been established, other events of September 1973 seemed – as often happens – simply to confirm it. Thus, in 'Thirty Years On', he takes from its shelf his copy of Francis Scarfe's *Auden and After* (1942) to look up its reference to the recently-deceased Kenneth Allott, and notices that the book was a Christmas present from his mother in its year of publication, when he of course was in Africa:

> Faint memory of Christmas of that year:
> A Whitmanesque night-passage through the camp;
> Ratings with branches, bottles; all dead drunk.

> It's certain that I never sent my thanks
> So as to touch my mother's worried heart;
> And now, in Allott's words, 'Too late. Too late.'[49]

It might be objected that Fuller compromises his emotional fidelity by quoting at the crucial moment some not very distinguished words of Allott's; yet on the contrary this exactly reaffirms and illustrates his sense of helpless reticence towards his mother.

Allott's and John Broadbent's deaths were swiftly followed by one which, for a poet of Fuller's age and allegiances, was still more momentous: that of Auden himself, on 29 September 1973. Writing in 'the dismal week when Auden died', Fuller briefly entertains notions of piety before concluding, with pragmatic frankness:

> And really more than holiness, it's booze
> And cigarettes make bearable our lives.
> Then cut them short; and leave us to the gods.[50]

Even the mention of cigarettes is typically double-edged. In an obituary article published in the following week's *Listener*, he recalled how, in June that year, he had introduced Auden at a Mermaid Theatre poetry reading:

> Going up the steps to the dressing-rooms backstage at the Mermaid, he had to stop to get his breath. Out of the complacency of one who'd recently stopped smoking, I worried about him. Up till then he'd seemed pretty indestructible. Now that only applies to the work.[51]

And in the next poem, a beautifully complex piece called 'Essential Memory', he reflects on the links between Auden's body, as it 'Breaks up beneath the top-soil of Kirschstetten', diminishing memories of the Auden 'world', and the peculiar intensity of that emotional bond which we can perhaps forge only with the dead:

> Can we love retrospectively the dead
> We never really knew? I start to think so;
> Especially since there is no question of
>
> Unwished for or unrequited love. And now
> The blood's all trickled to the ground; the voice
> Only on tape; speculatively warm the clasp.[52]

He was surely right, nevertheless, to judge the work 'pretty inde-
structible'.

Early in November, Fuller was briefly in hospital at Lewisham
for the surgical removal of two rectal growths, an episode
recounted in *Spanner and Pen* with a certain dry relish:

> Membership of BUPA only obtained for me a sort of small
> enclosure at the entrance to a general male ward, from which
> came the windy and other noises that took me disconcertingly
> back to messes in the Royal Navy during the war. Moreover,
> there was a ceaseless traffic past my enclosure. I asked for a
> sleeping-pill but, night having come, no one had authority to
> dispense it. I read until dawn, to the concern of the night sister.
> The day shift came on and the time drew near when I had
> been told by the consultant that surgery would take place.
> Though I remained unheeded in my semi-isolation, an oppor-
> tunity did arrive to tell a sceptical sister I was due to go to the
> theatre. But no one turned up to administer a pre-med, and
> when eventually the penny dropped I was wheeled off fully
> conscious, a state I did not at all mind, an easy chance to show
> *sang-froid*, and obtain confirmation that behind all institutions
> lies inefficiency. Towards evening I chartered a cab and had
> myself driven home.[53]

This helpfully explains three poems in *From the Joke Shop* which
may otherwise appear entirely baffling, so recessed are the events to
which they refer: 'Memories of War', 'The Other Side' and 'Post-
Operative'. Like 'Thirty Years On', the first of these suggests how
far beyond the scope of 'Long Time a Child' the autobiographical
project was to grow: as he listens to the 'uninhibited sounds,
among the groans' which emerge from the ward beyond his room,

> The feeling of a war-time mess returns
> So strongly as to occasion more alarm
>
> Than that tomorrow's probing will reveal
> Malignancy implanted deep within.[54]

Even the music in the headphones confirms this feeling. That a
thirty-year-old memory should prompt 'more alarm' than imminent surgery vividly reaffirms the traumatic nature of Fuller's war-
time experience.

The cumulative layer-on-layer character of the sequence is clearly suggested by a poem such as 'Fathers', which combines recurrent themes of dreaming, ageing, and the passage of time; that astonishing reach back into childhood from the end of 'Orphans'; and the question of our peculiar relationships with the dead from 'Essential Memory'. Although his father 'may be often in my dreams', the fact of his early death means that his features are now less easily memorable than certain familiar objects – for instance, his cut-throat razor. With a fine sweep across the generations, the poem modulates into reflections on both fatherhood and mortality:

> Did he imagine (as I sometimes do)
> His on would one day reach the age of sixty,
> Himself being almost *ipso facto* dead?
>
> Worse, in his final illness did he think
> How he would leave a foolish child of eight,
> Himself being hardly out of folly's years?[55]

Of course, another vulnerable aspect of Fuller's own ageing is the development of his retired colonel persona as a comic mask which may become a disconcertingly good fit. 'No wonder society is in a mess,' he grumbles, reasonably instancing ludicrous mid-1970s fashions in dress and the philistine dislike of classical music, before disarmingly classing himself among the 'reactionary chumps'.[56] And, indeed, a couple of poems later, he is reasserting his sympathies with the pacifist left and with 'hairy purchasers of stone-ground flour':[57] this irreconcilable dilemma was to recur, in very similar terms, in *Available for Dreams*.

The final poems in *From the Joke Shop*, bring us to the threshold of spring in 1974: as much as any in his work, they demonstrate how genuinely Fuller's poems deserve the over-used and often meaningless description 'life-affirming'. In 'The Future', the mild February prompts reflections which move easily through snow-drops (a 'Green-leotarded, white-capped *corps de ballet*'), robins, rhubarb, Mozart, Poulenc and Wallace Stevens to an optimistic yet wholly unsentimental conclusion:

> Better than I, birds sense the future's here
> And even in the sudden creamy snow,
> Cow-clapped next morning from a false-ceilinged sky

(Making the ballet's *décor* Muscovite),
Still swear to take the decades on and on.
Somehow they hear the *guzlas* dream: as ever,

Their love *alfresco* and their singing spry.[58]

At the beginning of March, Fuller told Arnold Rattenbury: 'I have
written 1600 lines since July – a sequence of a sort – but the stream
has now about run dry.'[59] He was, in any case, right to conclude an
often retrospective sequence with the anticipatory optimism of
spring: *From the Joke Shop* was an impressive start to his own 'late
period', and like major poems written around the middle of the
preceding two decades – such as 'The Ides of March' and 'Orders'
– it has the authentic air of a Wordsworthian 'timely utterance'.

★

The conflicts over cultural values which simmered during Fuller's
seven-year stint as a BBC Governor exploded far more dramatically
at the end of the year he spent as Chairman of the Arts Council's
Literature Panel in 1976-7. Once again, he must have seemed
exactly the right man for the job, despite – or, arguably, because of
– his lack of sympathy with many of the more experimental
projects funded by the Council. That he would bring to the position a degree of sceptical common-sense was predictable enough:
'Contemporary art is always almost all rubbish,' he wrote in 1974.
'And of the part that isn't rubbish, a substantial proportion is
doomed to fairly speedy extinction.'[60] Nevertheless, the Literature
Director, Charles Osborne, was an old friend – he had been
Assistant Editor to both John Lehmann and Alan Ross on the
London Magazine – whose musical and literary interests, from opera
to Auden (of whom he published a biography in 1980), had
obvious overlaps with Fuller's own. But if he allowed this to reassure him, the reassurance was to prove short-lived.

Of course, it was not his first association with the Arts Council.
He had been a member of its Poetry Panel in the 1950s, and in
January 1960 became a Director of the Poetry Book Society where
his congenial colleagues included Joseph Compton and Eric Walter
White; moreover, the PBS served an essentially uncontentious
purpose, in providing its members with four independently and
intelligently-chosen new collections of poetry each year. It satisfied
both Fuller's literary judgement and his business-like common-

sense: 'Those who have been subscribers from the start,' he wrote in 1968,

> now have on their shelves a not negligible hedge against infla-
> tion, first editions of many of the most notable books of the past
> fifteen years – *Hawk in the Rain, The Forests of Lithuania, Tares,
> The Nature of Cold Weather, The Whitsun Weddings* and *Ariel*, to
> name, as they say, but a few.[61]

The Literature Panel of 1976 was a different matter altogether: he had changed, no doubt, but so had the Arts Council.

From the outset, he found himself in a minority of one, surrounded by 'unregenerated lefties, naturally in favour of many things I had come to consider ghastly':[62] that typically coat-trailing formulation, incidentally, should not obscure the fact that Fuller, who presumably by then viewed himself as a *regenerated* lefty, never moved further right politically than the SDP.[63] The Arts Council, however, might almost have been specially invented to bring out the grumpy old buffer in him, vividly illustrating the dilemma which invariably haunts the ageing cultural arbiter: his dismay about the state of the arts may look merely like a reactionary and curmud-geonly dislike of the new, but who then is to judge when the arts truly are in decline? In his account of this affair in *Spanner and Pen*, he fails to do himself justice, overdoing the blimpish persona while omitting some of the detail with which he supported his case in an article called 'Taxpayers, the Arts and Big Balloonz', published in the October 1977 issue in *Encounter*; this had been commissioned by the magazine's co-editor, Anthony Thwaite, who was a member of the Literature Panel during Fuller's chairmanship and 'saw him fulminating against the "scroungers" and "remittance men"'.[64] Both versions cite a number of bizarre recipients of grants in the year 1975-6 – 'Performance Art' awards ranged from £10,138 for John Bull Puncture Repair Kit and £5,000 for Phantom Captain to £800 for Handbag, £744 for Forkbeard Fantasy and £300 for Amazing Professor Crump – but this is really a point about silly names, some of which are quite funny, rather than necessarily about artistic standards. Both versions also indicate his reservations about the mingling of art, education and social work under the guise of 'Community Arts' – a valid and still problematical matter, though not one which need have prompted Fuller's resignation from the Literature Panel in February 1977.

The *Encounter* article, however, listed specific instances of literary enterprises on which he felt public money had been bestowed foolishly or wastefully; many of these have not survived, although one that has (The Poetry Society) has subsequently more than justified Fuller's gloomy view of its management. His judgement was far from infallible: for instance, his description of the magazine *Ambit* as 'often pornographic, occasionally obscene' and 'likely to be highly offensive, in a non-artistic, non-literary way, to a substantial proportion of the public who paid for it'[65] has an air of wilful prissiness which conjures up the unlikely image of disgusted subscribers who had thought that they were buying, say, *Country Life*. Elsewhere he raised genuine if unfashionable matters of principle. Was it proper for the editors of the subsidised magazine *Fireweed* to include self-promotional material advertising their availability for readings funded by the (subsidised) National Poetry Secretariat? Perhaps, but it was the job of an acute, legally-trained mind to question the propriety of a manoeuvre which seemed to provide a self-perpetuating access to public funds. And was it appropriate for *Meridian* – 'It lacks editorial thrust and its purpose seems to be merely to print the work of unknown poets beside that of known poets'[66] – to receive a grant? Though this enabled it to pay its contributors, Fuller was unconvinced that 'getting money to poets', irrespective of merit, was a worthwhile aim. That sounds like the view of a comfortably-off writer untroubled by publication fees, but in fact his own parsimonious nature had been reinforced by his retirement just before the inflationary 1970s, and he didn't at all like magazines failing to pay *him*, as a circular letter he sent to various editors a little later demonstrates:

> Dear. . . . . . .
>
> Some periodicals commission work and then do not pay for it. This has been my experience with . . . .
>
> I'm rather thinking of taking the question up with The Society of Authors. Have you any comments I could pass on to them?
>
> Sorry about the bug letter, but I am writing to several editors.[67]

He elaborated on the point in a letter to Michael Schmidt: 'One of my beefs,' he wrote, is that there is all the difference in the world between a true little magazine, where contributors are very often not paid and do not expect to be paid, and ambitious and subsidised magazines which ought to pay unless announcing in their pages that they do not pay.[68]

Nevertheless, his opposition to *Meridian's* subsidy had a certain poignant edge to it, since in his earlier membership of the Poetry Panel he had argued for grants to little magazines, battling against John Hayward, who 'opposed their being doled out with all the maddening stubbornness for which he was notorious'.[69] In his later committee work, he clearly took Hayward's example to heart.

He was especially scathing about the apparent results of the Arts Council's benevolence towards The Poetry Society:

When the Poetry Society was a fuddy-duddy and decaying organisation housed in decaying premises, I believe the Literature Panel (with a grander title and new-found amplitude of money and freedom compared with the old poetry panel) conceived it to be an excellent object to revivify with cash. The result has been successive struggles for power within the Society, in the recent past mainly by people I would class as 'maniacs'. The subsidy to the Society is currently of the order of £50,000 a year and of course it is the benefits from this sum that are being quarrelled over.[70]

As he conceded, the 'maniacs' were successfully outflanked by the 'moderates' in that contest; and, as the Arts Council's Secretary-General, Roy Shaw, pointed out, it was somewhat unfair to speak of the Poetry Society 'as though the troubles in it were the responsibility of the Council'.[71] The note of affectionate nostalgia for the 'fuddy-duddy and decaying organisation housed in decaying premises' is consistent with his lifelong dislike of ostentation and his freely-admitted parsimony: as Alan Brownjohn recalls, 'Roy couldn't believe shabbiness was a bad thing in poetry organisations – "I *like* tat!" he said.'[72] Nevertheless, the financial fortunes or misfortunes of The Poetry Society over the past twenty years indicate just how well-founded his concerns were.

The more outrageous aspects of 'Taxpayers, the Arts and Big Balloonz' could only have shocked or surprised those who didn't know Fuller. For instance, his joke that having both Richard

Hoggart and Raymond Williams on the Council was 'rather more than bad luck', clearly an allusion to Wilde's line about the careless-ness of losing both parents, is utterly characteristic of his tendency to grumble about people with whom he actually had a good deal in common (like Dennis Potter in the BBC incident) rather than about those he considered wholly worthless; the feeling which underlies so many of his semi-humorous mutterings is *disappointment*, and it is a tricky one to manage. 'I know I have a fondness for the comic and occasionally for the vituperative,' he admitted, 'but that is just to add interest to the proceedings';[73] yet this – like 'Reactionary views, advanced mostly / To raise a laugh – taken as gospel!'[74] and the almost identical prose formulation in *Souvenirs*[75] – seems just a shade too easy a get-out, too reminiscent of the affronted child's 'I was only joking'. Certainly, it is hard to feel entirely comfortable about his response to Naseem Khan's report, *The Arts Britain Ignores*: he may or may not have described ethnic arts as 'a lot of wogs cavorting about in the street', as Jeremy Hutchinson claimed[76] – his reply to Hutchinson was cautiously ambiguous on this point – but his over-stated hostility to the notion of a multi-cultural society (something which Britain has arguably possessed at least since the Roman inva-sion) tended to blur his much more temperate and thoughtful view of the matter, stated in one of the more judicious passages of 'Taxpayers, Arts and Big Balloonz':

> I feel myself that the encouragement of ethnic minority arts on the scale envisaged by Naseem Khan is socially divisive, likely to be politically slanted, and in the last analysis pointless, for the conditions which led to the rise of those arts are not and will not ever (one hopes!) be present in Britain. But here, too, I felt views of this kind would never prevail round the Council table.[77]

He was probably right about that; all the same, it was a position which was worth expressing coherently and which was not much assisted by his resignation.

In a curious way, the pattern of his war-time experience – of idealism modified by disappointment – had been repeated. The BBC, he said, recreated his 'sense of the extent and diversity of British life, last felt to the same degree during war service with the Royal Navy';[78] yet he knew well enough that this was a sentimental view which conveniently eliminated his unpleasant memories of troopships and transit camps. The Arts Council recreated that other war-time feeling, of battered ideals and unfulfilled expectations. Fuller, as a skilled tactician, responded in terms which both drew on his own formative cultural self-education and turned his defeat into a fairly honourable one:

> Quite a lot of public money is now available for the arts and any government would find it politically difficult to cut it. There is no reason, for instance, why we shouldn't have the best symphony orchestras in the world; or a series of compact and elegant volumes of English literature like the French *Pléiade* editions; or a theatre that with modest seriousness played classic English drama.[79]

The scornful fury with which these proposals were dismissed by Jeremy Hutchinson and others demonstrated how effectively Fuller, in the retreat of his closing paragraphs, had hit his target. His suggestions, as he well knew, could never be adopted by an organisation primarily devoted to supporting contemporary arts, yet in arguing that the Arts Council devote more of its resources to making works of acknowledged excellence widely available, he remained true to his lifelong belief in a culturally enabling socialism. His opponents, on the other hand, with their fondness for encouraging small-scale arts entrepreneurs of varying quality, now curiously seem to have something in common with the 'enterprise culture' of the Thatcherite 1980s. As so often, the political labels of 'left' and 'right' prove to be unhelpfully slippery; and, not for the first time, Fuller's stance turns out to be the one which might more accurately be described as 'radical'.

His resignation prompted a lively debate beyond the pages of *Encounter* – most notably in *The Listener*, where Michael Schmidt's article 'The Fairy Godmother and her Bosses'[80] was followed by some excitable correspondence. 'Yes,' he told Anthony Thwaite,

> the Arts Council business was astonishing in the breadth of interest aroused. I turned down I should think at least half a dozen TV & radio appearances, & *did* get a bit cheesed off with the phone going, not least from the newspapers. All seems now to have died down – & I agree that to bring matters into discussion has been useful. Some nice intimations of support came – not *all* from maniacs! And I was glad in the end that I had got it off my chest.[81]

Off his chest it may have been, but Fuller returned to the episode two years later (in an article about the literary periodicals which had appeared to fill the gap left by a strikebound *TLS*), when his temper had cooled without at all affecting the fierce lucidity of his cultural values:

> Standards have slackened to an extent that alarms old fogies, and perhaps a few young fogies. The task of literary evaluation has obviously two parts. First, to try to find among the mass of current writing the good, the true, the beautiful. Secondly, to avoid trailing after what is merely fashionable, and to expose the dangerously phoney and pretentious.
>
> Oddly enough, the reluctance of some academics to commit themselves to straight questions of badness and goodness is paralleled by the extreme literary left, which denies the validity of pronoucements about value, judging works, on the whole, by their help or otherwise to the left's social and political aims. There are other strange, even alarming features of the present-day literary scene that seem insufficiently recognised in the first issues of the new magazines. I would instance the failure of postwar living standards and education to increase significantly the numbers of serious readers, let alone the numbers subscribing to literary magazines. Then there is the artistic apotheosis, mainly through Arts Council subsidy, of what is really amateur or crudely political activity, particularly in the theatre. Sometimes one has thought of the Arts Council as culture subsidising its own overthrow. And there is the ubiquity of pop and rock music, with its damaging volume and moronic words, which actually has its solemn reviewers in the so-called heavy Sundays and weeklies.[82]

Exasperated as he was by the Arts Council, the subversive side of Fuller's personality thoroughly relished his composite role of court jester and institutional saboteur. Literary committee-work gave full reign both to his efficiency and his eccentricity. Frank Kermode, who chaired the Poetry Book Society's Board of Management, remembers lunching with Fuller 'in Soho, at a favourite restaurant ruined, in RF's view, by an advertisement opposite (strident, visible) for DUREX'.[83] Jonathan Barker, too, recalls an apt image of the sunnier, dottier side of him on his way to a meeting of the Literature Panel, 'strolling leisurely down Piccadilly towards 105 wearing a wide brimmed hat looking rather like Robert Bridges...

He cut a fine figure in it.'[84] Perhaps the hat was the symbolic repository of his 'oddity', like that of the iconoclastic gardener in the Powys story; anyway, his liking for eccentric headgear remained happily undiminished. Alderman Broadbent would have approved.

★

During the late 1970s, Ian Hamilton's magazine *The New Review* ran a series of autobiographical essays called 'Family Life'; the fourth of these, 'Long Time a Child' by Roy Fuller, appeared in May 1977.[85] This compact childhood memoir developed partly from the retrospective glances scattered through *From the Joke Shop*; once he had begun to rummage about in his past, Fuller found he was disinclined to stop. The initial result was a book which he feared might be 'an old buffer's chain of consciousness',[86] *Souvenirs*: less a sequential autobiography than a series of variations ('if only one had been a composer!'),[87] it is the most entertaining and the most infuriating of his four volumes of memoirs. Apart from deploying the recurrent characteristics of his later prose – in which mischievous irony mixes oddly with solicitorial circumlocution – he here develops an especially teasing habit of forward reference: 'soon to be mentioned', 'I refer subsequently', and so on. *Souvenirs* is an easy book to read but a difficult one to make sense of, full of tortuous through-the-looking-glass chessboard progressions.

Fuller submitted the typescript, along with a new collection of poems (*The Reign of Sparrows*), to André Deutsch via his literary agent, Graham Watson of Curtis Brown. Though his relationship with Watson dated back to the mid-1950s – when, after the success of *The Second Curtain*, Curtis Brown would have felt that they were acquiring a writer of profitable literary thrillers – his use of an agent for so eccentric a book as *Souvenirs* was probably a mistake; one can't help feeling that a direct preliminary discussion with Diana Athill, his editor at Deutsch, might have averted or at least ameliorated the disastrous parting which was to follow. Fuller, however, with his habitual if often disappointed conviction that literary dealings should be as businesslike and orderly as the transactions of the Woolwich, sat back and waited for Graham Watson's reply. It was dated 18 January 1979, and with it was enclosed a copy of Athill's rejection letter: 'What it boils down to,' she wrote, 'is we think it would be a mistake for Roy to publish this book'; André Deutsch said, in a postscript, 'There is nothing I can add to this elegant, fearless, tactful letter.'[88] Watson, cautiously expressing his own agreement, remarked that 'there would certainly be publishers only too happy to include your name on their list but I don't believe it would really be in your interest to take such an action.'[89] Watson's implication was certainly worth taking seriously: at the time, Fuller had half a dozen books of poetry, two novels and two volumes of Oxford lectures in print with Deutsch; an abrupt change of publisher might complicate matters of rights and permissions as well as jeopardising the continued availability of this quite substantial backlist.

Fuller, however, reacted furiously. Although Deutsch would have been happy to publish the new book of poems, he severed his connections with the firm (an enormous risk, as his *TLS* review of Elizabeth Jennings's *Growing-Points* had suggested, in difficult times for even established poets). As with his resignation from the Arts Council, his departure from Deutsch engaged both his principles and his pride; it was, as he later admitted, 'a topic I was inclined to flog at the time'.[90] When, later in 1979, Deutsch published Julian Symons' *Conan Doyle: Portrait of an Artist*, Fuller wrote in exasperation to his old friend: 'I only hope the villain Deitsch – my hands tremble so much with wrath I can't even spell his name – gets it into the shops.'[91] Even a decade letter, when Symons edited *The Essential Wyndham Lewis* for Deutsch, Fuller's anger was undiminished: 'I can't come to your party on the 25th: my vendetta – the only one in my life – prevents me from risking confrontation with AD, to say nothing of Diana A; dirty dogs both (or rather dog & b*tch) in my book.'[92]

His next move was to offer *Souvenirs* to Faber, through Charles Monteith, with whom he served on the Library Advisory Council. Monteith's judgement, courteously expressed in a letter of 22 February 1979, was in effect much the same as Diana Athill's: the book's 'over-elaborate "musical" structure' gave it 'a superficial appearance of muddle – when of course the "muddle" is entirely deliberate'.[93] There was, however, one list – the publisher of such books as Maclaren-Ross's *Memoirs of the Forties* and Symons' *Notes from Another Country* – which seemed ideal for *Souvenirs*: Alan Ross's London Magazine Editions. Writing in May to Norman Lees, Fuller gave a stoical account of the book's publishing troubles and even hinted at some sympathy with Athill's and Monteith's judgement:

Have been hoping to write again; deferred doing so until I could give you news of the memoirs. My usual publisher turned them down: took ages over the decision, as did another publisher friend. They will be done, in fact, by a stauncher and older friend, Alan Ross, who runs a magazine and small publishing house. I can see – as I think I said to you – that people can easily have doubts about the book and it may well be received with opprobrium. But I feel it is better than much that gets in print, so have persevered.[94]

Souvenirs, and *The Reign of Sparrows*, duly appeared under the occasional yet indispensable LM imprint in February 1980. Though this was a happy solution to the problem, confirming one of his most durable literary associations, the suspicion must remain that a truly astute and businesslike author would have first sounded out Diana Athill, then offered *Souvenirs* to Ross and kept his poetry and fiction with Deutsch.

Fuller's patience would not have been improved by his ill-health. Some of his medical problems – essentially the visible or tangible ones – he was able to regard with wry amusement: they appealed to that almost scatological interest in the nose-picking aspect of humanity which so often appears in his fiction. In *Spanner and Pen*, he interrupts his chapter on the BBC to describe in enthusiastic detail the circumstances surrounding the surgical removal of two rectal growths,[95] while the sequence of 'Diary Entries' in *Tiny Tears* includes this cheerful quatrain:

> 'I'll burn it off now if you like,' said my GP,
> Apropos of the papilloma on my thigh,
> Bothersome of late. Would that all worries
> Disappeared in a whiff of over-done pork![96]

But it was harder to discover the comical side of other health matters. In August 1978, when he was still 'mucking about with a vol of poems, as well as the memoirs', he wrote to Lees:

> The old Chairman of my building society used to say all was better when one got through the 'sound barrier', which I seem to think he put at eighty! I do not ask the consultant about the prognosis of my heart 'condition', through cowardice. The strange thing is that I have always looked reasonably well – and indeed thought of myself as reasonably well – despite peptic ulcers, Graves Disease, insomnia, &c., throughout adult life.[97]

By the beginning of 1979, his state of health had become, like his row with Deutsch, a topic he was 'inclined to flog'. 'I have to admit,' he rather grudgingly told Arnold Rattenbury, 'being somewhat better with all my ailments, despite a cold & cough that started before Xmas. Did I tell you I have even had a recurrence of duodenal ulcer? In the intervening years, however, a magic pill therefor has been discovered – cimetidine.'[98] In April, he was 'struck down with 'flu & feel awful',[99] and the effects lasted through the following month. 'Have been over a week in bed – 'flu with the complications of a chest infection that has taxed my feeble heart,' he wrote on 7 May;[100] 'Begin to feel a bit better now.' Three weeks later, however, he was 'just getting over post-'flu complications, chest and cardiac unpleasantness – a new turn in my list of ailments'.[101]

The year 1979 had turned out to be in various ways a trying one for Fuller and, understandably, he was not altogether sorry to see the back of it. 'All good wishes for 1980,' he wrote to Alan Brownjohn, and added: 'Strange to think one may live into – even *write* into – yet another decade which will be given some poetic label.'[102]

3: The World in the Evening

❧❧ ❧❧ • ❦❦ ❦❦

'The poet who goes on writing into his old age,' observed Fuller after Auden's death in 1973, 'is singularly blessed.'[1] He could not have imagined how copiously this blessing was to be bestowed upon him, for the years of his last decade were only unremarkable in that special sense suggested by his own earlier poem 'The Unremarkable Year': years of grateful creativity spiced by the oddities of a world wryly observed through the windows of a Blackheath bungalow or a 53 bus.

The publication of three volumes of memoirs – *Souvenirs* in 1980, *Vamp Till Ready* in 1982 and *Home and Dry* in 1984 – undoubtedly contributed to the resurgence of his poetic productivity, enriching the characteristic mixture of everyday description and intellectual reflection with the vein of autobiographical reminiscence begun in *From the Joke Shop*. And the memoirs themselves were unexpectedly successful, well-reviewed and eventually reissued in slightly abbreviated form as a paperback, *The Strange and the Good*; *Souvenirs* even prompted a Granada TV programme about its author. Fuller was understandably delighted by this *succès d'estime*, though the actual hardback sales were modest enough to imply that on purely commercial grounds Deutsch and Faber may not have been entirely mistaken. He was especially pleased when reviewers such as Alan Brownjohn found *Souvenirs* 'very funny',[2] as indeed it is; and no one could blame him, in *Spanner and Pen*, for praising those who praised it. But an equally interesting view of *Souvenirs*, fundamentally friendly yet exasperated, is provided by John Lucas in his carefully detailed *TLS* review:

> Reading the book makes for a baffling experience. It is *so* determined to avoid a coherence that could be thought contrived, *so* unwilling to becoming anything as ambitious or deliberate as an account of the growth of a poet's mind, *so* ready to strike a self-deprecating pose.[3]

Lucas sternly suggests that many of the convenient blurs in *Souvenirs* – he cites the monstrously evasive opening of Chapter 5

('For a reason I never knew or have forgotten, phrase applicable to much of these reminiscences'⁴) – could have been clarified if Fuller had taken the trouble to ransack his memory, ask people, or simply look things up. He also very perceptively notices how slyly Fuller distances the self within the book from the self who is writing it, for example by talking about 'my character' when he means 'me'; yet perhaps we should expect no less from one who so often explores the idea of the double self. Most telling among Lucas's points, however, is his observation that for all Fuller's protestations in it that he never wished to be a lawyer, a lawyer's book is just what this is:

> ... *Souvenirs* seems to me very much a product of the legal mind: canny, utterly astute in its 'candid' admissions of weaknesses – 'I spent much of my childhood (and later life) missing connections in human affairs obvious to others', 'my dotty and priggish devotion to authority'; bufferish and game-playing to its own advantage in... the pedantic and not-quite-but-nearly absurd use of such words as rugeous, endentulousness, obstipated, minaciousness, oleaginous. What *is* one to make of them? Reading the book makes one realize afresh why David Copperfield had a hard time of it trying to fathom Mr Spenlow.

That question of Lucas's, even if intended rhetorically, invites an answer. Those words are buffers of another sort, protective and defensive gestures which help the author to elude or evade his reader: they have their precise meanings, which we may have to look up, but their chief strategic purpose is to qualify the informality of tone; they insist that this rambling elderly chap who is chatting away to us is not to be taken for granted, since he seems to use such out-of-the-way language *as a matter of course*. And the reason why this defensive mannerism is so recurrent in *Souvenirs* – and in *The Reign of Sparrows* – is clear enough: these are the books written closest to Fuller's Arts Council stint and the latter years of his BBC governorship, when he felt most embattled culturally, and their tone reflects this just as the over-insistent literariness of *Tiny Tears* reflects his response to Oxford.

There is an unsettling note in *The Reign of Sparrows*, which arises not just from one's uncertainty about whether Fuller is joking or not but, more disturbingly, from a sense that *he* is not always sure whether he is joking or not. He seems to be, indeed he insists that he is, in the section called 'Singing, 1977' from 'In his Sixty-Fifth Year':

> Of all my portraits I say: poor likeness.
> 'Colonel (Retired)' or 'Disgusted' stares out,
> Doomed to expire of apoplexy;
> Whitening moustache, jaw-line sagging.
> Like a woman, I think: I've lost my looks.
> Reactionary views, advanced mostly
> To raise a laugh — taken as gospel![5]

Perhaps; but that 'mostly' raises some awkward questions. When, shopping for trousers in Plymouth, the deferential courtesy of an assistant prompts him to declare 'Surely our England must be great again',[6] the intention is fairly unambiguously to 'raise a laugh'. On the other hand, when in 'On his Sixty-Fifth Birthday' he sets off for the 'Mini-Town Hall' (a 'tawdry building... set / In bogland off the A2') to collect his pensioner's bus pass, and finds people there talking about 'reduced-price Ovaltine / And other baksheesh of the State',[7] it is less easy to see anything humorous about the Retired Colonel persona.

Nevertheless, this is more than outweighed by poems where the elderliness which Fuller had been practising for so long is seen in terms of touching absurdity. The sequence 'Quatrains of an Elderly Man' — as so often, his diary-like observations work all the better for being organised into a neatly regular form — provides several effective examples, such as the wilfully punning misapprehension in 'Low Tide at Greenwich':

> BEWARE OF CRANES (it says) but all I see
> Are swans at the river's edge, past rusty wrecks
> Of piles and barges, preening on polished mud
> Their dazzling hulls with dislocated necks.[8]

Four lines seems about right for a relaxed joke like that to develop without outstaying its welcome. The length also suits a moment of Monsieur Hulot-like foolishness such as the one in 'Accident':

> My briefcase falls open in the street. Displayed:
> Aspirins for migraine, chocolates for my wife.
> Despite my 'Oh, bugger', strangers come to aid
> The old boy picking up his bits of life.[9]

That avoids both petulance and self-pity by artfully shifting its perspective so that the 'old boy' represents the bystanders' perception rather than his own. A very similar idea, though treated in a very different way, also occurs in a separate poem, 'The Old Toy', an appropriately small-scale *cri de coeur*:

> Bits of me keep falling off;
> bits don't work properly;
> and other bits are broken
> by the girl who owns me.
>
> O vanishing teeth that crunch
> things I still love; O part
> I know can't now be mended;
> O miniature heart![10]

The distant echo there of Yeats's scarecrow is, incidentally, confirmed by the appearance in the adjacent, trouser-buying poem, 'Crisis', of an unmistakably Yeatsian cadence: 'An ageing man, a man without much waist.'[11]

Yet the most perfect of the poems which explicitly address the matter of old — or oldish — age is 'Two Blond Flautists'. The knack here, deceptively simple-looking, lies in the absolute fidelity to observed experience with which Fuller supports his benign generalisation. The poet enters the bathroom recently occupied by his granddaughter, to find

> Bath-water still and tinted as lagoons;
> *Animal Farm* turned back behind the taps;
> Shampoo uncapped; all towels on the floor...[12]

He patiently remedies this disarray, as the sound of her playing Poulenc on the flute rises from beneath him. This occupies half the poem, which comprises a pair of eleven-line stanzas which feel like squashed sonnets; in the other, he contemplates another blond flautist, the goldcrest which 'probes the wall time has de-mortared'. Because both the poem's subjects are treated with such honest affection, Fuller's exclamatory gratitude — 'How blest are those / Destiny has engardened and grand-daughtered!' — seems fully earned and not at all excessive.

Of course, 'Two Blond Flautists' also brings together the two great preoccupations of the late poems, music and birds. It goes without saying that these concerns are interrelated – and also that they are not related in an entirely straightforward way. Anthony Storr, in *Music and the Mind*, usefully summarises the arguments for and against the notion that human music originated in birdsong – citing, for instance, Charles Hartshorne's interesting observation that 'birds sing far more than is biologically necessary for the various forms of communication'[13] – before opting for the probability that 'music developed from the prosodic exchanges between mother and infant which foster the bond between them.'[14] However, even if birds and music cannot with any certainty be anthropologically linked, they assumed parallel, closely connected roles in Fuller's later life. They consistently alleviated his disappointment in humanity's unsatisfactory conduct of its own affairs; by embodying forms of order beyond words, they symbolised the ideals to which his own language might aspire; and, for one whose early atheism never seriously wavered, they went some way towards filling the gap left by the lack of a faith. Consequently, readers who see in Fuller's poems on these subjects nothing more than an elderly man fussing among his record collection or pottering in the garden will completely misunderstand them.

He was naturally well aware of this possibility. 'I must not waffle on about gramophone records,' he resolves in *Souvenirs*,[15] typically offering himself advice which he has no intention of taking. So the poet who in *From the Joke Shop* managed to make the statement 'I come indoors and play my latest discs'[16] seem simultaneously commonplace and momentous here produces a sequence called 'Musical Offering': its final section, 'Ricercar',[17] is as densely allusive as the wonderful six-part fugue from Bach's work of the same name and seems to have its origin in Wilfrid Mellers' sleeve-note to its 1977 Enigma recording by members of The Yorkshire Sinfonia directed by Manoug Parikian. At such moments it may look as if Fuller is simply showing off, but the element of wilful obscurity in 'Musical Offering', like the arcane words and the retired colonel posturing, is a response to his sense of being culturally embattled – a version of Eliot's 'These fragments I have shored against my ruins'[18] – as well as an exploration of a perfectly genuine enthusiasm. The capacity of music to make sense when almost nothing else does becomes in this sequence a very personal kind of manifesto.

It is no accident that the next poem in the book, also a personal manifesto, is 'Hedge-Sparrows and House-Sparrows'. Here the

musical parallel is explicit – 'This couple trill as constantly as late /
Beethoven' – and so is Fuller's sense of his own identification with
the birds: 'I read, you nest in April.'[19] Yet 'identification' soon
becomes too simple a word for the poem's reflexive argument,
which typically ends by favouring the sparrows and by implying
that our generosity towards garden birds is one of the few good
things to be said for humanity:

> Instead, let there be sparrowdom, the reign
> Of sparrows, for sustaining your kin in name
> At least suggests some worth in human habitations.

Once again, the poem seems to invite misreading. Fuller is not
merely saying that the observable world of suburban wildlife is
enough; he is saying, far more ambitiously, that it possesses consum-
mate qualities which are quite beyond us. The point is made more
clearly in a brief, jotting-like piece called 'Notebook', which
consists of two six-line stanzas. This is the first:

> A seven-spotted ladybird
> Toddles across the sheet
> To which I feel I can't add a word.
> Then opening like some cute
> Trinket by Fabergé,
> It flies with angelic suddenness away.[20]

John Lucas, in the *TLS* review already quoted, cites the opening
lines as an instance of 'bufferdom', I think quite wrongly: for lady-
birds do indeed 'toddle' and then disconcertingly open their wings,
precisely as Fuller describes them. Like so many of his poems about
insects, this one is in the respectfully attentive tradition of Hardy's
'An August Midnight', which similarly consists of two six-line
stanzas. Hardy's second stanza, after he has describes the four
winged visitors which have landed on *his* page, is as follows:

> Thus meet we five, in this still place,
> At this point of time, at this point in space.
> – My guests besmear my new-penned line,
> Or bang at the lamp and fall supine.
> 'God's humblest, they!' I muse. Yet why?
> They know Earth-secrets that know not I.[21]

Fuller's second stanza, though necessarily more downbeat, nevertheless seems glancingly aware of its antecedent:

The book seems dead with things
I've left behind. I want
As ever to start again – on wings
Instead of feet. Yet aren't
To this new world the keys
Pedestrian particularities?

That rather fussy inversion perhaps slightly blurs the ambitious claim being made here, as in 'Hedge-Sparrows and House-Sparrows' for the transcendent potentiality of 'Pedestrian particularities'.

Reviewing *The Reign of Sparrows*, Robert Conquest noted that Fuller had 'always been to some degree a poet of melancholy, and he has taken on old age a trifle early', adding that the melancholy was surprisingly 'not very noticeable' in this collection: 'Indeed, he is often cheerful, one might even say smug, in depicting himself in this elderly role.'[22] Addressing the author, he shrewdly speculated that 'we may expect you to gather your talent into a great sunset masterpiece' in ten or even twenty years. 'The whole tone of this book,' he concluded, 'is, in an odd way, one of preparation for such a venture.' Such predictive assessments are always risky, but that one was just about right.

★

Ten years, but not twenty: Fuller's seemingly exaggerated hypochondria of the 1970s, which transformed the common cold into an obstacle to be heroically conquered for the sake of board meetings or grumblingly described to correspondents, was to prove all too well-founded. His long-term problem of hyperthyroidism had been treated, apparently successfully, by pills which had cured his hand tremor and palpitations; so successfully, indeed, that he was eventually taken off the pills. However, the palpitations then reappeared, this time incurably, 'for the heart's timing mechanism had broken down'; nor was he much reassured to learn 'that a number of people were happily walking about St Thomas' with atrial fibrallation, as the condition was called'.[23] In November 1980 he reported to Julian Symons:

Saw the Radio Active Iodine Fiend on Monday who, when sounding me, said I had still some 'crud' (could he have used this expression, quite unmedical?) on the lungs. He rather impressed me (first visit), despite your (just) criticisms of the tribe. My thyroid is greatly enlarged – with nodules attached, & shows vascular activity. My heart not only fibrillates but has also a mitral murmur. One is sorely tempted to have something done, on the lines it can't do harm, may do good. Had some further tests done, anyway, including sf scan of my throat – scene from Dr Who – & see the fellow again after Xmas, if I should live so long.[24]

Then, after a routine appointment with his doctor at St Thomas's Hospital in the autumn of 1981, he found himself abruptly packed off to the Royal Masonic Hospital in Hammersmith for a week. St Thomas's had no private room available, and his doctor tactfully and no doubt correctly 'said I would not like a public ward'; other patients might not have much liked his habit of reading throughout the night. He thought he had a minor chest complaint after a summer cold, but it emerged that he had suffered a slight heart attack: 'The episode served to increase, if that were possible, my phobia about the common cold.'[25] He was impressed by the Royal Masonic Hospital, though 'an alien among the ailing masons', and his stay there prompted the two poems called 'Home and Away', the first of which is particularly interesting since its opening image of the wandering convalescents in the garden anticipates (and may have suggested) the setting of his last novel, *Stares*:

> Garden enclosed on three sides by the sick,
> I move at last towards your health. As in
> The outer sequences of *Caligari*
> Some characters already stroll about;
> A white-capped Arab notably, in gown
> Of green, white-girdled, possibly a sheik.[26]

After a particularly agitated time in 1983, he was prescribed an unfamiliar anti-depressant called Mianserin:

> After a week or so my sleep and dreaming improved, and quite soon I wrote a sequence of twenty-one sonnets I called 'Mianserin Sonnets'... I gave Dr Y [his consultant at St Thomas's] a copy of 'Mianserin Sonnets': he was amused; hoped the drug manufacturers didn't exploit it. Another phrase of his has stuck in my mind: 'There are a lot of good drugs nowadays.' How much I agree, swallowing as I do nine pills a day, with nothing but benefit. Much tripe is talked about drug dependency.[27]

The generalisation has a defiant recklessness typical of the asides in *Spanner and Pen*, but about his own case he was probably right. Certainly, Mianserin enhanced not only his physical well-being but also his imaginative life. 'The drug Mianserin enchants,' says Jonathan Barker,[28] and the vivid dreams it encourages were to provide the perfect creative counterpart to Fuller's wry daylight observations.

The poems are largely in his loosely associative running journal style – they form a bridge between *From the Joke Shop* and the two later sonnet sequences, *Subsequent to Summer* and *Available for Dreams* – spiked with the dream-world's surreal re-orderings. Quite early on he writes: 'Ten days on Mianserin: amazing dreams / Begin – or perhaps from youthful years come back';[29] and these poems, which belong to his memoir-writing years, might have been expected in any case to include parallel excavations of his personal past. But here the memories are both heightened and superimposed:

> The place, my grandparents' house in Hollins Road.
> In the side lane the cat is crying to be
> Let in. So, riding my tricycle, I make
> A three-point turn and then proceed indoors.
> Some cars are swishing through the darkening snow:
> It's Guy Fawkes Night and in the pointed sky
> A rocket bursts. But why do I turn left
> And move away from where the cat will be,
> And try a strange, barred alley at the back?[30]

Clearly, these lines juxtapose disparate elements: cat, tricycle, snow and fireworks probably belong to different evenings; the anxious arrival at his grandparents' house may even have originated in that later winter night when, as a law student, he missed the last train home from Manchester and turned up on their doorstep. What is especially impressive is Fuller's fidelity to the way dreams actually work, combining bits of the recalled familiar world with completely inexplicable details like the 'pointed sky' and the 'strange, barred alley'. Equally striking is the reappearance of that most influential of figures from his childhood, Alderman Broadbent, whose Sunday high tea cheese and onion dish, 'The ichor, crumbled Lancastrian cheese',[31] is recalled in 'Curious Shapes', and whose wary first impression of Leopold Fuller is restated in 'Ancestry':

> My goy grandfather,
> Moreover, was (my mother told me) rather
> Inclined, when my exogamous sire appeared,
> To think him Jewish, with putative, black beard.[32]

Though interesting, these lines are far from distinguished – the metre is lame and the diction, lurching from 'goy' to 'exogamous', seems wayward even for Fuller of this vintage.

Such lapses are, however, relatively uncommon in this sequence. Literary friends – Cecil Day Lewis, Joe Ackerley, Allen Tate – are remembered; oddities of nature (ants at a bus-stop, foxes or cats in the garden) and of music (increasingly, the popular songs of his youth) are affectionately remarked on; and there is a wry self-assessment of his literary standing:

> I must return
> To the usual perils of longevity
> In the man of letters. Being out of date
> And out of print, and feeling orphaned, I
> Can't help a grin at my self-pity.[33]

The final sonnet, 'Dreams and Art', tackles the matter of what should be included or excluded in a poem. If, as Fuller here rather contentiously claims, 'Art is to try to impart a narrative / Less boring than dreams', then what needs to be edited out?

> Not all he personally lived and loved,
> Nor dotty twists; indeed, the latter give
> A deal of art its only excellence.[34]

There are other sorts of excellence in Fuller's poetry, of course, but this is nevertheless a well-aimed riposte to those who dislike his preoccupation with instances of his own – and others' – daftness.

Mianserin Sonnets appeared as a chastely elegant pamphlet published (like several others of his, including the invaluable *As from the Thirties*) by Alan Anderson's Edinburgh-based Tragara Press: it was a style of presentation of which he had grown very fond. When both he and Symons had first been published by the press, ten years earlier, he wrote: 'I think the Tragara's chaste and modest style v. agreeable, & suitable for us 60-year-olds.' And he added, with somewhat uncanny prescience: 'In a way one begins to feel that this kind of publication is all one wants – half way between meagre commercial sales & the desk drawer.'[35] For Fuller in the early 1980s, this was no longer altogether a matter of choice.

★

Early in the 1970s, Secker and Warburg had launched a poetry list under the advisory editorship of Anthony Thwaite: among its first titles, published in 1972, were John Fuller's *Cannibals and Missionaries* and James Fenton's *Terminal Moraine*. The list, handsomely and uniformly produced, diversified as it grew, but by 1980 a substantial strand of it — from Geoffrey Grigson and Kenneth Allott (to whose 1975 *Collected Poems* Fuller contributed an Introduction) through Alan Brownjohn to younger poets such as John Mole and George Szirtes — might almost have been chosen by Fuller himself. Although, when he suddenly found himself publisherless, Alan Ross had magnificently risen to the occasion, it would have been impossible for London Magazine Editions to undertake anything on the scale of, for instance, a new *Collected Poems*. But his old *Collected Poems*, published in 1962, was of course out of date, out of print, and — with Deutsch — out of favour. In March 1984, Jonathan Barker, whom Fuller knew through the Arts Council and Poetry Book Society, and who was by then running the Arts Council's Poetry Library, suggested to Thwaite that this might be a project for Seckers to undertake.

On 10 May, he wrote to Barker,

> to say that matters seem to be settled between S&W & me, re Collected Poems. It all started with your word in Thwaite's ear, so you will have to bear the responsibility for the enterprise. I'm enormously grateful to you for your practical & affectionate interest, not for the first time displayed. I would probably have let the Collected question drift along for years — perhaps to my demise — now I must face up to it.[36]

Fuller had almost nothing but praise for Seckers' in-house poetry editor, Helen Owen — although, by now hypersensitive to the merest whiff of publisher's adverse criticism, he did manage to be mildly offended by her comment that the book's 'manufacturing figures' were 'pretty frightening'.[37] They would have been: a 557-page hardback by a poet whose sales had seldom matched his reputation cannot have seemed an obviously viable project for a commercial publisher. However, the book appeared in June 1985,

and a memorably lavish party was held at Seckers' offices in Poland
Street to launch not only Fuller's *New and Collected Poems* but also
four other new titles in their poetry list, which had been not altogether happily redesigned; 'What a crush, what a hubbub!' he
grumbled to Julian Symons on the following day. 'Lovely to sink
back today into the calm of Langton Way & Safeway.'[38] At the party,
Peter Grose, then the firm's Managing Director, made an optimistic speech before piloting most of the poets on an airborne
reading tour, promoted with the ludicrous slogan 'POETRY
TAKES OFF'. But this was one invitation which Fuller had
already declined: 'I have refused the private plane, aiming to die in
bed – just going to Bristol & Oxford, but not till the end of June.[39]

The 'New' component in the book is substantial: some sixty
pages of run-on poems, more than a respectable slim volume's
worth, previously uncollected apart from those which had
appeared in Tragara Press pamphlets. Many are light or occasional
in nature: Fuller was inclined to over-indulge his fondness for
finding material, often transposed verbatim, in news items and
book reviews at this time; and there are also some fully intended
though not necessarily excusable descents into doggerel. The
dialect piece for Anthony Thwaite's fiftieth birthday is one, with
this deliberately excruciating conclusion:

> All t'same, 'e ne'er forgets 'is pals,
> And 'e keeps up thur pecker
> Printing thur prose, and 'awking round
> Thur books of verse to Secker.[40]

That, it may be noted, comes some pages later than the poem
about taking his 1964 Daimler V8 for its MOT test, with its
swiftly-broken resolution:

> At last he reaches Section VI.
> The windscreen-washer pisses. Nay,
> Even the horn appears OK.
> And so he slants the last few ticks.
>
> I vow that I shall never more
> Write thus...[41]

These are mildly problematical, and so are the recurrences of that
archness which in the memoirs seems less obtrusive. 'Mackerel in

the Athenaeum', for instance, is another pendant to the prose recollections of his grandfather, 'That long-dead Tory alderman', and in it Fuller makes a fair if cumbersome point about the 'Amazing decline in my lifetime of bourgeois standards' by observing that 'indolent grandpa', though far from well-off, employed a servant and refused to eat mackerel, which he called 'Scavenger of the ocean': 'But how the scaly item twixt me and Pall Mall / Would have upset him.'[42] That ridiculous paraphrase of the poem's title resembles neither verse nor prose, though it might pass for a crossword clue – as indeed might the equally quaint formulation in 'On the Demolition in 1980 of the Roxy, Old Dover Road SE3': 'bad action Hitler failed to bring off'.[43] One can see the pleasure to be had from inventing such dottily off-key constructions, but it remains an essentially private pleasure, like that of the marginal doodle (in which Fuller also delighted), and it has the effect of making the reader feel oddly intrusive.

There are two kinds of compensation for such disappointments. The major one is the inclusion of the 'Mianserin Sonnets' sequence, which forms a satisfactorily solid tailpiece to the book. The minor compensation occurs when, quite often, an occasional or personal poem hits exactly the right note. This happens in the bleakly consolatory 'New Year Blues', dedicated to Kathleen Symons: here he tries 'to take heart / From Hardy's example' but mercilessly admits that 'what has intervened' in the forty-five years of their friendship

> Is not just time, or blows
> Struck on ourselves, but loss,
> Absolute loss, and that
> In the end is the staunchless source
> Of our blues...[44]

Curiously, the unfudged honesty allied to the plainness of an unrhymed three-stress line *does* console, in spite of its apparently unrelieved pessimism. More predictably reassuring are the recurrent image of the fox in the garden – 'I draw the curtains, see a fox / Lying in winter sunlight, still'[45] – and the increasingly close connection between listening to music and writing poetry:

> Writing, I play some ancient discs I love,
> Certainly spun a hundred times or more,

And marvel at poetry coming in old age
And melody's persistent interest,
Like kissing one mouth inexhaustibly
Or the compulsive glancing at a face.

An almost identical motif of 'verse, discs, / *Et cetera*, owned, idly listened to, for years' figures in the fifth stanza of 'Autumn 1981', perhaps the most touching of all the personal pieces in the section. It is that comparative rarity in Fuller's work, a love poem to Kate – or rather, it is a poem about the tactful reticence which paradoxically embodies a special kind of honesty:

I nearly say: This is a happy time.
– You far from well; myself
With quite a shopping-list of fleshly ills,
And on the verge of seventy, you
Not far behind.

Our diary: dates with the dentist – putting off
Friends who'd put up with us;
Nor seeing even dearer ones enough.
Recluses who have very nearly
Ceased to mind

The world. Could be a mustering of milk
Bottles announces our end –
The sort of commonplace I often make
A jest of, though suspecting your
Grin's merely kind.[46]

Some quietly astonishing things are happening in these three opening stanzas: the lurch from happiness to illness (forcing one to wonder whether the 'happy' of line 1 isn't bitterly ironic, a doubt not fully resolved until much later); the unsparing, plainly honest account of engagements much like those of most elderly couples; and, above all, that extraordinary 'merely kind', whose apparent harshness neatly rebounds on the 'suspecting' poet. The clarification follows:

And always I refrain from mentioning
Happiness, unsure
Whether at bottom you don't feel a lack;
And also fearful that the word
Itself unbind

Some spell; and worse befall.

Such delicacy of feeling – and the Jane Austenish tone of that phrase seems perfectly appropriate – is so uncharacteristic of the late twentieth century that it may come almost as a shock. If so, it should be a salutary one: for this, surely, is the key which explains and vindicates Fuller's characteristic emotional reticence, his preoccupation with good manners, his dislike of vulgarity and obscenity. This tone, at once forthright and almost overwhelmingly tender, is (like so much in his later poetry) reminiscent of Hardy – here of the *'Veteris vestigia flammae'* poems of 1912–13. And indeed the final stanza of Fuller's poem is in its tone, movement and imagery utterly Hardyesque:

> Earlier, undoubtedly, I fiercely loved:
> Why else would I have lavished
> My miser's store, hung on through jealousy?
> Yet now appears the most delicate bloom,
> On the death-poised rind.

Those two startlingly simple words, 'bloom' and 'rind', are full of resonance: the flower emerging from a shrubby plant's bark as well as the glow of human skin. This is a perfect example of a kind of poem seldom associated with Fuller.

Having completed *New and Collected Poems*, he worked on a new sonnet sequence during the autumn of 1984. *Subsequent to Summer* was intended as a pamphlet but it grew into a book-length collection, and this appeared separately (somewhat to Seckers' irritation) from Salamander Press, later in 1985. Like Tragara, the Salamander Press was initially based in Edinburgh; it was run by Tom Fenton, James Fenton's brother and a friend of John Fuller's, and its publications were as handsome as Alan Anderson's though usually more ambitious in scale. 'The Salamander book,' Fuller recalled, 'was beautifully produced, but it did nothing for the fortunes of that firm, which fairly soon, like others which had taken me on, went bust.'[47] As so often in his later work, the sequence owes much of its success to his invention of an almost-familiar form, shaping but not inhibiting: the poems have fourteen iambic lines and so may conveniently be called sonnets, but they are sparsely and irregularly rhymed, and they are divided into couplets – a fairly arbitrary trick yet a surprisingly useful one. The effect is to isolate what might otherwise appear to be quite random

jottings and to provide them with an unexpected epigrammatic
bounce. For instance:

> Drops on the reddening leaves, such as depend
> In autumn's onset from my old man's nose.[48]

> Mild, sunny day; still-copulating flies.
> I go outdoors and find the garden wrecked.[49]

> I buy *The Browning Cyclopaedia* in
> Oxfam, feeling it better in my care.[50]

> I pick a fir-cone up, think: what's it like?
> Asymetrical; hooved its numerous legs.[51]

Of course, such syntactically complete couplets would soon become
wearisome, and Fuller's sentences usually run across his stanza-
breaks, but they add a useful piquancy to his quotidian observations.
Although he is predictably self-deprecating about his material –
'What bosh I dream up at the end of day!'[52] – his predominant theme
of the world in the evening seems apt and inevitable:

> Michaelmas daisies in the evening gloom
> Make now the only novel garden hue,

> Except some yellowing and reddening leaves
> Still too unnumerous to spread the blues.[53]

This notebooky kind of observation, typically written at dusk with
the evening's first drink at hand, is by no means confined to Fuller's
immediate domestic environment. Rather, this serves as a backdrop
to a series of little ironic excursions: to a funeral at St Michael and
All Angels, Wilmington, where he notes 'The crippled verger and
the single candle, / Bright coffin';[54] to Hextable School, where he
is consoled by 'Equal exchanges with a generation / I could with
ease grandfather';[55] and, of course, to the Woolwich, from whence
his return journey one day takes him on an unfamiliar route past
'"The Bricklayers' Arms Development" – an almost / Occult
phrase, denoting space and weeds.'[56] Meanwhile the spider, once
famously found in the bath and 'noted',[57] now spins through several
of these poems as an image of that autumnal creative regeneration
which prompts Fuller to 'marvel freshly, too, / At the amazing
pleasures of the human.'[58]

★

'Re-election', one of the later sonnets in *Subsequent to Summer* begins:

> I come up for re-election to the Board
> Of the old Woolwich; special wording, since
>
> I can't according to our rules see out
> The usual three years.[59]

Not only is this a curious and awkward start to a poem; it is also the most specific reference to his precise occupation in all Fuller's poetry. Of course, there are allusions and hints, which become increasingly explicit as time passes; and there is also the more-or-less fictional Saddleford Building Society in *Image of a Society*. But a crucial element of his tactfulness was the gentle yet firm demarcation line which he maintained between his two careers. Until he retired from his full-time employment at the Woolwich and joined the board, his jacket blurbs described him simply as 'Solicitor to one of the "big five" Building Societies': although it would have been easy enough for anyone to discover which one, there was no unseemly naming of names. So this sonnet represents a distinct departure from precedent, marking – or anticipating – an occasion which was indeed special. Because the Woolwich required its directors to retire at the age of seventy-five, Fuller's term of office would have to end on 11 February 1987; by that date he had 'served the Society over forty-nine years, and sentimentally would have liked to complete fifty'.[60]

The significance of this statement must not be underestimated. Fuller's Woolwich career – the crass expression 'day job' is for once quite precisely accurate – was both long and distinguished: it was, he said, 'the best kind of lawyer's life',[61] and it spilled over into such related areas as his membership of the Law Society's Working Party on Conveyancing and his Chairmanship of the Building Societies Association Legal Advisory Panel. Though this sort of committee work was much less publicly visible than that with the BBC or Arts Council, it was generally more to his taste: 'Through membership of the Working Party, and the work for the BSA, I began, against all the odds, and most of my previous experience, to enjoy the practice of the law.'[62] In his seventieth birthday BBC conversation with Anthony Thwaite, he added that through his involvement in these 'rather high-powered things' he had become 'actually inter-

ested in the law, rather too much for the health of literature, you
might say'; he also revealed an even more surprising kind of pleasure which he derived from his Woolwich career:

> I once nearly wrote, in collaboration, a book on mortgages, and
> I've always regretted I never did that, because I think it's a
> subject which verges in places on the poetic. Some great judge
> once said no-one understood the English law of mortgage in the
> light of nature or the light of reason, because the notion of
> property being conveyed as security for a debt and the borrower
> retaining an equity of redemption in the land is so full of artifi-
> ciality and metaphor – I mean, it probably arose round about the
> time of Donne.[63]

Coincidentally, Anthony Powell contributed to the pamphlet
Poems for Roy Fuller on his Seventieth Birthday a piece called 'Building
Society Drinking Song' which light-heartedly makes a similar point.
'Set me in my office where other books please,' he writes:

> There if ever allured by clandestine impieties,
> Drafting the terms where a mortgage pertains,
> Fuller's *Questions and Answers for Building Societies*
> Will tell me the Law and the Practice that reigns.[64]

Nevertheless, a close Woolwich colleague of Fuller's has expressed
mild surprise that, having quite gratefully escaped from his full-
time commitment to the Society, he should then have spent eighteen years conscientiously attending its board meetings;[65] yet the
Woolwich board was the last of the numerous committees on
which he had enjoyed serving, and he was reluctant to give it up.
He relished the paraphernalia of meetings, the ritual of corporate
lunches, the idiosyncrasies of colleagues – all of which furnished
material for poetry and, especially, for fiction. And he naturally
delighted in making the most of his elderly obstinacy, 'conscious of
the irony of having assumed the role of ancient, fuddy-duddy
director that in one's executive past one had looked on so pityingly
and exasperatedly'.[66] It was a role into which he could slip, with a
touch of self-mockery, even in writing to as old a friend as Julian
Symons:

> Thank God I have lived before the full onslaught of [electronic
> gadgetry]. Word processors, plastic cards, electronic transfer of

funds – all boring, & largely inconvenient. Have to deal with such topics to some extent on Woolwich board: the equipment is like drugs – the more you have, the more you have to have; & at ruinous expense. But mustn't rabbit on about such things in Retd Colonel vein.[67]

As David Blake recalls, Fuller increasingly saw himself as the lonely custodian of traditional values: at board meetings, he was the member who would on principle oppose every change. Some of these views were rationally and intelligibly rooted in his strong ethical convictions about the mutuality of building societies. He bitterly resented the dropping of the word 'Equitable', and he detested the Woolwich's new corporate headquarters, which have very much the style and scale of international big business, at Bexleyheath; and, as is clear from *Spanner and Pen*, he was appalled by the 1986 Building Societies Act, which enabled building societies to turn themselves from mutual organisations into public limited companies (the Abbey National was the first to do this, in 1988, whereas the Woolwich – whatever other reservations Fuller might have had about its development in recent years – remains the most staunchly committed of the major societies to the mutual principle). However, some of his other stands look like mere cussedness: for instance, he furiously sought to block a revolutionary proposal that the Woolwich board, which had traditionally met on the first Tuesday of the month at 2.30 in the afternoon, might sometimes meet on a Tuesday morning, if circumstances made this more convenient, or even on a Monday afternoon.

He also became liable to quirky variations on the theme of *droit du seigneur*. His great affection for his 1964 Daimler V8 is recorded in poems such as 'Getting his Daimler Out at Night'[68] and 'The Test'[69] as well as in his memoirs,[70] and he is to be seen seated in it in the jacket photograph on his *Crime Omnibus*; nevertheless, he had come to dislike driving much further than the mile or two from Langton Way to Equitable House. Instead, he was happy to be driven immense distances by senior colleagues such as David Blake (whose pleasurable chores included ferrying this 'sympathetic and amusing companion'[71] to and from Woolwich-sponsored concerts) or, better still, by a Woolwich chauffeur. Blake recalls his mistake in thinking that it might be a kindness for him to drive Fuller to a formal function which they both had to attend, rather than entrusting him to an impersonal chauffeur; whereupon Fuller spent much of the evening grumbling that, of all the important persons present, he was the only one not to have been provided with a proper chauffeur.

Still more eccentric was his behaviour when David Blake was diagnosed as suffering from a peptic ulcer, a complaint of which he had some knowledge through his own troublesome experience. Speaking from an unassailable combination of legal methodology and obsessive hypochondria, Fuller offered forceful advice and enquired about the specialist and the prescribed treatment. At his next appointment with the specialist, Blake was asked: 'Who is this Professor Fuller?' The doctor had naturally assumed him to be a medical academic – since Professor Fuller, who so seldom used his academic title, had phoned to instruct him on the correct treatment. That wilfully misleading claim of authority, characteristic of many a self-made man, represents a revealing lapse in Fuller's habitual discretion; and it vividly illustrates how tenaciously his sense of insecurity, and the corresponding need to prove his own competence, persisted even in his later life. Nevertheless, as David Blake ruefully admits, when Fuller warned him about the unpleasant side-effects of a particular drug and he passed on this warning anonymously to his doctor, it turned out that Fuller was absolutely right.[72]

As a board member, he was largely responsible for involving the Woolwich in its sponsorship of the arts, knowing the shortcomings (as he perceived them) of the Arts Council all too well; this included not only national musical and theatrical events but concerns closer to home. 'There is no doubt,' says his Blackheath neighbour, Neil Rhind,

> that he was influential in encouraging his then late employers...
> in a pump-priming donation to the Blackheath Concert Hall
> restoration appeal. Without the Woolwich and Roy's advocacy
> it is doubtful whether the local authorities would have
> supported the cause, and the Society's contribution encouraged
> other commercial groups to support the venture.[73]

Thus, in a typically unobtrusive way, some facets of the divided self – the legal, the cultural and the domestic – at last began to achieve a degree of synthesis. And when the time came for him to severe his formal links with the Woolwich, in February 1987, it was, apart from irritatingly falling just short of a fifty-year stint, probably the right time. Writing on that occasion to Mark Preston, Fuller with typical generosity thanked him for his 'care & conscientiousness' which 'complemented my slapdashery when we worked – so harmoniously – together', before adding with equally typical candour:

> No, I'm not altogether sorry to go. I feel b. societies are about to embark on a course full of dubieties, & in any case the old 'movement' idea – concern for the members & a modest style for the rulers – has gone for ever.[74]

★

On 12 February 1987, the day after his seventy-fifth birthday and his retirement from the Woolwich board, Fuller gave a reading at the Poetry Society in Earl's Court, introduced by Julian Symons, to launch his new collection of poems, *Consolations*. He was not in good health, and the event was further complicated by Seckers' astonishing inability to provide the Poetry Society Bookshop with copies of the book, whose initial print-run was already sold out. Nevertheless, everyone present seemed aware that it was a literary occasion of the rarest sort. Jonathan Barker recalls not only the reading but Symons' 'superb short talk on Roy Fuller's poetry with no note in sight', and adds: 'There was something about having these two men together which made the whole evening truly memorable.'[75] There was also the sense that with this book, mostly written since his *New and Collected Poems* of 1985, the hoped-for and anticipated late flowering of a major poet had indeed begun: fortunately, there are poems in *Consolations* to justify such heady expectations.

Although the book takes its place among the rag-bags rather than the sequences of Fuller's later collections, it is organised (as *Available for Dreams* would be) in loosely thematic sections. The first of these, 'Age', has its share of mildly barmy jottings – feeding chocolate drops to a dog outside a shop and mistaking a fox's turd in the lane for a mushroom – but also some more substantial and searching pieces; one notices almost immediately the relaxed assurance, the absence of those defensive mannerisms which were intermittently damaging in *The Reign of Sparrows* and in the final part of *New and Collected Poems*. In the opening poem, 'Down Kaunda Street', a guidebook prompts recollections of war-time Kenya and its subsequent changes – there is typically wry astonishment at the fact that Nairobi now has dual carriageways – before moving on to the genuinely unexpected discovery that he 'came to love / The strange land' where he experienced 'emotions / Perhaps I never truly owned again':

> What friendships torn in two, myself quite blind
> To anything (when at last the moment came)
> Save the long voyage to the *patria!*[76]

It is this sense of the author's train of thought evolving with the poem, and in doing so quietly surprising him, which gives much of Fuller's later work its peculiar integrity. If the poem as journal entry, often written almost literally on the hoof, has its moments of absurdity – 'And writing this, I still sit wearing / My kitchen apron...' he tells us in 'A Sort of Art', as the washing-up drips on the draining-board[77] – it also has the merit of discouraging the poem as predetermined artifact. Or, to put it another way, the inclusion of apparently inconsequential material may be a small price to pay for his free-ranging, self-surprising flow of ideas.

'Emperor's Tomb Found in China', its title borrowed from an article in *The Times*, provides a perfect example of this method, suggesting a parallel – and outrageously punning – form of archae-ological exploration:

> Deep in the attic of a kitchen cupboard
> A pile of plates is found, by time embrowned,
> Though not concealing gilt and dark-blue rims.[78]

For many writers, this neat jokiness would have been the end of the matter; but here it leads to recollections of the Fullers' other dinner-services and hence to the conclusion that this set must have been passed down to them by his mother:

> Among my infancy's mills and moors, my mother
> Girlish, what ghostly meals were served on those
> Platters, by servants dead as in old Cathay!

He manages to make this trick look deceptively easy, of course, but the distance travelled and the range of material embraced in the mere eighteen lines of this poem are extraordinary. The same is true of 'Born 1912', each of whose three sections contains an auda-cious chronological leap: from 'the tropical summer / Of 1911' which preceded his birth to the present with its 'permissive, self-styled "loose bananas"'; then from the present – this time a board meeting – back to the composition of *The Planets* (1914–16); and lastly from a Mendelssohn quartet to a contemporary supermarket.[79] An unsympathetic reader could of course see this merely as a lack of focus, a sort of elderly dithering; whereas what is happening is that intuitive synthesis of imaginative and everyday life towards which the earlier poems sometimes too effortfully strive. And that is something for which, as Fuller says, 'One renders faintly unbelieving thanks'.

The book's second section, 'Footnotes', has an unashamedly catch-all character, ranging from substantial pieces such as a strange desert island fictional monologue ('Booloo')[80] and a purportedly first-hand account of the *ur-Hamlet* ('The Marcellus Version')[81] to a not terribly funny squib about the unfortunate names of the American poets Adelaide Crapsey and Amy Clampitt.[82] The third section, 'Tenners', is a set of shortened sonnets, mostly in the now-familiar reminiscent-domestic mode: 'The robin's silence-breaking percussive song' juxtaposed with the Ampico rolls pedalled through on Uncle Alf's pianola,[83] 'The simple spud, provided of decent breed' commended at the vegetable counter.[84] And though the progress of the final section, 'Seasons', is familiar too, these poems are full of unexpectedly touching and vulnerable details.

For example, the little six-line poem called 'Preserving' at first glance may seem slight and entirely straightforward:

> Making the marmalade this year, I carve
> Some peel to form the initial of your name.
>
> Perhaps you'll come across it when I'm gone,
> For even in mourning mornings will go on.
>
> So such surprise as ancient love contrives
> Will change to the kind of shock that stunned our prime.[85]

There is further evidence of Fuller's devotion to marmalade both in his memoirs[86] and in a review – written at much the same time as this poem – of C. Anne Wilson's *The Book of Marmalade*. 'I once reckoned I had consumed over a ton of marmalade in my life,' he says, before surveying the field of commercial marmalade manufacturing and providing this pleasing account of its domestic alternative:

> Making marmalade at home is a bother, no doubt about it. In our early days my wife and I had my mother's marmalade-

cutter... but when my mother married again late in life it was
returned to her, and never recovered. It had to be clamped to
the edge of the kitchen-table, and the peel was fed to the hand-
operated to-and-fro blade through the body of the machine by
a short wooden baton, ending in a knob. As a boy, my sternum
was always sore after marmalade-making, due to pressing the
knob with my chest as I operated the peel-knife. No doubt at a
later date my stomach was similarly affected. Nowadays, I cut up
the fruit by hand.[87]

As, indeed, the poem confirms. The initial, we know, is K, a letter
conveniently and (one would imagine) durably made out of
orange-peel. The pun 'mourning mornings' is vindicated both by
its literary antecedents (Hopkins springs to mind) and by a clear
sense that any groans are meant to rebound on the poet himself: his
liking for puns has already been amply demonstrated earlier in
Consolations, and the *Book of Marmalade* review almost inevitably
includes the phrase 'a thin shred of objection'. Until we reach its
last line, the poem wears at least a mask of lightness, but 'the kind
of shock that stunned our prime' is a sturdily monosyllabic phrase
which carries a quite unexpected emotional force. It is also, for all
its simplicity, deeply ambiguous. For just what 'kind of shock' was
it that 'stunned our prime'? The intensity of love, or its failure, or
both? If Fuller had told us, this would have been a lesser poem.

Of course, it is neither necessary nor probably desirable to read
all his journal-poems so closely. Once again, he invokes the great
example of Henry James: 'As James said of the notebook habit: "To
catch / And keep something of life – that's what I mean".'[88] This is
just what Fuller does, but the trouble with writing continually
about a writer's life is that it can become maddeningly, or with luck
charmingly, reflexive:

> To hear the wind softly in the trees, yet fail
> To feel it on one's face – a test for summer.
> I carry a tea-tray to our (so-called) terrace:
> Peanut-butter or *patum peperium*;
> A freshly-out *London Mag* or *Private Eye*;
> A dish of soaked crusts for my pals the birds.
> A set of pleasures rather close to guilt.[89]

Though he sets out these props with such cheerful artlessness, even his fans might chance the mildest of grumbles about the absurd parenthetical 'so-called' (so-called by whom but himself?), the over-deliberate culture clashes between both spreads and magazines, the archness of 'pals'. Yet even here, typical of the refreshed confidence which so marks *Consolations*, he knows precisely what he is doing. No sooner has this exaggerated dodderiness been established than he cuts to 'children playing in the lane − / The start of their enormous evening', and with that lovely second phrase the contrast between apparently limitless child-time and his own finnickiness is crystallised. But then he goes indoors, to write among beautifully-evoked evening shadows and, in keeping with the collection's title, to conclude:

> July's more transient than children's games,
> Themselves untypical of the human lot
> As happiness. Yet even in old age
> Time sometimes lingers on a fabulous page.

The summer poems glow with this luminous feeling of time regained; and so, for a while at least, do the autumn poems, such as 'Images':

> The creeper knows when it must start to blush.
> As in a 'magic' painting book, the hose
> Reveals an unsuspected spider's web.
> Summer's about to end: let's hope to be
> Inspired by rotten weather, like Debussy.[90]

But the autumn of 1985 was to bring more than rotten weather. On 16 October he wrote to Julian and Kathleen Symons:

> Just a quick line to say that Kate is in hospital − whisked there on Sunday with a perforated gastric ulcer. Has been pretty bad, but now making good progress, as it seems, though living simply − so to speak! − on a saline drip.
> If you would like to send message she is in Ward 1G, Greenwich Hospital, Vanbrugh Hill, SE10. As she recovers she is likely to become more & more bored, so any scandal or news you can communicate would be appreciated. Will be in about another fortnight, they estimate.[91]

It was cruelly ironic for Kate to be afflicted with a complaint so like one which had formerly haunted her husband; and it was cruel,

too, for Fuller himself, his desolation trapped by his reticence (typically, whereas many people would have at once phoned and indeed
summoned their oldest friends, he sent that tactful note when Kate
was on the way to recovery). His timely utterance was the
restrained, melancholic poem 'Ward 1G', which ends *Consolations*,
setting 'Your scaffold-timed reprieve, that's also mine' against the
parallel image of 'a crew of wasps' taking 'A final sip of *nouveau*
apple-juice'.[92] In the hospital itself, he is struck by the distance
'between the *condition humaine* / And contemplative life' and by the
way in which 'the plaster that attaches you / To various tubes' is
oddly complemented by the band on a finger, 'your wedding-
ring'. Eventually, he is back home after dark, having navigated dogs
on the heath and a cat in the lane:

> And gratitude to enigmatic powers,
> Malevolent on the whole, wells up as I
> Return to music's marvels, while you lie
>
> Rather too closely to the realms of Dis.

★

One reader who apparently failed to respond to the unmistakable
qualities of Fuller's late poetry was Seckers' new senior editor, Robin
Robertson. 'I have been sacked by Secker,' Fuller told Alan
Brownjohn on Good Friday 1987. 'That fellow Robin Robertson
expressed no interest in an adumbrated new book – & presumably in
any new book.'[93] He had met Robertson for the first time over lunch
the previous summer, with Peter Grose, and in *Spanner and Pen*
provided a witheringly polite account of the occasion. Robertson

> turned out to be a young man with a designer stubble (as the
> unshaven look affected as a fashion had come to be known) and
> what I conceived to be a mid–Atlantic accent; perfectly amiable.
> He chose some faintly exotic dish from the menu of the up-
> market restaurant (within walking distance of Seckers' offices in
> Soho's Poland Street) to which Peter had taken us, possibly indi-
> cating quite a few lunches in that locale. He said one thing that
> struck me – that as an editor he liked to see (or had no objection
> to seeing) a book in its early, even inchoate, stage.[94]

The book Fuller had in mind was provisionally entitled *Sonnets and
'Sonnets'*; it would contain both true sonnets and other fourteen-

line poems, and he had planned it alongside *Consolations*, from which all such poems had been excluded. He sent his draft version off to Seckers in August 1986, but Robertson's final verdict did not arrive until March 1987, a month after the publication of *Consolations*:

> I have read through the sonnets three times now and given the whole project a great deal of thought. While there is much I admire here, I don't feel the collection would be right for the new Secker poetry list. You may have anticipated – if not already known – that I am moving the list in a new direction, and it is one that would not be appropriate for this work.[95]

This was really a more astonishing rejection than Deutsch's of *Souvenirs*: for, unlike that fascinating but oddly-constructed prose memoir, *Sonnets and 'Sonnets'* – or, as it was eventually called, *Available for Dreams* – was quite obviously a major late collection from an important poet, and precisely the book which his publisher might have been expected to welcome. Seizing on Robertson's statement that this was a 'completely personal decision', Fuller queried it with the Publishing Director, David Godwin, whose reply, while supporting Robertson's rejection, seemed nevertheless to distance him from it: 'your stature as a poet,' he wrote, 'is such that any publishing house lucky enough to publish your work should publish it with skill, commitment and drive.'[96]

Any satisfaction Fuller may have gained from these words was more than outweighed by their practical uselessness. He was, as he had been almost a decade earlier, once more without a publisher. Jackie Simms at Oxford University Press expressed interest, and raised the possibility of OUP buying the paperback rights in *New and Selected Poems*, but neither suggestion came to anything, 'although,' she said, 'I personally think many of the sonnets are wonderful, and perhaps in a smaller selection would make a good book.'[97] Anthony Whittome at Hutchinson was similarly deterred by the collection's length, though he would have been prepared to publish it if cut by a third. Finally, Alan Ross again provided the solution: not, on this occasion, by publishing the book himself but by introducing Fuller to Collins Harvill, from whom *Available for Dreams*, spaciously presented as a 150-page hardback, at last appeared in April 1989.

Reading the book one has, and not just retrospectively, the sense of a jigsaw nearing and possibly attaining its completion. It is so clearly the counterpart of that earlier book-length sequence, *From the Joke Shop*, and it is just as clearly the major achievement towards which slighter sequences – *Subsequent to Summer*, the 'Tenners' in *Consolations* – are pointing. The internal relationships are no less artful than these external ones: there are seven sections, of which the first and last ('Kitchen Sonnets' and 'The Cancer Hospital') start from very specific contexts; the second and sixth deal respectively with a progress through the seasons and with different kinds of social and personal decay; while the central three sections range more widely among Fuller's characteristic themes – domestic and suburban life, gardening and shopping, music and the arts, retrospects triggered by minor events. The effect is thus of a defined frame containing an increasingly complex interaction of themes as one moves in to the heart of the book.

Of all Fuller's late sequences, *Available for Dreams* is the one which demands to be read through as a kind of quasi-Proustian narrative, its details only resonating properly within that extended family of other details which accumulates during the book. It is also the one in which he most fully exploits his disarming knack of seeming intimately personal and utterly self-deflating at the same time. So, 'old Fauré, always a favourite' is 'Unhummable and yet all melody; / Rare but good way for ancient chaps to write.'[98] The formulation is exact, its potential smugness undercut by that sardonic 'ancient chaps'. That sense of an easy effect just nudged out of place by a subversive word or phrase is a recurrent one, as when the sequence-within-a-sequence called 'Lessons of the Summer' ends with these melodic (and almost hummable) lines:

> 6.45: an empty evening sky,
> Great calm, some robin-song. And then I spy
> A demi-moon, beginning just to glow;
> Of unexpected size, indifferent, low.
> If time stayed for emotion, what great tears
> Might occupy the hours, and moons and years![99]

Fuller very seldom permits himself such full-blooded eloquence in his rhymed iambics, but as ever the ego is not allowed to escape unmocked: 'spy' – mannered or archaic or childish, with its faint tang of his Lancastrian past – is the word which puts the ancient chap in his place, rescuing the lines from overblown romanticism while insisting (as his sly archaisms often do) on an unshakeable sense of continuity with the past.

One highly practical consequence of this stance is a plausible illusion of mellowness, purging self-pity from poems which might otherwise have seemed embittered. At its lightest, the bitterness surfaces in enjoyable grumbles about the toughness of lettuces, the price of that formerly 'demotic fish'[100] skate or the likely (poor) quality of '86 reds which he decides he won't survive to drink. More prevalent, though usually only recorded in glancing asides, is his sense of quiet despair about 'rotten times like these'[101] which erupts explicitly in the helpless conclusion of a poem about a once-despised and now-ruined cinema, glimpsed in 'Dans un Omnibus de Londres' from the window of the inevitable 53:

> The cinema itself is like a temple
> Of civilized antiquity after prolonged
> Years of barbarians. Too much is wrong.[102]

The moment of over-emphasis is uncharacteristic of this book: a few poems later, as if aware that this lapse into unqualified old-bufferdom is altogether too simple, he is sympathising with a young punk girl, her rejection of Thatcherite society, her vegetarian pacifist 'beliefs that he... / In principle supports'.[103] 'I play – I am! – the Shakespearean daft old man,' he insists,[104] tactfully leaving it for the reader to reflect that Lear and Polonius and Nestor – to say nothing of Prospero – are all something a good deal more complicated than 'daft'. He is in any case aware that elderliness provides the context, but not necessarily the cause, of alienation, as when he nips into an unfamiliar pub to use its lavatory on the way home 'after a West End day', and to make an image borrowed from the Venerable Bede very much his own:

> Music was playing, the tables mostly joined
> Mixed pairs. The marvellous relief was all
> Too quickly cancelled out by feeling like
> A sparrow flying through a feasting hall.[105]

If, despite this, *Available for Dreams* is not at all a gloomy book, it is because the themes of ageing and illness and despair are so perfectly balanced by the consolations of civilised suburban life. His attention is more than ever engaged and delighted by the honest oddity of things: spoons spooning 'behind closed drawers';[106] an unlighting oven ('one can't / Expect a pressed tit for respond for ever');[107] carrots 'haired sparsely as old age';[108] his father's ornately initialled hairbrush; a poodle wearing a Highland muff in the Post Office;[109] an 'out-of-season earwig' making its way 'towards the traffic-riddled road'.[110] Above all, as before, there is music: not only Mozart, Poulenc, Debussy, Duparc, Delius, but 'the neglected' Franz Schmidt, Alan Rawsthorne ('whom I might / Have actually met in deepest Lancashire'),[111] and the still-undervalued Gerald Finzi, but even jazz musicians – Sidney Bechet, Art Tatum, Bill Evans, and Ella Fitzgerald, with whom he proposes to 'sigh' in Gershwin. Though Fuller wryly asks himself, 'How did an old man's daily doings seem / Even remotely apt for poetry?',[112] the book provides a constant supply of answers.

Like *Consolations*, *Available for Dreams* concludes with poems, at once compassionate and stoical, about Kate's further absence in hospital. Because he has so completely earned his readers' confidence in his observation of ordinary life, these sonnets are all the more moving in their simple and truthful account of the slightly extraordinary, the jarring displacements of illness. The sense of habit knocked askew as he returns from the hospital needs only the plainest language:

> Back home, I have no doubt the door will be
> Unlocked, because I expect you always there;
> And have to search my pockets for the key;
> And find the flattened bed and vacant chair.[113]

Similarly, the symbols of Kate's absence – 'A long grey hair among the household dust', 'An empty room, two petals by the door' – are details much like those habitually noticed by Fuller, here transformed by their context which turns them into 'Relics of what mankind appears to trust / When flesh is failing';[114] though his scepticism is unfazed by times of emotional pressure, as the cautious 'appears to trust' demonstrates. The hospital itself provides other, stranger transformations: exploring, the visitor encounters first a book-cupboard ('some authors I knew once, now dead') and then hears from 'a "patients' sitting-room", played live, / The sounds of a Debussy arabesque'.[115] It is hard to imagine more unexpected or disconcerting evidence of Fuller's conviction that everyday life *is* poetic life, a point triumphantly reaffirmed and perfectly illustrated by the final sonnet, 'Postscript':

My hands are burnt with cooking, by roses scarred.
It's taken your illness and the carelessness
Of age to join me with the working-class,
Though in the war I used to skin my fingers
Crawling in aircraft beached in arching hangars.
The war! – unknown to possibly a third
Of present humans, including those whose wrong
Organs convey them to the Fulham Road
Early as middle-age. The way is long –
Shortish for some – and up and down for most.
Even insomniacs, if tired enough,
Eventually throw off their wearying load.
Available for dreams: a mighty cast
Of all the dead and living of my life.[116]

★

In 1988, after 'eighteen fictionless years',[117] Fuller completed his last novel, *Stares*. 'I kept it dark, being dubious about its passableness,' he told Julian Symons. 'Then Collins Harvill turned it down, so I kept it even darker. But the reckless but (as you say) virtuous S-S has signed on the dotted line.'[118] It was published in 1990 by the then new and independent firm of Sinclair-Stevenson; however, it is a seriously flawed book, and certainly not the starting-point for readers new to Fuller's fiction, even though it holds considerable interest for those who know his work.

The problems are easily illustrated. *Stares* is set in a convalescent home for the mentally ill, run by the mysteriously absent Dr Mowle (pronounced as in Hamlet's 'Well said, old mole' to his ghostly father), and narrated by one of the 'guests': a youngish homosexual actor called William Toyne, recovering from the trauma of his partner Sammy's suicide. Toyne's first-person prose style, however, is essentially that of an elderly heterosexual solicitor, compounded by a priggishness which seems entirely at odds with the character's age and profession. He is ludicrously edgy about the slightest allusion to his sexuality, which for an actor in the late 1980s is hardly anything to get excited about; when the outspoken Maida Brown says 'We were all married once', he has to be rescued 'from an embarrassing turn in the conversation';[119] yet when she later tells him 'I could do with a fag right now',[120] he seems strangely oblivious to the much more outrageous *double entendre* (of which conceivably his author was innocent). He is also readily bowled over by the barmy prejudices of others. When another fellow-guest, Mrs Stogden, recounts her horror on seeing from a bus her estranged sixteen-year-old daughter with 'her hand resting on the shoulder of a man not young, drinking from a can, in a black leather jacket, with outrageous dyed hair', he responds: "How truly harrowing!" I dared not ask the child's fate.'[121] The characterisation is so insecure that it is hard to tell whether or not this is meant sarcastically; the context gives no hint that it is. But clearly the incident described is *not* 'truly harrowing', though it may well have been upsetting and annoying; while Mrs Stogden's own speech is both syntactically strange – 'a man not young' is an absurd inversion, and the can momentarily appears to be wearing the leather jacket and dyed hair – and unidiomatic, for the solicitorial style has invaded dialogue as well as narrative. Problems such as these recur throughout the book.

Described in these terms, *Stares* may sound practically unreadable, and certainly it is a disappointment after *The Carnal Island*; but all Fuller's late work has its fascinations, and this is no exception. Firstly, there is its ingenious construction. At the heart of the novel is Toyne's production of a play-reading by himself and his fellow-patients: the idea is suggested by the *Lovers' Vows* episode in *Mansfield Park*, which is scarcely a happy precedent. 'In *Mansfield Park*,' Toyne recalls, 'the scheme went forward in the absence of the head of the family, with rather dire consequences',[122] and here the invisible Dr Mowle represents a dim parallel to Sir Thomas Bertram. The play chosen by Toyne is *The Seagull*, which provides ample opportunities for emotional ambiguity, mirrors in its setting the convalescent home itself (which is precisely described in Chekov's stage-directions for Act Two), and contains a play-within-a-play. The book is thus like a series of diminishing frames, or Chinese boxes: a play within a play within a novel, and the novel itself occupying an enigmatic position within Fuller's work as a whole.

For, secondly, this is a book which skews the interest in psychological oddity so prevalent in his fiction, since all the main characters are by definition slightly mad (those who are not 'guests' – the doctors, domestic staff, and a preposterous gardener who moves effortlessly from the botanical Latin of '*Prunus subhirtella autumnalis*' to the pure Mummersetshire of 'Always carry your seekatewers about with you'[123] – are not noticeably saner). This has enabled him to take his old theme of the divided self and fracture it into a multiplicity of selves. His legal background goes into Mr Boraston, a poetic solicitor ('Autumn has arrived in a day'),[124] his old bufferishness into Mr Chiswell; while William Toyne himself shares his author's creative consciousness: 'The somewhat Jamesian turn to my words brought home the part I seemed to be playing at Stares – the detached observer, outrageous emotions diluted by his judicious mind and balanced prose style.'[125] A highly literate actor such as Toyne might be expected to have read Henry James, but that formulation is not only writerly but utterly Fullerish. So, more painfully, is his reflection on the possible consequences of being orphaned:

> I said: 'At its simplest the thing works like this. An adult suffers a bereavement – the death of a spouse or an offspring – and that revives the devastating sense of loss suffered by that adult as a child when his mother or father – or both – died. So there is really a double – or treble – loss, and the adult fails to cope with the anxiety and pain and depression that can't wholly be accounted for.'[126]

Fuller seems to have intended, by creating a narrator who is clearly distinct from himself in age, sexuality and profession, to deal with matters which he found difficult or distressing to voice *in propria persona*. If this is so, then the intermittent flashbacks which chart the emotional estrangement of Bill Toyne and Sammy Rankin may cast an oblique light on Fuller's own mid-life marital tensions, whose existence – and resolution – is merely hinted at in the poems. Of course, the fictional estrangement, which is *not* resolved, ends in a violent death; and this causes a degree of imbalance within the novel, since the mismatched Bill–Sammy relationship, shown only in brief retrospective glimpses, is more powerful and engrossing than any of the flimsier relationships which develop among the inhabitants of Stares (of whom, given the brevity of the book, there are too many). In the end, life and art mirror each other, and themselves, in an endlessly reflexive manner which is thoroughly appropriate for such a frame-within-frame book: David Waddilove, a minor character introduced quite late into the proceedings, kills himself just before the final and complete play-reading, which is consequently cancelled. The suicide echoes both Sammy's, outside the chronological frame, and Trepliov's, in *The*

Seagull; while the abandonment of the play reminds us of the disastrous dramatic adventure in *Mansfield Park*, which prompted the
scheme in the first place. These symmetries, ingenious as they are,
seem creaky in a slight and lightly-characterised novel.

Stares was swiftly followed by Fuller's post-war memoirs, *Spanner
and Pen*. Some readers were puzzled by the book's fragmentary
nature, or the space devoted to not especially famous friends and
colleagues, or the relative absence of material about poetry, or the
obfuscatory prose style; while D.J. Taylor thought it 'rather a point
in the author's favour that he emerges from this short yet curiously
diffuse book as an entirely anachronistic figure'.[127] That, however,
strikes me – and would surely have struck Fuller – as a a curious
judgement: for in *Spanner and Pen* he is at pains to present himself
as a kind of retired suburban Everyman, grumbling about declining
standards in 'bread, schooling, dress, manners',[128] cutting back on
his engagements, giving up driving and finding consolation in the
virtues of the 53 bus-route, 'one of the few worldly things that
improved rather than degenerated during my latter life'.[129] He says
that he 'loved the uneventful suburban routine, really that of the
retired solicitor I was';[130] and while this may not be an entirely fair
statement of the case – in the same sentence he speaks of devoting
'only two or three hours a day... to literary activity', which is two
or three hours more than most retired solicitors – it accurately
describes a stance which is closer to ordinary life and less 'anachronistic' than that of many a full-time literary professional. It is also a
stance which enables him to move easily between the roles of
building society solicitor and literary-cultural figure, the 'spanner'
and 'pen' of his title.

Indeed, one of the paradoxical virtues of *Spanner and Pen* is that
it is something far more *ordinary* than a literary memoir: the people
who most engage Fuller's attention, and command his admiration,
are quite likely to be unknown to anyone outside the building
society world. The highest praise in the book – 'Indeed, his gifts of
various kinds were as great as any I encountered, though in the end
my acquaintance ranged among the highest in the land, as they
say'[131] – is reserved for Sandy Meikle; and this straightforward,
justly democratic ability to value his professional colleagues
provides a salutary contrast with those in the literary establishment
who assume that the only way to be at all creative or significant is
to do something or other in the arts. The chapters on specifically

cultural affairs are perhaps less balanced. His pages on the BBC and the Arts Council include remarks which, as we have seen, are at best coat-trailingly provocative and at worst counter-productively intemperate (even so, they may not be unrepresentative of the man on the Blackheath omnibus, the 53). As for the lack of material about the making of his poetry, Fuller himself provides one good answer and implies a still better one: 'I find,' he says, 'I can't enlarge to my own satisfaction about the business of being a poet.'[132] But of course he had done that already, in his Oxford lectures, in *The Carnal Island*, and above all in the poems themselves, for 'that is what a poet must finally feel: that his verse tells all if read with attention, hoping for intelligent readers – even one at a time – down the years.'[133]

★

By May 1990 Fuller was once again in St Thomas's: 'I've been in hospital – removal of cancerous prostate & follow-up surgery to stop further infection of the bones by the malignant cells. I'm slowly recovering,' he told me, 'but a biographer must be warned!'[134] He did recover for a while, but in the late autumn further complications occurred: 'Have been laid low with pleurisy since mid-November,' he wrote, adding that he had sent no Christmas cards and that he was 'glad to see the back of 1990'.[135] By this time, his declining health, and Kate's, had made them both virtually house-bound, 'our post, like other necessities of life, dependent on visiting neighbours'.[136]

'One knew old age was going to be a bugger,' he wrote to Kathleen Symons in January 1991, 'but the gory details are infinitely depressing.' She was in hospital for a hip-replacement (he, with typically glum humour, cheered her with an anecdote about the only instance he knew, that of John Lehmann, in which the operation had gone wrong); Kate meanwhile was 'very bad on her pins, & suffers from back-ache & hiatus hernia'; and as for himself:

> Chest pains better than they were, but breathlessness & dropsy bad – the latter in spite of my now taking a horse-pill-sized tablet in addition to my *six* diurnal Frumeside. But I mustn't go on about my ills, though they are pretty well the only events in my life at the moment.'[137]

A few days later, in his last letter to Julian Symons, he was his stoical self: 'It's awful for us all to be in the wars, though we're lucky it didn't happen long ago.'[138] And that, of course, was true: two brothers had died in infancy, his father at the age of thirty-six, and his mother at sixty-three; his own health had collapsed soon after the war and been problematical ever since; yet his astonishingly productive life was to stretch into his eightieth year.

By February 1991, however, he was back in St Thomas's Hospital, and after a long illness he died at home on 27 September 1991; his son was with him. Full and warmly appreciative obituaries appeared in the *Daily Telegraph*, *Guardian*, *Independent* and *Times*; though the latter, ironically confirming the degree of neglect and marginalisation which had afflicted much of Fuller's work, managed to remain unaware of any collections after *The Reign of Sparrows*. In the *Independent*, Anthony Thwaite, while undervaluing the novels, described him as 'among the most readable and striking English poets of the second half of the twentieth century';[139] while in the *Guardian* – after citing Fuller's self-doubting lines 'Is it possible that anyone so silly can / Write anything good?'[140] – I concluded: 'It was much more than possible, much better than good.'[141] After his cremation, conducted according to his wishes without benefit of clergy, the relatives and friends present returned to 37 Langton Way and 'saw from the living-room window the veritable fox in the garden, reddish-brown and sizeable, looking at us without alarm.'[142] A celebration of his life – including readings by John Fuller, Anthony Thwaite and Julian Symons, and music by the Duke String Quartet (led by his granddaughter, Louisa Fuller) – was held on 12 June 1992 in the Blackheath Concert Hall as part of the Greenwich Festival.

Fuller wrote few if any poems during the last eighteen months of his life; and, since he had published three substantial collections since the *New and Collected Poems* of 1985, it seemed unlikely that a vast store of uncollected work would remain to be discovered. Even John Fuller was surprised to find 'about 180 typescript pages, and many further poems in eight substantial notebooks used between December 1983 and July 1989',[143] from which he drew the posthumous collection, *Last Poems*. The echo of Yeats is not only in the title but also within the text ('We old men standing in a holy fire'),[144] though it has in any case a full-circle aptness for a writer who called his first book simply *Poems* and his innovatory mid-career volume *New Poems*. In assembling the collection, John Fuller rightly judged that it was not the occasion for drafts, fragments and footnotes: instead, the book is organised in a spirit of affectionate allusiveness. It opens with a sequence in *Joke Shop* triplets and closes, like *Brutus's Orchard*, with a remarkable set of sonnets; in-between are some seventy poems, mostly arranged in loose thematic clusters.

Most of the poems were written in the mid-1980s, alongside those published in *Consolations* and *Available for Dreams*, so their recurring concerns are familiar ones. There is a sizeable group about listening to music, which merges seamlessly into reflections on life, art, and nature:

> Happiness, the final aim of art,
> Is always, as we know, too good to last.
> How else came minor keys to mean the most?[145]

Another bunch, which might have been subtitled 'The Old Buffer Goes Shopping', extends the range of wry epiphanies already experienced in such places as Boots and Marks and Spencer, at once charming and wise:

> To be alive! Astonishing state of matter –
> Inherently, let alone at seventy-four.
> And yet I ponder whether or not to buy
> A two-pack of vests, singles for sale no more.[146]

There are characteristically attentive encounters with spiders, snails and, in 'On the Way to the Compost Heap', a dead field-mouse. And there are poems which treat with gentle stoicism the consequences of illness and age:

> Like November's great blue fly,
> If the day is mild go forth,
> Though the sole blossom (of
> The ivy) a mere green pseudo-flower.
>
> Keep house contentedly
> Should the April wind stay north:
> What will come your way of love
> Now past the exercise of power.[147]

That poem is called 'Advice to the Elderly', and the allusion (in tone, form and title) to Yvor Winters' 'To a Young Writer', though distant, is decisive and finely ironic. More allusive still, indeed quite fiendishly oblique, is the sonnet sequence which ends the book: adapting the fictional mode of Elizabeth Barrett Browning's 'Sonnets from the Portuguese', Fuller's dense, reflexive narrative entwines fragments of *Measure for Measure* and Freud's Vienna with more accustomed domestic themes; the texture of the verse, packed with rich detail and not amenable to brief quotation, confirms his enduring allegiance to Wallace Stevens.

But what is most striking in *Last Poems*, even more than in *Available for Dreams*, is the deep sense of resolution, of a life's disparate strands drawn together into a harmony which even (or especially) astonishes the author; and that is partly due to an auto-biographical range which is at once more intimate and more far-reaching than is usually the case in Fuller's poems. The reader of the memoirs will identify 'SHB', memorialised in 'Friendship',[148] as S.H. Birch, a musical contemporary from his Blackpool school-days, and 'AES' ('After a Cremation')[149] as Fred Shrimpton, his predecessor as solicitor with the Woolwich; in 'Maestro'[150] he recalls the piano-playing schoolmaster, Mr Tregenza, to whose performance of Chopin Ashkenazy's is unfavourably compared; and there is another unfavourable comparison in 'The Temple Revisited', which laments the present's 'malaises', in particular a feared 'discontinuance / In England's history', yet discovers in the juxtaposition of familiarity and exclusion a typically generous, complex irony:

> I see through casements chunky tomes left out
> Like toys, and striped-shirted arms with telephones
> Which formerly had me on the other end.[151]

'What shall I do with all these poems I'm writing?' Roy Fuller would often ask his son: he was, as John Fuller notes in his Preface, 'far from believing in inspirational mysteries and yet I suspect that privately he may sometimes have been ready for a mood of voca-tional thanksgiving like that of Rilke at Muzot.'[152] The suspicion is amply borne out by these poems. While Fuller's later prose is marred by patches of embittered cantankerousness, here the prevailing mood is one of unfeigned gratitude for 'the felicities of these / Fag-end years, that have almost come too late'.[153] In one poem, he wonders briefly whether Mozart wrote too much,

> And then comes one of many masterworks
> From that near-posthumous inspired

Summer – strange benefaction that even lurks
For artists less sublimely fired.[154]

In another, he delightedly reflects that 'I'm older than my grandfather / And most days making fresh discoveries'[155] – for instance 'That
Rimsky wrote Rachmaninovian songs'. Or there is the literally self-
sown though no less grateful astonishment of 'Surprised by Spring':

These bits of blue and yellow touch even me,
Who put them in the earth; at seventy-three
Surprised by what I half thought not to see.[156]

It is a sustained mood of thanksgiving for the incorrigible absurdity
as well as for the possible decency of the human condition; and,
like so much in Fuller's extraordinary last two decades, it is a tribute
to the incomparable consolations of minor keys, which resonate
through his final instincts of return and resolution:

Often I feel perhaps I don't mind death –
Still free from pain and lameness, despite old age;
And yet I blench to think some moment in
The story I shan't be there to turn the page.[157]

Appendix

→→ →→ • ←← ←←

As suggested above (p.62), Fuller's choice of material for his first collection, *Poems* (1939), was rather puzzling. The following table shows the distribution of his early work between *Poems* (1939), *As from the Thirties* (1983), and *New and Collected Poems 1934–84* (Part One).

Title	P	AFTT	NCP	Notes
I New Year	7			
The Channel			3	
II 'The murdered man was rumoured up again'	7		3	*NCP* The Rumour
III 'The swan that ploughs the lucid lake'	8		4	*NCP* Legends
Birthday Poem		★	4	
IV 'In the morning I visited her again'	8		5	*NCP* The Visits
V 'Reaching the rarer atmosphere of change'	9			
Future Fossils		★	5	
VI 'Torrid blossoms of snow lay on the trees'	9		6	*NCP* The Journey
VII 'The folded land a horse could stamp through'	11		7	*NCP* The Centaurs
VIII 'Sitting at desks in the silence of their exile'	12			
IX 'Birds in the pattern of a constellation'	13		8	*NCP* End of a City
X Ballad of the Last Heir	15		11	
XI 'The Leader denied his men were discontented'	22			
XII 'Your image in a mirror in a darkened room'	22			
XIII To M.S., Killed in Spain	23		9	
XIV 'The aborigines wore masks of old men's heads'	25			
XV Variations on a Theme by Donne	26			
XVI 'So many rivers in a land of mountains'	28			*Poetry in Wartime,* ed. Tambimuttu, 66

Bibliography

❧❧ ❧❧ • ❧❧ ❧❧

References in the text are to the first edition of works cited, except where a second or subsequent edition is also listed in this bibliography.

1: Works by Roy Fuller

Poems. London: Fortune Press, 1939.

The Middle of a War. London: Hogarth Press, 1942.

A Lost Season. London: Hogarth Press, 1944.

Savage Gold. London: John Lehmann, 1946.

With My Little Eye. London: John Lehmann, 1948.

Epitaphs and Occasions. London: John Lehmann, 1949.

Questions and Answers in Building Society Law and Practice. London: Franey, 1949.

The Second Curtain. London: Derek Verschoyle, 1953.

Fantasy and Fugue. London: Derek Verschoyle, 1954.

Counterparts. London: Derek Verschoyle, 1954.

Image of a Society. London: André Deutsch, 1956.

Brutus's Orchard. London: André Deutsch, 1957.

The Ruined Boys. London: André Deutsch, 1959.

The Father's Comedy. London: André Deutsch, 1961; Harmondsworth: Penguin, 1969.

Collected Poems 1936–1961. London: André Deutsch, 1962.

The Perfect Fool. London: André Deutsch, 1963.

Buff. London: André Deutsch, 1965.

My Child, My Sister. London: André Deutsch, 1965.

Catspaw. London: Alan Ross, 1966.

New Poems. London: André Deutsch, 1968.

Confrontation off Korea. Oxford: Sycamore Press, 1968.

Off Course. London: Turret Books, 1969.

The Carnal Island. London: André Deutsch, 1970.

To an Unknown Reader. London: Poem of the Month Club, 1970.

Owls and Artificers. London: André Deutsch, 1971.

Song Cycle from a Record Sleeve. Oxford: Sycamore Press, 1972.

Seen Grandpa Lately? London: André Deutsch, 1972.

The CCC. London: BBC, 1972.

Tiny Tears. London: André Deutsch, 1973.

Professors and Gods. London: André Deutsch, 1973.

An Old War. Edinburgh: Tragara Press, 1974.

Waiting for the Barbarians. Richmond: Keepsake Press, 1974.

From the Joke Shop. London: André Deutsch, 1975.

The Joke Shop Annexe. London: Tragara Press, 1975.

An Ill-Governed Coast. Sunderland: Ceolfrith Press, 1976.

Poor Roy. London: André Deutsch, 1977.
The Souvenirs of S.O.G. London: BBC, 1977.
Re-treads. Edinburgh: Tragara Press, 1979.
The Reign of Sparrows. London: London Magazine Editions, 1980.
Souvenirs. London: London Magazine Editions, 1980.
More about Tompkins, and other light verse. Edinburgh: Tragara Press, 1981.
The Individual and his Times: A Selection of the Poetry of Roy Fuller, ed. V.J.Lee. London: Athlone Press, 1982.
Vamp Till Ready. London: London Magazine Editions, 1982.
House and Shop. Edinburgh: Tragara Press, 1982.
As from the Thirties. Edinburgh: Tragara Press, 1983.
Howard Castled. London: BBC, 1983.
Home and Dry. London: London Magazine Editions, 1984.
Mianserin Sonnets. Edinburgh: Tragara Press, 1984.
Twelfth Night: A Personal View. Edinburgh: Tragara Press, 1985.
New and Collected Poems 1934–1984. London: Secker and Warburg, 1985.
Subsequent to Summer. Edinburgh: Salamander Press, 1985.
Outside the Canon. Edinburgh: Tragara Press, 1986.
Consolations. London: Secker and Warburg, 1987.
Crime Omnibus (With my Little Eye; The Second Curtain; Fantasy and Fugue). Manchester: Carcanet, 1988.
The Strange and the Good: Collected Memoirs. London: Collins Harvill, 1989.
Available for Dreams. London: Collins Harvill, 1989.
The World through the Window: Collected Poems for Children. Glasgow: Blackie, 1989.
Stares. London: Sinclair-Stevenson, 1990.
Spanner and Pen. London: Sinclair-Stevenson, 1991.
Last Poems. London: Sinclair-Stevenson, 1993.

2: Other works cited in the text

Abse, Dannie (ed), *Poetry Dimension 2*. London: Abacus, 1974.
Alexander, Peter F., *William Plomer*. Oxford: OUP, 1989.
Auden, W.H., *Collected Poems*. London: Faber, 1976.
Auden, W.H., *The English Auden*. London: Faber, 1977.
Bergonzi, Bernard, *Reading the Thirties*. London: Macmillan, 1978.
Birkenhead, Sheila (ed), *Essays by Divers Hands*, New Series, XXXV. London: OUP, 1969.
Cloud, Yvonne (ed), *Beside the Seaside*. London: The Bodley Head, 1934.
Daiches, David, *Literary Landscapes of the British Isles*. London: Paddington Press, 1979.
Danby, John F., *Shakespeare's Doctrine of Nature*. London: Faber, 1958.
Eliot, T.S., *Collected Poems 1909–1962*. London: Faber, 1963.
Forster, E.M., *Howards End*. London: Arnold, 1910; Harmondsworth: Penguin, 1941.
Forster, E.M., *Where Angels Fear to Tread*. London: Arnold, 1905; Harmondsworth: Penguin, 1959.
Fuller, John (ed), *Poems for Roy Fuller on his Seventieth Birthday*. Oxford: Sycamore Press, 1982.
Gittings, Robert, *Young Thomas Hardy*. London: Heinemann, 1975; Harmondsworth: Penguin, 1978.

Greene, Graham, *Brighton Rock*. London: Heinemann, 1938; Harmondsworth: Penguin, 1975.

Greene, Graham, *A Sort of Life*. London: The Bodley Head, 1971; Harmondsworth: Penguin, 1972.

Hamilton, Ian (ed), *The Modern Poet*. London: Macdonald, 1968.

Hamilton, Ian, *Robert Lowell: A Biography*. London: Faber, 1983.

Hardy, Thomas, *Complete Poems*. London: Macmillan, 1976.

Heath-Stubbs, John, *Hindsights*. London: Hodder, 1993.

Hennessy, Peter, *Never Again*. London: Cape, 1992.

Hewison, Robert, *Under Siege*. London: Weidenfeld and Nicolson, 1977; Quartet Books, 1979.

Hynes, Samuel, *The Auden Generation*. London: The Bodley Head, 1976.

Isherwood, Christopher, *Goodbye to Berlin*. London: Methuen, 1939; Harmondsworth: Penguin, 1945.

Isherwood, Christopher, *The World in the Evening*. London: Methuen, 1954; Four Square Books, 1960.

Isherwood, Christopher, *A Meeting by the River*. London: Methuen, 1967.

Kermode, Frank, *Wallace Stevens*. Edinburgh: Oliver and Boyd, 1960

Lambert, Constant, *Music Ho!*. London: Faber, 1934.

Larkin, Philip, *The North Ship*. London: Fortune Press, 1945; Faber, 1966.

Lehmann, John, *I am my Brother*. London: Longmans, 1960.

Maclaren-Ross, Julian, *Memoirs of the Forties*. London: Alan Ross, 1965.

Motion, Andrew, *The Lamberts*. London: Chatto and Windus, 1986.

Motion, Andrew, *Philip Larkin: A Writer's Life*. London: Faber, 1993.

Parker, Peter, *Ackerley*. London: Constable, 1989.

Plomer, William, *Collected Poems*. London: Cape, 1973.

Ross, Alan, *Blindfold Games*. London: Collins Harvill, 1986.

Ross, Alan, *Coastwise Lights*. London: Collins Harvill, 1988.

Scannell, Vernon, *A Proper Gentleman*. London: Robson, 1977.

Schofield, Sim, *Short Stories about Failsworth Folk*. Oldham, 1905.

Shenton, Kenneth, *History of Arnold School*. Blackpool, 1989.

Sherry, Vincent B. (ed), *Dictionary of Literary Biography*, 40. Detroit: Gale, 1985.

Skelton, Robin, *Poetry of the Forties*. Harmondsworth: Penguin, 1968.

Storr, Anthony, *Music and the Mind*. London: Harper Collins, 1992.

Symons, Julian, *Confusions about 'X'*. London: Fortune Press, 1939.

Symons, Julian, *Notes from Another Country*. London: London Magazine Editions, 1972.

Tambimuttu, M.J. (ed), *Poetry in Wartime*. London: Faber, 1942.

Thwaite, Anthony, *Poetry Today 1960–1973*. Harlow: Longman, 1973.

Thwaite, Anthony (ed), *Selected Letters of Philip Larkin*. London: Faber, 1992.

Tolley, A.T. (ed), *Roy Fuller: A Tribute*. Ottawa: Carleton University Press, 1993.

Tomlinson, Charles, *Seeing is Believing*. London: OUP, 1960.

Tredell, Nicolas, *Conversations with Critics*. Manchester: Carcanet, 1994.

Vaughan, Keith, *Journals and Drawings*. London: Alan Ross, 1966.

Wain, John, *Strike the Father Dead*. London: Macmillan, 1962.

White, Eric W. (ed), *Poetry Book Society: The First 25 Years*. London, 1979.

Winters, Yvor, *Forms of Discovery*. Denver: Alan Swallow, 1967.

Yeats, W.B., *Collected Poems*. London: Macmillan, 1950.

Notes

❧❧ ❧❧ • ❧❧ ❧❧

Abbreviations

AFD	*Available for Dreams*	*MW*	*The Middle of a War*
B	*Buff*	*NCP*	*New and Collected*
BO	*Brutus's Orchard*		*Poems 1934–1984*
C	*Counterparts*	*NP*	*New Poems*
CI	*The Carnal Island*	*OA*	*Owls and Artificers*
CO	*Crime Omnibus*	*P*	*Poems*
CP	*Collected Poems*	*PF*	*The Perfect Fool*
	1936–1961	*PG*	*Professors and Gods*
CS	*Consolations*	*RB*	*The Ruined Boys*
EO	*Epitaphs and Occasions*	*RS*	*The Reign of Sparrows*
FC	*The Father's Comedy*	*S*	*Souvenirs*
FTJS	*From the Joke Shop*	*SAP*	*Spanner and Pen*
HAD	*Home and Dry*	*SG*	*The Strange and the*
IS	*Image of a Society*		*Good*
LP	*Last Poems*	*SS*	*Stares*
LS	*A Lost Season*	*STS*	*Subsequent to Summer*
MCMS	*My Child, My Sister*	*TT*	*Tiny Tears*
MS	*Mianserin Sonnets*	*VTR*	*Vamp Till Ready*

Preface
1 Arnold Rattenbury to NP, 1 October 1991
2 *SAP*, 116
3 Frank Kermode, *Wallace Stevens*, 19
4 'A Conversation with Philip Larkin', *Tracks*, 1, 1967, 5–6
5 *S*, 118; *SG*, 71
6 *SAP*, 176
7 *S*, 119; *SG*, 72
8 RF to NP, 8 April 1990
9 RF to NP, 7 June 1990
10 The first three volumes were collected in slightly abbreviated form as *The Strange and the Good* (1989); the fourth volume is *Spanner and Pen* (1991).

Part One: North and South

1: Northern Boy
1 *FTJS*, 17; *NCP*, 373
2 *PF*, 40

3   S, 20; SG, 10
4   S, 17; SG, 8
5   W.B. Yeats, *Collected Poems*, 234
6   *SAP*, 164
7   *MS*, 18; *NCP*, 537
8   *SAP*, 164
9   David Daiches, *Literary Landscapes of the British Isles*, 186
10 S, 17; SG, 7
11 S, 80; SG, 47–8
12 Sim Schofield, *Short Stories about Failsworth Folk*, 32
13 S, 22; SG, 11
14 John Stafford to NP, 24 March 1993
15 S, 25; SG, 13
16 *PF*, 6
17 *PF*, 8
18 S, 33; SG, 16
19 S, 28; SG, 15
20 S, 19, 50; SG, 9, 28
21 S, 181; SG, 111
22 In *Souvenirs*, the occasion is given as New Year's Eve (*S*, 88; *SG*, 53); in *Spanner and Pen*, as New Year's Day (*SAP*, 163). Curiously, the joke works equally well in either case.
23 S, 181; SG, 111
24 S, 81; SG, 48
25 *VTR*, 63; *SG*, 151
26 Emily Broadbent, 'Reflections on Life', *The Standard* [Oldham], 23 September 1933
27 *SG*, 44
28 S, 75; SG, 44
29 S, 76; SG, 45
30 S, 77; SG, 45
31 RF and Anthony Thwaite, 'Penny Numbers', BBC, 8 February 1982
32 S, 27; SG, 14
33 S, 31; SG, 17
34 'The Need for the Non-Literary', *TLS*, 10 November 1972
35 S, 62–3; SG, 36
36 S, 38; SG, 21
37 *VTR*, 171
38 *RB*, 247
39 'The classrooms were at the rear of these two houses, in a single-storey building erected where the property was bounded by a back street. This building was extended during my early days at the school to make a science laboratory, perhaps the school's last gesture of prosperity and expansion' (*S*, 40; *SG*, 22). Those 'early days' would be 1923–4. Blackpool High School's advertisement in *Hampton's Scholastic Directory* for 1925 boasts of 'Excellent Chemical and Physical Laboratories equipped for Practical Work to Inter-B.St. and Pre-registration in Physics and Chemistry for Medical and Dental Students.'
40 RF to Kenneth Shenton, 16 October 1984

41   *RB*, 14
42   *RB*, 39
43   *RB*, 42
44   *RB*, 43
45   *RB*, 84
46   *RB*, 246
47   *RB*, 247
48   *S*, 46; *SG*, 25–6
49   Fuller was fond of inventing perilously thin disguises for friends and
     colleagues, both in his memoirs and in his fiction (see also the discussion of
     Image of a Society, pp.163–70); the case of Burt Briggs, who is happily still
     alive, is characteristic and telling. After the publication of *Souvenirs* in 1980,
     Fuller received from his Blackpool High School contemporary S.H.Birch,
     among much other information, 'a cutting from the local rag showing that the
     saviour recently of the Grand Theatre was none other than the boy called in
     Souvenirs "Byng" – "Chuck it, you rotten beggar, Byng." Good job I changed
     the name. The newspaper photo showed the somewhat simian features quite
     recognizable, though weight added and hair taken away' (RF to Norman
     Lees, 29 December 1980). The matter was still on his mind in his next letter
     to Norman Lees: 'Burt Briggs comes into *Souvenirs* as the simian-faced boy
     who teases Ames. I changed his name in case he was still alive (as he turns out
     to be – I was sent a cutting showing him in relation to the Grand Theatre
     rescue operation' (RF to Norman Lees, 21 January 1981). Not only was
     Briggs, a retired bank manager, very much alive; by 1985, he had also read
     Souvenirs and its sequel, *Vamp Till Ready*: 'Even after 60 years or so it is still
     interesting to hear of one's incarceration in a small private preparatory
     academy... I was amused to think that my antics could have produced such
     an unusual impression on another young boarder under the Boss's care' (Burt
     Briggs to RF, 3 August 1985). After recalling a cricket match against
     Southport College, he innocently added that Fuller could have a seat named
     at the Grand Theatre for £350: perhaps irony was somehow on the Blackpool
     curriculum. Fuller responded with a long and warmly reminiscent letter: 'I
     fear I often depicted the seamier side of life in Alexandra Road, but you have
     taken the account of our doings in those days very calmly' (RF to Burt Briggs,
     21 August 1985). He concluded: 'This is just a preliminary to saying that I
     would like my name on the back of a seat, in memory of those ancient days –
     just ROY FULLER – and enclose a cheque for £350.' (Briggs had addressed
     his letter to Roy Broadbent Fuller Esq CBE.)
50   'Roy Fuller in Conversation with Brian Morton', *PN Review*, 50, 1986, 10
51   Blackpool High School Magazine, VI:2, 1926, 9
52   *S*, 63; *SG*, 37
53   *S*, 65; *SG*, 38
54   *S*, 42; *SG*, 24
55   *RB*, 110
56   *S*, 47; *SG*, 26
57   *RB*, 64
58   *S*, 57; *SG*, 32
59   *EO*, 33; *NCP*, 106

60 *S*, 59; *SG*, 34
61 *S*, 57; *SG*, 33
62 *S*, 60; *SG*, 35
63 SS, 45
64 *S*, 90; *SG*, 54
65 *S*, 122; *SG*, 74
66 *PF*, 75
67 *S*, 154; *SG*, 93
68 *S*, 97; *SG*, 58
69 *S*, 91; *SG*, 54
70 RF to Julian Symons, 20 July 1939
71 Yvonne Cloud (ed), *Beside the Seaside*, 167–8
72 *S*, 13; *SG*, 5
73 *S*, 31–2; *SG*, 17
74 *S*, 68–9; *SG*, 39–40
75 Vincent B.Sherry (ed), *Dictionary of Literary Biography*, 40, 145
76 *S*, 48; *SG*, 26
77 *S*, 96; *SG*, 57
78 Andrew Motion, *Philip Larkin: A Writer's Life*, 21
79 *S*, 122; *SG*, 74
80 *S*, 124; *SG*, 75
81 'Roy Fuller in Conversation with Brian Morton', *PN Review*, 50, 1986, 10
82 'From Blackheath to Oxford', *London Magazine*, New Series, 8:12, March 1969, 24
83 Sheila Birkenhead (ed), *Essays by Divers Hands*, New Series, XXXV, 1969, 68
84 *S*, 42; *SG*, 23–4
85 *S*, 93; *SG*, 55
86 *S*, 118; *SG*, 72
87 *S*, 169; *SG*, 103
88 *S*, 146; *SG*, 89
89 RF and Anthony Thwaite, 'Penny Numbers', BBC, 8 February 1982
90 *S*, 100; *SG*, 60
91 This may well have been derived from Arthur Anderson, who was 'always immaculately dressed' (Kenneth Shenton, *History of Arnold School*, 80). Another former pupil, Neil Kitchingman, in a letter to the *West Lancashire Evening Gazette*, recalled: 'Arthur Anderson imbued me with a desire, at an age when scruffiness was more of a tendency than sartorial elegance, always to be turned out as neatly as he was' (13 June 1989).
92 *S*,99; *SG*, 60
93 *S*, 105; *SG*, 63
94 *S*, 110; *SG*, 66–7
95 RF to Norman Lees, 21 January 1981
96 RF to Norman Lees, 18 February 1980
97 *S*, 105; *SG*, 63
98 Robert Gittings, *Young Thomas Hardy*, 55
99 *S*, 103; *SG*, 62
100 RF to Norman Lees, 18 August 1978

101 *S*, 44
102 RF to Norman Lees, 6 August 1957
103 *S*, 111; *SG*, 68
104 *S*, 114; *SG*, 69
105 *S*, 130; *SG*, 79
106 Andrew Motion, *The Lamberts*, 158
107 *S*, 49; *SG*, 27
108 *S*, 161; *SG*, 97
109 *CO*, 367
110 Fuller records his purchase of *Dubliners* in March 1930, and continues: 'When I met John Davenport, I rather think in the summer following this very winter...' (*S*, 128; *SG*, 78). This seems a likelier date − closer to Davenport's involvement with *Cambridge Poetry* and more consistent with his undergraduate status, pre-dating Fuller's first spell in London − than 1931, implied later in *Souvenirs*: 'her [Muriel George's] film debut was in 1932, the year after I was introduced to her by Bobby' (*S*, 163; *SG*, 99).
111 *S*, 167; *SG*, 102
112 *S*, 168; *SG*, 102–3
113 *S*, 129; *SG*, 79
114 *VTR*, 50; *SG*, 140
115 *VTR*, 160
116 RF and Anthony Thwaite, 'Penny Numbers', BBC, 8 February 1982
117 Samuel Hynes, *The Auden Generation*, 23–4
118 *S*, 169; *SG*, 103
119 RF and Anthony Thwaite, 'Penny Numbers', BBC, 8 February 1982
120 *S*, 149; *SG*, 90
121 RF to Julian Symons, 29 January 1989 (probably misdated for 1990)
122 *S*, 151; *SG*, 92
123 *S*, 152; *SG*, 92

2: Southern Man
1   *VTR*, 32; *SG*, 128
2   *VTR*, 22; *SG*, 120
3   *VTR*, 24; *SG*, 122
4   *VTR*, 24; *SG*, 122
5   *SG*, 138
6   RF to Norman Lees, 31 December 1946
7   *SAP*, 8
8   *VTR*, 45; *SG*, 137
9   *VTR*, 29; *SG*, 126
10   *VTR*, 31; *SG*, 127
11   *VTR*, 25; *SG*, 122
12   *SAP*, 9
13   *VTR*, 39; *SG*, 131
14   *VTR*, 30; *SG*, 130
15   *VTR*, 33; *SG*, 129
16   *VTR*, 33–4; *SG*, 129–30
17   *VTR*, 41; *SG*, 133

18 The other cases were Carhill vs. Carbolic Smokeball Company (1893) and Rylands vs. Fletcher (1866).
19 *VTR*, 67; *SG*, 158
20 *S*, 118; *SG*, 71
21 *VTR*, 50; *SG*, 141
22 *VTR*, 52; *SG*, 142
23 *VTR*, 54; *SG*, 144
24 *VTR*, 54; *SG*, 144
25 *VTR*, 79; *SG*, 166
26 RF to Norman Lees, 8 August 1937
27 *VTR*, 80; *SG*, 167
28 *VTR*, 91; *SG*, 178
29 *CO*, 23
30 RF to D.S. Savage, 12 March 1936
31 *VTR*, 83; *SG*, 170
32 RF to D.S. Savage, 12 December 1936
33 RF to Norman Lees, 8 August 1937
34 *VTR*, 84–5; *SG*, 171
35 *P*, 23; *NCP*, 9
36 RF and Anthony Thwaite, 'Penny Numbers', BBC, 8 February 1982
37 *VTR*, 86; *SG*, 173
38 Julian Symons, 'The Enterprise of St Mary's Bay', *Roy Fuller: A Tribute*, 112
39 Julian Symons, *Notes from Another Country*, 59
40 RF to Julian Symons, 23 February 1938
41 George Woodcock, 'The Habit and the Habitat', *Roy Fuller: A Tribute*, 99
42 Kirby pad ms., c.1933
43 RF to NP in inscribed copy, 1983
44 *NCP*, 5
45 *Roy Fuller: A Tribute*, 112
46 RF to Julian Symons, 22 June 1938
47 *VTR*, 87; *SG*, 173
48 *VTR*, 88; *SG*, 174
49 Julian Maclaren-Ross, *Memoirs of the Forties*, 113
50 John Heath-Stubbs, *Hindsights*, 89
51 *Roy Fuller: A Tribute*, 112
52 RF to Julian Symons, 11 March 1938
53 RF to Julian Symons, 22 June 1938
54 Julian Symons to RF, 24 June 1938
55 RF to Julian Symons, 1 July 1938
56 RF to Julian Symons, 6 July 1938
57 RF to Julian Symons, 8 July 1938
58 RF to Julian Symons, 11 July 1938
59 RF to Julian Symons, 14 July 1938
60 RF to Julian Symons, 6 September 1938
61 RF to Julian Symons, 1 September 1938
62 *VTR*, 93–4
63 *P*, 30
64 *CP*, 31

65 *NCP*, 19
66 *P*, 29; *NCP*, 19
67 *VTR*, 93
68 Julian Symons to RF, 'Saturday', September 1938
69 *NCP*, 20
70 *VTR*, 88; *SG*, 175
71 *VTR*, 102
72 *VTR*, 103; *SG*, 186
73 *VTR*, 106; *SG*, 189
74 'Living in London – IV', *London Magazine*, NS, 9:10, January 1970, 40
75 RF to D.S. Savage, 24 November 1938
76 RF to D.S. Savage, 2 December 1938
77 'Living in London – IV', *London Magazine*, NS, 9:10, January 1970, 39
78 RF and Anthony Thwaite, 'Penny Numbers', BBC, 8 February 1982
79 RF to Julian Symons, 27 October 1938
80 A.T. Tolley, 'The Fortune Press and the Poetry of the Forties', *Aquarius*, 17/18, 1987, 92
81 RF to Norman Lees, 18 March 1940
82 Julian Symons, *Notes from Another Country*, 60–1
83 Philip Larkin, *The North Ship*, 2nd edition, 7
84 Julian Maclaren-Ross, *Memoirs of the Forties*, 97–8
85 *VTR*, 99; *SG*, 182
86 *VTR*, 98; *SG*, 182
87 *P*, 7
88 *P*, 7; *NCP*, 3
89 *P*, 8; *NCP*, 5
90 *P*, 13; *NCP*, 8
91 *P*, 28
92 M.J.Tambimuttu (ed), *Poetry in Wartime*, 66–7
93 *New Statesman*, 11 May 1940

Part Two: Writer and Society

1: War Poet

1   Julian Symons, 'Roy Fuller: After the Obituaries', *London Magazine*, NS, 31: 11/12, February/March 1992, 41
2   *VTR*, 126; *SG*, 204
3   *VTR*, 124; *SG*, 202
4   *TT*, 67; *NCP*, 34
5   *VTR*, 182; *NCP*, 33. For Fuller's subsequent reflections on the work of Julien Benda, see *PG*, 113–16.
6   *MW*, 7; *NCP*, 31
7   *VTR*, 129; *SG*, 206
8   RF to Norman Lees, 18 March 1940
9   *VTR*, 136; *SG*, 212
10 RF to Julian Symons, 28 April 1941
11 RF to Julian Symons, [?] May 1941
12 W.H.Auden, *The English Auden*, 79–81
13 *MW*, 23; *NCP*, 42–3

14 *VTR*, 147
15 *VTR*, 144; *SG*, 219
16 RF to Julian Symons, 5 June 1941
17 *RS*, 52; *NCP*, 471
18 RF to Julian Symons, 17 June 1941
19 RF to Julian Symons, 9 July 1941
20 RF to Julian Symons, 17 June 1941
21 *VTR*, 142; *SG*, 217
22 *VTR*, 151; *SG*, 223
23 *MW*, 36; *NCP*, 49
24 RF to Michael Schmidt, 20 August 1976
25 Eric Homberger, 'Roy Fuller: "In the Paralysis of Class"', *Poetry Nation*, 6, 1976, 96
26 *VTR*, 154
27 RF to Julian Symons, 31 July 1941
28 *VTR*, 157; *SG*, 226
29 RF to Julian Symons, 16 September 1941
30 *VTR*, 160
31 RF to Julian Symons, 17 August 1941
32 RF to Julian Symons, 23 August 1941
33 RF to Julian Symons, 16 September 1941
34 *VTR*, 167
35 RF to Julian Symons, 3 October 1941
36 *MW*, 32; *NCP*, 47
37 *VTR*, 163; *SG*, 231
38 As had the Reverend Harold Davidson, ex-Rector of Stiffkey, on Blackpool's Golden Mile (see *VTR*, 59; *SG*, 149).
39 *MW*, 33–4
40 *NCP*, 47–8
41 *VTR*, 162; *SG*, 229
42 *VTR*, 164; *SG*, 232
43 RF to Julian Symons, 4 March 1942
44 *MW*, 35; *NCP*, 48
45 *MW*, 37; *NCP*, 49
46 *MW*, 38; *NCP*, 50
47 *VTR*, 164; *SG*, 232
48 RF to Julian Symons, 19 February 1942
49 RF to Julian Symons, 18 March 1942
50 RF to Julian Symons, 24 May 1982
51 Alan Brownjohn to RF, 1 June 1982
52 RF to Julian Symons, 18 March 1942
53 *HAD*, 11; *SG*, 252
54 *VTR*, 178; *SG*, 240
55 *MW*, 46; *NCP*, 55
56 *HAD*, 2; *SG*, 244
57 *HAD*, 3; *SG*, 245
58 Journal, 13 April 1942; cf. *HAD*, 2–3
59 *PF*, 116–17

60   *PF*, 119
61   Journal, 16 April 1942
62   *HAD*, 5; *SG*, 246
63   *CI*, 41
64   Journal, 18 April 1942
65   Journal, 26 April 1942
66   *MW*, 48; *NCP*, 55
67   *PF*, 117
68   *HAD*, 12; *SG*, 253
69   *HAD*, 12; *SG*, 254
70   *PF*, 123
71   *HAD*, 8–9; *SG*, 250
72   Journal, 1 May 1942
73   Journal, 5 May 1942
74   Journal, 11 May 1942
75   *HAD*, 16; *SG*, 257
76   Journal, 19 May 1942
77   *HAD*, 16; *SG*, 257
78   Journal, 23 May 1942
79   Journal, 5 June 1942
80   *HAD*, 19; *SG*, 260
81   *HAD*, 20; *SG*, 261
82   *HAD*, 20; *SG*, 261
83   Journal, 19 June 1942
84   Journal, 20 June 1942
85   *Savage Gold*, 18
86   Journal, 21 June 1942
87   *HAD*, 22; *SG*, 263
88   *LS*, 11 (quoted); *NCP*, 67
89   *PF*, 130–7
90   *HAD*, 36; *SG*, 269
91   Journal, 15 August 1942
92   *HAD*, 40; *SG*, 274
93   Journal, 27 July 1942
94   *HAD*, 41–2; *SG*, 275
95   Journal, 23 September 1942
96   *HAD*, 48; *SG*, 280
97   Journal, 23 September 1942
98   RF to Julian Symons, 1 December 1942
99   *Observer*, 22 November 1942
100 Robert Hewison, *Under Siege*, 134–5
101 John Lehmann, *I Am My Brother*, 197
102 *LS*, 9; *NCP*, 56
103 RF to Norman Lees, 5 September 1942
104 RF to Norman Lees, 13 October 1942
105 RF to Norman Lees, 13 June 1943
106 *HAD*, 44; *SG*, 277
107 *HAD*, 52; *SG*, 284

108 *HAD*, 54; *SG*, 285
109 *HAD*, 59; *SG*, 288
110 *LS*, 16; *NCP*, 60–1
111 *HAD*, 67; *SG*, 295
112 *PF*, 142
113 *LS*, 41; *NCP*, 76
114 *LS*, 45; *NCP*, 79
115 *PF*, 144
116 *HAD*, 67; *SG*, 296
117 *HAD*, 69; *SG*, 297
118 *HAD*, 71; *SG*, 298–9
119 *AFD*, 75
120 *LS*, 47; *NCP*, 80
121 RF to Julian Symons, 3 June 1943
122 *HAD*, 157–65
123 *Penguin New Writing*, 19, 1944, 23–4
124 RF to Julian Symons, 7 July 1943
125 *HAD*, 74
126 *HAD*, 77; *SG*, 301
127 Journal, 27 July 1943
128 Journal, 29 July 1943
129 *HAD*, 92; *SG*, 315
130 RF to Julian Symons, 10 November 1943
131 *HAD*, 80; *SG*, 303
132 *LS*, 52–3; *NCP*, 84–5
133 *HAD*, 81; *SG*, 303–4
134 RF to Julian Symons, 3 December 1943
135 *HAD*, 94; *SG*, 316
136 RF to Symons, 19 May 1944
137 *LS*, 55 (quoted); *NCP*, 86–7
138 *LS*, 55; *NCP*, 86
139 *LS*, 57; *NCP*, 88
140 *LS*, 57; *NCP*, 88
141 *HAD*, 95; *SG*, 317
142 *PF*, 146–7
143 RF to Julian Symons, 5 January 1944
144 RF to Julian Symons, 13 April 1944
145 RF to Julian Symons, 19 April 1944
146 RF to Julian Symons, 30 April 1944
147 RF to Julian Symons, 26 June 1944
148 *HAD*, 118; *SG*, 338
149 *NP*, 19; *NCP*, 281
150 Alan Ross, *Blindfold Games*, 240
151 *HAD*, 120; *SG*, 340
152 *HAD*, 121; *SG*, 341
153 *HAD*, 121; *SG*, 341
154 *HAD*, 122; *SG*, 342
155 *HAD*, 124; *SG*, 343

156 *HAD*, 137; *SG*, 355
157 RF to Julian Symons, 8 April 1944
158 *HAD*, 141–2; *SG*, 258
159 'Living in London – IV', *London Magazine*, NS, 9:10, January 1970, 43
160 *HAD*, 136; *SG*, 353
161 John Lehmann, *I Am My Brother*, 254
162 *HAD*, 100; *SG*, 323
163 *HAD*, 101; *SG*, 323–4
164 *Time and Tide*, 29 July 1944
165 *PG*, 172
166 *HAD*, 131; *SG*, 350
167 William Plomer, *Collected Poems*, 129
168 *HAD*, 126; *SG*, 345
169 *The Listener*, 2 November 1944
170 Peter Parker, *Ackerley*, 180
171 *The Listener*, 14 December 1944
172 Peter Parker, *Ackerley*, 180
173 Peter Parker, *Ackerley*, 181
174 Peter F. Alexander, *William Plomer*, 241
175 *S*, 130–1
176 *HAD*, 128; *SG*, 348
177 *HAD*, 143; *SG*, 360
178 *Our Time*, October 1945, 47

2: Images of a Society
1   *EO*, 23; *NCP*, 91
2   *HAD*, 140
3   *EO*, 22; *NCP*, 91
4   *EO*, 59; *NCP*, 118
5   *CO*, 7
6   *CO*, 15
7   *CO*, 21
8   *CO*, 19
9   *CO*, 46
10   *CO*, 71
11   *CO*, 32
12   *CO*, 83
13   *CO*, 10
14   *CO*, 108
15   *CO*, 150
16   *CO*, 23
17   *CO*, 53
18   *CO*, 59
19   *CO*, 74
20   'From Blackheath to Oxford', *London Magazine*, NS, 8:12, March 1969, 24
21   *VTR*, 69; *SG*, 158
22   *S*, 84; *SG*, 50. See also 'Chinoiserie': 'a fixation / At the irrelevant anal stage of existence' (*NP*, 17; *NCP*, 279).

23 *EO*, 21; *NCP*, 99. See also *OA*, 112
24 *EO*, 22; *NCP*, 91
25 *EO*, 51; *NCP*, 114
26 *EO*, 20; *NCP*, 90
27 *EO*, 12; *NCP*, 98
28 Julian Symons, 'Roy Fuller: After the Obituaries', *London Magazine*, NS, 31:11/12, February/March 1992, 35
29 *EO*, 25; *NCP*, 101
30 *VTR*, 182–3; *NCP*, 33
31 *MW*, 11
32 *EO*, 44; *NCP*, 110
33 *Times Literary Supplement*, 30 December 1949
34 *Manchester Guardian*, 30 December 1949
35 G.S. Fraser, 'Some Notes on Poetic Diction', *Penguin New Writing*, 37, 1949, 128
36 Nicolas Tredell, *Conversations with Critics*, 330
37 *SAP*, 10
38 *SAP*, 11
39 'Living in London – IV', *London Magazine*, NS, 9:10, January 1970, 43
40 Alan Ross, *Coastwise Lights*, 124
41 RF to Julian Symons, 26 August 1952
42 RF to Julian Symons, 9 December 1952
43 *CO*, 8
44 Steven Smith, 'The Curious Generation of Roy Fuller', *London Magazine*, NS, 33:7/8, October/November 1993, 40
45 *CO*, 8
46 *VTR*, 21; *SG*, 119
47 *CO*, 159
48 *CO*, 162
49 *CO*, 164
50 *CO*, 167
51 *CO*, 168
52 *CO*, 171
53 *CO*, 171
54 *CO*, 177
55 Graham Greene, *A Sort of Life*, 9
56 *CO*, 182
57 *CO*, 185
58 *S*, 179; *SG*, 109
59 *CO*, 198. 'Mr and Mrs Veneering were bran-new people in a bran-new house in a bran-new quarter of London' (*Our Mutual Friend*, I:2).
60 *CO*, 203
61 Alan Ross, undated postcard to NP, 1993
62 *CO*, 210
63 *CO*, 211
64 *CO*, 214
65 *CO*, 218
66 *CO*, 220–1

67 *CO*, 225
68 *CO*, 232
69 *CO*, 234
70 RF to Julian Symons, 29 August 1952
71 *CO*, 245
72 *HAD*, 140–1; *SG*, 357
73 *CO*, 247
74 *CO*, 256
75 *CO*, 290
76 RF to Julian Symons, 24 August 1954
77 *CO*, 293
78 *CO*, 8
79 Barbara Gabriel, 'The Corpse in the Library', *Roy Fuller: A Tribute*, 87
80 *CO*, 412
81 *CO*, 404
82 *CO*, 405
83 *CO*, 387
84 *CO*, 427
85 *CO*, 218
86 *CO*, 417
87 *CO*, 367
88 *CO*, 231
89 *CO*, 233
90 *CO*, 359
91 *CO*, 377
92 *HAD*, 64; *SG*, 292
93 *CO*, 377
94 See p.107 above
95 *HAD*, 74
96 *CO*, 379
97 RF to Norman Lees, 11 July 1957
98 'From Blackheath to Oxford, *London Magazine*, NS, 8:12, March 1969, 27–9
99 Bernard Bergonzi, *Reading the Thirties*, 60–1
100 *SAP*, 58
101 Peter Hennessy, *Never Again*, 319
102 Robin Skelton, *Poetry of the Forties*, 29–30
103 Ian Hamilton, 'A Generation Ago', *The Listener*, 25 September 1969
104 Anthony and Ann Thwaite to NP, 5 October 1994
105 Alan Brownjohn to NP, 1 June 1994
106 *SAP*, 62–3
107 *SAP*, 63
108 Alan Brownjohn to NP, 1 June 1994
109 *SAP*, 59
110 Alan Brownjohn, 'The High Style and the Low Style', *Roy Fuller: A Tribute*, 39
111 Bernard Bergonzi, 'The Poet in Wartime', *Roy Fuller: A Tribute*, 17
112 *C*, 19; *NCP*, 119
113 *C*, 19; *NCP*, 126

114 *C*, 20; *NCP*, 126
115 *C*, 34; *NCP*, 138
116 *C*, 39; *NCP*, 141
117 *Roy Fuller: A Tribute*, 39
118 *C*, 35; *NCP*, 139
119 *C*, 33; *NCP*, 137
120 *SAP*, 12
121 *SAP*, 12
122 *S*, 177; *SG*, 108
123 *IS*, 27
124 *IS*, 28
125 *IS*, 14
126 *IS*, 23
127 *IS*, 65
128 *IS*, 67
129 *IS*, 69
130 *SAP*, 63
131 *IS*, 25
132 *IS*, 31
133 *IS*, 181
134 *IS*, 9
135 *IS*, 12–13
136 Jeremy Lewis, Introduction to 1986 reprint of *Image of a Society*, unnumbered prelims
137 *IS*, 77
138 *IS*, 7
139 *SAP*, 57
140 *SAP*, 45
141 *SAP*, 47
142 *SAP*, 161
143 John Dyer to NP, 6 July 1994

3: *The Middle of a Career*

1 Julian Symons to NP, 24 November 1993
2 RF to Julian Symons, 1 December 1942
3 Alan Brownjohn, 'The High Style and the Low Style', *Roy Fuller: A Tribute*, 40
4 RF and Anthony Thwaite, 'Penny Numbers', BBC, 8 February 1982
5 *BO*, 43; *NCP*, 167
6 *BO*, 40; *NCP*, 165
7 *EO*, 59; *NCP*, 118
8 *EO*, 25–6; *NCP*, 100–1
9 *BO*, 12–13; *NCP*, 153–5
10 *BO*, 66–75; *NCP*, 181–9
11 *BO*, 46–7; *NCP*, 169–70
12 *BO*, 48–9; *NCP*, 171–2
13 *Julius Caesar*, II:i:111–13
14 *BO*, 50; *NCP*: 172

15   *BO*, 51; *NCP*, 173
16   *BO*, 56; *NCP*, 176
17   *SAP*, 63
18   *BO*, 28
19   *BO*, 14–15; *NCP*, 150–1
20   *BO*, 34–5; *NCP*, 161–2
21   'Poetry in my Time', *Essays by Divers Hands*, XXXV, 78
22   Anthony Thwaite (ed), *Selected Letters of Philip Larkin*, 259
23   'Poetry in my Time', *Essays by Divers Hands*, XXXV, 78
24   *FC*, 17
25   *FC*, 77
26   *FC*, 150
27   *FC*, 136
28   *FC*, 86–7
29   *FC*, 89
30   *FC*, 91
31   *FC*, 96
32   *FC*, 108
33   *FC*, 111
34   *FC*, 112–3
35   *FC*, 123
36   *FC*, 166–7
37   *FC*, 168
38   *FC*, 169
39   *FC*, 204
40   *FC*, 216
41   *FC*, 216
42   *FC*, 222–3
43   *FC*, 223
44   *MCMS*, 110
45   *Twelfth Night: A Personal View*, 6–9
46   *MCMS*, 23
47   *MCMS*, 29
48   *MCMS*, 30–1
49   *MCMS*, 45
50   *MCMS*, 48
51   *MCMS*, 90
52   *MCMS*, 86
53   *MCMS*, 81
54   *MCMS*, 88
55   *B*, 29; *NCP*, 242
56   *MCMS*, 89
57   *MCMS*, 94
58   *MCMS*, 103
59   *MCMS*, 106
60   *MCMS*, 106
61   *MCMS*, 108
62   *CO*, 247

63 *MCMS*, 121
64 *MCMS*, 124–5
65 *MCMS*, 155
66 *MCMS*, 165
67 *FC*, 87
68 *MCMS*, 166
69 *MCMS*, 175
70 *NP*, 38; *NCP*, 292–3
71 *MCMS*, 179
72 *MCMS*, 175
73 *MCMS*, 180
74 *MCMS*, 181
75 *MCMS*, 185
76 *London Magazine*, NS, 5:9, December 1965, 99
77 Julian Symons to NP, 18 March 1994
78 RF to Alan Brownjohn, undated postcard
79 *OA*, 104–5
80 Ian Hamilton (ed), *The Modern Poet*, 31
81 'Context', *London Magazine*, NS, 1:11, February 1962, 33
82 *C*, 22; *NCP*, 130
83 *BO*, 66–75; *NCP*, 181–9
84 *CP*, 238–48; *NCP*, 214–24
85 *B*, 9–19; *NCP*, 227–36
86 *B*, 52–64; *NCP*, 254–64
87 *Off Course*, unnumbered pages; *NCP*, 265–72
88 Donald E. Stanford, 'The Poetry of Roy Fuller 1959–1980', *Roy Fuller: A Tribute*, 21
89 *CP*, 244; *NCP*, 219
90 *CP*, 238; *NCP*, 214
91 'Poetry in my Time', *Essays by Divers Hands*, XXXV, 79
92 Julian Symons to NP, 18 March 1994
93 RF to Julian Symons, 2 November 1989; cf. Wallace Stevens, *Collected Poems*, 254
94 Alan Brownjohn, 'The High Style and the Low Style', *Roy Fuller: A Tribute*, 41
95 'Lancastrian Syllabics', *Times Literary Supplement*, 10 September 1976
96 *B*, 9; *NCP*, 227
97 RF to Arnold Rattenbury, 9 May 1967
98 *B*, 20; *NCP*, 236
99 *B*, 21; *NCP*, 237
100 *CP*, 232; *NCP*, 208
101 *B*, 23; *NCP*, 238

Part Three: Blackbirds and Debussy

1: The Double Nature of Nature
1 *NP*, 38; *NCP*, 293
2 Ian Hamilton, 'Loosening the Screws', *Observer*, 25 August 1968
3 *OA*, 44–68

4   *PG*, 81–97
5   *Thames Poetry*, 1:1, 1975, 42–58
6   *Thames Poetry*, 1:3, 1977, 33–49
7   'Poetry in my Time', *Essays by Divers Hands*, XXXV, 79–80
8   *OA*, 54
9   *NP*, 3
10   *NP*, 54: *NCP*, 304
11   RF to Michael Hamburger, 13 September 1968
12   *NCP*, 302
13   *NP*, 46; *NCP*, 198
14   *PG*, 116
15   *NP*, 42; *NCP*, 295
16   John F. Danby, *Shakespeare's Doctrine of Nature*, 15
17   *The Tempest*, I:2, 365–6
18   *The Tempest*, IV:1, 188–9
19   *RS*, 55; *NCP*, 474
20   *NP*, 43–4; *NCP*, 296–7
21   *NP*, 15; *NCP*, 277
22   *NP*, 12; *NCP*, 276
23   *NP*, 57; *NCP*, 306
24   Quoted by George Woodcock, 'The Habit and the Habitat', *Roy Fuller: A Tribute*, 103
25   Jonathan Barker to NP, 12 May 1994
26   *TT*, 14; *NCP*, 314
27   *NP*, 29; *NCP*, 288
28   *NP*, 61; *NCP*, 310
29   Stephen Wall, 'Chairing the Bard', *The Review*, 20, 1969, 57
30   Ian Hamilton, *Robert Lowell: A Biography*, 346–7
31   *SAP*, 81
32   RF to Norman Lees, 20 November 1968
33   RF to Norman Lees, 18 January 1969
34   Mark Preston to NP, 17 June 1994
35   'Poetry in my Time', *Essays by Divers Hands*, XXXV, 84
36   *OA*, 14
37   Constant Lambert, *Music Ho!*, 235
38   *OA*, 18
39   'From Blackheath to Oxford', *London Magazine*, NS, 8:12, March 1969, 27
40   'The Revolution of the Equitable Man', *Guardian*, 24 September 1970
41   *PG*, 15
42   *PG*, 23
43   RF to Arnold Rattenbury, 25 February 1970
44   Arnold Rattenbury to RF, 14 March 1970
45   RF to Arnold Rattenbury, 21 March 1970
46   Philip Larkin to Robert Conquest, 19 August 1968, in Anthony Thwaite (ed), *Selected Letters of Philip Larkin*, 404–5
47   Anthony Thwaite, *Poetry Today 1960–1973*, 29
48   'Context', *London Magazine*, NS, 1:11, February 1962, 33
49   'Poetry 1970', *Tracks*, 8, 1970, 8

50   *SAP*, 88
51   Yvor Winters, *Forms of Discovery*, 347
52   *SAP*, 91
53   *SAP*, 91
54   *SAP*, 91
55   RF to Michael Schmidt, 19 February 1973
56   RF to Michael Schmidt, 30 August 1978
57   RF to Norman Lees, 12 February 1970
58   'The Revolution of the Equitable Man', *Guardian*, 24 September 1970
59   Robert Gittings, *Young Thomas Hardy*, 313
60   'Roy Fuller in Conversation with Brian Morton', *PN Review*, 50, 1986, 9
61   *CI*, 28
62   *CI*, 10
63   *HAD*, 128; *SG*, 348
64   *CI*, 9
65   *CI*, 51–2
66   *VTR*, 108–9; *SG*, 191–2
67   *CI*, 22
68   *CI*, 100
69   *CI*, 68
70   *CI*, 102
71   *CI*, 35
72   *CI*, 15–16
73   *CI*, 68
74   *HAD*, 113; *SG*, 334
75   *CI*, 33
76   *CI*, 34
77   *CI*, 35
78   *CI*, 36
79   *CI*, 35
80   *CI*, 40
81   *CI*, 41–2
82   *CI*, 47
83   *CI*, 59
84   *CI*, 61
85   *NP*, 17; *NCP*, 279
86   Fulke Greville, *Caelica*, VII
87   *CI*, 62
88   *CI*, 64–5
89   *CI*, 66
90   Charles Tomlinson, *Seeing is Believing*, 30
91   *CI*, 72
92   *CI*, 73
93   *CI*, 80
94   *CI*, 97
95   *CI*, 108
96   *CI*, 134
97   *CI*, 122

98 *CI*, 128
99 *CI*, 135
100 *CI*, 140
101 *CI*, 143
102 *CI*, 145
103 *CI*, 151
104 Eric W. White (ed), *Poetry Book Society: The First 25 Years*, 25

2: Part Managerial, Part Poetic

1   Jonathan Barker to NP, 12 May 1994
2   RF to Julian Symons, 11 November 1970
3   *SAP*, 146
4   *SAP*, 150. Philip Larkin had expected Fuller himself to become Poet Laureate on the death of C. Day-Lewis. On 31 May 1972 he wrote to Robert Conquest: 'Roy Fuller for my money. After all, there's nothing about the PL having to be any good at poetry. "Have you ever considered writing about corgis, Mr Fuller?"' (Anthony Thwaite (ed), *Selected Letters of Philip Larkin*, 458).
5   RF to Julian Symons, 11 November 1970
6   *EO*, 58; *NCP*, 117
7   W.B. Yeats, *Collected Poems*, 243
8   John Dyer to NP, 6 July 1994
9   'Roy Fuller: After the Obituaries', *London Magazine*, NS, 31:11/12, February/March 1992, 37
10   Alan Brownjohn to NP, 2 June 1994
11   *SAP*, 95
12   *SAP*, 94
13   *SAP*, 96
14   *The CCC*, 3
15   *Howard Castled*, 3
16   *SAP*, 103
17   *SAP*, 104
18   RF and Anthony Thwaite, 'Penny Numbers', BBC, 8 February 1982
19   *SAP*, 111
20   RF to Julian Symons, 28 February 1972
21   RF to Julian Symons, 23 March 1974
22   *SAP*, 99
23   *SAP*, 100
24   *SAP*, 100
25   *SAP*, 105
26   *SAP*, 105
27   *Howard Castled*, 1
28   *Times Literary Supplement*, 4 July 1975
29   *FTJS*, 34; *NCP*, 389
30   *Poetry Book Society Bulletin*, 85, Summer 1975, 2
31   *TT*, 13; *NCP*, 313
32   *TT*, 32; *NCP*, 325
33   *TT*, 40; *NCP*, 330

34 *TT*, 41; *NCP*, 331
35 *TT*, 43; *NCP*, 333
36 *TT*, 44; *NCP*, 333
37 *Poor Roy*, 49
38 *TT*, 39; *NCP*, 329
39 *TT*, 34; *NCP*, 326–7
40 *TT*, 85; *NCP*, 354
41 *Hamlet*, I:5:196
42 *FTJS*, 15; *NCP*, 370
43 *FTJS*, 17; *NCP*, 373
44 *FTJS*, 19; *NCP*, 374
45 *FTJS*, 42; *NCP*, 396
46 *FTJS*, 48; *NCP*, 402
47 *FTJS*, 50; *NCP*, 404
48 *FTJS*, 23; *NCP*, 378
49 *FTJS*, 29; *NCP*, 384
50 *FTJS*, 34; *NCP*, 389
51 *The Listener*, 4 October 1973
52 *FTJS*, 35; *NCP*, 390
53 *SAP*, 117
54 *FTJS*, 40; *NCP*, 394
55 *FTJS*, 46; *NCP*, 400
56 *FTJS*, 52; *NCP*, 405
57 *FTJS*, 54; *NCP*, 407
58 *FTJS*, 61; *NCP*, 415
59 RF to Arnold Rattenbury, 4 March 1974
60 Dannie Abse (ed), *Poetry Dimension 2*, 152
61 *Times Literary Supplement*, 14 March 1968
62 *SAP*, 122
63 In the programme for a Poetry Society reading at the Royal Albert Hall in May 1987 (one of that month's series of *Poetry Live* events), Graham Staines printed various poets' replies to the question, 'How will you vote in the General Election?' Fuller wrote: 'Living in the Greenwich constituency, I'm siding with Rosie [Barnes, who had won the seat for the SDP in a by-election].'
64 Anthony Thwaite to NP, 12 September 1994
65 *Encounter*, XLIX:4, October 1977, 47
66 Ibid., 45
67 RF to various editors, 14 October 1977
68 RF to Michael Schmidt, 8 November 1977
69 *Times Literary Supplement*, 14 March 1968
70 *Encounter*, XLIX:4, October 1977, 45
71 *Encounter*, XLIX:5, November 1977, 91
72 Alan Brownjohn to NP, 1 June 1994
73 *Encounter*, XLIX:6, December 1977, 94
74 *RS*, 46; *NCP*, 466
75 *S*, 119; *SG*, 72
76 *Encounter*, XLIX:6, December 1977, 92
77 *Encounter*, XLIX:4, October 1977, 46

78   *SAP*, 111–2
79   *Encounter*, XLIX:4, October 1977, 48
80   *The Listener*, 20 October 1977. On poetry and subsidy, see also Vernon
     Scannell's account of his experiences as a 'Resident Poet', *A Proper Gentle-
     man*, and Neil Powell, 'The Poet, the Public, and the Pub', *PN Review*, 7,
     1978, 44–6.
81   RF to Anthony and Ann Thwaite, Christmas card, 1977
82   *The Listener*, 6 December 1979
83   Frank Kermode to NP, 29 September 1994
84   Jonathan Barker to NP, 12 May 1994
85   *The New Review*, 38, May 1977, 33–8
86   *S*, 13; *SG*, 6
87   *S*, 14; *SG*, 6
88   *SAP*, 136
89   *SAP*, 136
90   *SAP*, 138
91   RF to Julian Symons, 21 November 1979
92   RF to Julian Symons, 3 March 1989
93   *SAP*, 137
94   RF to Norman Lees, 29 May 1979
95   *SAP*, 116–18
96   *TT*, 31; *NCP*, 325
97   RF to Norman Lees, 18 August 1978
98   RF to Arnold Rattenbury, 20 January 1979
99   RF to Michael Schmidt, 27 April 1979
100 RF to Julian Symons, 7 May 1979
101 RF to Norman Lees, 29 May 1979
102 RF to Alan Brownjohn, 29 December 1979

3: The World in the Evening

1   *The Listener*, 4 October 1973
2   *SAP*, 137
3   *Times Literary Supplement*, 7 March 1980
4   *S*, 90
5   *RS*, 46; *NCP*, 466
6   *RS*, 41; *NCP*, 461
7   *RS*, 54; *NCP*, 473
8   *RS*, 50; *NCP*, 469
9   *RS*, 53; *NCP*, 472
10   *RS*, 41; *NCP*, 462
11   *RS*, 40; *NCP*, 461
12   *RS*, 34; *NCP*, 456
13   Anthony Storr, *Music and the Mind*, 5
14   Ibid., 23
15   *S*, 96; *SG*, 57–8
16   *FTJS*, 61; *NCP*, 414
17   *RS*, 21–2; *NCP*, 445–6
18   T.S. Eliot, *Collected Poems 1909–1962*, 79

19 *RS*, 23; *NCP*, 446–7
20 *RS*, 34; *NCP*, 456
21 Thomas Hardy, *Complete Poems*, 147
22 *London Magazine*, NS, 20:3, June 1990, 73
23 *SAP*, 158
24 RF to Julian Symons, 27 November 1980
25 *SAP*, 159
26 *NCP*, 493
27 *SAP*, 158–9
28 Jonathan Barker, 'The Amazing Pleasures of the Human', *Roy Fuller: A Tribute*, 31
29 *MS*, 9; *NCP*, 533
30 *MS*, 6: *NCP*, 531
31 *MS*, 11; *NCP*, 534
32 *MS*, 18; *NCP*, 537
33 *MS*, 17; *NCP*, 541
34 *MS*, 24; *NCP*, 541
35 RF to Julian Symons, 25 October 1974
36 RF to Julian Symons, 10 May 1984
37 *SAP*, 139
38 RF to Julian Symons, 11 June 1985
39 RF to Julian Symons, 29 May 1985
40 *NCP*, 506
41 *NCP*, 496
42 *NCP*, 499
43 *NCP*, 504
44 *NCP*, 499
45 *NCP*, 523
46 *NCP*, 500
47 *SAP*, 139
48 *STS*, 9
49 *STS*, 11
50 *STS*, 13
51 *STS*, 19
52 *STS*, 15
53 *STS*, 30
54 *STS*, 18
55 *STS*, 39
56 *STS*, 51
57 *C*, 22; *NCP*, 130
58 *STS*, 58
59 *STS*, 53
60 *SAP*, 77
61 RF and Anthony Thwaite, 'Penny Numbers', BBC, 8 February 1982
62 *SAP*, 74
63 RF and Anthony Thwaite, 'Penny Numbers', BBC, 8 February 1982
64 *Poems for Roy Fuller on his Seventieth Birthday*, unnumbered pages; a pamphlet printed by John Fuller at the Sycamore Press, Oxford. The other contributors

were Jack Clark, Aedamair Cleary, John Fuller, John Lehmann, Alan Ross, Stephen Spender, Julian Symons and Anthony Thwaite.

65 Mark Preston to NP, 17 June 1994
66 *SAP*, 79
67 RF to Julian Symons, 18 January 1985
68 *RS*, 42; *NCP*, 463
69 *NCP*, 495
70 *SAP*, 154–6
71 *Woolwich World*, February 1987, 2
72 David Blake to NP, 20 September 1993
73 Neil Rhind to NP, 20 April 1994
74 RF to Mark Preston, 13 February 1987
75 Jonathan Barker to NP, 12 May 1994
76 *CS*, 4
77 *CS*, 12
78 *CS*, 7
79 *CS*, 9–10
80 *CS*, 22–4
81 *CS*, 25–6
82 *CS*, 27
83 *CS*, 34
84 *CS*, 37
85 *CS*, 44
86 *HAD*, 16; *SG*, 257
87 *London Magazine*, NS, 25:4, July 1985, 108
88 *CS*, 43
89 *CS*, 50
90 *CS*, 52
91 RF to Julian and Kathleen Symons, 16 October 1985
92 *CS*, 55
93 RF to Alan Brownjohn, 17 April 1987
94 *SAP*, 140
95 *SAP*, 142
96 *SAP*, 142
97 *SAP*, 143
98 *AFD*, 87
99 *AFD*, 51
100 *AFD*, 65
101 *AFD*, 98
102 *AFD*, 117
103 *AFD*, 125
104 *AFD*, 75
105 *AFD*, 67
106 *AFD*, 11
107 *AFD*, 23
108 *AFD*, 37
109 *AFD*, 74
110 *AFD*, 88

111 *AFD*, 102
112 *AFD*, 95
113 *AFD*, 137
114 *AFD*, 140
115 *AFD*, 146
116 *AFD*, 151
117 *SAP*, 145
118 RF to Julian Symons, 18 February 1990
119 *SS*, 38
120 *SS*, 113
121 *SS*, 78–9
122 *SS*, 14
123 *SS*, 114–15
124 *SS*, 191
125 *SS*, 78
126 *SS*, 93
127 *Independent*, 16 March 1991
128 *SAP*, 77
129 *SAP*, 154
130 *SAP*, 153
131 *SAP*, 46
132 *SAP*, 177
133 *SAP*, 177
134 RF to NP, 7 June 1990
135 RF to NP, undated card, January 1991
136 RF to Julian Symons, 12 January 1991
137 RF to Kathleen Symons, 7 January 1991
138 RF to Julian Symons, 12 January 1991
139 *Independent*, 28 September 1991
140 *NP*, 61; *NCP*, 310
141 *Guardian*, 30 September 1991
142 Julian Symons, 'Roy Fuller: After the Obituaries', *London Magazine*, NS,
     31:11/12, February/March 1992, 42
143 *LP*, vii
144 *LP*, 45
145 *LP*, 18
146 *LP*, 57
147 *LP*, 67
148 *LP*, 48
149 *LP*, 41
150 *LP*, 22
151 *LP*, 43
152 *LP*, vii
153 *LP*, 44
154 *LP*, 24
155 *LP*, 82
156 *LP*, 61
157 *LP*, 83

Index